STUDIES IN THE HISTORY
OF CHRISTIAN MISSIONS

R. E. Frykenberg
Brian Stanley
General Editors

STUDIES IN THE HISTORY OF CHRISTIAN MISSIONS

Alvyn Austin
China's Millions: The China Inland Mission and Late Qing Society, 1832-1905

Michael Bergunder
The South Indian Pentecostal Movement in the Twentieth Century

Judith M. Brown and Robert Eric Frykenberg, *Editors*
Christians, Cultural Interactions, and India's Religious Traditions

Robert Eric Frykenberg
Christians and Missionaries in India:
Cross-Cultural Communication Since 1500

Susan Billington Harper
In the Shadow of the Mahatma: Bishop V. S. Azariah
and the Travails of Christianity in British India

D. Dennis Hudson
Protestant Origins in India: Tamil Evangelical Christians, 1706-1835

Ogbu U. Kalu, *Editor,* and Alaine M. Low, *Associate Editor*
Interpreting Contemporary Christianity:
Global Processes and Local Identities

Donald M. Lewis, *Editor*
Christianity Reborn: The Global Expansion of Evangelicalism
in the Twentieth Century

Jon Miller
Missionary Zeal and Institutional Control: Organizational Contradictions
in the Basel Mission on the Gold Coast, 1828-1917

Andrew Porter, *Editor*
The Imperial Horizons of British Protestant Missions, 1880-1914

Dana L. Robert, *Editor*
Converting Colonialism: Visions and Realities in Mission History, 1709-1914

Wilbert R. Shenk, *Editor*
North American Foreign Missions, 1810-1914: Theology, Theory, and Policy

Brian Stanley, *Editor*
Christian Missions and the Enlightenment

Brian Stanley, *Editor*
Missions, Nationalism, and the End of Empire

Kevin Ward and Brian Stanley, *Editors*
The Church Mission Society and World Christianity, 1799-1999

The South Indian Pentecostal Movement in the Twentieth Century

Michael Bergunder

WILLIAM B. EERDMANS PUBLISHING COMPANY
GRAND RAPIDS, MICHIGAN / CAMBRIDGE, U.K.

Published 2008 by
Wm. B. Eerdmans Publishing Co.
2140 Oak Industrial Drive N.E., Grand Rapids, Michigan 49505 /
P.O. Box 163, Cambridge CB3 9PU U.K.

Printed in the United States of America

13 12 11 10 09 08   7 6 5 4 3 2 1

Library of Congress Cataloging-in-Publication Data

Bergunder, Michael.
[Südindische Pfingstbewegung im 20. Jahrhundert. English]
The South Indian Pentecostal movement in the twentieth century /
Michael Bergunder.
p.   cm.
Includes bibliographical references and index.
ISBN 978-0-8028-2734-0 (pbk.: alk. paper)
1. Pentecostalism — India, South — History — 20th century.
2. India, South — Church history — 20th century.
I. Title.

BR1644.5.I4B4713   2008

275.4′082 — dc22

2007005978

www.eerdmans.com

Contents

Acknowledgments   ix

A Note on Transliteration and Conventions   xi

INTRODUCTION: Constructing Indian Pentecostalism   1

HISTORY   21

1. Early Beginnings   23

2. Kerala   37

3. Tamil Nadu   58

4. Karnataka   86

5. Andhra Pradesh   92

6. Evangelists, Interchurch Fellowships, and Marginal Movements   107

BELIEFS AND PRACTICES   121

7. Context   123

8. Themes   130

9. Ordo Salutis   138

10. Gifts of the Spirit   146

11. Ethics   181

12. Ministry   191

13. Church Life   209

14. Social Structure and Ecumenical Relations   231

PROSPECTS   245

15. Pentecostalism and Contextualization of Christianity   247

APPENDIX 1: Selected Biographies   255

APPENDIX 2: Missionaries and Leadership Positions   301

APPENDIX 3: Church Statistics   305

List of Interviews   311

Bibliography   321

Maps   357

Index   365

Acknowledgments

Such a study was possible only with the help of others. Herewith, I would like to express my thanks to all of them. In the first place, I would like to thank my interview partners, who as a rule took time willingly to answer all my questions. This readiness can in no way be taken for granted, and without it the present work would not have been possible. Moreover, I would like to thank in a special way the many Indian Pentecostal pastors and evangelists who allowed me to take part in the congregational life of their churches. I would like to thank Helmut Obst, for the professional and personal support that he untiringly offered in every stage of the project. Similarly, I owe thanks to Theodor Ahrens for the manifold important inspirations that I experienced through him. My approach to the Pentecostal movement is in certain aspects influenced by the work of Walter J. Hollenweger. Hence, I feel the special need to express my gratitude to Prof. Dr. Hollenweger for his energetic support for this undertaking. Thanks also to my friends Andreas Nehring and Daniel Jeyaraj, whose help has contributed greatly to my successful stay in India. Further, I express my thanks to the many church institutions in India that extended hospitality, and to the Evangelical Lutheran Mission Society in Leipzig for the support extended to me. A few archives of the western Pentecostals have made material available to me. To them also I would like to express my thanks. I thank E. Antony for his untiring and valuable help in the translation of texts from Malayalam.

My sincere thanks go to Father Ralph Woodhall, S.J., who translated almost the whole German manuscript into English without ever being asked. Without him the study would have never been available in English. My thanks go also to Allan Anderson, who supported the translation in many ways and to Father Gomez, who translated a part of the manuscript. I thank

Ellen Weinel for her untiring efforts in correcting the manuscript and organizing the index. I am also deeply indebted to Jörg Haustein, who undertook a thorough proofreading of the whole manuscript. My special thanks go to the publisher for very careful editorial work.

Without the endless patience, immense encouragement, and help of Robert Eric Frykenberg this book would never have been published. My sincere thanks go also to Brian Stanley the co-editor of the series, and the reviewers, especially Robert Fox Young, who all helped me to substantially improve the English manuscript.

A Note on Transliteration and Conventions

To avoid misunderstanding, we shall observe certain rules of speech: "Pentecostal movement" will be treated as a general category including those independent churches and independent organizations that call themselves "charismatic." Only where it is quite clear from the context, "Pentecostal movement" will be used in a narrower sense. "Classical Pentecostal churches" is the usual designation in the USA for the big Pentecostal unions, especially the Assemblies of God, the Church of God, and the Church of God of Prophecy. "Charismatic movement" will be used only for inner-church organizations (Protestant or Catholic). When not stated otherwise, technical terms like conversion, Spirit baptism, immersion baptism, and so on are used in a descriptive way according to the self-understanding of the Pentecostal movement. For practical reasons, some churches will be designated with slightly shortened names: the "Indian Pentecostal Church" has the full title Indian Pentecostal Church of God;[1] "Church of God" designates the Church of God (Cleveland, Tennessee), which in India is registered as Church of God (Full Gospel) in India; "British Assemblies of God" means Assemblies of God of Great Britain and Ireland. To avoid unnecessary confusion for those who are not experts, Indian geographical names are generally given according to their modern usage, excepting some grave anachronisms (e.g., Kerala, Tamil Nadu, Karnataka, Andhra Pradesh). An exception is the use of Madras (instead of Chennai), Bombay (instead of Mumbai), and Calcutta (instead of Kolkata). Indian names are mostly given in the usual popular English transliterations,

---

1. "India Pentecostal Church of God" is an authorized synonym, as the church statutes expressly lay down (Indian Pentecostal Church 1991: 1).

and scientific transliterations are avoided wherever possible. Square brackets within quotations always indicate additional explanations by the author.

Introduction: Constructing Indian Pentecostalism

In the course of the twentieth century, the Pentecostal and Charismatic movement developed into one of the most dynamic elements of Christianity and has spread over the whole world, split into innumerable different churches and groupings. In not quite one hundred years, a Charismatic Christianity developed that now comprises between 15 and 25 percent of the worldwide Christian population, with the main regions of its growth being in Latin America, Africa, and Asia, and not in the West. However, the extent and significance of Pentecostalism stands in contrast to the still-inadequate academic research.[1] Basic issues concerning appropriate methodology and representation are not yet resolved. The academic study of and the discussion within the Pentecostal movement up to now show that what is meant by Pentecostalism and how to define it are hotly debated questions. A wide range of answers has been given so far, reaching from extremely narrow definitions to broad ones. Certain circles of white Pentecostalism in the United States, for instance, sometimes try to narrow down Pentecostalism to a subcategory of American evangelicalism.[2] In sharp contrast to that stands the approach of David Barrett, who considers a broad variety of churches, organizations, and networks as representative of Pentecostalism.[3] Current Pentecostal and non-Pentecostal academic study tends to use such a broad understanding of Pentecostalism; and when it comes to statistics even Pentecostals, who otherwise count themselves as Evangelicals,

1. Here, Pentecostalism is understood as a general term that includes Charismatics, Neo-Pentecostals, Faith Movement, and so on.
2. See e.g., Robeck 1990. It is noteworthy that also in recent sociological literature Pentecostals will often be lumped together with Evangelicals. See e.g., Freston 2001.
3. See Barrett 1990.

refer to Barrett's findings that about 25 percent of world Christianity is Pentecostal.[4] Admittedly, a narrow understanding has some real advantages. It would enable a comprehensive definition of Pentecostalism, because a clear-cut dogmatic basis could be formulated (e.g., evangelicalism plus tongues-speaking as initial evidence of Spirit baptism) and an institutional framework assigned (e.g., Pentecostal member-churches of the National Association of Evangelicals). Nevertheless, its heuristic value would be limited as it is absolutely counterintuitive and arbitrarily separates phenomena that belong together. As the acceptance of Barrett's figures already indicates, even the most evangelical-oriented Pentecostals refer in certain contexts to more inclusive identities of Pentecostalism.

From an academic point of view there is no alternative to a broad understanding of Pentecostalism, but so far not much has been done to substantiate this approach in a methodologically satisfying manner. The most serious problem lies in the fact that a broad understanding of Pentecostalism refers neither to a common dogmatic basis nor to a common institutional framework. International umbrella organizations like the Pentecostal World Conference only cover tiny fragments of the Pentecostal movement. Nevertheless, academic research of the last decades has proved the usefulness of a broad understanding of Pentecostalism as a single global phenomenon. However, its unity can't be described in the way traditional church history deals with confessional families like Orthodoxy, Catholicism, Lutheranism, and so on. Other ways have to be found to trace the international discursive network called Pentecostalism. This could be done by having a closer look at the global dimensions of the beginnings of the movement and by describing Pentecostalism in a meaningful manner without referring to specific theological tenets as a basis for definitions.

Global Beginnings of Pentecostalism

In the last few decades, vigorous historical research into the beginnings of the Pentecostal movement has started. To a great extent this has been done by Pentecostal scholars themselves, who have tried to overcome an uncritical, more or less hagiographical tradition of telling about the beginnings, as was common within their churches. This tradition, often called the "providential ap-

4. The recent statistics are found in Barrett et al. 2001: 4 (table 1-1). For a broad understanding of Pentecostalism in modern Pentecostal scholarship see e.g., Hollenweger 1997; Anderson & Hollenweger 1999; Anderson 2001; but see also the critique by McGee 1994: 277.

proach,"[5] was based on the belief that Pentecostalism was "a spontaneous, providentially generated, [worldwide] end-time religious revival, a movement fundamentally discontinuous with 1900 years of Christian history";[6] but such a notion is hardly compatible with academic history. Therefore the "'new' Pentecostal historiography"[7] is trying to relate the emergence of Pentecostalism to nineteenth-century theological roots and to its contemporary social and cultural context. It was Donald Dayton's *Theological Roots of Pentecostalism* (1987) that set the standard for this new endeavor.[8] Dayton argued in a richly textured historical analysis that the theological patterns of Pentecostalism could be traced back to nineteenth-century Wesleyan, Reformed, and Higher Life holiness circles in the United States. At the turn of the twentieth century, this vast network of holiness institutions and movements constituted "a sort of pre-Pentecostal tinderbox awaiting the spark that would set it off."[9] Numerous important studies have come out more recently that further prove he continuity between Pentecostalism and nineteenth-century popular American evangelicalism, though there are discussions about the details (e.g., Wesleyan versus Reformed roots).[10] Pentecostal and non-Pentecostal historians now consider Topeka and Azusa Street as the outcome of a specific American (and to some extent British) religious history.

As a side effect, this strict historical approach rejects the notion that Pentecostalism was a worldwide revival from its very beginnings. This assumption of multiple, worldwide origins of Pentecostalism was the popular self-understanding of early Pentecostals and became an integral part of the providential historical self-understanding in Pentecostal circles (e.g., it is part of the famous popular histories of Donald Gee and Stanley H. Frodsham).[11] Nevertheless, from an academic point of view, this kind of Americanization of Pentecostal historiography seemed to be inevitable, as Robeck rightly states: ". . . without wishing to be triumphalistic, the evidence gathered in all

---

5. Cerillo 1997: 31-36; Wacker 1990: 69-76; Cerillo & Wacker 2002: 397-99.

6. Cerillo 1997: 32.

7. Cerillo 1999: 229.

8. See Dayton 1987.

9. Dayton 1987: 174.

10. See e.g., MacRobert 1988; Faupel 1996; Wacker 2001.

11. "One remarkable feature of the Latter-Rain outpouring in the early days was the way the Spirit of God fell upon one and another in different parts of the world who had never come in contact with anyone who had received the Pentecostal experience" (Frodsham 1946: 53). ". . . yet there was also occurring a truly spontaneous and simultaneous Revival on Pentecostal lines in widely separated places. The only agency was a deep hunger for such a Revival produced in the hearts of Christians by the Holy Spirit Himself" (Gee 1967: 29-30).

serious quests for origins of the modern Pentecostal movement appears inevitably to point to North America."[12] However, it is not without problems, as that historiography now runs counter to the early Pentecostal self-understanding as a global movement and that worldwide Pentecostalism becomes necessarily the result of Pentecostal missionary work from North America. Especially among scholars who focus their research on the non-western Pentecostal movement, there is a certain uneasiness with such an American-centered history, as this does not seem to do justice to the multifaceted and global nature of the Pentecostal phenomenon.

In the following, we would like to offer a way out of the dilemma, when we argue that there is an additional historical root of Pentecostalism that has been somewhat neglected as a distinctive category so far: the *missionary movement*. The nineteenth century and early twentieth century, up to the beginning of the First World War in 1914, was the heyday of colonialism. Under the brutal rule of colonial powers nearly the whole world was brought into the reach of the West. In that situation, parts of western Christianity reacted with missionary initiatives to spread the Christian faith in Africa and Asia, and a huge number of missionary societies were founded for that purpose.[13] The specific conditions on the "mission fields" brought many Protestant missionary societies into close contact with each other, and in the course of time a global missionary network beyond denominational boundaries developed. This emerging global network led to the famous World Missionary Conference at Edinburgh in 1910 that is arguably the beginning of the ecumenical movement.[14]

Religious revivals always played a crucial role in the missionary movement, as they influenced many of the missionary recruits. However, in the second half of the nineteenth century a development took place that is of special interest in regard to Pentecostalism. It was during this time that premillennialism permeated evangelical circles in Britain (first in the Brethren movement) and in the United States (in the prophecy conferences, starting in New York in 1878). This was accompanied by a new missionary awareness: "On the great missionary movement hangs the appointed hour of the millennial dawn, of the marriage of the Lamb, of the glory of the resurrection, of the time of the restitution of all things."[15] As a result, several so-

---

12. Robeck 1993: 170. See Nichol, who called the United States the "Birthplace of Twentieth-Century Pentecostalism" (Nichol 1966: 25).

13. See Neill 1964; Hutchison 1987. For the connection between western missionary activities and colonialism see Gründer 1992.

14. See Rouse & S. Neill 1994.

15. Annual Report of the International Missionary Alliance 1892: 62, quoted in Fiedler 1992: 364 n. 77.

called "faith missions" were founded.[16] The idea of faith missions (strictly interdenominational, no fixed salary, missionaries as members not employees of the mission, and so on) was first formulated in Hudson Taylor's China Inland Mission (London 1865), but became widely popular through the work of Fanny and Grattan Guinness, who founded the East London Training Institute in 1873. The Guinnesses influenced A. B. Simpson and the Christian and Missionary Alliance (1887), and, during a journey through the United States in 1889, Fanny Guinness was instrumental in starting the Boston Missionary Training Institute (A. J. Gordon) and the Chicago Evangelization Society (later Moody Bible Institute). Another enthusiastic promoter of faith missions was Arthur Tappan Pierson, a Christian journalist, who edited the *Missionary Review of the World* from 1886 (in 1891 joined by Gordon as co-editor). The Student Volunteer Missionary Union (1886) was also part of this premillennial-oriented evangelical missionary network, and was inspired by Dwight L. Moody and led by John R. Mott. The latter chose the motto "the evangelization of the World in this generation" (originally coined by Pierson) for this organization.[17] Through this vast network, American holiness circles became part of the global missionary movement and this in turn affirmed a strong missionary awareness among them. It was this missionary awareness that became a decisive theological root for Pentecostalism, and it gives some clues as to why tongues-speaking became so important for the movement.[18]

Charles Parham created the threefold theological formula that was used at Azusa Street: "1) Tongue speech as the initial evidence of Holy Spirit Baptism, 2) Spirit-filled believers as the 'sealed' Bride of Christ, and 3) xenoglossic tongues as the tool for dramatic end-time revival."[19] It is arguable that the idea of xenoglossic tongues ("missionary tongues") was the most important aspect among these three points. In the early days, Pentecostals thought that their glossolalia was actually foreign tongues for missionary purposes. This was hitherto rather overlooked, as the Pentecostal movement quietly gave up the idea of xenoglossy later. Nevertheless, a number of sources point to the fact that Parham got his emphasis on tongues-speaking from the missionary movement.

---

16. See Fiedler 1994: 65-102, 359-70.

17. See Rosenkranz 1977: 218-19.

18. Dayton did not identify a theological root for tongues-speaking: "Nearly every wing of late nineteenth-century revivalism was teaching in one form or another all the basic themes of Pentecostalism except for the experience of glossolalia, or 'speaking in tongues'" (Dayton 1987: 167). The following reflections are mainly based on the findings of Goff 1988; Faupel 1996; and McGee 2001: 118-23.

19. Goff 1988: 173.

William Faupel shows convincingly the deep influence of the missionary movement on Parham.[20] The premillennialist missionary strategy was not aiming at converting the whole world to Christianity, but to be a witness to all nations and to give the chance to as many people as possible to accept the Christian message before Christ's Second Coming. Within such a perspective, time was running out and it became an urgent question as to how successful missionary work could be possible in such a limited timeframe. For one thing, the extremely time-consuming learning of foreign languages was felt to be a major obstacle. In this connection, isolated reports about the occurrence of the gift of xenoglossy spread in missionary circles.[21] Prominent was the tale of a young woman called Jennie Glassey, who had received African languages through the Holy Spirit in 1895.[22] The Glassey case became known to Charles Parham and impressed him very much, as it seemed to prove that God could enable missionaries by giving them the necessary foreign languages.[23] Furthermore, in premillennial circles the idea was widespread that the Second Coming of Christ would be preceded by a worldwide revival that would greatly enlarge missionary work. Through the influence of Frank Sandford, Charles Parham accepted this notion and then brought it all together into the new Pentecostal "Latter Rain" concept.[24]

These two points, which Parham developed under the influence of the missionary movement (missionary tongues and worldwide revival), became part of the core self-understanding of the Azusa Street Revival in 1906, as can be seen from its periodical, *The Apostolic Faith*.[25] For the participants of Azusa Street it was clear that tongues-speaking meant missionary tongues for a worldwide end-time revival that now had started in Los Angeles. To prove this claim it was of utmost importance that the revival would develop into a global phenomenon within a short time. This pressure gave Azusa Street an extremely global outlook from its very start.

As already mentioned, many evangelicals at home and in the "mission fields" shared the idea of a worldwide end-time revival. Moreover, Azusa Street falls in a time when many thought that such a revival had already

20. See Faupel 1996: 115-86.
21. See McGee 2001.
22. See Goff 1988: 72-73; Hunter 1997; McGee 2001.
23. See Faupel 1996: 174.
24. See Faupel 1996: 167.
25. "This is a world-wide revival, the last Pentecostal revival to bring our Jesus" (*Apostolic Faith*, vol. 1., no. 1, Sept. 1906: 4). "God is solving the missionary problem, sending out new-tongued missionaries on the apostolic faith line, without purse or scrip, and the Lord is going before them preparing the way" (*Apostolic Faith*, vol. 1., no. 3, Nov. 1906: 2).

started. The revival chronicler Edwin Orr speaks of a global "Fifth General Awakening" between 1900 and 1910 (including Keswick, the Torrey and Alexander evangelistic ministry, the Welsh Revival, the Khasi Hills Revival, the Mukti Mission, and the Korean Revival).[26] During that time, the global missionary movement that was connected through a dense network of extensive correspondence and personal contacts was much focused on revival matters: "What was remarkable was that missionaries and national believers in obscure places in India, the Far East, Africa and Latin America seemed to move at the same time to pray for phenomenal revival in their fields and worldwide."[27] Contemporary outsiders, like Frederick Henke, saw Azusa Street simply as a small part of this revival: "This speaking in tongues is but one of a series of such phenomena as 'tongues of fire,' 'rushing of a mighty wind,' 'interpretation of tongues,' jerking, writhing, and falling to the ground, which are occurring in connection with a world-wide religious revival."[28] Moreover, Orr is of the opinion that during this "Fifth General Awakening," Pentecostalism was not a crucial factor, but only an indirect by-product.[29]

It is important to keep in mind the relatively small impact of the Azusa Street Revival at that time, because it contradicts the self-understanding of the Pentecostal movement. Azusa Street claimed to be the definitive formula for and sure beginning of the end-time revival, fulfilling all revival hopes that were transmitted through the missionary movement. They thus claimed the whole ongoing revival movement for themselves: "The present world-wide revival was rocked in the cradle of little Wales. It was 'brought up' in India, following; becoming full grown in Los Angeles later."[30] In this situation, it became crucial to get their views accepted within international evangelical circles. Azusa Street went global from the very start and began to channel its message through the vast international evangelical and missionary network that was receptive to revivals. As the Azusa Street participants were themselves part of this network and the Pentecostal formula contained mainly ele-

26. "It was the most extensive Evangelical Awakening of all time, reviving Anglican, Baptist, Congregational, Disciple, Lutheran, Methodist, Presbyterian and Reformed churches and other evangelical bodies throughout Europe and North America, Australasia and South Africa, and their daughter churches and missionary causes throughout Asia, Africa and Latin America, winning more than five million folk to an evangelical faith in the two years of greatest impact in each country" (Orr 1976: 99). See also Orr 1973; Orr 1976: 99-106.

27. Orr 1976: 100.

28. Henke 1909: 193-206 (193).

29. "Indirectly it [the Fifth General Awakening] produced Pentecostalism" (Orr 1976: 99). See also Faupel 1996: 190.

30. Bartleman 1980: 19.

ments that were familiar to those circles (fivefold gospel and end-time revival), they found easy access.

It is amazing to see how quickly the Azusa Street Revival received positive responses in different parts of the world. However, as Joe Creech has rightly emphasized,[31] joining the Azusa Street Revival movement was not necessarily connected with formal changes in institutional structure and ethos or theological traditions; nor did this establish formal institutional ties with Azusa Street. It spread because individuals and organizations generally accepted that a second Pentecost with the experience of tongues-speaking and other spiritual gifts like healing and prophecy had happened, and they declared themselves to be part of it. In that way, different and divergent streams could join the Pentecostal movement, as nearly everybody who desired it could become part of it. Because of that, internal tensions and splits were a fundamental part of the movement right from its beginnings. The spread of the Azusa Street Revival was essentially a kind of networking within evangelical and missionary circles. It took place in at least three different ways: correspondence and magazines; evangelistic journeys and other personal contacts; and missionary work. Some examples to emphasize this threefold global outreach may illustrate this.[32]

In September 1906 Azusa Street started its first journal, *The Apostolic Faith,* with 5,000 copies; half a year later it was already printing 40,000. Numerous new Pentecostal periodicals started and existing ones became Pentecostal all over North America and far beyond. It is said that, within the first year of the Azusa Street Revival, vernacular Pentecostal newspapers were printed in Norway, Germany, China, Japan, Palestine, and Brazil.[33] This publication network was accompanied by immense and intensive correspondence. In January 1907, it was reported that up to fifty letters reached Azusa Street alone every day.[34] Nearly all Pentecostal groups in the early years maintained extensive international mail networks. One gets the impression that each corresponded with everyone. Through these written channels an imagined global Pentecostal community was created that assured the individual believer of the international success of the revival and made it attractive to join in.

But it was also through personal contacts that the message was spread. Right from the beginning, the specific worship practice of Azusa Street —

---

31. See Creech 1996: 405-24.
32. For a good concise overview see Faupel 1996: 212-27.
33. Wacker 2001: 263.
34. See *Apostolic Faith,* vol. 1, no. 5, Jan. 1907: 4.

heavily shaped by black spirituality[35] — was passed on through common worship when people flocked from all over the country and even abroad to Los Angeles to "get their Pentecost." Besides, quite a number of Pentecostal leaders undertook global evangelistic tours, so that "Pentecostals' geographic restlessness seemed so pronounced that the movement eventually became synonymous with itinerancy."[36] For instance, Anseln Howard Post was an early member of Azusa Street who in 1907 started travels abroad that took him as far as South Africa, England, Wales, and Ceylon.[37] Thomas Ball Barratt had come from Norway to the USA and became Pentecostal after visiting Azusa Street in 1906; and in 1908-1909 he traveled through much of Europe and undertook a journey to India.[38] Daniel Awrey circled the globe in 1909; in 1910/1911 he was in India and China, and he died in Liberia in 1913.[39] Frank Bartleman, after he had already traveled extensively in the USA, started in 1910 on a round-the-world trip via Europe, Palestine, Egypt, India, Ceylon, China, Japan, and Hawaii.[40] These evangelists and several others traveled along established evangelical networks, and in the "mission fields" they tried to impress their beliefs on missionaries open to the evangelical revival teachings.

However, the most spectacular global outreach of early Azusa Street were the missionaries who went out in confidence that they were equipped with foreign tongues to preach the Pentecostal message in the vernaculars. Quite a few former faith missionaries participated in Azusa Street (e.g., Samuel J. Mead and George E. Berg) and even helped to identify specific African or Asian languages allegedly being spoken by some in worship services, as is amply reported in *The Apostolic Faith*. Boosted by the impression that he had spoken Bengali at Azusa Street, A. G. Garr and his wife (who supposedly spoke Tibetan and Chinese) started for India, where they arrived at the beginning of 1907.[41] S. J. Mead, former missionary with William Taylor in Africa for twenty years, organized a missionary party that allegedly had received African languages to go to Africa, and the group embarked in December 1906.[42]

---

35. On the question of black spirituality at Azusa Street and its difference from Parham's teachings see MacRobert 1992; Hollenweger 1997: 31-56; Daniels 1999: 222-52. But see also Taves (1999: 328-37), who opens up new perspectives to explain the different spiritualities between Parham and Azusa Street.

36. Wacker 2001: 215.

37. See Gitre 2002.

38. Barratt 1927; Bloch-Hoell: 68.

39. *Apostolic Faith,* vol. 1, no. 2. Oct. 1906: 4; Hunter 2002; Bartleman 1980: 83.

40. Bartleman 1980: 146.

41. *Apostolic Faith,* vol. 1, no. 1, Sept. 1906: 4; *Apostolic Faith,* vol. 1, no. 2, Oct. 1906: 2.

42. Faupel 1996: 220-21.

In September 1907, M. L. Ryan collected a dozen men and women to go to Japan, clearly confident that they would be equipped with the necessary languages through missionary tongues.[43] When these missionaries arrived at their "mission fields," they naturally became disillusioned because missionary tongues were not available,[44] but it seems that only a few abandoned their Pentecostal objectives. Some returned early; some, like the Garrs, concentrated on revival preaching among western missionaries; and others stayed and turned to traditional methods.[45] In that way they played an essential role in establishing an international Pentecostal network.

This threefold global networking of early Pentecostalism was not without success. Many faith missionaries (especially from the Christian and Missionary Alliance) joined the new Pentecostal network. So did quite a few indigenous workers and adherents of faith missions,[46] and it will become crucial for further research to concentrate on their contribution to the making of global Pentecostalism.[47] Rewriting Pentecostal history in such a way will probably bring new and unforeseen insights that might change quite a few of the established views.[48] At the end of 1908, the Pentecostal movement had taken root in around fifty countries all over the world,[49] and it could be stated that it had virtually "circled the globe."[50] A truly worldwide network was thus estab-

---

43. See Wacker 2001: 86.

44. As Pentecostal theologian Gary McGee clearly stated: "Evidence of any early Pentecostal missionary ever receiving a new language in this manner does not exist" (McGee 1986: 45). See also Henke 1909: 205-6. A theological reflection on the failing of missionary tongues is now going on within Pentecostal theology; see Powers 2000: 39-55.

45. It seems to be not entirely clear whether all early Pentecostal missionaries initially believed they were equipped with missionary tongues. Further research should bring clarification, because already at Azusa Street we find the clear notion that tongues were not necessarily for use in a foreign field "but as a sign to you of Pentecost," as G. A. Cook wrote to T. B. Barratt in October 1906 (Bundy 1992: 164). Robeck gives further examples from the early times where speaking in tongues was not connected to foreign languages. (W. F. Carother, Nov. 1906; Report of Chicago Revival, summer 1907; C. H. Mason, Feb./Mar. 1907). See Robeck 1999: 8.

46. From China we know that in addition to that indigenous workers from established missions joined the Pentecostal fold — see Bays 1999: 61; for India see below.

47. See, for instance, Anderson 2007.

48. See, for instance, the Indian case. Histories of early Indian Pentecostalism that focus on the work of western Pentecostal missionaries are still in vogue (see, e.g., Burgess 2001: 85-98), but, when the Indians write themselves about their history, the picture changes completely (see Saju 1994; George 2001: 215-37).

49. See Faupel 1996: 15 n. 6.

50. *Apostolic Faith* (Ore.), July-Aug. 1908: 1; *Latter Rain Evangel*, Mar. 1909: 5; quoted in Wacker 2001: 263.

lished. Only then had Azusa Street proved to be the start of a worldwide revival, because without an immediate global establishment, the revival would have fallen short of all expectations according to its self-image.

Putting the Pentecostal beginnings into such a global context means that only this worldwide network could be called Pentecostalism in the true sense. Azusa Street was the prelude, but the beginning of Pentecostalism was reached when a global Pentecostal network was established. The beginning of Pentecostalism is neither a creed, an institution, nor a place, but a vast and vague international network; and in that specific sense Pentecostalism was a global movement right from its beginnings. And it is in this context that the beginnings of Pentecostalism in India have to be understood, as will be shown later.

Outlining a Definition of Pentecostalism

Pentecostalism could not keep its initial promises. As Faupel has emphasized, by the end of 1908 it became clear that Pentecostal expectations had not been realized.[51] "The delay of the parousia and inability to speak in known tongues forced most Pentecostals to reassess their mission."[52] Unlike many others, the Pentecostal revival did not vanish after the initial promises had to be revised. The global network that was established within a few years marked the beginning of a movement that would vigorously shape world Christianity in years to come. This divergent, multi-voiced, and fragmented movement kept the idea of a common Pentecostal identity, but it appears that it is very difficult for scholars to define the phenomenon appropriately. As Everett Wilson has pointed out, there is no institutional setting of Pentecostalism: "At no time, within the ranks, did adherents make up a discrete, readily identifiable group."[52] Moreover, Wilson also disputes the existence of an essential theological agenda: "By almost any standard, Pentecostalism presently is not what Charles Fox Parham or any of his successors had pronounced it to be, but rather what contemporary Brazilians, Koreans and Africans demonstrate that it actually is."[53] Nevertheless, there are certainly things that form a distinctive Pentecostal identity, however vague it might be. One might guess that it has something to do with a certain spiritual practice (intuitive, experiential, Spirit-centered devotion; oral liturgy; firm biblical orientation; narrative theology and testimonies; strong lay participation; healing, and so on), but even

51. See Faupel 1996: 228.
52. Faupel 1996: 308.
53. Wilson 1999: 108-9.

then it is rather something that is subject to constant change and dependent on mutual affirmation because "every generation is the first generation" in Pentecostalism.[54] The vigorous debates about Pentecostal identity that are going on within Pentecostal theology will therefore rather help to shape, create, and reaffirm this identity than to discover essential categories that could be used as a starting point for a scholarly definition.[55]

If there are no institutional or theological avenues for definition, then it might be a good idea to look for a non-essential way of mapping the Pentecostal network as global discursive formation. We suggest applying two criteria for outlining Pentecostalism: historical connections and synchronous interrelations. Both of these criteria have to be applied within a global context, as Pentecostalism has been a global movement right from its very beginning. The first criterion demands that everything we count as Pentecostal must be connected within a vast diachronous network that goes back to the beginning of Pentecostalism. That means that the question of direct historical influences becomes a crucial one and that all parallel phenomena without historical connections (e.g., Irvingites, cargo movements) must not be called Pentecostal. In addition to historical connections, the second criterion demands that only that which is linked together in a synchronous network can be called Pentecostalism. This purely descriptive definition corresponds, as far as we see, to the way most Pentecostal and non-Pentecostal scholars who prefer a broad definition of Pentecostalism are using the term, though they seldom make their use explicit. Moreover, this definitory proposal doesn't seem to be counterintuitive to common Pentecostal self-understanding. Although the definition is very much based on common sense, it has some rather harsh consequences for actual research, because without establishing a diachronous and synchronous network one must no longer speak of Pentecostalism.

For the establishment of the diachronous network a critical, strictly historical perspective has to be applied. Tracing historical connections usually means focusing on churches that have split and on pastors that changed their affiliation from one Pentecostal denomination to another, often taking with them whole congregations or even a set of churches. It is precisely these frictions that are most important for the historian who tries to sketch a diachronous network. The problem is that this approach is usually not in line with the common stereotyped pattern of testimonies and hagiographies that church leaders like to tell. Especially in many popular accounts of denomina-

54. Wilson 1999: 106.
55. For that debate, see e.g., Johns 1995: 3-17; Smith 1997: 49-71; Chan 2000; Coulter 2001: 38-64; Kärkkäinen 2002: 187-98.

tional histories, the illusion is fostered that the respective church started under direct godly providence and splits or contacts with other churches or leaders, and so on, are not thoroughly analyzed. But then, such accounts do not contribute much to a general Pentecostal history. If we want to write a history of Pentecostalism, we have to trace historical connections, and this information is often hard to get. They are usually not found in oral testimonies or written documents and are in danger of getting lost when the respective generation has died. It will never be possible to reconstruct the full diachronous interconnections; but it is necessary to keep the gaps in mind carefully, because without a diachronous network there is no Pentecostalism. In this context, it is of utmost importance that the bias of western archival sources and indigenous hagiographical traditions is not reproduced by the historian but is critically broken up and put under hermeneutical suspicion.

Similarly, establishing a synchronous network is very demanding. The description of a major denomination that calls itself Pentecostal does not contribute much to the research of Pentecostalism. Instead, it is necessary to map a communicative network between different churches, organizations, and individuals that share the same diachronous network at the specific time period the research is focusing on. Through this synchronous network, theological styles and oral tradition will be made or kept compatible with each other. Theologoumena can be subjected to comparative control and be mutually assimilated, so that some sort of common Pentecostal identity will be created. This synchronous network is very fluid and is in no way a closed structure, and it remains open to discussion because it is subject to rapid historical change. But that does not mean that the power of representation is equally distributed within the synchronous network. On the contrary, representational power depends very much on the control of material and intellectual resources, so that dominant discourses shape the synchronous network and need to be thoroughly analyzed. Moreover, constructing the Pentecostal network is not only a scholarly enterprise, but those who undertake it may themselves exercise discursive control over Pentecostalism by doing so.

Within the one ideal global synchronous network there are many partial networks (e.g., regional networks, Charismatic movements, white American evangelical Pentecostal churches) and, if some church or organization is part of the historical but not of the contemporarily existing synchronous network, then this is purely a descriptive statement that may be subject to change. It could be the case that it was part of the synchronous network in the past and/or became (again) part of the network afterward. The synchronous network has always tested boundaries, as shown by the case of the African Instituted Churches, which share in many aspects common historical roots with the Pentecostal movement and were at a time, at least to some extent, loose parts of a synchronous network;[56] and there are many signs that some of them will reclaim a Pentecostal identity and re-enter the synchronous network.[57] Accordingly, this study will understand Indian Pentecostalism as a constructed category that must be established as both a diachronous and a synchronous network. This approach can open new ways in dealing with the complex methodological problems of regional studies on Pentecostalism, and hopefully, the present study will serve as an example.

Scope of the Study

Cultural geography may divide India roughly into three main regions, distinguished historically, culturally, religiously, and politically: northeast India, north India, and south India. Also the situation of Christianity in the three regions is quite distinct. While the northeast, inhabited by so-called tribals or adivasis, has a more Christian presence, Christianity in north India represents a vanishingly small minority. In south India, where nearly two-thirds of Indian Christians live, Christianity represents a relatively strong minority and has reached a relatively high proportion of the general population, as for example in the southern part of Kerala and the southern tip of Tamil Nadu. This study thus limits its research to south India, because this is not only the center of Indian Christianity but of Indian Pentecostalism too. Notwithstanding the overall minority situation of Indian Christianity, the percentage of Pentecostals in the south Indian Christian population is relatively high with a growing trend. Already 20 percent of south Indian Protestants are Pentecostals. While we have quite good information on the history and present condition of the established churches, there is hardly anything known about the Pentecostal movement in India.[58] Despite its numerical strength and its hundred years of history, Indian Pentecostalism has remained rather invisible in the academic writing on Christianity in India. Hopefully, the present study will help to change this situation.

56. See Maxwell 1999: 243-64.
57. See Anderson 2001.
58. Compare, however, the important works of Hoerschelmann 1977 (condensed English edition in 1998) and Caplan 1987; Caplan 1989; and Saju 1994. Since the second half of the 1990s several articles were published on the south Indian Pentecostal movement that show a new awareness of the issue, though these texts contain, as a rule, only few new findings; see Bayly 1994; Burgess 2001; Burgess 2002; George 2001; Hedlund 2001; Hedlund 2002a; Hedlund 2002b; Leembruggen-Kallberg 2002; Matthew 2002; McGee 1996a; McGee 1996b; McGee 1999; McGee 2002; Morgan 2002; Pulikottil 2001; Sullivan 2002.

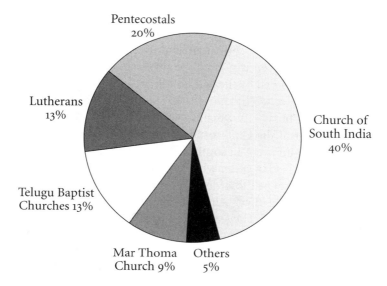

South Indian Protestantism (1994)

There are some social and denominational peculiarities in south Indian Christianity that need to be mentioned. Christianity in south India traces its origin to the apostle Thomas who, according to the legend, landed on the coast of present-day Kerala in the year 52 CE. Historical evidence dates from the fourth century. When the Portuguese reached India in the sixteenth century, they found a Christian church in Kerala which remained in communion with the east-Syrian Catholikos in Baghdad. There followed massive efforts for reunion by the Catholic Church with the support of Portuguese colonial rulers. These efforts were crowned with success only to the extent that, in an extremely painful confrontation marking the sixteenth and seventeenth centuries, they led to a splitting of the Thomas Christians; resulting from this, one section belongs to the Catholic Church and another to the Syrian Orthodox patriarchate of Antioch. In the nineteenth century, under the influence of Anglican missionaries, a Protestant section separated from the Syrian orthodox church and founded the Mar Thoma Church. Further divisions followed when many Thomas Christians went over to the Brethren at the end of nineteenth century and then to the Pentecostal movement in the twentieth. The high proportion of Christians in southern Kerala is mainly due to the Thomas Christians.[59]

59. On the history of the Thomas Christians see Verghese 1974; Joseph Thekkedath 1982: 19-140; Mundadan 1984; Visvanathan 1993.

A specialty of the Thomas Christians is that, in spite of their divisions, they maintain a common identity, analogous to Hindu castes *(jatis)*. They practice an extraordinarily consistent endogamy (even across denominational lines), and they keep very much to themselves in churches dominated by them. This is intensified by the fact that they claim to come from Brahmin families formerly converted by the apostle Thomas.[60] This elitist claim, made against the Christian majority which mostly comes from the lower classes, is also shared by most of the Pentecostals coming from this community.

Another important event in south Indian church history was the conversion of part of the Nadar caste, which is mostly found in southern Tamil Nadu.[61] The Nadars earned their livelihood mainly by harvesting palms; socially and economically they belonged to the most discriminated-against groups of the population. They were also considered as a very low caste. In the course of the nineteenth century there was a liberation movement among the Nadars that developed into a massive conversion to Christianity, by which many Nadars gained economic advantages as well as overcoming discrimination by caste. According to a 1969 estimate, at least a quarter of the Nadars converted to Christianity;[62] probably even more than this did.[63] A large proportion of the Christians in Tamil Nadu are Nadars. The fact that nearly 40 percent of the whole population of Kanyakumari District in the southern tip of Tamil Nadu are Christian is mainly due to the Nadar Christians.[64] The Christian Nadars hold strongly to their Nadar identity, as shown for instance by their strict endogamy. Alongside the Thomas Christians, they represent the second closed grouping within south Indian Christianity.

In the northern part of Tamil Nadu and in Andhra Pradesh were the so-called Dalits, who largely turned to Christianity.[65] Here again it was largely in mass conversions, especially in Andhra Pradesh. They are divided into various groupings, occasionally in dispute with one another. In Andhra Pradesh

60. On the Thomas Christians' understanding of themselves see Forrester 1980: 97-117.

61. On their history see Hardgrave 1969.

62. See Hardgrave 1969: 270f.; Frykenberg 1976.

63. Parallel to this development, in the second half of the nineteenth century, there was also a liberation movement among the Hindu Nadars. Within a hundred years, they became, economically and politically, one of the most influential groups in Tamil Nadu. This was accompanied by the claim to belong to the second highest Hindu caste, the Kshatriyas.

64. Census of India 1981; see Church Growth Research Centre 1992: 596.

65. "Dalit" is today the generally recognized name for those population groupings that in Brahmanic Hinduism are treated as untouchable or without caste. The positively intended name *Harijan* (children of God), proposed by Gandhi, is today felt by Dalits to be discriminating. On the situation of Christian Dalits see Webster 1992; Evangelisches Missionswerk in Deutschland 1995.

there is a longstanding conflict between the Malas and the Madigas, who both belong to Dalit communities. Besides, there are also many Christians from other Hindu communities, but these mostly appear regionally as special groups.[66]

Among south Indian Christians there is still a strong awareness of their different socio-religious ancestries, with the result that caste discrimination persists in Christian churches, although in a very modified form. The Pentecostal churches are no exception. However, it should not be forgotten that at the same time, there are many individual Indian Christians who give faithful witness through their lives that for them caste distinctions play no role. Since this problem is a delicate matter, conflict conditioned by caste has only been approached where it was absolutely necessary in this presentation. In general, the author has been very reserved in order not to risk aggravating confrontations or provoking new ones.

More than half of south Indian Christians are members of the Catholic Church. The remainder belong to a number of different churches. The non-Catholic Thomas Christians, as already mentioned, belong mostly to the Syrian Orthodox Church and the Mar Thoma Church. The other non-Catholic Christians belong, for the most part, to the Church of South India, a union of various western mission churches. The Lutheran churches, among which the Tamil Evangelical Lutheran Church and the Andhra Evangelical Lutheran Church should be mentioned, did not join this union. The Baptists also, strongly represented in Andhra Pradesh, remained independent. Next to these, there are Methodists, many smaller evangelical churches, and of course the Pentecostal movement.[67] The confessional boundaries in south India are traditionally much less strict than in Europe and exchanges between particular churches not uncommon.[68] This situation is also, of course, connected with the fact that there is a strong tradition of proselytism, beginning with efforts of the Catholic Church for union in the sixteenth century, continuing in the nineteenth with the embittered competitive struggles of the mission churches to win adherents.[69] These unhappy developments contributed to the fact that a genuine sense of confessional tradition was only rarely formed. And this was surely one reason why various missionary churches came together to form the

66. So, e.g., the Ezhavas (related to the Nadars) in southern Kerala, the Mukkulathor communities in the districts of Usilampatti and Thanjavur (Tamil Nadu), and Vellalas in Thanjavur District (Tamil Nadu). In Andhra Pradesh, it is especially the Kammas and Reddis who have come to Christianity from the higher-caste Hindu population.

67. A good overview of the Protestant churches in India is given by Grafe 1981.

68. See, e.g., the experience of a south Indian Christian in Sundkler 1954: 31-33.

69. Baago 1966: 17-35; Bergunder 2000a.

Church of South India in 1947.[70] After Indian independence, south Indian Christianity could no longer increase its percentage of the whole population but only with difficulty maintain it. An exceptional case is Andhra Pradesh, where there was a dramatic fall from 4.19 percent in 1971 to 2.68 percent in 1981. But since these figures come from the official census, there is ground for suspicion that many Christian Dalits ceased to confess their Christianity in order to enjoy the privileges reserved for Hindu Dalits.[71] The south Indian Pentecostal movement shows rapid growth against the generally known trend.

Our historical and systematic presentation of the south Indian Pentecostal movement is based on extensive empirical research between 1993 and 1995. During long stays in south India, the author had the opportunity to get to know the life of various Pentecostal congregations and to take an active part in worship and other community events.[72] Formal interviews were conducted with 191 leading pastors and evangelists as well as prominent laypeople who served as sources for the research.[73] The author managed to question nearly all the key figures in the south Indian Pentecostal movement. The interviews were informal but based on a list of questions. The order and manner of questioning depended on the situation only insofar as many important questions, for instance about caste problems and church divisions, were seen by many as too delicate. The interviews lasted on average for one and a half to two hours and proceeded always in a very good atmosphere. Additionally, written material of all kinds was collected: address lists, leaflets, letters, prospectuses, souvenirs of jubilee celebrations, edifying literature, testimonies, and so on.[74] Material from western mission archives was also used. For the history of the south Indian Pentecostal movement, however, written material is much less significant than information from interviews. Usually the former is of a very propagandist character and can therefore only be brought into use where it is a question of making sure of historical dates or questions of self-presentation. Much in the south Indian Pentecostal movement is only transmitted as oral tradition.

The first part of this study follows the history of the south Indian Pentecos-

---

70. See Sundkler 1954 for the history of the development of this church.

71. Prabakaran 1990: 4-28.

72. Most of the material was collected during visits in India from November 1993 to November 1994 and from January 1995 to April 1995. Some updating was done in subsequent visits.

73. Since the author promised confidentiality to his informants, the quotations in the text cannot be attributed.

74. The author could himself make use of material in English or in Tamil. For Malayalam texts, he had the help of translators. Texts in Telugu or in Kannada could not be considered.

tal movement. Based on the theoretical background explained above, a new style of Pentecostal historiography will be proposed where denominational perspectives are overcome, indigenous agencies are put into the center, and frictions, splits, and conflicts are not suppressed and omitted but consciously brought into the focus of discussion. Accordingly, special attention is given to describing the many independent churches and groups in their relations with one another. The divisiveness should not obscure the extent of networking within the south Indian Pentecostal movement. International contacts and partnerships between churches are described wherever possible. Such a historical overview will create the framework that is a presupposition for any future research into individual churches. The numerical importance of any church or organization was taken as a decisive criterion for its presence in this historical presentation.[75] Exceptions were made where a particular indigenous church or organization, which might be of slight statistical significance, has made some original contribution to the development of the south Indian Pentecostal movement.[76] Biographical sketches of several Pentecostal leaders are put in appendix 1, in order to make the historical part more readable. Because these biographical outlines are based on the available sources they often remain fragmentary, but even so they are vital for a comprehensive understanding of a Pentecostal network based on personal interconnections.

The second part of the study presents a systematic profile of the south Indian Pentecostal movement. This will cover the question of how Pentecostal spirituality relates to the Indian context and to the living folk religiosity shaped by Hinduism. But the foreground is taken by a synchronic description closely guided by the concrete practice of the communities. This takes into account that Pentecostal teaching and spirituality are strongly related to experience and praxis.[77] Only so can the special characteristics of the south Indian Pentecostal movement be explicated.[78] Wherever the author recognized original theological positions taken by south Indian Pentecostals, he has quoted them, if possible.

---

75. The attention given to churches that originated in American missionary work, especially the Assemblies of God, is also related to their statistical significance. In some particular cases the greater availability of sources in churches coming from western missions has led to a slightly more detailed presentation. But altogether the proportions, especially in the main texts, have been preserved.

76. See, e.g., Christian Fellowship Centre, Bangalore, or Maranatha Visvasa Samajam, Vijayawada.

77. See Land 1993: 32-47; Parker 1996: 20-28.

78. The description presupposes the present state of discussion concerning the worldwide Pentecostal movement but, in some places, it has reference to literature that takes the issues further.

HISTORY

CHAPTER 1

Early Beginnings

India played an important role in the worldwide revival that took place in the first decade of the twentieth century, especially through the events in the Khasi Hills and at the Mukti Mission. At the end of the nineteenth century, expectations for a new revival were high in India too.[1] In 1898, Pandita Ramabai attended the Keswick convention and requested the people there to pray for a missionary awakening among the Indians.[2] Ramabai, a Marathi Brahmin convert, led a missionary and charity organization in Kedgaon (Maharashtra) called the Mukti Mission. It was backed by foreign help, and many western missionaries took part in its work.[3] In the year 1903 she sent her daughter Manoramabai to Australia along with her close coworker, the American Minnie F. Abrams, to monitor the evangelistic efforts of the Torrey and Alexander team.[4] Influenced by the revival in Wales (1904-1906), the Welsh Presbyterian mission in the Khasi Hills of northeast India experienced a great awakening that introduced Christianity to the whole region.[5] The news of these events soon spread throughout India and abroad, and it also caught the keen attention of Ramabai. Under the influence of events in Australia and Wales, she started a special prayer circle in 1905 that led to a great revival at the Mukti Mission in Kedgaon.[6] In the years 1906-1907, it was ac-

1. See Orr 1976: 107-11; McGee 1999: 651-53.
2. See Orr 1976: 144; McGee 1999: 651.
3. For Pandita Ramabai and the Mukti Mission see MacNicol 1926; Dongre & Patterson 1969; Adhav 1979; Kosambi 2000; Blumhofer 2001.
4. See Orr 1976: 144.
5. See Downs 1992: 95-96.
6. See MacNicol 1930: 161-62; Orr 1976: 143-48.

companied by various manifestations such as speaking in tongues. Different Americans, who worked for the mission and had heard from Azusa Street, also started speaking in tongues, and interpreted the Mukti Mission as proof for the worldwide Pentecostal end-time revival.[7] Moreover, as McGee and Blumhofer have emphasized,[8] the Mukti Mission also shows that even among its very Pentecostal protagonists, the role of tongues-speaking as initial evidence and as missionary tool was considered less important in India than at Azusa Street. However, Ramabai and the Mukti Mission as an institution later definitely backed out of the Pentecostal movement and interpreted the revival there as part of the larger evangelical awakening in the first decade of the twentieth century, as Orr has shown. This fact is often overlooked in popular Pentecostal hagiographical appropriation of the Mukti Mission.

The Mukti Mission became a vital link for the global Pentecostal network that was to be established, and it helped create Pentecostalism in India, but other events were similarly important. Pentecostal revival ideas got an important boost in India when the first active participants from Azusa Street landed there. In the beginning of 1907 the Garr couple arrived and held meetings in English for "missionaries and Christian workers" in Calcutta, and as a result regular Pentecostal gatherings at the Carey Baptist Chapel (Bow Bazaar) are reported.[9] Of course, they also visited the Mukti Mission. Although their stay was quite controversial among missionaries, it certainly further established the Pentecostal network.[10] In 1908, George E. Berg, another active participant at Azusa Street, landed in India and settled at Bangalore, a British civil and military center at that time.[11] He had already been a missionary in India before, and he immediately used his contacts in the Brethren mission in Kerala. In the same year, T. B. Barratt was invited to India by sympathizing missionaries to tell them more about the Pentecostal experience.[12] Most of the time Barratt stayed at Coonoor, a so-called hill station, where most of the western missionaries had gathered to take refuge from the hottest months of the year.

7. See McGee 1999.
8. See McGee 1999; Blumhofer 2001.
9. Moorhead 1920.
10. Probably the Garrs stayed from January to October 1907 in India, and in that time they also visited Ceylon. See McGee 1990a; McGee 2002.
11. Little is known about the life of George E. Berg. Apparently, he had already been a missionary to India before he became a Pentecostal at the Azusa Street Revival. In Azusa Street he held the post of a secretary (see Robeck 2002: 347).
12. Barratt 1927: 157-67. T. B. Barratt stayed in India from 3 April till 15 August 1908. The invitation came from A. N. Groves, together with Maud Orlebar and Max Wood Moorhead.

During his stay some missionaries and Indians received the new baptism of the Spirit, though there were also seemingly outspoken negative reactions. During his stay in India, Barratt also held meetings at Bombay and Calcutta, and he visited the Mukti Mission.

Within a very short time, a widespread and diffuse Pentecostal network was established that could be called the beginning of Pentecostalism in India. It was from this network that a Pentecostal movement got established on the subcontinent through different initiatives. The most far-reaching missionary initiative came from Berg and Robert F. Cook, who joined him in 1913; however, they were part of a wider Indian network. There were links between Cook and the Mukti Mission. Cook's second wife, Mrs. Bertha Fox, worked in Dodballapur near Bangalore along with Mary Bai Aiman, who had once belonged to the Mukti Mission. Albert Norton, an American missionary who was present during the awakening in the Mukti Mission, also had contact with Cook.[13] There are many other connections. One example is the founding of the Madras Pentecostal Assembly, which can be attributed to two Swedish missionaries, Karin Andersson and Ida Nilson, who in north India had probably been in close contact with the Mukti Mission. It is said that, as they waited for their ship in Madras on their way back to Sweden in 1913, they did evangelistic work there in Guindy; and, as a result, a Pentecostal congregation started there led by the Tamil Benjamin Jacob.[14] Two female English missionaries, Miss Bouncil and Miss Aldwinckle, probably received the baptism of the Spirit through the work of Barratt in Coonoor. They worked in Thanjavur and had a good contact with Berg. Miss Bouncil died in Thanjavur, perhaps in 1914, and was buried there by an Indian coworker of Berg, Pandalam Mattai. Later, Miss Aldwinckle worked together with Mary Chapman, a female missionary of the Assemblies of God in south Kerala.[15] The American missionaries Christian Schoonmaker and Herbert Coxe, to give another example, had originally come to India with the Christian and Missionary Alliance and then became Pentecostals under the decisive influence of the Mukti Mission, eventually working for the Assemblies of God in north India.[16] Moreover, it must also be pointed out that at least two American missionaries who became Pentecostals in In-

13. See Cook 1955: 52. See also McGee & Rodgers 2002; Wilson 1990; Shinde 1974: 143.

14. There are conflicting reports about the details. See *Balm of Gilead,* vol. 50, no. 9, Dec. 1988: 5; Vasu ca. 1950: 15; Andreasson & Andreasson 1989: 33. See also p. 34.

15. See Saju 1994: 32, 38-39, 56, 58, 61, 81, 268. In Cook 1955: 172, Miss Aldwinckle is mentioned as a member of his church convent in 1930.

16. See Ketcham 1973; Schoonmaker 1908; Frodsham 1946: 111-13; Robinson 1990a: 770-71; Wilson 1990: 641.

dia influenced the Pentecostal movement in other parts of the world: Minnie Abrams in Chile and Alice E. Luce in Mexico and among Hispanic Americans.[17]

Kerala

The activity of George E. Berg in Kerala became crucial for the making of the Pentecostal movement in south India. As already mentioned, Berg settled in Bangalore in 1908, where he resumed contact with the Brethren in Kerala, whom he apparently knew from his previous stay as a faith missionary in India. In 1909 he was invited as one of the guest speakers by the Brethren for the convention they organized annually in Kottarakara, Kollam District. In the following year, when he also visited that convention,[18] an open discussion on his Pentecostal views took place, and as a result the Brethren discontinued their contact with him. However, some members of the Brethren congregations remained with Berg, and they founded the first decidedly Pentecostal Brethren assemblies in South India in Kottarakara and in Adur in 1910.[19]

When Berg left for Kerala for the third time, in 1911, Robert Cumine, a Tamil-speaking Anglo-Indian from the Kolar Gold Fields near Bangalore, who had been converted to the Pentecostal faith under Berg's influence, accompanied him, and again they also stayed in the region of Kottarakara and Adur most of the time. In Thuvayur near Adur they met a small prayer group that had close contact with the Brethren and was under the leadership of Paruttupara Ummachan. This group invited Berg to Thuvayur and as a consequence accepted the Pentecostal faith. It thus became the first Pentecostal congregation in south India.[20] During the Kerala tour of 1911, Berg also got acquainted with a few young people who followed him to Bangalore, where he held Bible studies for them and instructed them in the Pentecostal belief. Among them were Umman Mammen and Pandalam Mattai, who began to work as Pentecostal evangelists after they returned to Kerala.[21]

17. See Gee 1967: 57; Hollenweger 1965/1967: 1136; McGee 1999: 664-65.

18. It was established practice among westerners to take shelter from the heat of the summer and during the monsoon time in the pleasant hilly climate of Bangalore and to travel through the land in the cooler time of the year (November to February) only.

19. See Saju 1994: 30-31.

20. See Saju 1994: 33-35.

21. Not much is known about Umman Mammen. He was a member of the Church

In 1912, Berg returned to the USA and took part in the First World Wide Pentecostal Camp that was organized by the Apostolic Faith Mission in Azusa Street. There he met with Robert F. Cook, whom he asked to follow him to India.[22] Both of them met in Bangalore in 1913. Cook planned first a mission of his own among the Tamils in Kovilpatti, Chidambaranar District. He proceeded to that place in December of the same year along with Robert Cumine. In January, he proceeded farther to Kerala with a view to accompanying Berg on a preaching tour.[23]

A few months after that journey, there was a conflict between Berg and Cook. As a result, Berg left India in 1914, and Cook continued the mission work.[24] He was, however, very much restricted in his activities during the time of the First World War. He lived mainly in the safe garrison city of Bangalore, but undertook an evangelistic tour to Kerala, along with Robert Cumine, in the winter of 1916/1917, intending to renew the contacts made by Berg. During this tour it became evident that the congregation in Thuvayur had developed its own lively mission activities under the leadership of Paruttupara Ummachan. Umman Mammen and Pandalam Mattai, two disciples of Berg, had also been active as Pentecostal missionaries in Kerala. Cook undertook a few journeys to Kerala in the years that followed. However, the actual mission work was conducted by the congregation in Thuvayur and by other indigenous evangelists who were financially supported by Cook. He also bought a plot of land in Thuvayur on which a Pentecostal church was built.[25] Thuvayur remained the only Pentecostal congregation in Kerala until the beginning of the 1920s.

It was not until the 1920s that the Pentecostal movement was firmly established in Kerala. Cook's decision to settle permanently in Kottarakara after he had toured Kerala again in 1921 played no insignificant role in this. In addition, Mary Chapman, a missionary of the Assemblies of God, came to Trivandrum at the same time. She and Cook, who himself had joined the As-

---

Missionary Society and the son of Umman Padiri, who was archdeacon there. In the years before World War I he conducted several Pentecostal rallies around Punalur. See Saju 1994: 31-33.

22. See Cook 1955: 16.

23. See Saju 1994: 65.

24. According to his own statement, Cook broke his relationship with Berg because of Berg's "unholy life" (Cook, 1955: 21). A few Indian authors are of the opinion that Berg had to leave India with the beginning of the First World War because he was a German (see Saju 1994: 37; Abraham 1990: 52; Mathew 1990: 33). This version seems to take its origin from a text of K. E. Abraham (1955: 9-11), which unfortunately is not available to the author. However, the most probable reason that Berg left was the conflict with Cook.

25. See Saju 1994: 42.

semblies of God,[26] worked closely together. In the first half of the 1920s a great number of Brethren went over to the Pentecostal movement, and many of them became its future leaders.

When Cook was on furlough from 1924 to 1926, a first quest for independence appeared among the indigenous Pentecostal leaders. K. E. Abraham, who had joined the Pentecostal faith in 1923 and was heading a small congregation in Mulakuzha near Chengannur, stood in the forefront of these aspirations. He became the speaker for the indigenous coworkers of the mission. During the absence of Cook, a quarrel developed between Mary Chapman and K. E. Abraham and his followers on the question of financing a church building. She made her financial help dependent on the registration of the property in the name of the Assemblies of God. Against this, Abraham insisted that the plot of land must be registered in the name of the local congregation.[27] The conflict led to disruptions in the relationship between Mary Chapman and the followers of Abraham. When Cook returned to India in 1926, he sided not with Mary Chapman but with Abraham, who demanded that the autonomy of the indigenous coworkers and their congregations be accepted. That demand was certainly influenced by the extreme congregational understanding of the Brethren, to whom most of the Indian coworkers had previously belonged. Though he remained a missionary of the Assemblies of God, Cook founded the Malankara Pentecostal Church along with Abraham, which was formally associated with the Assemblies of God but in reality acted fully independently. With that, the close cooperation between Cook and Mary Chapman, who continued her work in the name of the Assemblies of God, came to an end.

In 1927, Cook moved to Abraham's locale in Mulakuzha and opened a Bible school by the name of Mount Zion Bible School. For the years 1928 and 1929, a series of Pentecostal awakenings were recorded among the Brethren, and as a result, whole congregations went over to the Pentecostal movement.[28] However, when in 1929 a regional Council of the Assemblies of God for South India and Ceylon was formed in order to bring about a better synchronization of the work of the missionaries, this meant a decisive turning point.[29] Abraham and his coworkers were not ready to accept any regional restrictions and administrative handicaps by a mission society. They therefore urged Cook to give up his membership in the Assemblies of God, which he did.[30]

26. See Saju 1994: 108-9.
27. See Abraham 1983: 143; Saju 1994: 74-75, 277. The outcome of the conflict is not known to the author.
28. See Saju 1994: 84ff.
29. See Assemblies of God 1929.
30. The main point in the discussion was probably about regional allocations. In order

Further events, however, were less favorable to Cook. At the end of the 1920s the Ceylon Pentecostal Mission, which originated in Ceylon in the middle of that decade, began to be noticed in Kerala. Its leaders P. Paul and Alwin were invited as guest speakers to the evangelizations by Cook and Abraham. The fact that the Ceylon Pentecostal Mission was working without any support from the West apparently impressed Abraham. In March 1930, he left along with his followers, the Malankara Full Gospel Church, which was led and financially supported by Cook. Abraham moved to Kumbanadu near Chengannur, joined the Ceylon Pentecostal Mission, and was ordained as a pastor by P. Paul. Cook was left with only a few of the faithful. It is hard to understand the background of the separation of Abraham from Cook in 1930.[31] The reason given by Abraham, i.e., that the pastors and the congregations were not given enough freedom in their work with Cook, is rather an excuse. Indeed, Cook had accepted demands for freedom as much as possible, and he had even separated from the Assemblies of God. Perhaps it was the explicit refusal of any foreign control and influence that led Abraham to take this step. In that respect, he was very much influenced by the example of the Ceylon Pentecostal Mission, which was completely under indigenous leadership. In the Malankara Pentecostal Church, however, the American Cook functioned as president while the Indian Abraham was only vice-president. In addition, Robert F. Cook apparently extended regular financial support to the indigenous coworker, which was not agreeable to the faith principles demanded by the Ceylon Pentecostal Mission. Moreover, the charismatic Abraham was very conscious of his power and influence, and he probably wanted to become the sole leader. That became manifest when the liaison between Abraham and the Ceylon Pentecostal Mission broke after three years. Finally, Abraham founded his own church, the Indian Pentecostal Church, which was fully controlled by him.

In these splits and turmoils Thomas Christians were able to establish themselves as the first leadership generation in Kerala's Pentecostalism, and thus the distribution of administrative power was similar to that of the established churches very early on. In the beginnings of the 1920s the majority of Pentecostals in Kerala were mostly from a "low caste" or "untouchable" background, people who would call themselves Dalits today. Cook received posi-

---

to avoid competition and rivalry the Council wanted individual missionaries to restrict their area of operation to mutually agreed geographic regions. See Saju 1994: 108-10 (Saju cites opinions that Abraham and Cook had published in their journal — *Suvisesha Prabasakan*, vol. 2, no. 12, July 1929). Chacko 1986: 60-61, names seventeen congregations that left the Assemblies of God.

31. See Saju 1994: 115-17.

tive reactions from different independent Dalit groups and their leaders at that time. He was, for example, invited to Kumbanadu near Chengannur in 1922 by someone named Choti, who was a religious leader of a big group of Dalits. According to Cook, Choti had been a Christian and had worked in a mission station for a while, but then had left because of continuous discrimination, and hence remained without any link to a church or missionary society. When Cook came to Kumbanadu, about one thousand people gathered in order to listen to him.[32] A little later, he received an invitation from Poykayil Yohannan of Eraviperoor near Tiruvalla, a man who was still more influential as a leader among the Dalits than Choti.[33] After having been a member in the Church Missionary Society, in the Mar Thoma Church, and lastly with the Brethren, he founded his own church in 1907. Cook had met him during his stay with Choti in Kumbanadu. Poykayil Yohannan invited Cook to a central convention of his church in 1923 in which more than a thousand people gathered.[34] There too Cook found keen listeners, and as a result, further invitations followed. However, these intensive contacts did not bring about the conversion of Dalit leaders to the Pentecostal movement. Saju, a leading Pentecostal journalist from Kerala, who himself belongs to the Thomas Christians, has written openly about this subject.[35] He points out that in about the mid-1920s many Thomas Christians, who had worked as congregational leaders in the Brethren movement, moved to the Pentecostal movement together with their congregations, and thus became leading Pentecostal figures almost automatically. The Thomas Christians could also utilize the two-year absence of Cook, who had gone on furlough from 1924 to 1926, to establish themselves in leading church positions. According to Saju, it was this emerging dominance of the Thomas Christians that prevented Dalit leaders such as Choti and Poykayil Yohannan to join the Pentecostal movement. At that time it would have been hardly possible for Pentecostal Dalit pastors to reach leading church positions. With regard to caste, the Pentecostal movement in Kerala practiced discrimination similar to the established churches from the very beginning.

As a result of the different separations that took place in the 1920s, four Pentecostal churches originated before the mid-1930s: Assemblies of God, Ceylon Pentecostal Mission, Indian Pentecostal Church, and Church of God. Hereafter, all these new churches developed and acted fully independently of

32. See Cook 1955: 98-105.

33. For Poykayil Yohannan see Hunt 1920/1933: II, 235; Hoerschelmann 1977: 152-55; Fuchs 1992: 236-38; Saju 1994: 51.

34. See Cook 1955: 120-24.

35. See Saju 1994: 50-51; see also 45-46, 49.

each other. It should be particularly noted that two of them were independent, indigenous churches.

After ending her collaboration with Robert F. Cook, Mary Chapman settled down at Mavelikara, Alappuzha District, in 1926, where her close Indian coworker A. J. John was in charge of a congregation. This would become the beginning of an established work by the Assemblies of God. In the same year, she received support through the arrival of John H. Burgess, who had to continue the work alone in the years that followed the death of Mary Chapman in 1927, the year in which Burgess opened the Bethel Bible School in Mavelikara with the help of A. J. John and P. V. John,[36] probably the oldest Bible school of the Assemblies of God that still exists outside the USA.[37] The separation of Cook from the Assemblies of God in 1929 seems to have affected the work of Burgess, because it was not until 1934 that the Bible school started to function continuously.[38] From that time onward, John H. Burgess and the other missionaries staying in Kerala concentrated mainly on the Bible school, while the work in the congregation was left in the hands of the Indians. The sole exception was the missionary Martha Kucera, who had worked in Trivandrum since the end of the 1920s and carried on a successful mission work along with the young A. C. Samuel, who became her successor in 1932.[39] From that time until after the Second World War, Burgess was the most important integrative person of the Assemblies of God in south India. He preserved the church from further separations and was responsible for the formation of the South India District Council in 1933. This was a kind of forerunner of the South India Assemblies of God, in which there was already a measurable participation of indigenous pastors in leading positions, although Burgess himself kept the chairmanship.[40]

The Ceylon Pentecostal Mission increased its mission efforts in Kerala at the end of the 1920s. Not much is known about its beginnings. Probably around 1923, P. Paul, who hailed originally from Kerala, left the Church Missionary Society in Colombo and started an independent Pentecostal ministry along with the Singhalese Alwin, the Ceylon Pentecostal Mission. In the first one or two years, at least, they had contacts with a Pentecostal congregation in Colombo (Glad Tidings Hall at Wellawata) that was started by the Danish missionary

---

36. For P. V. John see p. 276.

37. See McGee 1986: 98.

38. See Shinde 1974: 116.

39. Until the beginning of the 1950s, half of the congregations in Kerala were in the region of Trivandrum and the other half in Kollam District (see McLeish & Watts 1951: 217). Only after that did the Assemblies of God spread to the whole of Kerala.

40. See Reginald 1995: 32-33.

Anna Lewini and later run by the English missionary Walter Clifford.[41] However, the character of this relationship is difficult to establish,[42] because, so far, hardly anything is known about the early years of this church. The church was met with great acceptance among the leading Pentecostal pastors and evangelists of Kerala. P. M. Samuel was converted to the Pentecostal faith in Ceylon, and K. E. Abraham joined the Ceylon Pentecostal Mission in 1930, after he and his followers parted ways with Robert F. Cook. However, that cooperation did not have a future, since the Ceylon Pentecostal Mission was completely under the leadership of Paul and Alwin, and Abraham was not willing to submit.[43] Paul and Alwin created a centrally led denomination in the subsequent period, which was perhaps one of the most successful Pentecostal churches in Kerala in the 1930s and 1940s. Its centralized organization, which differed substantially from the majority of the strictly congregational south Indian Pentecostal movement, promoted the development of a few special, radical teachings in the subsequent period. That tendency, however, came to full force only after the death of Paul in 1945, when the openly radical-minded Alwin took on the leadership of the Ceylon Pentecostal Mission all alone.

After the three-year cooperation with the Ceylon Pentecostal Mission, K. E. Abraham founded his own, independent church.[44] Since 1934 it had been called the Indian Pentecostal Church, and in the following year it was officially registered.[45] Kumbanadu became the headquarters where, immedi-

41. Walter Clifford worked as a missionary in north India and visited Colombo briefly in 1924 when he went on furlough, but came permanently to Ceylon as a missionary of the British Assemblies of God in 1925. He joined the American Assemblies of God in 1929 (see Assemblies of God 1929). See Burgess ca. 1934; Redemption Tidings, vol. 1, no. 12, Dec. 1925: 11; Frodsham 1946: 115-16.

42. Especially John 1976: 122-23 (see also Shinde 1974: 28; Varghese 1982: 28) reports about such a collaboration and Y. Jeyaraj (see Rajamani n.d.: 1, 3), who informs about Walter Clifford. According to Johnson 1976: 123, the Ceylon Pentecostal Mission separated itself from the Assemblies of God in 1927. Leembruggen-Kallberg reports that the Ceylon Pentecostal Mission broke away from Glad Tidings in 1923 but that in 1925, when Clifford took over the congregation, another group left and joined the Ceylon Pentecostal Mission (see Leembruggen-Kallberg 2002a: 248-49).

43. In the opinion of the author, this is the most probable version for the short duration of the cooperation. However, a difference in the teachings that could not be bridged was cited by Abraham as the crucial reason (see Abraham 1983: 234-35; see also Abraham 1990: 61), but it is hardly possible that the Ceylon Pentecostal Mission advocated any church-dividing doctrine at that time.

44. According to a statement of Abraham, the South India Pentecostal Church of God was constituted under his leadership in 1933 and changed its name to Indian Pentecostal Church a year later. See Abraham 1983: 236; also Abraham 1990: 63.

45. The registration was done in 1935 in Eluru, Andhra Pradesh, which (unlike central

ately after his separation from Cook, Abraham had previously opened a
school called the Hebron Bible School. The pastors of the Indian Pentecostal
Church were trained there over several decades. The financial condition of
the newly founded church was bad. However, K. C. Cherian, a close coworker
of Abraham, met the Swedish Pentecostal missionary Carl Swahn while staying in Mangalore in 1934 and won him over as the guest speaker for the
church convention in the beginning of 1935 at Kumbanadu. Swahn was indeed much impressed by what he saw in Kerala. As a result, he made arrangements for Abraham and Cherian to be invited to Sweden by Lewi Pethrus of
the Filadelfia Church. In the spring of 1936, both of them left for Sweden,
where they completed an eighteen-month-long journey of preaching.[46]
Abraham and Cherian arrived back in India in the beginning of 1938. During
the journey, which became the start of a longer cooperation with the Swedes,
the Indians received a considerable number of donations, and after their return they received the support of the Filadelfia Church. As promised, the
Swedes did not place any conditions on their financial support.[47] As a result,
Abraham, whose responsibility was to distribute the money that came from
Sweden, developed his leadership position further in the subsequent period.
In the 1930s he made the Indian Pentecostal Church the strongest Pentecostal
church in Kerala, much stronger than the western mission churches.

After Abraham and his followers left him, times became very difficult for
Cook. His financial condition worsened dramatically because of the worldwide economic crisis. Many people in the USA who had supported his work
until then were forced to stop their help.[48] As Abraham and Cherian started
their journey to Sweden, he feared that this would result in the migration of
his coworkers to the Indian Pentecostal Church: "Since two of the brethren
of the Indian Pentecostal Church of God were taken to a foreign country, we
sensed the danger that lay ahead on their return, especially if they were
backed by foreign finances. . . ."[49] In these difficult circumstances he met
with J. H. Ingram from the Church of God in Ooty, Nilgiris District. Ingram
was spending time in India in 1936 on the occasion of his famous Golden Jubilee World Tour.[50] As a result, Cook and his Indian coworkers decided to
join the Church of God. In this way Cook secured a future for the mission he

---

and south Kerala) belonged to Madras Presidency, where the British Society's Act was in
force.

46. See Verghese 1974: 33-47. See also Andreasson & Andreasson 1989: 18-19.
47. See Abraham 1983: 275-77. See also Abraham 1990: 69; Verghese 1974: 35.
48. See Cook 1955: 206.
49. Cook 1955: 211.
50. See Cook 1955: 211-12; Ingram 1936. See also Conn 1959: 218-19.

had started. However, this affiliation with the Church of God initially did not have any administrative consequences. Cook led his mission, along with his close Indian coworker T. M. Verghese,[51] in the same way he had done before.[52]

Beginnings Outside Kerala

The south Indian Pentecostal movement established itself outside Kerala only in the second half of the 1940s. However, a few remarkable mission activities had taken place in the period before. Unfortunately, little is known about it. The first attempts in Tamil Nadu had been restricted to Madras. Presumably in 1913, as already mentioned, the two Swedish women Karin Andersson and Ida Nilson founded a Pentecostal congregation there. They seem, however, to have stayed in Madras only for a short while.[53] Soon the young Benjamin Jacob assumed leadership of the small congregation in the area of Royapettah. Mary Chapman, who had come to India as a missionary of the Assemblies of God in 1916, stayed for a long time in Madras and worked closely with Benjamin Jacob.[54] In 1926, the young John Vasu joined the congregation and soon became one of the most important coworkers and noted followers of Benjamin Jacob. In 1934, a big church was built and registered as the Madras Pentecostal Assembly.[55] In 1938, the congregation started to bring out its own magazine, *Balm of Gilead*,[56] and in the 1930s and 1940s the church stood in close contact with the British Assemblies of God.[57]

51. T. M. Verghese (1898-1985) belonged to the Thomas Christians. He joined Robert F. Cook in 1927 and was the foremost Indian leader of the Church of God till his retirement in 1965 (see Saju 1994: 100).

52. The four-year stay of Hoyle Case and his wife, who were sent to India in 1938, was overshadowed by sickness and war and therefore did not make any impact (see McCracken 1943: 139-41).

53. See Vasu ca. 1950: 15; Andreasson 1989: 33.

54. See Shinde 1974: 107, 110.

55. In 1933, the congregation was mentioned in a church directory as an independent church with the name The Pentecostal Assembly (see Philip 1934: 184, 205).

56. See Vasu ca. 1950: 15-17; Balm of Gilead, vol. 50, Dec. 1988, no. 9: 6-7. "Balm of Gilead" appears in both Tamil and English and it was still published in the 1990s, which made it the oldest still-existing Pentecostal magazine in India.

57. The church building was financed by the sisters Mrs. E. M. Dickens (ca. 1876-1961) and Miss J. Robinson (died in 1936) who functioned also as the trustees. Both women lived in Yercaud, Salem District, and were missionaries of the British Assemblies of God. See Madras Pentecostal Assembly 1934; Vasu ca. 1950: 17. It is also recorded that the church had

From the beginning of its existence the Madras Pentecostal Assembly was an important center for the south Indian Pentecostal movement.[58] Its missionary radiation was minimal, but it remained the one and only big Pentecostal congregation in Madras until after the Second World War. The Ceylon Pentecostal Mission also started its mission work in Tamil Nadu in the 1930s. During that time, congregations arose in Tuticorin, Nazareth, and Palayankottai.[59] It is also to be mentioned that the British Assemblies of God were running a mission in Coimbatore and Pollachi in the 1920s and stood in close contact with Robert F. Cook.[60] Their work, however, did not show any tangible results until the second half of the 1940s. Cook also undertook missionary efforts in Tamil Nadu, and after he had won M. Benjamin as his coworker, a congregation was started in Madurai. After some turbulent conflicts, it became the foundation stone for further work of the Church of God in that area.[61]

In Karnataka, however, no Pentecostal missionary work worth mentioning took place till the end of the 1930s, and that in spite of the fact that Bangalore was the place where many western missionaries had stayed since the time of George E. Berg. It was not until Carl Swahn came to Bangalore in 1941 that the situation changed somewhat.[62] After that time the Swedish missionaries supported a few independent pastors, but even that was without tangible results.[63] In Andhra Pradesh, Lam Jeevaratnam founded the first

---

contacts with the Liveseys in Coimbatore and with Lam Jeevaratnam in Gudivada (see Vasu ca. 1950: 16-17).

58. Gopal Daniel (see Balm of Gilead, vol. 50, Dec. 1988, no. 9: 5) and M. Murugesan (see Madras Pentecostal Assembly 1934, where he was shown as the trustee and pastor of Bethelpuram Church, Basin Road, Washermanpet Post) were also attached to that church. Gopal Daniel later joined the Church of God, probably through his contacts with M. Benjamin (see Cook 1955: 150).

59. See The Pentecostal Mission 1984 (Tuticorin); Samuel 1980: 14-15 (Nazareth); Christopher Asir 1975: 48-49 (Palayankottai).

60. For the contact with Robert F. Cook see the preface of Lawrence Livesey to Cook 1955.

61. See also Cook 1955: 150-53.

62. See Andreasson & Andreasson 1989: 22, 24.

63. An exception is the Full Gospel Church in India, which was founded by Stephen Andrew and was supported by Carl Swahn from the beginning of the 1940s and then by Arthur Conney. After the death of Stephen Andrew in 1965, the church was led by his son S. A. George. George became a well-known pastor because he was much involved in developing Pentecostal networks in Bangalore. The small but lively Full Gospel Church in India is the oldest Pentecostal church that still exists in Bangalore. See George n.d. Further, it must be noted that in the 1950s, the Gospel Prayer Hall and also the Philadelphia Church in Kolar Gold Fields came into existence with Swedish support.

Pentecostal church with the Eastern Full Gospel Mission. He had been converted to the Pentecostal faith during his stay in England, and from there returned to India in 1926 as a recognized missionary of the British Assemblies of God. His work remained without successor and was dissolved once for all after his death in 1960. M. Murugesan, who was a pastor of an independent church in Washermanpet, took up a few mission journeys into Andhra Pradesh in the 1920s and 1930s, but they too were without significant results.[64] In contrast, the missionary efforts of the Indian Pentecostal Church under the leadership of P. M. Samuel, begun in Kerala in 1932, were successful. In 1936, Samuel and P. T. Chacko founded an Indian Pentecostal Church in Eluru, West Godavari District, and developed an intensive mission activity. For the success of the church in later years, however, it was not insignificant that they were able to win over the cooperation of many Telugu-speaking Indians who had experienced conversion to Pentecostal confession in other places. Thus, K. S. Joseph, who later founded a Pentecostal center in Narasapur, was converted in north India. Among those Indians who had fled to their native places in Andhra Pradesh from Rangoon due to the Japanese invasion, there were a number of Pentecostals who later became pastors of the Indian Pentecostal Church. Here mention must be made of P. Rajaratnam, who became active as pastor of the Indian Pentecostal Church immediately after his return from Rangoon and started a mission in Antarvedipalem.[65]

64. However, see pp. 260, 285.
65. See Komanapalli ca. 1991: 12-13; Samuel 1980: 53.

CHAPTER 2

Kerala

Four Main Pentecostal Churches

In the course of progressing consolidation, each of the four already-existing larger Pentecostal churches in Kerala developed its own identity beginning in the 1940s. Despite waning missionary pressure and many bitter internal quarrels that badly affected church activities, the churches showed considerable growth. What was common to all of them was that they were dominated by Thomas Christians. In 1947, both the leaders of the Indian Pentecostal Church in Kerala, K. E. Abraham and K. C. Cherian, received a fresh invitation to Stockholm from Lewi Pethrus of the Filadelfia Church.[1] They traveled along with P. M. Samuel from Andhra Pradesh to Sweden and undertook a preaching journey of many months. During that journey, Swedish-American pastors translated their English-language sermons into Swedish. When those translators invited them to America, it was the fulfillment of a long-cherished dream for the Indians.[2] The following year, the three leaders of the Indian Pentecostal Church went to America. Their stay was mediated to a great extent by Joseph Mattsson-Boze,[3] a prominent Swedish-American pastor in Chicago and simultaneously a leading coworker in the Latter Rain Movement that was taking its origin just then.[4] He also helped the Indian guests establish contacts with representatives of the Latter Rain Movement, among which an acquaintance

---

1. See Saju 1994: 177; Samuel 1980: 92ff.; Verghese 1974: 48ff.
2. See Samuel 1980: 102 and Verghese 1974: 50.
3. See Samuel 1980: 103 and Verghese 1974: 50.
4. For the Latter Rain Movement see Riss 1987.

with Ivar Q. Spencer from the Elim Bible Institute in New York proved to be specially fruitful in the years to come. By the time Abraham and Cherian returned to India in 1949, they had won a number of sponsors, and as a result the Indian Pentecostal Church would have considerable financial means for implementing its tasks.[5] However, it was not prepared personnel-wise at that time for an adequate administration and distribution of those new resources. In addition, Abraham tried to ensure his personal control over these foreign funds, in order to secure his leading position within the church. As a consequence, serious quarrels on leadership and distribution arose that almost threatened to break the church. In the beginning of 1950s the conflict worsened when influential pastors of the church settled in and around Kumbanadu, the center of the Pentecostal church where, until then, Abraham had resided alone, and they tried to take over leadership roles in the Indian Pentecostal Church.[6] Among them was Cherian, who apparently was the first to start an extremely bitter quarrel with Abraham, accusing him of autocratic leadership over the whole church in Kerala.[7] In 1953, many pastors openly broke with Abraham. The Indian Pentecostal Church within Kerala divided itself into two parties, a parallel church leadership was formed, and the congregations in Andhra Pradesh also sided against Abraham.[8] After a reconciliation in 1957, the conflict broke out openly again and this time lasted until 1966. These long years of conflict restricted the progress of the church work considerably. Even after the split, Abraham remained the indisputable leading figure within the Indian Pentecostal Church. The leaders of the local centers, however, attained great autonomy, especially when they had found their own foreign sponsors.

After the death of K. E. Abraham, his son T. S. Abraham took his position in Kumbanadu. Under his rule a further decentralization took place, and the leaders of the local centers acted fully independently with regard to questions of property. Through the contributions of non-residential Indians, especially of those who had worked for a longer time in the Gulf countries, the congregations received a solid financial basis. In addition, a series of Bible schools were started that helped to train sufficient numbers of workers. That enabled a considerable growth during the 1980s and 1990s. The rather nominal unity of the church and also the alleged misuse of church positions for private interests caused, however, a great embarrassment among many pastors. It became man-

5. See Saju 1994: 177, 181.
6. See Saju 1994: 181-82.
7. See Saju 1994: 131. See also Verghese 1974: 111 and Saju 1994: 181, where accusations against K. E. Abraham regarding immorality and stealing are mentioned.
8. See the list of names in Abraham 1990: 88. See Daniel 1981: 32ff.

ifest at last, when T. S. Abraham wanted to run the central Hebron Bible School as an institution independent from the church and solely controlled by him. The separation of that traditional establishment from the Indian Pentecostal Church let loose a protest wave that even went to the extent of taking the dispute to court. The outcome of that protest was limited, however, since the plaintiffs did not have sufficient financial means. Though the Indian Pentecostal Church in the 1990s was still nominally the largest Pentecostal church in Kerala, with some remarkable growth, in administrative terms it presented itself only as a loose and badly organized community. According to its statutes, the administration of the Indian Pentecostal Church is structured with a central General Council under which the different regional State Councils — Kerala, Andhra Pradesh, Tamil Nadu, Karnataka, and the Northern Region — are organized.[9] Most of the time only Kerala and Andhra Pradesh played an important role, and the General Council functioned as a place where both regions (represented by K. E. Abraham and P. M. Samuel respectively) could reconcile their interests. As the example of Tamil Nadu shows, this was still the case in the mid-1990s. When K. E. Abraham died, the leading offices exercised by him (Kerala State President; General President) did not go over to his son, but were given to other persons. At first, T. S. Abraham only attained the post of a Kerala State Secretary but remained the head of the Hebron Bible School. But in 2000, he could win over the position of the General President and secure his dominant administrative influence on the church.

One of the most striking examples of the administrative problems within the Indian Pentecostal Church is the K. E. Abraham Foundation. Probably in order to withdraw the ministry at Kumbanadu from the control of the Indian Pentecostal Church and to bring it under his individual control, T. S. Abraham established the foundation in 1975. To his advantage, some of the land at the headquarters in Kumbanadu, which K. E. Abraham had acquired for the Indian Pentecostal Church, was not registered in the name of the church but as private property. K. E. Abraham had explained in an interview in 1971, however, that these properties should be considered as belonging to the Indian Pentecostal Church:

> About 50 years before, I decided not to accumulate treasures in this world and I still maintain this view. At Kumbanadu there are 6 acres of

9. P. M. Samuel was the General President during the registration in 1935, but probably in 1939 K. E. Abraham took over the post. From 1953 to 1957 and 1964 to 1966, Samuel acted most of the time as a parallel General President. Thereafter only Abraham was really recognized by all as the General President.

land and a few buildings in my name for the Church. They are not mine or my children's. My two sons earn their living through the work of their own hands. What I gave them, as a father, was their education.[10]

However, T. S. Abraham made preparations to transfer those lands and buildings to a trust that had him as the founder and president. As a result, the leadership of the Indian Pentecostal Church would lose any claim to those properties. Since the Hebron Bible School existed on the above-mentioned plot, it was also claimed for the K. E. Abraham Foundation. This claim was legalized with the official registration of the K. E. Abraham Foundation in 1989. The designated successor in the leadership of the K. E. Abraham Foundation was Valson Abraham, the son of T. S. Abraham. However, the pastors and laity, who were concerned about the well-being of their church, raised their critical voices. Through prolonged court cases they fought for a ruling that no longer allowed T. S. Abraham to call the school run by the K. E. Abraham Foundation the Hebron Bible school. Therefore the name was changed to India Bible College, but buildings and land were acknowledged as lawful properties of the K. E. Abraham Foundation. However, in practice this verdict meant nothing but the end of the Hebron Bible School. For continuing it under the leadership of the Indian Pentecostal Church, money as well as will were lacking. And again, T. S. Abraham apparently used his influence to hinder the reopening of the Hebron Bible College on the Kumbanadu plot, which still belonged to the Indian Pentecostal Church.[11] In the meantime, other leading pastors of the Indian Pentecostal Church also started to do the main part of their work through organizations that were registered in their own names. The problem with this development was that it led to the disintegration of the Indian Pentecostal Church into different small denominations, the overall name of the church being used only to collect funds abroad for their own individual organizations. This accusation by a member of the Indian Pentecostal Church in a letter written to the author of this study states accordingly:

> If you come to Kerala I can show you several churches owned by individuals and at the same time they claim that they are standing for India Pentecostal Church. When Convention season comes they get together to preach. Money making is the main business of the church leaders.[12]

10. Verghese 1974: 114.
11. See IPC News, no. 1, May 1993: 4.
12. Letter dated 7.11.1994.

In spite of their efforts, the many committed pastors and the laity were not able to stop this development, which was caused mainly by a few of their church leaders.

A somewhat different development took place in the Ceylon Pentecostal Mission, which distanced itself from the rest of the Pentecostal movement in Kerala in the 1940s and 1950s — a move, however, that does not seem to have affected its further growth. This was mainly due to the extraordinary charismatic power of Alwin, who led the church after the death of P. Paul in 1945. The Jaffna Tamil Benjamin Selvaratnam, who was widely known for his brilliant style of preaching in English, stood by his side. The dogmatic radicalization pursued by Alwin led to increasing isolation, but even though this caused a number of splits in Tamil Nadu,[13] it had little negative impact in Kerala. This was mainly due to the fact that the Pentecostal movement in Kerala as a whole shared comparatively radical views, and important differentiations of the ecclesiastical landscape had already taken place in the 1930s. However, the church suffered a strong setback in 1962, when Alwin was accused of moral misbehavior and was dismissed under scandalous circumstances. The sudden fall of their leader, who was also one of the two founding fathers of the Ceylon Pentecostal Mission, shook the centrally established church to its roots. The situation became still worse when internal tensions within the church, which were till then only below the surface, broke out openly, and when Alwin tried to regain his position by all means.

It is rather difficult to reconstruct the context of Alwin's removal, since there were several conflicts that ran parallel to each other. Though the available information is contradictory in certain points, a general picture can be drawn. Around 1960, when Selvaratnam, the second-ranking person after Alwin, unexpectedly married a French woman and left the Ceylon Pentecostal Mission, a gap at the leadership level arose.[14] As no one could be found to replace Selvaratnam, Alwin's decision-making capacity increased, but so also did his workload. It seems that Alwin was unable to cope with that situation, and his already autocratic leadership style turned gradually into a still more self-glorifying and unpredictable one.

The conflict unleashed when Alwin attempted to introduce Singhalese as the only language for the worship in the congregations in Ceylon in the spring of 1962.[15] Until then, worship services were held generally in three lan-

---

13. See pp. 64ff.

14. Selvaratnam became a member of the Apostolic Church in France and was working as a missionary of this church at Madras from 1969 to 1978.

15. See Williams 1962, for the following description of the events in Ceylon.

guages (Singhalese, English, and Tamil), among which Tamil was mostly the main language. As the official explanation for his plans Alwin remarked that although until then Tamils were the main members of the church, in order to win more Singhalese, there would be a need to increase the missionary efforts. Hence, it was necessary to give up Tamil, so that the Singhalese, too, would feel at home. Practically, however, the tense political situation in Ceylon at that time, heated up by the murder of President Bandaranaike in 1959, would have led Alwin to take such a step. There were strong political demands by the Singhalese majority to oust Tamil from public life and to foster the Singhalese language.[16] For this reason, one may well understand that Alwin took it very seriously when in April 1962 in front of the headquarters in Colombo an anti-Tamil demonstration was staged, an event that led Alwin to immediate action. Many coworkers raised objections against the changes brought about by Alwin. They did not understand why the Tamil language should not be used despite the fact that many visitors to the worship were Tamils. When Alwin felt that coworkers were following his instructions only with reservations, he reacted in an incomprehensible manner. Wherever he suspected that a pastor was not obeying him, he ordered an immediate transfer. His main anger was directed against Freddy Paul, the son of P. Paul, whom he saw unjustly as the ringleader of a rebellion against his authority. As the situation went fully out of his control, Alwin even went to the extent of falsely accusing, humiliating, and excommunicating Freddy Paul, who in fact had always been loyal to him. This altercation then spread throughout the Indian mainland, though with a completely different content there. After the events reached a peak in Ceylon, the Malayali A. C. Thomas, who was stationed in France and was responsible for the work in Europe, came from Europe to Madras. He presented the letter of a famous and much-respected sister from a Faith Home in London, in which she accused Alwin of a sexual attack on her. The matter was described in a way suggesting that it was a false insinuation, though it remains unclear whether Thomas knew this or whether he himself had forged the letter. Simultaneously a rumor was spread that Alwin went around preaching a new doctrine called Edenic Perfection that supported unchaste practices,[17] undermining faith in Alwin's moral integrity and adding credibility to the letter. Though many details remain vague, it seems certain that Thomas tried to overthrow Alwin on the basis of these accusations and

16. See Houtart 1974: 244-49.

17. According to many rumors, Alwin had introduced a sort of "holiness test" in the Faith Homes to see whether the men had really overcome their worldly desires. In order to test it, men were exposed to the sight of naked sisters. However, it is difficult to decide whether such Adamite practices really existed.

to win the support of the Malayali pastors with the hope of succeeding Alwin. This plan failed, however, because of the opposition of the Tamil pastors and of those Malayalis who suspected the ambitions of Thomas. It was thus agreed to have Freddy Paul as Alwin's successor. At the time of the conflict any reconciliation with Alwin was no longer possible. The conflict had taken on a life of its own, and Alwin had lost any sense of reality. From his side, nothing was done to placate the parties, and he uttered only hate-ridden tirades against his supposed opponents. Even in preaching he preferred to speak belligerently about the conflict. As he also refused to accept the last offer of retreating for a little while to America till the heated atmosphere cooled down, Alwin was officially excommunicated by Freddy Paul in 1962. In Ceylon, the congregations that were dominated by the Tamils, which were in the majority, also joined Freddy Paul. However, for quite some time, there were bitter quarrels with Alwin regarding property rights on the Faith Homes, and they had to be settled legally. For the most part, the few Singhalese congregations joined Alwin. In Tamil Nadu a few followers also remained loyal to Alwin for a short period, but most of his Tamil sympathizers soon turned their backs on him.

Eventually, Freddy Paul as a person of integrity became the successor of Alwin. At least in Kerala, the missionary dynamics of the church broke down after the conflict, though in the end, the Thomas Christian–dominated Kerala church stood united behind Freddy Paul. Still, the church consolidated itself in the 1960s and 1970s and even showed considerable growth again. At the same time, sectarian tendencies grew stronger and the fostering of exclusive traditions came to the fore. This became particularly manifest in 1984, when the name for the Indian section of the church was changed to the Pentecostal Mission.[18] In order to retain the old name to which they attributed a great part of their identity, a massive opposition arose against it, especially in Kerala. However, the deeper reason for this opposition should be sought in the fact that, as a reaction to the lost missionary dynamics, pastors and congregation members had started to glorify the early period of the church under the leadership of P. Paul. The present situation was seen as a decline, a constantly increasing deviation from the original will of the founder P. Paul, who was supposed to have composed an instruction of ten points in which he laid down the ways and means of church leadership after his death. One of those points was that the name Ceylon Pentecostal Mission should never be changed. The existence of such an instruction is, however, highly improbable. It is all the more so, since

18. See p. 73. However, the church in Sri Lanka, where the central headquarters is situated, retained the old name.

branch churches all over the world probably started very early to act under different names. The quarrel over the name was vehement and at times even turned violent. A serious incident took place at Kottarakara, where the Tamil Philip Chandrapillai, who belonged to the highest leadership level of the church, had come as a mediator. A heated exchange of words led to a hand-to-hand fight in which Chandrapillai had a bad fall and died from the after-effects of this accident. Finally, in 1984, a handful of congregations made themselves independent under the leadership of A. Chandy and retained the name Ceylon Pentecostal Mission. Though the group was small in number, the step found a surprisingly great sympathy among the members, who formally accepted the change of name. Apart from these internal differences, the church's general rejection of education also became more and more a problem. The majority of the pastors were without any formal training or education, with the few exceptions of those who already held academic degrees before they entered the church ministry. This was also one of the reasons for the general stagnation of the church, particularly when we compare this situation to the comparatively highly educated and well-trained pastors in the other Pentecostal churches in Kerala in mid-1990s.

Remarkably different was the development of the Assemblies of God. In 1947, the American missionaries of the Assemblies of God in India decided on a new administrative structure in their church. As a result, they merged the Malayalam-speaking region with the Tamil-speaking Kanyakumari District as an independent administrative unit. The experienced Indian pastor A. C. Samuel was elected to lead that unit. Shortly afterward, Samuel and the most important Indian leader next to him, C. Kunjummen, were invited to the United States, where they undertook a long preaching tour from 1947 to 1948. That journey was successful and aroused great interest among the American partner churches in the work in India. Thus, after the journey enough funds were available to acquire built-up land in Punalur around 1949 for the Bethel Bible School which, despite its long tradition, had been run only provisionally for many years.[19] In the midst of this atmosphere of new beginnings, John H. Burgess unexpectedly returned to the USA in 1950, due to the bad health of his wife. Burgess had considerably influenced the work of the church for almost twenty-five years. Since no other American missionary was immediately available as a substitute, the leadership roles of Samuel and Kunjummen, who was appointed as new director of the Bible school, became of special importance. In a certain sense, the year 1950 marked the beginning of indigenous leadership in the Assemblies of God in Kerala. Ernest A. Sorbo,

19. See Sam 1983: 37-39, 71-72; Saju 1994: 180.

44

who came to India as successor of Burgess in 1951, was able to cooperate in harmony with the Indian leadership and concentrated his activities on the trans-regional work of the south Indian districts as well as on the mobilization of the necessary financial means.[20] After the retirement of Samuel in 1967, Kunjummen assumed Samuel's office too, and thus became the uncontested leading figure in Kerala. In the 1960s and 1970s, the Assemblies of God attained a steady but modest growth. Though the administration during this time seemed to be stable externally, internally there was a high conflict potential that came to erupt openly at the end of the 1970s. In 1975, Earl Stubbs, son-in-law of Ernest A. Sorbo, had come to the Bible school as a new American missionary. His attempts to raise the academic level and to extend the capacity of the Bible school as well as to increase the missionary strength of the church soon brought him into conflict with Kunjummen, who felt himself attacked in his leading position.[21] In addition, a long-swelling conflict between the Malayalam-speaking areas and the Tamil-speaking Kanyakumari District broke out openly in 1978, and the American missionaries were dragged into the conflict. Soon the situation escalated to one of the most difficult crises in the history of the Assemblies of God in India. The occasion that triggered the controversy is not known to the author, but the deeper reason was a tension that had been lying beneath the surface till then and was made public for the first time. The Tamil-speaking students, who hailed from the south and belonged predominantly to the Nadar caste, started a massive protest. But the same sentiments were also shared by the Malayalam-speaking Dalits under the leadership of P. D. Johnson. Since Kunjummen did not undertake any real step to solve the conflict, the governing body of the school appointed Stubbs in his place.

This led to the revolt of the Thomas Christians who remained in solidarity with Kunjummen, who was still the head of the district, and whose supporters took legal action to challenge his voting out of the Bible school.[22] Moreover, replacing Kunjummen by the comparatively younger Earl Stubbs was a blatant breach of the principle of seniority that is very pronounced in India. Extremely hostile voices were raised against the American missionaries, demanding that they leave Kerala. At the same time, the Tamil-speaking pastors energetically engaged themselves in favor of retaining these missionaries in Kerala. They were supported in these efforts by a few Thomas Christians from Malabar in the north, whose missionary work had been strongly

---

20. See Assemblies of God 1977: 4, 8, 14; Rajamoni n.d.: 4; Reginald 1995: 41.
21. See Assemblies of God 1977: 17.
22. See Reginald 1995: 56.

promoted by the missionaries. Soon after the breakout of the conflict, the Tamil-speaking pastors combined their protest with a demand to separate the Kanyakumari District from Kerala and to make it independent.

In the midst of such chaotic conditions and hardening frontiers, it was all the more surprising that it was possible to resolve the conflict soon and somewhat amicably. First, the South India Assemblies of God as the higher administrative authority provisionally took over the leadership of the district. It should be noted that continuing adaptations of the administrative framework took place within the Assemblies of God. In 1947, preparations were begun to organize the work in south India independently, and as a result, the South India Assemblies of God were founded in 1949 in Coonoor, with the American missionary Carl D. Holleman as the first General Superintendent.[23] The South India Assemblies of God formed an umbrella organization for largely independent districts.[24] Such an organization proved itself especially suitable to settle crises in and between the districts if necessary.[25] As another important measure in solving the crisis, John Thannickal from the Southern Asia Bible College in Bangalore was invited to become head of the Bethel Bible School. He was a Thomas Christian and an intellectual head of the south Indian Pentecostal movement. He was successful in significantly improving the academic level, as was intended by Stubbs before. The death of Kunjummen soon afterward in 1979 de-escalated the conflict further. As successor, an able and widely recognized pastor was found in P. D. Johnson, who had been the elected deputy of Kunjummen. He was not a Thomas Christian, but he was respected by them. At the end, the administration of the Assemblies of God proved itself capable of mastering a situation that temporarily had become chaotic. In 1980, Johnson was officially elected as Kunjummen's successor, and this change set free a considerable growth potential in Kerala. Under Johnson and T. J. Samuel, who followed him in 1991, the church expe-

23. See Rajamoni n.d.: 7, 4.

24. In the course of time the following districts came into existence: 1947: Malayalam District, till 1981 South West District (corresponds somewhat to Kerala); 1948: Tamil District (corresponds to Tamil Nadu without Kanyakumari District); 1953: Maharashtra District; 1957: Central District (corresponds somewhat to Karnataka); 1981: Southern District (formerly part of the South West District); 1987: Andhra Pradesh (formerly with Central District).

25. In February 1995, the three churches of the Assemblies of God (South India Assemblies of God, Assemblies of God of North India, and Assemblies of God of East India), which were functioning independently of each other in India, decided to form one General Council of the Assemblies of God. Y. Jeyaraj was elected as the first General Superintendent. An official registration was in preparation in 1995. See Jeyaraj 1995; Assemblies of God 1995.

rienced a steady and solid growth, which, however, was far from reaching the dynamics of the Assemblies of God in Tamil Nadu. However, the American missionaries left Kerala over the crisis, disappointed and also personally hurt. Sorbo went back to the USA in 1982, and Stubbs found a new field of operation in Andhra Pradesh. Since then there have been no more American missionaries of the Assemblies of God in Kerala. As another result of the conflict, the Tamil-speaking pastors were pacified by the establishment of a new district. In 1981, the Tamil-speaking South became independent from Kerala and formed the Southern District, whose area corresponded somewhat to the Kanyakumari District.[26] However, objections were raised from the powerful Tamil District, which would have liked to include these southern Tamil-speaking congregations in its own administration.[27] Though this would make sense both from the linguistic and the political point of view, the South did not support such a union. Hence, the new district was approved by the South India Assemblies of God. With its independence, the southern district soon displayed a breathtaking growth. In 1989, however, there arose a severe quarrel in which the then newly elected leadership was criticized for nepotism. Temporarily, a parallel leadership board was formed by the critics. Though the quarrel was severe, it did not hinder the growth of the church, as was stressed by informed observers:

> Ironically or miraculously (depending on the perspective), the problems of the southern district did not affect the church growth much, because both the parties vigorously worked to prove their ministry.[28]

Eventually, both parties subjected themselves to an arbitration of the South India Assemblies of God, and the conflict was basically solved in 1990. However, another conflict could not be solved as easily. The Tamil district of the South Indian Assemblies of God founded numerous new churches in the Kanyakumari District and did not leave this part of Tamil Nadu completely to the southern district.

The last of the four old larger Pentecostal denominations in Kerala, the

---

26. The present Kanyakumari District belonged to the princely state of Travancore during the British colonial period. In 1956, the Tamil-speaking part of Travancore was incorporated into Tamil Nadu as Kanyakumari District (with some important exceptions — Shenkottai, for example, was added to the Tirunelveli District). Besides Tamil, Malayalam is also spoken widely in the Kanyakumari District. The remaining Travancore became southern Kerala.

27. See for the following Reginald 1995.

28. Reginald 1995: 95.

Church of God, initiated by Robert F. Cook in 1936, had a difficult time during the end of the 1940s. In 1947, the American headquarters of the Church of God sent the missionary C. E. French to India with the goal of cooperating with the central church leadership in Kerala and finally to relieve Cook, who was about seventy years old.[29] Up till then Cook had determined the destiny of the church single-handedly, and apparently he was not prepared to share leadership or to hear anything about retirement. Instead, he attempted to persuade his long-time Indian coworker T. M. Verghese to work for a separation from the Church of God and to form a new independent church.[30] At the last minute, separation was averted through the refusal of Verghese to follow Cook's wishes. Moreover, to solve the problem, the Malayalam-speaking son of Robert F. Cook, Paul Cook, who stayed in India at that time, intervened on behalf of the Church of God, and finally, the General Overseer of the Church of God paid a visit to India.[31] As a result, Robert F. Cook submitted and left India in 1950. The church ministry had suffered considerably during the crisis, and the administration that had been tailored totally to suit Robert F. Cook needed thorough changes.[32] The reorganization of the church was pushed forward by the missionary Miss Dora P. Myers. Shortly after her arrival in India in 1950 she had undertaken the reopening of Mount Zion Bible School, which was rich in tradition but had lain closed for years. Through their long ministry in India, she and William Pospisil, who arrived soon after her, ensured continuity in the ministry, and the church showed a considerable growth in Kerala. When Verghese retired in 1965, the required change in the leadership was used as an opportunity to bring in a necessary regionalization. Till 1965, the Church of God in India had a central administration that was led by Verghese as Field Secretary. After he retired, it came to a regionalization of the organization. The Church of God was divided first into three districts: Kerala, Tamil Nadu, and Andhra Pradesh.[33] Each district got a separate State Representative (later called State Overseer). In 1969, a Northern Region was added in which a Regional Overseer was appointed, with headquarters at Bombay. In 1972, Kerala was divided into two districts: Kerala State and

---

29. See Saju 1994: 178-80; Conn 1959: 223-24; Myers 1960: 55-56; Varghese & George 1973: 31-32; Cook 1955: 254-57; Varghese 1982: 43-44 (based on an interview with T. M. Verghese).

30. See Myers 1960: 55; Saju 1994: 178; Varghese 1982: 45-46. See also Pentecostal Fellowship of India 1991: 38. The Church of God was registered first in 1949 by C. E. French (see Church of God 1979: 52).

31. See Myers 1960: 56; Varghese 1982: 46.

32. See Varghese 1982: 68.

33. See, however, p. 61, n. 11.

Kerala Division. These districts or regions were actually placed directly under the Far East Superintendent. After Verghese, a pan-Indian leadership no longer existed, though P. A. V. Sam held the newly created post of Field Representative (instead of the former Field Secretary) for the whole of India between 1966 and 1971. The post was without power or competence and was abolished in 1971. A specialty of the administration of the Church of God is the direct influence of the American headquarters on decisions about persons and other important areas of church life. Thus, for example, all the State Overseers were appointed by the American headquarters. The decisions taken there were often bad or at least not sufficiently coordinated with the Indian partners, a circumstance that bore considerable potential for conflicts.

As a result of this reorganization, Kerala became a separate district, with an indigenous representative as the head. On the whole, however, the church leadership in Kerala remained substantially controlled by the American missionaries until William Pospisil left India in 1972. Pospisil was also responsible for the founding of a new and separate caste-based administrative unit, the Kerala Division, within Kerala in 1972.[34] As a result, the part that remained as Kerala State district became an exclusive church of the Thomas Christians. After the complete transfer of the church leadership into indigenous hands, the church developed continuously and showed considerable growth in the 1970s and 1980s.[35] The assuming of power by Sam in 1988, however, led to a severe crisis in the internal church leadership that went on till the 1990s.

The conflict around Sam offers a good example of the problem of American influence on personnel policies in the Indian Church of God. In 1986, Sam gave up a good post in industry and took up full-time ministry in the Church of God with a lot of evangelical verve. He drew the attention of the American headquarters, which saw in him a new, extremely capable leading personality, so much so that it placed great hopes in him and did everything to support his ambitions about coming to a leading position in the church. Unfortunately, a wrong assessment of the Indian situation was made when M. V. Chacko was removed from his office in 1988 to make the way free for Sam. Chacko did not feel properly treated, and many pastors of some standing had reservations about Sam, who was brought into office through the back door. The situation became worse in the course of time and an opposition party was formed that set up a parallel church leadership. Legal actions were undertaken and church conventions had to be held under police protection. The behavior of Sam did not contribute to reconciliation. His hasty in-

---

34. See pp. 55-56.
35. See Church of God 1993; Varghese & George 1973.

troduction of modern methods of administration, his authoritarian leadership style, and severe procedures against his critics met with protests in many places. Unmindful of the tragic division within the church, he officially celebrated great successes, above all in church growth. Thus he reported that the number of congregations had doubled in the first five years since his taking charge of office. The truth of this statement, however, is doubtful. In the mid-1990s, Sam emerged successfully out of the legal quarrels and power struggles within the church. His opponent Chacko went over to the Indian Pentecostal Church at the beginning of 1995. However, the reputation of the Church of God in Kerala was significantly damaged in this conflict.

New Churches

Since the larger already-existing four Pentecostal churches in Kerala suffered from many internal quarrels, they were not in a position to offer an adequate framework for integrating younger leading personalities with new ideas. That led to the founding of new churches under the leadership of young Pentecostal Thomas Christians. In 1952, P. J. Thomas returned to his native Kerala after studying long years in Australia and in the USA. At that very time, violent inner-church power struggles broke out in the Indian Pentecostal Church whose pastor he was. That caused him not to engage himself again in the Indian Pentecostal Church, but to open a small, independent Bible school, the Sharon Bible School, in Tiruvalla in 1953.[36] In the same year, he arranged a big twenty-three-day program for the couple J. C. and M. A. Daoud, two prominent American faith healers.[37] That program left a great impression in Kerala, and Thomas became a well-known figure. Moreover, he could establish contacts with many sponsors abroad and traveled regularly to the USA during that time. Many pastors who were dissatisfied with the situation in the Indian Pentecostal Church associated themselves with him, and he supported them. He also made arrangements for financial assistance to those who had passed through his Bible school and who had founded their own congregations but wanted to stay in fellowship with him. In 1957, Thomas organized another big campaign in Tiruvalla, this time with the controversial American faith healers A. A. Allen and his two coworkers Robert W. Schambach and John E.

36. In his autobiography, K. E. Abraham makes some mention of a quarrel with P. J. Thomas about the registration of a plot of land that was bought by Thomas. However, the background of the conflict is not given (see Abraham 1983: 386). See also Mathew 1990: 74; Abraham 1990: 90.
37. For the Daoud couple see Hewett 1990a.

Douglas.[38] This evangelization proved itself to be of great importance, since it seemed to have awakened great interest in India in Douglas.[39] A little later, after he had founded his own organization called World Missionary Evangelism, Douglas devoted a great part of his activities to India. Thomas received manifold assistance from Douglas in the 1960s and 1970s.[40] With that assistance he was able to open an orphanage, to extend considerable financial support to pastors, and to build a few prayer houses. More and more pastors, most of them formerly connected with the Indian Pentecostal Church, sought to associate themselves with these newly arising churches. However, Thomas kept up loose contact with the Indian Pentecostal Church for a long time, and only in 1975 did he finally decide to formally register the congregations that were in fellowship with him under the name Sharon Fellowship.[41] Unlike the Indian Pentecostal Church, Sharon Fellowship remained free from bigger internal conflicts. One reason for that is the extremely congregational structure of the church, without a hierarchical central administration but firmly grouped around the charismatic personality of Thomas. It was of special importance for further developments that at the end of the 1970s T. G. Koshy, returning from the USA after finishing his theological studies, wanted to work with Thomas. In 1970 in the neighborhood of Adur, Pathanamthitta District, Koshy founded a Bible school, the Faith Theological Seminary. Thanks to his manifold contacts with sponsors abroad, it developed into one of the most academically prestigious Pentecostal formation places in India and was still the best showpiece of the church in 1990s. Consequently, Koshy became the successor to Thomas in 1998.

Another new church was founded by V. A. Thamby, who hailed from the Cananite group of the Thomas Christians.[42] He had converted to the Pentecostal faith in 1962, and from that time on he had worked as a full-time evan-

---

38. See Mathew 1990: 76-77. For A. A. Allen see Harrell 1975: 66-75, 175, 194-206.

39. See World Missionary Evangelism 1989: 10 (Letter of greetings by R. Courts).

40. It is not certain exactly when P. J. Thomas broke his relationship with John E. Douglas. Most probably, this might have happened in the second half of the 1970s, when C. S. Mathew and his church, which was similarly supported by Douglas, formally joined World Missionary Evangelism, while Sharon Fellowship remained independent.

41. See also Warren 1959: 119. Here, P. J. Thomas is still recorded as pastor of the Indian Pentecostal Church in Tiruvalla for the year 1959.

42. The Thomas Christians are divided into two endogamous groups: the Kananites or inhabitants of the south (referred to as Knanayites, Suddhists, or Southists) and the inhabitants of the North (referred to in English as Northists). The Cananites represent the more elitist and tradition-conscious subgroup. See Brown 1956: 175-77; Mundadan 1984: 95-98; Kariyil 1995, 42-43. According to the knowledge of the author, Pentecostal Thomas Christians belong mainly to the Northists.

gelist. Apart from the fact that he was instrumental in founding two independent Pentecostal house congregations among the Cananite Thomas Christians, he could not show any notable missionary success until the beginning of the 1970s. This situation changed in 1973 when he met the Australian Pentecostal pastor Cliff Beard in Kerala and both opted for close cooperation. With the recommendation of Beard, Thamby undertook a long preaching journey through the USA in the following year, making it possible to win sponsors for the starting of a new church which he registered shortly afterward as the New India Church of God. For some years he contemplated concentrating his activities fully in north India. He gave up that idea, however, by the beginning of 1978 at the latest, when he acquired a big built-up piece of land in Chengannur with assistance from abroad, with a view of establishing the headquarters and a Bible school there. At the same time, he commissioned his brother-in-law to begin a missionary work for the church in north India. Since the end of the 1970s, the New India Church of God developed a number of missionary activities that led to a steady growth of the church. Big evangelistic events with intensive follow-up programs that were organized jointly with partners from abroad seem to have been comparatively effective. Through Mariamma Thamby, the dedicated wife of Thamby, the ministry received a special emphasis. After completing half a year of further studies in Australia in the 1980s, she opened a special Bible school for women in 1983. Women who had completed their formation in it took part in many decisive ways in founding new congregations.[43] In 1988, Thamby transferred the headquarters of the church to Chingavanam, Kottayam District, the traditional episcopal residence of the Cananites. On the extensive land acquired for this purpose, he put up, among other things, a big prayer hall and started in that small place an intensive missionary activity among the Cananite Thomas Christians. He had some success, and after a few years Chingavanam became the largest local congregation of the New India Church of God. At the end of the twentieth century, no other single Pentecostal church had challenged its "mother church" to the same extent as the New India Church of God.

The New India Bible Church is another important organization founded by young Pentecostals with a Thomas Christian background. When Thomas Philip was converted to the Pentecostal faith in 1969, he was earning his livelihood as a teacher in a small secular evening school in the neighborhood of Changanacherry. After his conversion he was engaged in evangelical work, and for obvious reasons began to concentrate his efforts on Christian instruction. The Bible courses that he conducted for the children and the youth during the

43. See Thamby 1993: 4, 6.

holidays found approval. Such good experiences caused him to found a small Bible school of his own in 1972. In that effort he was financially supported by his brother Abraham Philip, who was studying in the USA at that time. In 1974, after finishing his studies, Abraham Philip returned to India, took over the Bible school founded by his brother, and developed it further. As a result, the New India Bible College was started. From the beginning there were young people among the students who wanted to found their own congregations. For such cases, Thomas Philip and his brother began to build up an independent organization, the New India Bible Church. The Bible school and the church were brought under a single umbrella organization, the New India Evangelistic Association. Abraham Philip was the head of the latter, and besides his responsibility for the Bible school, he made successful efforts to win financial sponsors abroad. His brother Thomas Philip was mainly engaged with the church work. Though both the brothers belonged to the Thomas Christians, the members of the newly founded congregations, according to their statement, were exclusively Dalits. The New India Bible Church showed a modest growth over the years, and by the end of the twentieth century it had secured a firm place within the Pentecostal movement of Kerala. The early death of Abraham Philip in 1992, however, meant a big setback.

One of the most influential new foundations in the second half of the twentieth century was Gospel of Asia. In 1978 K. P. Yohannan, an Indian who was working as a pastor in the USA, began to financially support ten pastors in India.[44] Within a short time he developed a large missionary society with the name Gospel for Asia. The professed goal of Gospel for Asia is to support indigenous missions. It opposes direct mission work of western churches because it sees in them the danger of religious neo-colonialism.[45] Yohannan writes: "My message to the West is very simple. Everywhere God calls Christians to recognize that it is He Himself who builds His church in Asia. Indigenous missionaries need support. God calls in order to establish His Kingdom, but not to impose western control and teachings on the Asian church."[46] Besides, Gospel for Asia explicitly stands against any social engagement. Yohannan writes:

> The social gospel tries basically to fight a spiritual battle with weapons of flesh, even if it is clothed in a religious garb and operates within the Christian institutions. Our battle is not against flesh and blood, or

44. See Yohannan 1994a: 209.
45. See Yohannan 1994b: 148.
46. Yohannan 1994b: 149.

against the symptoms of sins such as poverty and disease. It is directed against Lucifer and innumerable demons which fight day and night in order to drag the human souls into an eternity without Christ. ... When we have plans to fight the biggest problem of the human being, the separation from the eternal God, through supplies of food, then we throw to a drowning person a life-belt, however, we do not take him out of the water.[47]

In 1981, Yohannan started an official branch of the organization in his native Kerala, and in 1983 the Indian headquarters in Tiruvalla were set up in order to take over the distribution of the money received mainly from the USA. Donations were constantly increasing and made Gospel for Asia into one of the most financially powerful mission undertakings in India in the 1980s. The Indian headquarters, which have been housed in a modern new office building since 1990, enabled it to do administrative work in an efficient manner. The self-professed goal was to provide material support to the existing missions and churches without interfering in the internal affairs of any organization. Though a great part of the funding went to north India, many churches in south India also received support. In the beginning of the 1990s, however, Yohannan changed his strategy. New local Bible schools run directly by Gospel for Asia were opened in different parts of the country. Graduates of these institutions were offered financial support to found new congregations. In 1993, Gospel for Asia created its own church administrative structure, the Believers' Church, where newly founded congregations supported by Gospel for Asia were grouped together. Because of the great financial means and the efficient administration at the disposal of Gospel for Asia, the Believers' Church has the potential to develop into an important Pentecostal church in India.

However, it was not only young Pentecostal leaders with a Thomas Christian background who founded important new churches in Kerala. Since the 1940s new Pentecostal churches were also initiated by Dalits and Nadars. The main reason for this was the inability of the churches led by the Thomas Christians to integrate Dalit or Nadar leaders. As a result, a caste compartmentalization became manifest also within the Pentecostal movement in Kerala, as it was already practiced in the other Malayalam-speaking churches. While the churches that were dominated by the Thomas Christians fostered comparatively closer contact among themselves, they seldom had any close contacts with churches led by Dalits or Nadars. The first major church foundation by a Dalit goes back to C. S. Mathew, an active member

47. Yohannan 1994b: 92.

with the Brethren, who received the baptism of the Spirit in 1946 and immediately began to spread the Pentecostal faith within his mother church. This soon led to a conflict with the Brethren, who were anti-Pentecostal, and a year later Mathew founded the Independent Church of God in India, which received a big influx from those who were once members of Brethren congregations. During that time, Mathew, who was an outstanding preacher and an excellent composer of songs, stood in close contact with K. E. Abraham and the Indian Pentecostal Church, which, however, did not lead to a real collaboration between them. The elite leaders of the Indian Pentecostal Church, who had a Thomas Christian background, were not at all ready to share church leadership with a Dalit. As a reaction to the rejection by the Thomas Christians, Mathew started his own missionary activities among Dalits. Though hardly any financial assistance from abroad was available, the church grew fast under his able leadership. When John E. Douglas came to Andhra Pradesh in 1962, with the intention of offering direct support from World Missionary Evangelism to Indian pastors,[48] Mathew belonged to the first who accepted that offer. That cooperation worked to his advantage and the new financial possibilities led to a consolidation of the work. On the basis of that good experience, Mathew gave his consent to transfer the whole property of the church to the organization led by Douglas and to change the name from Independent Church of God in India to World Missionary Evangelism. It was the one and only case in all of India that an entire church organization formally joined World Missionary Evangelism, which gave Mathew and his work in Kerala a special position within the organization. Until his death in 1985, the church showed a gradual but steady growth. O. M. Rajakutty was elected as his successor. He was the son-in-law of Mathew, who did not have any male offspring. Rajakutty kept the course of his predecessor, characterized by its continuity and stability. For this reason, World Missionary Evangelism in Kerala was hardly affected by the turbulent inner conflicts of the organization that broke out in Andhra Pradesh in 1990,[49] and it remained one of the most important and most stable Pentecostal churches in Kerala.

A remarkable development has taken place within the Church of God in Kerala since the 1960s. Traditionally the Church of God had a big proportion of Dalits among its members, but the indigenous leadership was in the hands of the Thomas Christians only. After Kerala formed a separate administrative unit in the second half of the 1960s,[50] the Dalits started to raise their voices

---

48. See pp. 95-96.
49. See p. 98.
50. See p. 48.

and complained of discrimination vis-à-vis ordination of pastors and assignment of administrative posts in the church. Apparently, for the Thomas Christians these complaints were no reason to make changes. In the beginning of the 1970s, however, a group of pastors from the ranks of the Dalits came together and urgently demanded equal representation for all the key positions of the church. They thereby put pressure on the American missionary William Pospisil. The situation escalated when the Thomas Christians turned down the demands of the Dalits by saying they did not have sufficient trained leading personalities. For the Dalits, however, this seemed to be a tactical, fictitious argument, and they began to issue an ultimatum for an immediate participation in the leadership. Pospisil and the representatives, who had come from the American headquarters, did not find any other way than to divide the church. Hence, in 1972, the Dalits were allowed to form their own administrative unit which came to be known as the Church of God (Kerala Division), and K. J. Chacko was elected to be its leader. Because at that time there was hardly anyone among the Dalits with higher education, it was hard to build up an able administration in the beginning. The church showed considerable growth, however, and in 1984 it was able to open its own Bible school in the neighborhood of the headquarters at Pakkil near Kottayam. Since the mid-1980s, new highly motivated leaders from the younger generation arose who had undergone a comparatively good education. Those young pastors made the church grow noticeably and gave it considerably greater missionary dynamics than in the parallel organization, the Church of God (Kerala State), which was dominated by the Thomas Christians.

In the second half of the 1940s, the members of a prayer circle, mainly Nadar Christians that had close contact with the Pentecostal movement, left the London Missionary Society in Kovalam, Trivandrum District. They founded an independent church, there and T. Stephen, who had been leader of the group for many years, was made a pastor.[51] It drew more people from the surrounding area, and after a short time another congregation was founded in Neyyatinkara. However, in 1952, the Neyyatinkara congregation separated itself from T. Stephen under the leadership of K. N. Stephen, who founded an independent organization that was registered under the name Zion Sangham. K. N. Stephen had converted from Hinduism to Christianity

---

51. Lois Timothy, the mother of T. Stephen, had founded a prayer circle in the 1920s after her husband was cured of a sickness through prayer. That circle came under the influence of the Pentecostal movement and gradually estranged itself from the London Missionary Society. The opposition against infant baptism seemed to have been the reason for an open separation. T. Stephen (ca. 1903-1986) was working as a teacher, but gave up his job in order to assume the leadership of the church.

at the end of the 1940s, and had become a close coworker of T. Stephen. However, the cooperation continued only for a few years. The Zion Sangham showed a modest growth in the following decades. Its gains came to an unexpected end near the end of the 1980s when people attempted to dethrone K. N. Stephen, who until then had led the Zion Sangham without disputes, toward the end of the 1980s. Afterward the organization was divided into at least two parts that quarreled with each other and even went to court. As a result, Zion Sangham ceased to play a significant role by the mid-1990s. The congregation in Kovalam always remained with T. Stephen, and in the 1950s four more branches were founded in the wider surroundings. In 1958, T. Stephen went to Madras where his younger sister was working and left the work in Kerala temporarily in the hands of one of his brothers. He founded another congregation in Madras and registered the whole church there under the name International Zion Assembly in 1962, but returned to Kerala soon afterward. The church stagnated in the 1960s and 1970s. Only when T. Stephen resigned due to old age in 1981 and his son Edwin K. Raj entered the pastoral ministry did the International Zion Assembly experience a new impetus.[52] Edwin K. Raj took over the congregation in Kovalam and a leading position in the church. From 1984 onward he secured financial support through Gospel for Asia, giving new missionary impulse to a church that had previously survived on donations from its members only. The church leadership was in the hands of Nadars; Dalits were also among the congregational members, but no Thomas Christians. In the southern part of Kerala, the International Zion Assembly became one of the most important Pentecostal churches.

52. Edwin K. Raj (b. 1947) had worked as an employee in the office of the Christian Medical College, Ludhiana, since 1968. He resigned his job in 1981 in order to succeed his father.

CHAPTER 3

Tamil Nadu

Despite a series of earlier missionary activities, the Pentecostal movement gained a foothold in Tamil Nadu only after the Second World War. Two distinct phases can be observed. First in the 1940s and 1960s, there were increased missionary attempts by foreign mission societies (Assemblies of God, Church of God, and British Assemblies of God) and indigenous churches. Since the 1960s, the foreign missions had been taken over by indigenous leadership, and it became increasingly possible for indigenous churches to win their own international partners. As a result, many large inter-regional and regional Pentecostal churches with strong indigenous leadership arose, well connected to the global Pentecostal movement and showing enormous increases from the 1980s onward.

Foreign Missions

The American couple Doris and Robert Edwards came to K. P. Valasai near Shenkottai in southern Tamil Nadu in June 1948 with the intention of introducing the work of the Assemblies of God in Tamil Nadu.[1] In the beginning, two young Indian Pentecostal pastors, M. O. John and C. T. David, accompanied them as Tamil-translators and local experts. The Edwardses began with a simple street-evangelization in the surrounding villages and conducted Sunday worship in their house. To the worship services they invited those whom they had made contacts with through street-evangelization. Within a

---

1. See Rajamoni n.d.: 1. See also Rajamoni 1989: 9.

year a small worshiping community was created. As a result, the Edwardses took up the building of a prayer house. A plot of land became available, and after a few months a small church was solemnly consecrated in June 1949. For the opening of that church they organized a convention of several days' duration, in which many Pentecostal pastors and Pentecostal Christians from the wider area took part. On that occasion, the young Y. Jeyaraj, who also hailed from a Pentecostal parental house, consented to receive baptism. The Edwardses immediately won him as an urgently needed translator, giving a big impetus to the mission. Another deciding factor for the further progress of the mission might have been the opening in December 1952 of a handicraft school,[2] which received state approval two and a half years later in 1955,[3] a considerable boon to the working conditions in many respects. On the one hand, the school increased overseas spending for the mission so that the financial situation of the Edwardses, which was difficult in the beginning, improved.[4] Further, the acceptance of the mission among the people increased through that social involvement, and every year some of the pupils became Pentecostals. The handicraft skills of the people also made it possible to put up church buildings for the Assemblies of God in Tamil Nadu using their own skilled labor. Further, it was possible to receive visas for American missionaries on the grounds that they were needed for the school in K. P. Valasai.

At the same time as the Edwardses but independently from them, Oliver Foth came as another missionary from the Assemblies of God to Tamil Nadu. When he met with the Tamil Pentecostal pastor Benjamin, who had just separated from the Church of God, both of them agreed to open up a Bible school of the Assemblies of God in Madurai, which they did in 1948. Thanks to a property-broker acquaintance, Benjamin was soon able to negotiate the purchase of a suitable piece of land somewhat outside the town, where they built some homes. At the same time, on another piece of land somewhat more in the center of Madurai a church was built where Benjamin became the pastor. From its beginning, the Bible school influenced the development of the whole Pentecostal movement in Tamil Nadu. It stood in close contact with the mission of the Edwardses in K. P. Valasai. In the first three years Richard Edwards took great pains to go to Madurai once every two weeks in order to teach there.[5] However, in the third year of his mission a severe crisis arose that became a major setback for the work of the Assemblies of God in Madurai for some time.

2. See Edwards n.d.: 16.
3. See Rajamoni n.d.: 1.
4. See Edwards n.d.: 20.
5. See Edwards n.d.: 14.

The crisis in the Bible school began when Oliver Foth left Madurai, probably in 1950, after he had familiarized his successor H. W. Lowry with the work. In contrast to Foth, Lowry was apparently less capable of coping with difficult situations in which diverse interests were at play. In particular, he could not accept that the south Indian Pentecostals refused to wear jewelry of any kind. Foth had accepted it, and as a result he had not even worn his wedding ring in public. But obviously, Lowry was not ready to be pragmatic on this point, in spite of the people's general acceptance of his western lifestyle. It seemed that Lowry also underestimated the charismatic Benjamin, who in no way was ready to subordinate himself to an American missionary. Because of the quarrel Benjamin left the Assemblies of God and went back to the Church of God, claiming for himself the newly built church, since it was built on a private piece of land owned by him. In the conflict over the church building, attempts were even made to call the police. However, in a later agreement the Church of God offered a compensation payment to the Assemblies of God. Without Benjamin, Lowry stood somewhat on lost ground. When he went back to the USA in 1953,[6] he left behind a Bible school that was no longer functioning properly. The Bible school did not recover from this setback for quite some time. However, Clarence W. Roberts, who took up the school in 1954, could achieve at least a temporary consolidation.[7] With the help of the students from the Handicraft School in K. P. Valasai, a chapel was built on the campus, since the Assemblies of God had lost their church in Madurai when Benjamin left. When Roberts left India in 1957, the school suffered again and its management changed almost every year until 1965.

With the return of M. Benjamin to the Church of God, the church in Tamil Nadu experienced a new surge of activity.[8] It was of some advantage here that the passionate quarrels about the succession of Robert F. Cook had just come to an end.[9] Benjamin, who became the undisputed leading figure of the Church of God in Tamil Nadu for the next twenty years, gathered around him a handful of pastors and their congregations who had stood loyal to him and had not remained with the Assemblies of God, but accompanied him when he rejoined the Church of God. In 1953, Benjamin founded a Bible

6. See McLeish & Watts 1951: 163.

7. See McLeish 1995: 136 and Warren 1959: 154.

8. M. Benjamin (d. 1971) was a high school teacher and was converted by Gopal Daniel to the Pentecostal faith. In the 1930s and 1940s he had already worked under Robert F. Cook in the Church of God. Cook referred to him at that time as "our general evangelist of the Tamil Field" (Cook 1955: 215, see 251-52). It is not known why he then joined the Assemblies of God. See also Samuel 1980: 16.

9. See p. 48.

school for the Church of God in Tamil Nadu on the church premises. The Bible school was simple at the beginning, functioning more in the form of a guru-shishya relationship. This changed completely at the end of the 1950s, when the Communists came to power in the newly formed Kerala State and the American missionaries of the Church of God thought it advisable to move to Tamil Nadu for a while. Thus, Dora P. Myers went to Madurai at the end of the 1950s[10] and closely collaborated with M. Benjamin. Dora Myers, who had already headed the Bible school in Mulakuzha in Kerala, initiated the opening of an orderly Bible school in 1959. Since the Bible school still functioned in the church building, the question of space became an urgent problem. She purchased a piece of land at the railway station on Kodai Road, a distance of about forty kilometers from Madurai, and the school was transferred to a newly erected building there in 1961. However, that place proved to be too remote from the centers of the Church of God. Hence, it was sold in 1967 and, after one interim year at Vickramasingapuram, Tirunelveli District, the Bible school was again transferred to a newly bought piece of land at Coimbatore. In spite of such turbulent changes, the Bible school produced quite a few capable pastors. In 1965, Tamil Nadu became an independent district of the Church of God, and Benjamin was elected as the first State Representative,[11] a post he held till his death in 1971. He died in Madras, where he had transferred the headquarters of the district from Madurai at the end of the 1960s.[12] Thanks to the charismatic leadership qualities of Benjamin, the Church of God became an important factor in the Pentecostal movement in Tamil Nadu in the 1950s and 1960s.

The British Assemblies of God concentrated their work around Coimbatore. At first sight it produced hardly any notable results. In the end, however, it led to the origin of two important independent Pentecostal churches that became a dominating force in Coimbatore in the 1990s. Margaret and Lawrence Livesey took over the work in Coimbatore from Spencer E. May at the beginning of the 1940s. In 1947, they had already succeeded in putting up a small church in the town area of Tatapad.[13] The Tamil couple

10. See Myers n.d.: 34.

11. See however Varghese & George 1973: 52, where the year 1962 is given. If that is right, Tamil Nadu State had been constituted already in 1962.

12. See Varghese & George 1973: 52; Benjamin 1981: 16.

13. The British missionary Spencer E. May came to south India in the first half of the 1920s and worked continuously in Coimbatore since 1931. The mission couple Margaret and Lawrence Livesey came to India in 1935 and settled down in Vadugapalayam near Pollachi, till they took over the work from May in Coimbatore. See also Gnanaprakasam 1995: 1, 2-3.

Lily and J. C. Isaiah worked with them actively in the congregation. Both of them were brought to the Pentecostal faith by the Liveseys and were long-time members of the congregation. Job Gnanaprakasam was working in the newly erected church as the indigenous pastor. He was one of the Hindus converted by the Liveseys and the most intelligent student out of five young men who had been trained in an improvised Bible school in the mid-1940s.[14] In 1954 the Liveseys decided rather suddenly to put an end to their work in India and to return to Europe.[15] The church in Coimbatore was handed over to a committee under the leadership of the Isaiah couple as trustees, and Job Gnanaprakasam was appointed as pastor. The division of power between a pastor and a committee is atypical in Indian Pentecostalism and soon led to a conflict. On the one hand, Gnanaprakasam did not accept the obligation of being accountable to a committee. On the other hand, in opposition to the Liveseys and influenced by indigenous Pentecostals, he now radically opposed wearing jewelry. Gnanaprakasam left this church in 1957 and founded an independent congregation. At this time, he intensified his contact with the more radical indigenous Pentecostals, especially with John Rose,[16] and apparently, his theological understanding also shifted more and more in this direction. Unexpectedly, the Liveseys returned to India as missionaries of the British Assemblies of God, and this created new confusions. The church committee at Tatapad was afraid it would be forced again to give up its independence to the European missionaries, to which it was opposed. This conflict, especially between the Isaiah family and the European missionaries who were highly respected by them, was a great tragedy that intensified further. Hence, the Liveseys left this church and diverted their attention to a suburb of Coimbatore, the Saibaba Colony, where they attempted a completely new beginning. They succeeded in winning over Gnanaprakasam, who had been converted and trained by them, to work with them. In spite of all the problems, they did not become discouraged and started their new work with great energy. Fourteen months after their arrival, on 30 December 1961, they consecrated a newly built prayer house in their new place, the Zion Assembly of God. However, the church did not win many members, though they had some success as they extended their activities to a neighboring agricultural school. One person who was converted to the Pentecostal faith there was Peter Arumainayakam, who later revived the stagnating work of the Liveseys. After some time the Liveseys achieved a reconciliation with the Tatapad com-

14. See Livesey n.d.: 16.
15. See Livesey n.d.: 42.
16. See Gnanaprakasam 1995: 3.

mittee under the leadership of the Isaiahs,[17] but there was a further blow when Gnanaprakasam left the Liveseys in 1963 and became the pastor of the Pentecostal Church of India in Coimbatore.[18] Formally, Gnanaprakasam's departure happened in a mutual agreement, but it restricted the outreach of their work considerably. After continuing their modest work in the newly established congregation for a while and consolidating it to some extent, the Liveseys left India for good in 1965.

Indigenous Churches

After the end of the Second World War, indigenous Pentecostal churches also developed vigorously in Tamil Nadu. In the 1950s, the Indian Pentecostal Church in Andhra Pradesh started some missionary work here that was coordinated by P. M. Samuel, though he resided in the neighboring Andhra Pradesh. He succeeded in convincing many able Tamil pastors to join the Indian Pentecostal Church. In southern Tamil Nadu, this affected above all the followers of Sadhu Kochukunju, an influential leader of the Indian Pentecostal Church in Kerala. A series of Tamil pastors, mainly from Kanyakumari District, which was politically united with Kerala till 1956, had joined Sadhu Kochukunju and lived the Sadhu ideal although with different degrees of commitment. Two years after the death of Sadhu Kochukunju and after some serious internal quarrels, many of his Tamil congregations affiliated themselves with P. M. Samuel in 1959.[19] In Thanjavur, a town that had been well known to him for a long time, Samuel convinced the young Victor P. D. Kay to join him at the beginning of the 1950s. In 1959, during a visit of Kay in Thanjavur he met with M. O. John, who stayed for some time with Kay, and they came to an agreement that John should start a mission in the name of the Indian Pentecostal Church in T. Kallupatti. John was to become the most important supporter of Samuel in Tamil Nadu in the future.

In the 1940s and 1950s the Ceylon Pentecostal Mission became, as already mentioned, more and more radical in its positions. However, despite its radical stand the Ceylon Pentecostal Mission was able to reach a surprising growth in Tamil Nadu till the end of the 1950s. Almost in all the big towns, centers were founded or built up, so that the Ceylon Pentecostal Mission was the strongest Pentecostal group in Tamil Nadu at that time. The church was

17. See Livesey n.d.: 46.
18. See Gnanaprakasam 1995: 3.
19. See Samuel 1989: 69; Samuel 1980: 16.

rigidly and centrally organized under the leadership of Alwin, and celibacy was made an obligation for newly appointed pastors. Likewise the common living of the pastors and sisters in Faith Homes was institutionalized. In addition, the radical doctrinal statements were explained to be binding for members of the church, a policy that separated the Ceylon Pentecostal Mission from the rest of the south Indian Pentecostal movement. Alwin was probably responsible for the Ceylon Pentecostal Mission's formulation of special teachings that caused its split from other Pentecostal churches. Those teachings were propagated in a series of publications. As a result, the Ceylon Pentecostal Mission is the only south Indian Pentecostal church that has laid down its teachings almost fully in writing. The special teachings of the Ceylon Pentecostal Mission are concentrated on a very sacramental understanding of ecclesiastical offices. The office-holders are not allowed to marry and are obliged to keep celibacy. A very holy way of life is expected of them. They must live in the Faith Homes, are not allowed to have any personal possessions, and must be attired in white. The justification for this is drawn from a typological interpretation of the Old Testament priesthood.[20] Only these ministers belong to the 144,000 that will stand on Mount Zion near Christ in eternity. However, they are only a part of the bride of Christ who will be carried away before tribulation. Those Christians who have received the baptism of the Spirit, who wait for the Second Coming of the Lord, and who distinguish themselves through a holy life will also be carried away with them. These faithful will go into the New Jerusalem.

> The overcoming Church (the human child — Rev. 12:5) which will be caught up to Zion and the New Jerusalem will share the throne of God and His Son Jesus Christ and rule over all principalities and power and might and dominion in the heavenly places throughout eternity (Eph. 1:21-23).[21]

This means, that according to the teachings of the Ceylon Pentecostal Mission, all other Christians must go through the tribulation. However, if they are born again, they will be saved from damnation.[22] Thus, the baptism of the Spirit is a condition for the carrying away before the tribulation, so that

20. See The Pentecostal Mission 1993.
21. The Pentecostal Mission ca. 1985: 29.
22. See The Pentecostal Mission ca. 1985: 21-29. However, one should not overestimate the intensity of Ceylon Pentecostal Mission members' expectation of the world's imminent end. According to the impression of the author, it was in no way particularly acute in the 1990s.

it is considered to be a necessity for salvation. Consequently, the immersion baptism is only recognized if it is administered by a pastor who has received the baptism of the Spirit.[23] In light of the sacramental understanding of ecclesiastical offices, it is not surprising that, contrary to the general Pentecostal teaching, immersion baptism is considered to be necessary for salvation.[24] Further, the Ceylon Pentecostal Mission holds a radical notion of holiness and forbids any medical treatment of its members.

Quite a few important Tamil pastors turned their back on the Ceylon Pentecostal Mission in the 1940s and 1950s because they rejected the dogmatic radicalization that characterized it at the time. It was probably in the 1940s that John Rose came into conflict with the Ceylon Pentecostal Mission. He worked there as a pastor and had founded several congregations in southern Tamil Nadu. As the quarrel became more heated and Rose was excommunicated by the Ceylon Pentecostal Mission, many congregation members stayed with him and he founded an organization of his own that he registered as the Full Gospel Pentecostal Church. It soon grew rapidly.[25] In Palayankottai a certain K. C. James worked as a pastor of the Ceylon Pentecostal Mission, but at the same time he held a private registration for his congregation and also a marriage license in the name of the Pentecostal Church of India. In the 1940s, when the situation of married pastors in the Ceylon Pentecostal Mission became more and more difficult, S. Ponraj, who worked in Coimbatore, also obtained a private marriage license with the help of K. C. James in the name of the Pentecostal Church of India.[26] However, such independent activities were tolerated less and less in the Ceylon Pentecostal Mission at that time. Therefore, S. Ponraj and also James were forced to leave the Ceylon Pentecostal Mission once their actions became known.[27] Both of them joined together to run their congregation independently under the already-registered Pentecostal Church of India. James died in 1948. After that, S. B. Daniel, who still worked as a pastor for the Ceylon Pentecostal Mission in Palayankottai, left his church and took over James's congregation. Like his predecessor, Daniel worked closely together with Ponraj in Coimbatore. When Ponraj died in

---

23. See The Pentecostal Mission 1987b: 12. According to the unpublished bylaws, the immersion baptism must even be administered by a "consecrated servant," that is, by one who lives in celibacy (see The Pentecostal Mission 1984: 3). However, in practice, this seems to be of less importance, as this demand is not found in the printed teachings of the church. See also Easow 1991: 63.

24. See The Pentecostal Mission 1987b: 26.

25. See Gnanaprakasam 1995.

26. For the Christian marriage laws in India see also p. 224 n. 34.

27. See Christopher Asir 1975: 37, 49.

1952, this cooperation came to an end, and hereafter, despite sharing the same name, the churches in Coimbatore and Palayankottai worked independently of each other. The further development of the Pentecostal Church of India in Coimbatore turned out to be difficult. The congregation committee was led by Mrs. Thangamma Cherian Jacob (d. 1990), a learned woman from Kerala. Her husband had a well-paid job in Coimbatore. A suitable successor for Ponraj could not be found for a long time, and the pastors went on changing often. The church experienced a positive impetus when Job Gnanaprakasam was pastor there from 1963 to 1975. When he got into conflict with the committee and went away after some quarrel, the church again was in crisis. Then Paul Ponraj (b. 1945) took over the leadership of the church in 1977. A nephew of S. Ponraj, he had previously run a small workshop for repairing electrical appliances. He held the small congregation together and brought continuity without getting any help from abroad.

In 1948, there were two families in Madras that had left the Ceylon Pentecostal Mission and were now without any church affiliation. Both families had contacts with pastor S. Ponraj from the Pentecostal Church of India in Coimbatore. When Ponraj heard of the situation in Madras, he decided to come and start a new congregation with those two families. However, S. Ponraj had begun to grow old and suffered from severe asthma that forced him, after only six months, to return to Coimbatore to the care of his wife, who had not gone with him to Madras.[28] In his absence, his friend G. Sunderam had led the congregation in Coimbatore. After the forced return of Ponraj, he sent Sunderam to Madras to continue the newly started work. Sunderam, who like S. Ponraj had previously been a pastor in the Ceylon Pentecostal Mission, used that chance and founded the Apostolic Christian Assembly. Two young enthusiastic members of the congregation, P. S. Chelladurai Sr. and Henry Joseph, were employees in the public service and had secure and comparatively well-paid jobs. Both of them devoted all their free time to the young congregation. Thanks to their assistance a stable core congregation was established after only a few years. However, Chelladurai left the congregation in 1951 and founded his own church, which later gained importance as Apostolic Fellowship Tabernacle. At the end of the 1950s, the college student Sam Sunderam, whose father belonged to one of the two families that had once brought S. Ponraj to Madras, showed a strong interest and talent to enter full-time ministry, and he became a pastor in the late 1950s. During the New Year's service in 1961, he was ordained as pastor in the Apostolic Christian Assembly and appointed as assistant to G. Sunderam. Their cooperation was firmly sealed immediately after-

28. See John & Palavesamuthu ca. 1990: 12.

ward when Sam Sunderam married the youngest sister of G. Sunderam's wife. In Sam Sunderam, a suitable successor had been found. Hence, the Apostolic Christian Assembly enjoyed considerable administrative stability that surely later facilitated its breathtaking growth. Henry Joseph, who had been the right hand of G. Sunderam for a long time, finished a course in a Bible school in England, just about the time of Sam Sunderam's ordination. When he returned in 1962, his place was filled by Sam Sunderam to some degree. Since he had found new contacts during his stay in England, he decided to found a separate independent organization called Maranatha. It is to be especially noted that John Rose, G. Sunderam, S. B. Daniel (Palayankottai), S. Ponraj, and a few others had found their way to the Pentecostal movement around 1930 in Malaysia and thus had met there.[29] All of them came back to India between the beginning and the middle of the 1930s and first became pastors of the Ceylon Pentecostal Mission. Later, though each one of them founded independent churches, they kept in close contact and worked together to some extent. Even after the death of their founders, the Full Gospel Pentecostal Church and the Apostolic Christian Assembly, for example, still considered themselves to be sister organizations, and did not conduct missionary work in each other's territories.

Another indigenous church that would play an important role in the future was the Madras Pentecostal Assembly. Toward the end of the 1940s, the actual leadership of the Madras Pentecostal Assembly was virtually in the hands of John Vasu, and he succeeded in further developing the existing contacts with foreign missions.[30] In that regard, the meeting with Donald Gee during his journey to India and China in 1948 was of great importance.[31] As a result, John Vasu became a member of the organization committee of the World Pentecostal Conference in Paris in 1949, and after the conference a preaching tour through Europe was organized for him, which lasted several months.[32] In 1952 a Bible school was opened,[33] and in the course of time, a series of branch congregations were founded in the rural surroundings of Madras. Though the work was supported in many respects by foreign agencies,

---

29. Among others, the names that are also sometimes mentioned are: Silvanus, G. Jacob, Premraj (see also Christopher Asir 1975: 34; Tan 2002a: 170).

30. For the origin of the Madras Pentecostal Assembly see pp. 34-35.

31. See Gee & Woodford 1948; Livesey n.d.: 24f.

32. See Pentecost, no. 8, June 1949: Front Page. See also Vasu ca. 1950: 24-25, where feedbacks from the pastors of the congregations he had preached to are printed.

33. See Andreasson & Andreasson 1989: 33. The Bible school was first supported by the Swedish Pentecostals.

the leadership of the church continued to be wholly in the hands of Vasu. The work, however, suffered a certain blow with his early death in 1962.

The south of Tamil Nadu was to become an important center of indigenous Pentecostal churches, not least because of the influence of Sadhu Yesudhason. Sadhu Yesudhason probably converted to Pentecostal Christianity under the influence of Sadhu Kochukunju in the beginning of the 1940s. As a result, he became a traveling evangelist in southern Tamil Nadu until he settled down in a village in Kanyakumari District after a few years.[34] There he founded a church called Kirubasanam, which developed into one of the most important indigenous Pentecostal churches of Tamil Nadu. Kirubasanam is a loose community of pastors and is held together solely by Sadhu Yesudhason. In spite of his very old age no successor had been appointed as of the 1990s. Yesudhason has never actively supported any cooperation with other Pentecostal churches, but at the same time, he hasn't propagated any church-dividing special teachings. A distinctive feature of his otherwise traditional Pentecostal ministry is that he himself has administered baptism only in a few exceptional cases, generally leaving it to his co-pastors. Though there had always been isolated contacts with foreign partners, Kirubasanam had hardly received any foreign assistance worth mentioning. To some extent, an offspring of Kirubasanam is the Jehovah Salvation Church. The young Y. S. Devasundaram came into contact with Kochukunju and Yesudhason through Charismatic prayer circles in the Church of South India. One of these prayer circles developed into an independent church when Devasundaram, together with the leading woman of this prayer circle, Soorna Packiam, founded the Jehovah Salvation Church, which soon attracted pastors from other Pentecostal churches.[35] One of the closest coworkers of Yesudhason, Sadhu Nesamony, also went over to the Jehovah Salvation Church.[36]

Inter-Regional Churches

Since the 1960s, the foreign missions were generally taken over by indigenous leadership and became inter-regional churches. Within the Assemblies of God, the transition from an American mission to an indigenous church in Tamil Nadu took place as an organic process, with surprisingly little tension. This smooth transition was certainly a cause for the great success of this

34. See Hoerschelmann 1977: 271-72.
35. For Jehovah Salvation Church see p. 84.
36. See Devasundaram 1981: 13.

church. The transition took place in two phases. In the early 1960s, only the church leadership passed into indigenous hands. It was still many years before the Bible school in Madurai was taken over completely by Indians.

In a formal sense, leadership of the church was in Indian hands right from the beginning. But as long as Robert Edwards resided in K. P. Valasai, he exercised effective oversight. His increasingly bad health made it necessary for him to leave for the USA in 1960. He did not find healing there and died in 1961. Then, although his wife, Doris, returned to India at the end of the same year, as a single woman she could no longer resume the role in leadership she had formerly played alongside her husband. Instead she concentrated on the management of the industrial school in K. P. Valasai. In this way, the Indian church leadership gained considerable autonomy unexpectedly early. Since Y. Jeyaraj was chosen as superintendent of the Assemblies of God in Tamil Nadu already a year before the Edwardses' departure for America, a capable indigenous leader was already available.[37] Under him the church leadership became generally independent of the American partners in their work. Jeyaraj resided in K. P. Valasai with Doris Edwards. This enabled him to become a figure of integration, both within the church and in relation to the American mother church. However, it should be noted that the American missionaries, by their financial contribution and through their Missionary Fellowship acting in parallel with the indigenous church leadership, still exercised strong influence. It was only at the end of the 1970s, when most missionaries had left Tamil Nadu, that the churches were really independent.[38] By the 1970s, the Assemblies of God had experienced a breathtaking and stable growth, and at the end of the twentieth century they were by far the strongest force in the Tamil Pentecostal churches. The growth of the Assemblies of God showed in rural as well as urban districts. Some urban congregations reached a considerable size in the course of time. A first breakthrough occurred in 1967 when the congregation of S. Adamdurai in the small town of Kovilpatti, Chidambaranar District, registered rapid growth.[39] By the end of the 1970s, it was mainly the work in the urban areas that sustained the growth. The American David Stewart, who came to K. P. Valasai in 1965 as a missionary of the Assemblies of God, played an important part here.[40] He concentrated on mission to college students and on founding congregations in the major towns, and he managed to raise adequate financial support from abroad. The large urban congregations, with

---

37. See Rajamoni n.d.: 8, 4.
38. See Zechariah 1981: 56ff.
39. See Jeyaraj 1995: 26.
40. See Rajamoni n.d.: 2.

their greater income from donations, apply themselves to mission in their regions, thus having a multiplying effect. Some of the urban congregations have
attained considerable numbers. In 1994, the Assemblies of God in Tamil Nadu
included five congregations with more than a thousand worshipers: Madras,
6,000 (D. Mohan); Madras, 1,500 (Charles Aaron); Trichy, 1,000 (Norman
Basker); Kovilpatti, 1,200 (S. Adamdurai); and Palayankottai, 1,600 (Ratna
Paul). Special mention must be made of the Madras congregation founded by
D. Mohan (b. 1948) in 1973 and called the New Life Assembly of God. In the
course of only twenty years, it developed into the biggest Pentecostal congregation in India. Through the mediation of David Stewart it secured sufficient
financial means from overseas to buy a big estate in the south of Madras and
there, in keeping with the growth of the congregation, gradually erected impressive church buildings. Beginning in 1990, the methods of the Church
Growth movement were consistently and systematically applied in this
congregation. In that year they entered into partnership with Trinity Christian
Centre in Singapore.[41] Naomi Dowdy, leading pastor at the time, organized a
systematic lay formation program, which sought to ensure strong participation by laypeople in the life of the congregation. The distinguishing mark of
the program was that existing house prayer groups were changed into Care
Cells (prayer cells). The distinctiveness of these care cells, as compared to the
house prayer groups, was their formal organization. Everyone in the Care Cells
attended the common prayer every Wednesday. With D. Mohan as leading
pastor, there were eight district pastors under whom were several so-called
section leaders. The section leaders exercised oversight over perhaps three
Care Cells. Then, in each Care Cell, there would be a leader and a deputy. Except for the pastors, it was the business of laypeople. There was special training
for all who held posts in the system. New members were put in the care of Care
Cells, where "spiritual parents" were specially designated. The cell members
were trained as missionaries. Every member personally acquainted with a
group could be assigned to this group if he or she wished it. But it must be
added that only about one-third of the congregation were enrolled in a Care
Cell.[42] As the system seemed to be successful, it was also introduced in other
congregations of the Assemblies of God in Tamil Nadu.

The Assembly of God's Tamil Bible Institute in Madurai remained much

41. See New Life Assembly of God Church 1994: 39.
42. In 1994 for 6,000 worshipers only 145 Care Cells were established (see New Life Assembly of God Church 1994). Because the Care Cells split after they have reached a certain
size to increase their missionary effectiveness, they can scarcely exceed a maximum of 10-
15 members per cell. Therefore, in 1994, they would cover at most 24-36 percent of the congregation.

longer under the oversight of the American missionaries who, however, after the departure of Clarence W. Roberts never saw themselves in the position to provide a long-term director. It was the nurse, Colleen Guinn, working ten years previously in various social institutions as a missionary of the Assemblies of God, who undertook the difficult task of directing the Bible school in 1966. She was active as principal until 1977; in this she was supported almost the whole period by her colleague Fern Ogle. With this stable leadership, the Bible school was able to give future pastors some training. But the work suffered a certain setback when the American missionary Paul Williams assumed the leadership of the school in 1977. In contrast with Colleen Guinn, he was also engaged in church work in Madurai, and here he came into serious confrontation with the local indigenous leadership; he left Madurai a year later. The conflict with Williams was most of all related to holiness matters. When at the end of 1977 the experienced and well-established pastor A. R. Thangaiah took refuge in India from Sri Lanka and became pastor of the newly established First Assembly of God in Madurai, Williams found in him a likeminded person who also rejected certain views handed down by the Indian Pentecostal tradition — especially rules concerning women covering their heads at worship and the wearing of jewelry. Williams and Thangaiah tried to overcome these traditions, and a severe conflict arose. The Indian leadership refused to accept views in accordance with western practices if they contradicted the Indian norms of Christian behavior. As a result, Williams left Tamil Nadu and moved to Bangalore, while Thangaiah was excommunicated by the Assemblies of God at the peak of the conflict. He founded an independent church in Madurai, the New Life Assemblies. The crisis around Williams had no further consequences for the Bible school, since in C. Zechariah there was already an Indian ready to take over from the missionaries. Under him the academic standard in the school was significantly raised, although the practice-oriented training remained entirely directed toward mission and the planting of new churches. As an expression of this new development, in 1982 the Tamil Bible Institute was renamed Tamil Nadu Bible College. It is not least due to this institution that the Assemblies of God had an almost inexhaustible reservoir of leadership personalities in the 1990s.

The work of the Church of God in Tamil Nadu came under prolonged pressure with the death of M. Benjamin in 1971, since no suitable successor was available. The outstanding presence of Benjamin had prevented an open display of conflict. But immediately after his death, a power struggle broke out. This was the reason that Pratap Singh, who had returned from a Bible school in America and was thereby predestined for the succession, refused to assume the leadership position. Only thirty years old, he had the justified fear of becoming the object of interplay between the various interests of older pastors. In this crisis, they called upon the young, inexperienced, and largely uneducated Abraham to be temporary State Overseer for Tamil Nadu for one year in 1972. Then, in 1973 when Joseph Navamoni was officially made State Overseer for Tamil Nadu, Abraham was not in agreement. He refused to back down and brought the case to court. When funds from America were stopped, he tried to compensate by mortgaging the building of the Bible school in Coimbatore. A five-year legal battle followed and, in the end, the Bible school building was regained. The school had been temporarily shifted to Madras in 1973, but in 1978 when it was reopened at its old place in Coimbatore, the conflict came to a formal end. The church, however, had suffered deeply, and Joseph Navamoni was not in a position to give it a new missionary impetus; instead he strengthened his authority with some kind of nepotism. The abuse made it possible for Wellesley Solomon, who for thirteen years had been Navamoni's right hand, to persuade the majority of the pastors together with the American headquarters to name him the new State Overseer. In contrast to the less-educated Navamoni, who did not speak English, Solomon was a graduate and had traveled. He made numerous efforts to reorganize the church and, to some extent, with considerable success.[43]

After the scandal concerning Alwin in 1962, the Ceylon Pentecostal Mission in Tamil Nadu needed somewhat longer than in Kerala to extricate itself from the confusion. The rivalry that broke out through the conflict between Tamils and Malayalis induced some Tamils to support Alwin for a time even after his excommunication. A group of laypeople with the engineer P. C. Martin stuck by him. In 1962 they registered an organization with the name *The* [sic] Ceylon Pentecostal Mission, with Alwin as president and Martin as secretary. In Madras at least, this group achieved good growth, but Alwin was no longer capable of a new start. His thought and behavior were completely taken up with the dispute, so that even his sermons could deal with nothing else. So most of his followers, including Martin, left him and returned to the Ceylon Pentecostal Mission.[44] In Tamil Nadu too, Alwin lost almost all his following, but he remained president of the Ceylon Pentecostal

43. Wellesley Solomon (b. 1951) came from the Kanyakumari District. His father already belonged to the Church of God. He was converted in 1967 at a missionary campaign by Sarah Navroji in Nagercoil. He received immersion baptism by M. Benjamin in 1968. He graduated as B.Sc. and B.Ed. Immediately after the completion of his studies he became assistant to Joseph Navamoni in 1973.

44. In the middle of the 1990s, P. C. Martin was the Indian National Director of the Full Gospel Business Man's Fellowship.

Mission until his death in 1967. His successor was S. J. Dhass, who acted as president until his death in 1997, though the church was practically reduced to a congregation in Nagercoil and did not affect the work of the main Ceylon Pentecostal Mission in any way. However, as in Kerala, so also in Tamil Nadu the dynamic and power of the Ceylon Pentecostal Mission had suffered as a result of the conflict. After all, from the 1960s, the rapid Pentecostal growth generally observed in Tamil Nadu was also to the advantage of the Ceylon Pentecostal Mission. Differently from Kerala, it registered some growth in Tamil Nadu, although it did not keep pace with the general increase of Tamil Pentecostalism. In this period the center of gravity of the work of the Ceylon Pentecostal Mission shifted from Kerala to Tamil Nadu. The official headquarters for India became Madras. A storm of protest was unleashed in 1984, by the decision to change the name of churches in Indian territory to the Pentecostal Mission. The name of the mother church in Sri Lanka remained unchanged.[45] The name change occurred against the background of escalating struggle between separatist Tamils and the government in Sri Lanka through which, especially in Tamil Nadu, an extremely hostile feeling developed against Sri Lanka. In some isolated cases it came to the stoning of prayer houses, and to avoid all misunderstanding the name was changed. But since for many, church identity was bound up with the name, there were many objections. Although there were no open protests in Tamil Nadu, there was much discontent — especially among the older people — and this had negative effects on the generally high loyalty to their church among pastors and people.[46] Despite some pastors changing to other Pentecostal churches, the centralizing structure of the church was hardly threatened. When at the end of 1993 several leading pastors died in quick succession, it was quickly and unanimously decided upon the succession of the vacant posts. However, C. K. Lazarus, who was appointed as Chief Pastor in 1994, was hardly capable of giving a new impetus to the church. The administration of the Ceylon Pentecostal Mission has a whole range of peculiarities. It is strongly centralized. At the summit is the Chief Pastor, who has the last word in questions of doctrine and in all other aspects of the church. At his side stands the Deputy Chief Pastor and an Assistant Deputy Chief Pastor. These three form the leading group for the church. The Chief Pastor designates his successor, whom he appoints Deputy Chief Pastor. The Assistant

---

45. To avoid confusion, the name The Pentecostal Mission is not used here. But it should be noted that from 1984 this was the only official name for the Indian branch of the church.

46. See also p. 44.

Deputy Chief Pastor in the 1990s was the American Donald M. Spiers, who formerly had worked with Oral Roberts.[47] He was especially competent for work abroad. Under the leading group are several centers where the full-time workers in the Faith Homes live together. Women also can be active in full-time service as Sisters; like the men, they are committed to celibacy. However, women may not be ordained as pastors. Men and women live together in the Faith Homes. The centers are led by a Center Pastor, with a Center Mother at his side who has authority over the sisters. Typical of the Ceylon Pentecostal Mission is the frequency of moves for pastors and sisters, including the Center Pastors. Future pastors do not receive any formal education but are prepared for their future tasks by helping experienced pastors, according to the guru-shishya system. For all men and women who devote themselves to full-time ministry in the church, it is desirable to sell their property and leave the proceeds to the church. The Ceylon Pentecostal Mission has worldwide connections, although the overwhelming majority of centers are in Kerala and Tamil Nadu. Members outside India are largely migrants from India.

Until his death in 1981, the Indian Pentecostal Church in Tamil Nadu was indisputably under the influence of P. M. Samuel, who had his headquarters in Andhra Pradesh. His most important Tamil partner during this time was M. O. John. Just as in Andhra Pradesh, Samuel only allowed financial help to the people who suited him; the others were almost without any support. By the end of the 1960s, there was a whole range of new established churches. After that, the Indian Pentecostal Church in Tamil Nadu experienced only modest growth. Within the Indian Pentecostal Church, Tamil Nadu has never been completely independent. Until his death, Samuel led the church in Andhra Pradesh as president, but also in Tamil Nadu to all intents and purposes; he formally made Paul Perinbam president there, but without executive competence. Paul Perinbam died in April 1981, and apparently Samuel had chosen P. Philip from Andhra Pradesh as successor. But before P. Philip was effectively appointed, P. M. Samuel also died, in June 1981. The Tamils took advantage of this opportunity and chose Sadhu Abraham from Nagercoil as president. Surprisingly, they were supported in this by P. M. Samuel's son, Abraham Samuel. M. O. John, as P. M. Samuel's favorite, found himself without much backing but tried to prevent this development, and for a time there was a rival leading group with P. Philip as president. But the latter group had no support from the majority of the Tamil pastors, and after some time it was dissolved. At this point, John left the Indian Pentecostal Church

47. See Harrell 1985: 263.

disillusioned.[48] Sadhu Abraham died a year later and his followers turned to the respected M. S. Joseph, an experienced pastor from Kerala who had long been working in Tamil Nadu. In 1985 Abraham Samuel was elected president in place of M. S. Joseph. Thus Tamil Nadu was again entirely under leadership from Andhra Pradesh.

When Abraham Samuel died in 1993, some concerned pastors and lay people resolved to make their district really independent. They called a full assembly for 18 February 1994 in order to elect as their president K. C. Abraham, a rich Malayali businessman from Kodaikanal, Dindigul District. He was connected neither with T. S. Abraham nor with Noel Samuel, the son of Abraham Samuel. Thereupon the leadership of the General Council (that is, the umbrella organization for the Indian Pentecostal Church) called a meeting even earlier, for 8 February, a procedure to which they were not entitled according to the constitution. The Tamils successfully went to court and got a stay against this and held their own meeting correctly. In spite of the legal action, the other party decided to have their meeting at a later date, 15 March 1994. At this rival meeting, the Malayali R. Muttu was elected president. There were now two parallel leadership groups. The background to this action by the General Council must be seen in that both T. S. Abraham in Kerala and Noel Samuel in Andhra Pradesh wished to exercise influence in Tamil Nadu.

With World Missionary Evangelism, founded by John E. Douglas, a new American organization started to make its inroads in Tamil Nadu in the 1970s. Douglas made good contacts in Tamil Nadu, especially through P. M. Samuel. It was not so much pastors of the Indian Pentecostal Church but rather leaders of independent churches who most gratefully accepted his support. This consisted, more than anything, in helping to build and maintain orphanages and schools, and financial subsidies for pastors and evangelists, without World Missionary Evangelism being involved administratively in any way in the work of the churches they supported. It was simply that "in fellowship with World Missionary Evangelism" should be added to the name of the churches, and the orphanages in Tamil Nadu were usually called "Douglas Memorial Children's Home." In view of these generous conditions, it is not surprising that at the start of the 1970s nearly all the larger independent churches in Tamil Nadu were supported by World Missionary Evangelism. Job Gnanaprakasam, pastor of the Pentecostal Church of India in Coim-

---

48. Maybe John, coming from a Mukkulathor community, was against a Tamil leadership because in his opinion that would mean a Nadar domination. When Abraham Samuel backed the election of Sadhu Abraham he might have feared that Malayali domination would also continue. In any case, this meant that John would lose his influence.

batore, became a key figure. With the financial help of World Missionary Evangelism, he supported a great number of pastors and evangelists and managed a variety of social works, so that he was the de facto chief responsible agent of World Missionary Evangelism in Tamil Nadu. The restructuring of World Missionary Evangelism in 1978 meant that help was no longer available with no strings attached, so that it became mandatory to join the organization to receive support.[49] In Tamil Nadu this led to decisive change since, almost without exception, all independent churches decided against an administrative merger with World Missionary Evangelism.[50] Even Gnanaprakasam, who coordinated most of the work in Tamil Nadu, separated from the organization. Since there were no temporary regulations for the transition period, all these churches faced financial crises and hard decisions had to be made without delay. The attitude of preferring to renounce assured financial support rather than allowing administrative interference by a third party must be taken as typical of the greater part of the south Indian Pentecostal movement. There is no doubt that their strength lies in seeing themselves as strongly independent of any external influences. After the departure of the independent churches, the remaining activity of the World Missionary Evangelism was minimal, especially with regard to the churches. The only exception was in Madras, where two significant representatives were found in N. Jeevanandam and Nataraja Mudaliar. After the latter's death, his wife Padma Mudaliar took up the succession. However, after the 1990 change in the Indian leadership of the World Missionary Evangelism, N. Jeevanandam and Padma Mudaliar also left the organization, and with this, it lost its last significant partners in Tamil Nadu.

One of the strangest missionary activities in Tamil Nadu in the 1970s was Siloam. Shortly after the founding of Siloam in Germany, the president Karl Becker looked for involvement in India.[51] In 1972 he met A. Jacob, an active part-time evangelist and member of the Church of God in Trichy. This led to significant cooperation between a definitely evangelical organization and a Pentecostal partner. The sister organization founded in India by Jacob had a clear self-understanding as a Pentecostal church. The Germans made consid-

---

49. See also p. 96.

50. The following churches left World Missionary Evangelism: Indian Pentecostal Assemblies, Maranatha, Full Gospel Pentecostal Church of India, Apostolic Christian Assembly.

51. Siloam worked under the name "Siloah-Mission" in Germany and it called itself evangelical in the sense of the conservative German confessional movement (Bekenntnisbewegung). See Reimer 1991: 70-71, where it is also stated: "It is commonly known that there were judicial inquiries against Siloah-Mission in several cases."

erable financial resources available, and so Siloam made rapid progress. Church work was supported by various social activities, and Siloam, in the short term, became one of the largest Pentecostal churches in Tamil Nadu. But the loyalty of its pastors was principally based on the material support. When at the beginning of the 1980s, suspicion of financial irregularity in Jacob's management activity arose and investigations by the Indian tax authority began, Siloam collapsed like a house of cards. Efforts at damage control were scarcely effective, given that at the same time there were similar investigations against the mother organization in Germany. After frequent changes of leadership there is now a successor organization for the work of Siloam in India, whose self-understanding is explicitly evangelical.[52]

Regional Churches

From the 1960s onward certain Pentecostal churches with no wide outreach began to play dominant roles in certain regions, for instance, in the big cities of Madras, Coimbatore, and Madurai and in the southern tip of Tamil Nadu. In Madras, the Pentecostal movement experienced big growth in the 1970s, and the city became the most important center of the movement in south India. Apart from the especially strong representation of the Assemblies of God, the scene was increasingly marked by many independent regional churches. The most significant was the Apostolic Christian Assembly. It was initially focused on its main congregation with G. Sunderam as its sole leader. Branches in and around Madras represented the accidental result of his charismatic influence rather than any deliberate strategy of church growth. He developed many young pastors who began their own church work, and who greatly valued spiritual fellowship with Sunderam and wanted to remain part of the Apostolic Christian Assembly. Very soon there were thirty branch congregations under Sunderam. No later than by the 1960s, the Apostolic Christian Assembly had acquired numerous overseas contacts. Indeed it had become so well known that it was a sort of staging post for foreign visitors. Through these contacts, there was a flow of financial contributions; this was in addition to support from World Missionary Evangelism. However, this did not induce Sunderam to start ambitious proj-

---

52. A. Jacob's work was extended through his son Gideon, married to a German. The son lives in Germany and leads the mission agency Christliche Initiative für Indien (Christian Initiative for India) based in Hamburg. Communities supported by Gideon Jacob work in India under the name Good Shepherd Evangelical Church, with headquarters in Trichy.

ects that would depend entirely on money from overseas. He kept things in proportion. After Sunderam's death in 1989, the long-prepared succession of Sam Sunderam brought changes that in many respects had big consequences for the missionary work of the church. In 1990 Sam Sunderam had bought land in the district of Otteri, in the heart of Madras, for the main congregation, which until then had only rented accommodation. A special fund was set up for the purchase and considerable expenditure was undertaken. Sam Sunderam also did not hesitate to take out a loan. This showed how much Sam Sunderam differed from his predecessor, for G. Sunderam was categorically against any kind of borrowing, which, for him, was incompatible with the faith principle.[53] Sam Sunderam set up the administration of the Apostolic Christian Assembly in a modern and effective form. Establishing branch congregations was undertaken as the most important task. In only five years the number of worshipers in the main congregation was tripled, so that it became the biggest Pentecostal congregation in Madras. The number of branch congregations was also tripled. It remained to be seen whether, in view of the church growth Sam Sunderam pursued, he would retain due moderation. The extremely rapid church growth was not accompanied by the necessary structural alterations in administration. Moreover, a proportion of the many new congregations were former independent churches that had decided to join the Apostolic Christian Assembly. It was only in 1993 that its own Bible school was established, because under G. Sunderam the only training for future pastors and evangelists was in the guru-shishya system. By the 1990s, the Apostolic Christian Assembly had become a small denomination entirely under the leadership of one person. The administrative relationship with the branches is not yet clarified. On the one hand, there is mention of a loose association of independent churches that seek only spiritual fellowship; on the other hand, these branches in the yearly report are listed as official branch members and their membership statistics are included.[54] It must be stressed that though the Apostolic Christian Assembly is backed by powerful overseas sponsors, it also has a very high income through the offerings from the main congregation. The Apostolic Christian Assembly is also engaged in social work. In 1969 an orphanage was established with the support of World Missionary Evangelism. When this support ceased in 1978, Intermission stepped in and the work was even extended.[55] In

53. For the faith principle see pp. 195-96.

54. See Apostolic Christian Assembly 1994.

55. Intermission is a German interconfessional missions agency, supported both by Pentecostal-Charismatics and by evangelical circles. The center of gravity of its work is In-

1980, a project for drug addicts called Divine Deliverance Movement was funded with the help of World Vision. After this source of help ceased, the work was carried on at a reduced scale supported by the income of the main congregation. When in 1990 the church bought land for its main congregation, it faced the problem that there were many slums in the immediate environment. Immediately after the purchase, it was decided to initiate a special project to better the social condition of people in the neighboring slums. Help for this came from World Vision. This project, called New Life Development, certainly helped to avoid social tension between the church and the slum dwellers. At the same time, it is one of the very few examples of a Pentecostal church engaging in a comprehensive way with the social needs of slum dwellers.

Another important Madras-based church was Maranatha. Not long after his return from Bible school training in England, in 1963, Henry Joseph founded the Maranatha Bible Training Institute. This extremely improvised Bible school gave its graduates the possibility, under the supervision of Joseph, to found their own churches. This marked the beginning of Maranatha as a separate church. A special characteristic of Maranatha is its numerous contacts with overseas organizations. The Bible school was opened by Joseph in collaboration with a missionary from Northern Ireland, John A. Prentice, with whom he had studied in England. The Bible school began on the property of the Apostolic Christian Assembly but soon moved into its own premises, which also meant an official break with the church of G. Sunderam. In the 1970s Maranatha had support from World Missionary Evangelism and organized seminaries and evangelism for overseas evangelists. There was an especially close partnership in 1970 with the Elim Pentecostal Church in Britain. In spite of this, Maranatha remained a completely independent organization. In the course of time, through his many overseas contacts, Henry Joseph became a central figure in the Pentecostal movement in Tamil Nadu. Even when in the 1980s, through his mediation, representatives of the controversial Faith Movement introduced seminaries in Madras, his position remained unthreatened. The actual church work of Maranatha remained rather modest, though it did have branches throughout Tamil Nadu. This had

dia, where the German Jochen Tewes has coordinated its activities since 1973 (see Reimer 1991: 244f.). The beginnings of Intermission need further clarification, since a year after its foundation in 1964 it was affected by a scandal. There was embezzlement of expenses at a time when they cooperated with the controversial evangelist Richard Schley. But apparently the founder of Intermission, Achim Schneider, was not involved so that Intermission came through these turbulent early years relatively unscathed. See Sesselmann 1988. On Richard Schley see Hutten 1989: 376.

much to do with the fact that, in the course of time, some important pastors left Maranatha and founded independent churches. Unfortunately, Joseph, who led his church in a rather patriarchal way, never made rules for succession, and his two grown-up sons had practically no authority in the church. There was also destructive rivalry between the two. Henry Joseph introduced his two sons at a very late stage to the leadership. His eldest son, Charles Finney Joseph (b. 1955), married a daughter of P. M. Paramjothi. He studied from 1974 to 1976 at Elim Bible College in Capel, Surrey. When he came back from England, Henry Joseph gave him a teaching post in the Bible school. In 1983 he became pastor of a small branch church in Anna Nagar. The second son, Alex Joseph (b. 1957), studied at the Continental Bible College, Brussels (1976-1977), and at Elim Bible College in Capel, Surrey (1978-1981). When he returned to India, there was internal tension between the brothers, since Alex openly sought a position of leadership while his elder brother was quite satisfied with the position assigned him by his father. The deeper cause of the conflict must be found in the fact that Henry Joseph did not allow either of his sons a definite field of activity within the church. In the 1980s the tension took on an embittered form and was dragged out into the open. Henry Joseph at last saw the need to manage the affair, especially after he underwent a serious heart operation in 1992. The administration of the church was decentralized in that greater competence was allowed to the district pastors. Charles Finney Joseph was made responsible for pastoral work while Alex Joseph was assigned full authority over the Bible school. However, Henry Joseph still held control over the finances in the 1990s. The public dispute was put aside and the grievances were redressed to a great extent, but the problem of the succession was still not solved.

In 1951, after P. S. Chelladurai Sr. had separated from G. Sunderam's Apostolic Christian Assembly, he founded his own church, the Apostolic Fellowship Tabernacle. However, it was not until the very end of the 1960s, when he was able to make closer contacts with the USA,[56] that he gave up his employment to devote himself full time to work for the church. With financial help from abroad, he started his own Bible school.[57] In the course of the 1970s the number of branch churches was growing and social institutions were founded, so that the Apostolic Fellowship Tabernacle attained a significant size in the Pentecostal movement of Madras. In this period P. S. Chelladurai Sr. was in close contact with the American Faith Movement. His son Sam P. Chelladurai Jr. became a convinced adherent of this controversial trend

---

56. See Chelladurai Sr. 1995: 69ff., 83ff.
57. See Chelladurai Sr. 1995: 68; see also 59.

within the Pentecostal movement. In the first half of the 1980s, Sam P. Chelladurai Jr. staffed a whole range of seminaries with American representatives of the Faith Movement. In the middle of the 1980s the main congregation got its own buildings, and Sam P. Chelladurai Jr. was given full responsibility for this congregation.[58] Thereupon he began to reorganize pastoral work consistently on the principles of the Faith Movement. Since the majority of the older members were not ready for such change, they left. But this was more than compensated for by the growth in new membership, so that within a decade it became one of the biggest Pentecostal congregations in Madras, with a considerable income, and it expressly considered itself as part of the Faith Movement.

When Henry Joseph and Sam Chelladurai Jr. independently of one another organized seminaries in the 1980s with representatives of the American Faith Movement, this had decisive influence on Justin Prabakaran, who was at that time working for the Assemblies of God. He became a strong adherent of this movement, which brought him into conflict with the Assemblies of God, who were very much opposed to it. Since Prabakaran would not renounce his new conviction, he had to leave the Assemblies of God. At the beginning of 1989 he founded his own church, the Rainbow Church, entirely in line with to the principles of the Faith Movement. Tailored to his own unique charismatic outreach, Prabakaran emphasized unconventional modern forms of worship, faith healing, a prosperity gospel, and church growth. Concerning the last of these, he set himself the incredible aim of one million members.[59] The church did indeed have rapid growth immediately after its founding and grew week by week. Sunday worship took place in cinemas and concert halls specially hired for the purpose; and in the course of time, progressively larger premises were hired. After two years about 1,500 came to the services, and it seemed as if the Pentecostal landscape of Madras was about to be fundamentally changed. Prabakaran's sudden tragic death ended the ambitious project. There followed years of painful confrontation during which most members left the Rainbow Church. A significant proportion found a common refuge in the Shekinah Church under Paul Moses, a pastor hardly to be reckoned as belonging to the Faith Movement but rather stemming from the traditional Pentecostal spectrum.

Another important regional church of Madras is the Madras Pentecostal Assembly. After the early death of John Vasu in 1962, his son and designated successor Prabhudoss Vasu was too young to take up leadership, so the expe-

---

58. See Chelladurai Sr. 1995: 92, 86, 89; Samuel 1988.
59. See Rajendran 1992: 72; Prabakaran 1989 and Prabakaran 1990.

rienced pastor G. N. Chockalingam took over this position.[60] Prabhudoss Vasu, only twenty years old at the time of his father's death, underwent Bible school training to prepare himself for the future leadership of the Madras Pentecostal Assembly. Under Chockalingam the church showed a certain amount of stagnation but apparently was spared splitting. When in 1971 this leader died, Prabhudoss Vasu became his successor. Thereafter the church experienced growth. The Bible school was reactivated and the central church convention, after a long interval, was taken up again so that the church took a stronger missionary stance. The close contacts with Scandinavia that had been formed at the time of foundation were extended and new relations with overseas missions established. With the support of these, the Madras Pentecostal Assembly financed social projects and parts of its church work. This enabled the founding of a considerable number of new branches that showed notable increase, as did the main congregation. Prabhudoss Vasu died unexpectedly in 1995, at a time when no successor was ready. However, his twenty-three-year-old son Stanley Vasu immediately took over the responsibility of his father and became a young, energetic leader of the church.

In 1980 Pratap Singh, who had been active for nearly twenty years in a leading position in the Church of God and more recently had directed the Bible school in Coimbatore, came to Madras to found the independent Trinity Full Gospel Church. Clearly, the longstanding conflicts within the Church of God in Tamil Nadu were among the reasons that led him to this step. Existing overseas contacts enabled him in 1982 to buy land and in the same year to found a Bible school. In parallel with this, there was steady growth in his congregation that soon reached a good amount of income from donations. Especially through graduates of his Bible school, he soon had branch foundations throughout Tamil Nadu. Especially notable was the growth in his main congregation, which was combined with extensive building work so that by the 1990s the Trinity Full Gospel Church counted as one of the biggest Pentecostal churches in Madras.

In Coimbatore, in contrast to the general trend, the Assemblies of God until the 1990s did not belong to the larger Pentecostal churches. At the end of the 1970s two independent churches became dominant here, the Zion Assemblies of God and the Indian Pentecostal Assemblies. Interestingly, leaders of both came from the work of the British Assemblies of God. When in 1965 the Liveseys from the British Assemblies of God finally left India, the newly founded Zion Assemblies of God were taken over by an Indian committee with Peter Arumainayakam, an employee of the neighboring agricultural

---

60. *Balm of Gilead* (50) Dec. 1988, no. 9: 4.

school, as secretary. The church stagnated for a long time until in 1973 Arumainayakam finally gave up his employment and became its pastor. After this appointment, the situation changed at once. Within a few years the congregation had grown so much that an extension of the small church building was necessary. This trend continued to the 1990s. In parallel with the growth of the main congregation, whose well-to-do worshipers were capable of considerable expenditure, went the establishment of branches. In 1986 the Zion Assemblies of God was registered as an independent church. Since it was regarded by the British Assemblies of God as a partner organization, the Zion Assemblies of God had sufficient support to undertake a social project in the form of an orphanage. The story of the other large independent church in Coimbatore is quite complicated. To preserve his independence, Job Gnanaprakasam had left World Missionary Evangelism in 1979 and had, after a short period of uncertainty, found several new overseas sponsors. This enabled him, in a very short time, to start an independent church organization, the Indian Pentecostal Assemblies. Overseas support made many social projects possible, as well as the establishment of a larger number of branch churches. One of the most imposing church buildings in Tamil Nadu was consecrated for the main congregation in 1991. A special emphasis in the work was marked in 1981 by the erection of a large Bible school. The responsibility for this was given to Job's eldest son David Prakasam, who stands ready to succeed his father.

In Madurai, it was the Living Word Church of J. Harris that stood out among the independent churches there in the 1990s. When at the end of the 1970s J. Harris gave up teaching at the Tamil college of the Assemblies of God in Madurai, he began to found churches in the name of Henry Joseph's Maranatha. As a result of seminars in conjunction with representatives of the Faith Movement in Madras at the beginning of the 1980s, Harris was impressed and subscribed to this movement. Although formally a member of Maranatha, Harris formed a congregation entirely tailored to his own personality from the beginning. The congregation grew rapidly and soon attained a special status within Maranatha because of its size. On account of this special status and size, it was just a question of time when it would leave Maranatha. It was not at all unexpected when in 1994 Harris cut all his formal links with Maranatha and continued on his own, with the result that the group became numerically the greatest in the region and, in addition, received no financial help from overseas.

In the south of Tamil Nadu, several independent regional churches showed considerable growth since the 1960s. In Palayankottai, M. Rajendran directed an orphanage and a small church under the name of the Indian

Christian Assembly at the beginning of the 1970s. It is said that the founder of the Indian Christian Assembly was S. B. Daniel, a Brahmin from Tiruvannamalai who had converted from Hinduism to Christianity. With the help of Intermission he built up the Indian Christian Assembly in the beginning of the 1970s, and his organization managed schools and orphanages but also had some congregations, especially in the Arcot District. Daniel died in 1980(?), whereupon the organization broke up with internal strife and sank into insignificance.[61] In 1980 after the death of the founder, Rajendran declared his work independent as Good News Mission. He was able to find good overseas sponsors so that the social projects could be extended. The pastoral work was concentrated on the main congregation, which grew into one of the biggest Pentecostal congregations in Palayankottai. The Good News Mission had a wider outreach through its yearly International Levites Camp (instituted about 1980). This was a retreat for pastors and laypeople, a ministry of preaching set up in collaboration with the Dutch evangelist Ben Hanegraaff and enjoying great popularity. But in 1994 it was decided to no longer conduct these retreats as a large central meeting but rather to decentralize them for local communities in different places. So the International Levites camp almost lost all of its significance. After this, the center of gravity of the work became the Bible school founded in 1992 under R. Rajendran, who was the eldest son and designated successor.

In Nagercoil, Y. S. Devasundaram of the Jehovah Salvation Church sought to strengthen contact with Canadian partner organizations in the mid-1970s. But it was only in early 1978 that an inquiry reached him from Jean Christensen, a Canadian missionary, whether she could spend some time with the Jehovah Salvation Church. This opened up a new perspective for him. The missionary only stayed for a few months, but she developed a specially close contact with Soorna Packiam, the joint founder of the church. During her stay, Jean Christensen showed a genuine interest in the church's problems, especially the unfinished building. She came on a second visit in early 1979 and brought with her sufficient funds to finish the building. From 1983 to 1994 she stayed almost continuously in Nagercoil and, through her mediation, the church received adequate funding from Canada. A whole range of branch churches was established in this way and a Bible school founded. In 1991 an extensive estate outside the locality was bought and a large building erected to hold the Bible school.

The Full Gospel Pentecostal Church had its center of activities in the Kanyakumari District. When its founder John Rose died in 1977, the leader-

---

61. Benjamin 1981: 20.

ship of the Full Gospel Pentecostal Church was taken over by the comparatively young but educated N. Thomas. This change coincided with separation from World Missionary Evangelism. The consequent decrease in financial support gave the church a rather useful stimulus. The new leader did not have at his disposal the multiple overseas contacts of his predecessor, but he managed, mainly with indigenous resources, to help the church strengthen its effectiveness in mission. In consequence, the Full Gospel Pentecostal Church remained, against the general trend, bound up with the tradition of radical Pentecostal holiness ideas. This might be partially attributed to the indigenous orientation and to the relatively isolated situation of headquarters in Kattathurai in Kanyakumari District.

CHAPTER 4

Karnataka

The Pentecostal movement in Karnataka remained numerically weak right into the second half of the twentieth century. It was limited almost exclusively to migrants from Tamil Nadu, Kerala, and Andhra Pradesh, and it scarcely touched the Kannada-speaking population. Until the 1990s, there were no major Pentecostal centers in Karnataka except in Bangalore and in the neighboring Kolar Gold Fields. In 1951 the Assemblies of God opened an English-speaking Bible school in Bangalore, the Southern Asia Bible Institute. The aim was to establish a training institute in India that would be at a standard comparable to their schools in the USA. The foundation arose from a combined initiative of the American headquarters and missionaries residing in India. This coordinated undertaking resulted in the acquisition of land in the center of Bangalore and erection of the necessary building within a short time. The Bible school soon gained good repute. Already in the 1950s many students were studying there who would later be important leaders in the south Indian Pentecostal movement.[1] Heartened by this success, they decided at the end of the 1960s to make more comprehensive provisions, and as a first expression of this resolve they renamed the institute Southern Asia Bible College. In 1969 a large estate was bought in northwest Bangalore outside the city.[2] After five years the most important extensions to the building were completed, and by 1975 there were 120 students, a number that was only slightly surpassed in the 1990s.[3] In the 1970s,

1. For example, Ernest Komanapalli, T. C. George, A. C. George, George Oommen, P. J. Titus, and John Thannickal.
2. See Southern Asia Bible College 1991: 13.
3. See Southern Asia Bible College 1991: 13, 32.

86

an increasing number of Indians who had acquired theological doctorates in the USA were on the teaching staff, and in 1983 the first Indian principal, A. C. George, was appointed.[4] Until the beginning of the 1980s, the Southern Asia Bible College was the Pentecostal training institution with the best academic reputation in south India. This position was somewhat weakened later, as the college did not significantly raise its standards, whereas in the meantime other good Pentecostal training institutes had appeared.

The quick success of the Southern Asia Bible Institute (or College) contrasted with the slow development of church work of the Assemblies of God in Bangalore; at the start it was even a hindrance.[5] The property bought for the training institute had already been rented by the missionaries of the Assemblies of God to accommodate an English-speaking as well as a Tamil-speaking congregation. Now the English-speaking congregation also had to care for the students of the newly founded Bible school and hence developed an unstable character. Even after the move of the Bible school outside the city, this congregation did not recover and remained inhomogeneous, which became apparent from a split in 1994. For the Tamil-speaking congregation, which had been started in the mid-1940s by the missionary Constance S. Eady,[6] things also became difficult after the foundation of the Bible school. Its pastor, K. R. Paul, left the Assemblies of God in 1952 in order to found his own independent church.[7] His place was taken by M. V. Lamech, another Tamil pastor, but only after accommodation was acquired outside the Bible school in 1953.[8] The congregation grew steadily under Lamech. By 1970 it had its own church building and till the end of the 1970s it was the biggest congregation of the Assemblies of God in Bangalore.[9] The beginning of the 1980s was the start of remarkable growth, leading to the widespread development of large congregations that made the Assemblies of God by far the strongest Pentecostal force in Bangalore. However, it hardly attained the dynamic to be observed in Madras, for instance. Moreover, although in 1957 the Assemblies of God had already formed a district covering the whole of Karnataka (and Andhra Pradesh until 1987), the work of the church remained largely confined to Bangalore until the 1990s. One exception worth mentioning was the successful mission in the region of Bellary, among the Telugu-speaking population, started by Gera Peter in 1976.

4. See Southern Asia Bible College 1991: 25-26.
5. George 1975: 27-28 draws attention to the problem.
6. Benjamin 1981: 24f.; Shinde 1974: 126.
7. See Paul & Paul 1977: 19.
8. See Rajamoni n.d.: 8, 3.
9. Benjamin 1981: 25.

A noteworthy Pentecostal contribution to the contextualization of the Christian message within the Assemblies of God in Bangalore is the ashram project by John Thannickal, the founder of Nava Jeeva Ashram. The ashram project originated in Thannickal's dissertation, in which he looked at Hindu and Christian ashrams and sought some stimulation for a contextual proclamation of the Christian message.[10] He was concerned with a way of communication proper to the ashram, including "the guru-shishya principle, the community principle, the power encounter principle, the place of non-verbal (ritual) communication, dialogue and monologue principle, the principle of dynamic and functional substitute."[11] However, this project always remained in its initial stage. From his base in Bangalore Thannickal financially supported a pastor in the north of Karnataka and undertook evangelical training in the ashram style there. But in the 1980s the Nava Jeeva Ashram had gradually become rather a conventional Pentecostal Bible school, and the congregations in northern Karnataka were taken over by Korean pastors. The failure of Thannickal's ideas must certainly also be attributed to the opposition from the southern Pentecostal movement itself, which he could not persuade to accept his project. Thannickal, however, remained a fighter for an indigenous Christianity. In an open letter of 1994, he complains that too many guest preachers from overseas speak at evangelization campaigns and in seminaries. He says: "It looks like we are contributing to the accusation that Christianity is a foreign religion. . . . Unless we project an indigenous image of the church our mission in India will not succeed. St. Paul was careful to employ men of local culture for his mission among the gentile churches."[12]

Apart from the Assemblies of God, several independent churches came up in Bangalore in the course of time. One of the most important of these was the Gospel Prayer Hall. After K. R. Paul left the Assemblies of God in 1952 and started his own church, he had a difficult time in the beginning, since the members who left with him were scarcely able to provide for him. But the new independent Gospel Prayer Hall, which he established quite close to the Southern Asia Bible Institute with the efficient help of his wife, grew rapidly, and Swedish missionaries in Bangalore became aware of him, especially Mrs. Signe Andersson. He bought a plot in 1959 with Swedish money and established a prayer hall there, called Gospel Prayer Hall. Cooperation with Signe Andersson was so close that for two years in the mid-1960s she lived on the same plot and maintained a small orphanage until she moved to Kotagiri in

10. Thannickal 1975.
11. Thannickal 1975: Abstract (emphasis deleted — M.B.).
12. *New Life Herald* Dec. 1994: 16.

Nilgiris District in 1967.[13] A foundling from this orphanage was adopted as his own son by the childless K. R. Paul. In the 1960s and 1970s, the Tamil-speaking Gospel Prayer Hall was the biggest and most important Pentecostal church in Bangalore. With the early death of K. R. Paul in 1983, the church suffered a severe crisis. His adoptive son and designated successor T. Daniel Paul was very young at the time but immediately took up the succession. He overcame a long, difficult transition phase, and by the 1990s Gospel Prayer Hall was again among the most dynamic churches in Bangalore.

Among the newer independent churches, which were gaining increasing influence in Bangalore in the 1980s, the Shekinah Gospel Prayer Fellowship, founded in 1966 by Robert Sandy, certainly stands out.[14] Significant growth only took place after T. Yeswanth Kumar came into full-time ministry in 1979 and established a separate Tamil-speaking congregation that quickly developed into one of the bigger Pentecostal congregations in Bangalore. In 1987 they bought their own land and in 1993 consecrated a church building. This was accomplished largely out of their own resources, although Shekinah Gospel Prayer Fellowship maintained good contacts throughout, especially with Indian migrants in the USA. At the beginning of the 1990s, Kumar's brother also started a congregation in Bangalore in the name of Shekinah Gospel Prayer Fellowship.

The Christian Fellowship Centre, formed around Zac Poonen in Bangalore, deserves special attention. In the first half of the 1970s, Poonen was a welcome guest preacher at many evangelical events and retreats. He then made closer contact with Charismatic circles, and in 1975 he received baptism in the Spirit. This happened while praying with Michael Harper, a leader of the Charismatic movement in England,[15] who was visiting India at that time. As Poonen belonged to the Baptist community of Bangalore when he had his Charismatic experience, he entered a period of tension, eventually leading to his founding of an independent church with some like-minded people, the Christian Fellowship Centre. Since the group had sufficient means, they were able to build their own meetinghouse by 1991. By the 1980s some branches were also established. When the Christian Fellowship Centre was founded, it was decided that pastors were not to be paid by the church. It

13. See Andreasson & Andreasson 1989: 37.

14. Robert Sandy came from Kerala and grew up in Andhra Pradesh. His parents belonged to the Church of South India. He gave up his job in 1973 and studied for about half a year in the Hebron Bible School, Kumbanadu. He is pastor of the main church in Krishnarajapuram, Bangalore.

15. See biographical article on Harper by Hocken 2002b. The visit to India is also mentioned in Balasundaram 1990: 249.

was insisted that Paul was just as good an example as Peter in that the full-time ministry was not the only valid way of working as pastor. As a result, Poonen invested in shares, which proved so successful that he was able to provide for his family. Another fellow worker set up a joinery business with equal success. In this way Christian Fellowship Centre claimed to be financially independent from the start. The group also stressed the importance of personal holiness from its beginning. This brought them into close contact with the so-called Smith's Friends (Den Kristelige Menighet) from Norway, with whom they found themselves in agreement.[16] Strong perfectionist tendencies and a long-lasting partnership with the exclusivist Smith's Friends led to the isolation of the Christian Fellowship Centre from the Pentecostal movement. This isolation diminished in 1982 when Joseph Balachandran secured Poonen as preacher for an evangelization event, which in turn was followed by invitations to other Pentecostal churches. Around 1990, all relations with the Smith's Friends were broken off. In spite of these developments, the Christian Fellowship Centre remained somewhat distant from the Pentecostal movement in the 1990s, although Poonen had good personal contacts with representatives of the movement. Together with the general perfectionist tendency, there was sharp criticism of particular Pentecostal practices, especially tithing, which was met with rejection and misunderstanding in the south Indian Pentecostal movement. On the other hand, Poonen with his high profile and his numerous publications gained recognition by many Pentecostals.

Among the Tamil-speaking population in the Kolar Gold Fields beyond Bangalore, a whole range of Pentecostal churches was started since the 1950s. However, among them it was only the Philadelphia Church that had any inter-regional outreach.[17] In 1954 a Methodist lay preacher, G. Nickelson, attended a big rally organized by an independent Pentecostal church near his house, to which a guest preacher from England had been invited. He was converted to the Pentecostal faith there and became a member of the congregation. However, later in the same year he separated and founded his own independent church. Like K. R. Paul in Bangalore, after some time he made contact with Swedish missionaries, whose financial help enabled him to build a big church in 1963. Later, Nickelson was able to widen his relations with overseas sponsors. The marriage of his daughter to the German Jochen Tewes, representative of the German aid agency Intermission was of some significance here. With financial aid readily available, he realized various social

---

16. Contacts between Zac Poonen and the Smith's Friends date back to 1971. For the Smith's Friends see Hutten 1989: 266-69.

17. A summary is given by Jeyanesan 1990.

projects, and in 1983 he founded a small Bible school. He became a widely known pastor, not least because of his numerous international contacts. However, until the 1990s, his success in the actual church work was relatively modest.

CHAPTER 5

Andhra Pradesh

For a long time the Indian Pentecostal Church was the only distinct force of Pentecostalism in Andhra Pradesh. It was only in the 1960s that World Missionary Evangelism offered a new alternative, but this brought about splits in the Indian Pentecostal movement with serious consequences. A real pluralization of the ecclesiastical landscape began at the start of the 1970s as new churches arose in various situations.

Establishment of Local Centers of the Indian Pentecostal Church

In the second half of the 1940s, Pentecostalism in Andhra Pradesh entered a new phase. The missionaries from Kerala and the new recruits from Andhra Pradesh, who were practically all with the Indian Pentecostal Church, gave up moving about and became settled. Financial assistance from overseas made it possible for them to build their own churches and to set up local centers, which acted very independently. In this way, the Indian Pentecostal Church in Andhra Pradesh developed a rather decentralized structure. It proved to be of special significance that the missionaries from Kerala, especially P. M. Samuel in Vijayawada and P. T. Chacko in Hyderabad, had far more overseas contacts than their colleagues from Andhra Pradesh. As a result an unfair distribution of resources went along with the establishment of local centers, and this prepared the ground for the recruitment campaigns by World Missionary Evangelism in the 1960s. The most important local centers will be described in what follows.

In Vijayawada, P. M. Samuel, the uncontested leader of the Indian Pentecostal Church in Andhra Pradesh, set a good example in the establishment of local centers. He arrived in Vijayawada in 1940,[1] and in the beginning he lived in conditions of extreme poverty.[2] However, in 1947 he received an invitation to Sweden, together with the leaders of the Indian Pentecostal Church in Kerala, that completely changed his situation. The visit to Sweden was extended by a preaching tour of several months in Europe and the USA. As a result he brought back a considerable amount of money and many new contacts when he returned in 1948.[3] With this he bought a new plot and erected a big building, the Zion Home.[4] He was now in a position to give material support to other pastors. Through further extensive foreign tours in the following years, he was able to acquire a number of different overseas sponsors for the work in India. In 1960 Samuel bought another big plot in Gunadala on the outskirts of Vijayawada in order to found a permanent Bible school for the Indian Pentecostal Church in Andhra Pradesh. He also erected an orphanage and an elementary school on the same plot, so that an impressive campus resulted.[5] The Bible school gave Samuel additional influence in the church. Moreover, it strengthened his position of leadership, since he had personal responsibility for spending the money and he shared it out at his own discretion. Equally, however, this was a principal cause for the later severe crises that the church encountered.

P. T. Chacko established a local center in Secunderabad when he came there in 1940.[6] In comparison with P. M. Samuel, he maintained much closer relations with the Indian Pentecostal Church in Kerala. This was evident in the marriage of his daughter to T. S. Abraham, the son of K. E. Abraham, in 1950. T. S. Abraham often spent half the year in Kerala and the other half with his father-in-law in Andhra Pradesh, thus ensuring active contact between the two regions.[7] Relations with P. M. Samuel were similarly strengthened. In 1956 Abraham Samuel, the son of P. M. Samuel, married Chacko's second daughter. Church work in Secunderabad took a decisive turn in 1952 when Chacko was able to go to the Pentecostal World Conference in London. As often happens, there were numerous invitations leading to a preaching tour of several months in various locations, including the USA. On his return to In-

---

1. Samuel 1980: 38.
2. Samuel 1980: 38-44.
3. Samuel 1980: 82, 92f., 102ff.
4. Samuel 1980: 82, 112.
5. It seems that the property in Gunadala was not registered in the name of the Indian Pentecostal Church.
6. See Pastor Chacko's family members 1980: 11.
7. See Pastor Chacko's family members 1980: 70.

dia, he had received sufficient contributions for the purchase in 1954 of a large
site on which a church was built in 1959.[8] Although Chacko was the same age
as P. M. Samuel, was far better educated, and maintained good relations with
all the leaders of the Indian Pentecostal Church, his influence was in general
restricted to the Hyderabad-Secunderabad District.

P. L. Paramjothi arrived in Antarvedipalem in 1942, in order to support
the work in the Godavari Delta, which had been started just before by
P. Rajaratnam.[9] Although still quite young, he already had years of experience
as a pastor. This fact as well as his close relationship with P. M. Samuel soon
made him one of the leading personalities of the Indian Pentecostal Church
in the Godavari Delta.[10] A crucial event was a one-month Bible study course
arranged together with the leading pastors of the Indian Pentecostal Church
in Andhra Pradesh that took place in Antarvedipalem in 1942.[11] Quite a few
participants from the established churches let themselves be rebaptized and
thus made an open break with their mother churches. This was the origin of
the first large congregation of the Indian Pentecostal Church in the Godavari
Delta, with Paramjothi as pastor. Soon after, with the help of the Swedish
Pentecostal missionary Karin Cométh, they acquired their own building site
in Antarvedipalem.[12] When the provisionally erected accommodation fell
victim to a storm in 1945, one of the first permanent buildings for the Indian
Pentecostal Church in Andhra Pradesh took its place.[13] Under these more favorable conditions, Paramjothi was able to develop successful missionary activity.

Among the Telugu-speaking coworkers that P. M. Samuel was able to win
for the Pentecostal faith, K. R. David, along with P. L. Paramjothi, was certainly one of the most prominent. After some apparently not very successful
attempts to gain a footing for the Indian Pentecostal Church in Rajahmundry,
Samuel decided in 1945 to send David, who succeeded in founding a congregation there and subsequently erecting his own church building.[14] Not least
due to this achievement, David won the confidence of Samuel and an important position in the Indian Pentecostal Church of Andhra Pradesh. However,

8. Chacko noted expressly that the plot was bought in his own name in 1954 but in 1964
the whole property was transferred to the Indian Pentecostal Church (see Pastor Chacko's
family members 1980: 23).

9. See also p. 36.

10. See Komanapalli ca. 1991: 13; Samuel 1980: 52ff.

11. See Samuel 1980: 55ff.; Komanapalli ca. 1991: 16, 38.

12. See Samuel 1980: 57.

13. See Samuel 1980: 57.

14. See Samuel 1980: 64f.

since he did not have particular contacts with overseas partners at his disposal, he depended on Samuel's support for sufficient financial resources. In the 1960s he went over to World Missionary Evangelism.

In Narasapur, K. S. Joseph, another Telugu Pentecostal evangelist, had successfully won his closer relatives over to the Pentecostal faith, and he proceeded in 1951, with the united resources of the family and probably without support from overseas, to commence his own church, the Bethel Church. In his pastoral work he was in close fellowship with P. M. Samuel and the Indian Pentecostal Church in Andhra Pradesh. But at the same time, he engaged in lively exchange with the American-Swedish missionary couple who had first led him to Pentecostal faith. In the mid-1950s he broke with Samuel and the Indian Pentecostal Church and a few years later became a member of World Missionary Evangelism.

Campaigns for Recruitment by World Missionary Evangelism

P. M. Samuel's authoritarian leadership style and arbitrary administration of financial resources led to tensions within the Indian Pentecostal Church, which proved heavy with consequences. As it appeared to many Telugu-speaking pastors presiding over local centers, Samuel was seeking to ban any contact with overseas partners that was not strictly controlled by him. They were also under the impression that the resources coming from abroad for church work were not fairly shared out with Telugu-speaking fellow workers. The dissatisfaction with Samuel's leadership turned to the advantage of World Missionary Evangelism, an American organization founded by John E. Douglas in 1958.[15] On the invitation of Samuel, Douglas took part as guest speaker in the central conventions of the Indian Pentecostal Church in Andhra Pradesh in 1959 and 1960.[16] He was urgently looking for Indian partners for his new organization, which had considerable financial resources. Apparently he was very interested in the possibility of direct support without going through Samuel. In India he got to know P. L. Paramjothi. When the latter came to the USA at the invitation of Thomas Wyatt, Douglas contacted him and asked him for help in acquiring direct contacts in Andhra Pradesh.[17] In 1962 Douglas again came to Andhra Pradesh and probably took part in the central convention of the Indian Pentecostal Church. He

15. For John E. Douglas (d. 1988) see also Hewett 1990c.
16. See Samuel 1980: 35.
17. See Komanapalli ca. 1991: 41; World Missionary Evangelism 1989: 9.

spent some time with P. L. Paramjothi and decided on some support for certain projects. The dissatisfaction of the Telugu pastors and the generous offers of financial support for orphanages, pastors, and evangelists brought acclaim to Douglas. By his 1962 Indian visit he had formed partnerships with many of the more significant Telugu-speaking pastors of the Indian Pentecostal Church and, in addition, found many partners in Tamil Nadu and Kerala. In the following years the number of persons who received support from World Missionary Evangelism increased further. At first the pastors supported by World Missionary Evangelism remained members of the Indian Pentecostal Church. With this ready supply of money many new branch congregations were founded, but they were treated as part of the Indian Pentecostal Church. It was only the orphanages, called Douglas Memorial Children's Homes, that were outwardly recognizable as supported by World Missionary Evangelism. It seems that P. M. Samuel stood in opposition to the help provided by World Missionary Evangelism because it reduced his influence in the Indian Pentecostal Church, but also because it was in contradiction to the ideas of faith mission he was propagating. The relationship problems resulted in John E. Douglas gradually coming to desire that the work he financially supported should go under his own name. The open break between the two organizations came about, apparently, in connection with the Indian registration of World Missionary Evangelism in 1969.[18] In Andhra Pradesh, as distinct from Tamil Nadu and Kerala, Douglas desired that all pastors supported by him should join World Missionary Evangelism. The result of this tension was that, with the exception of Paramjothi, almost all the important Telugu leaders in the Indian Pentecostal Church went over to World Missionary Evangelism, which suddenly became the biggest Pentecostal church in Andhra Pradesh. Although there were other examples of large secessions for financial reasons in the Pentecostal movement in south India, this recruitment campaign of World Missionary Evangelism was unique in its extent.

Further Developments within the Indian Pentecostal Church and World Missionary Evangelism

Through the break with World Missionary Evangelism, the Indian Pentecostal Church suffered a severe setback, but it consolidated its position relatively soon and remained one the bigger Pentecostal churches in Andhra Pradesh.

18. See Indian Pentecostal Church 1974: v. The split was finally completed in 1974.

After the departure of the Telugu-speaking leaders to World Missionary Evangelism, the Indian Pentecostal Church was more than ever dominated by missionaries from Kerala, which strengthened P. M. Samuel's leadership role. However, at the same time, P. L. Paramjothi's significance also increased as mediator with Telugu-speaking pastors and leaders in the Godavari Delta, a traditional center of Pentecostalism in Andhra Pradesh. P. L. Paramjothi enjoyed a secure position and built up his private relationships with overseas partner organizations and with south Indian churches, not least by a successful marriage policy. However, he always remained a declared member of the Indian Pentecostal Church. After the death of P. M. Samuel in 1985, his son Abraham Samuel was chosen as successor for the church in Andhra Pradesh. However, Paramjothi became president of the General Council of the Indian Pentecostal Church, and in the time following P. M. Samuel's death a significant change of generations occurred. Three key positions held by pastors of Kerala were to be occupied anew, because the incumbents had just died and their children, who had in the meantime migrated to the USA, made no claim to the succession. Telugu-speaking pastors now took these posts.[19] This trend was strengthened when Abraham Samuel died in 1993 and his son Noel Samuel was too young for any prominent post in the church; in consequence, G. R. Purushottham, a Telugu pastor, was chosen as the new president of the Indian Pentecostal Church in Andhra Pradesh. With the exception of P. L. Paramjothi, the leading Telugu pastors did not have outstanding leadership qualities or overseas contacts like their colleagues from Kerala. Hence the prospects of the Indian Pentecostal Church in Andhra Pradesh were not so favorable for the time to come.

It is noteworthy that through P. M. Samuel and his successors, some social projects were called into existence. In 1961 Christian Mission Service made it possible for him to open two orphanages. One he gave to M. O. John in T. Kallupatti in Tamil Nadu, and the other he administered himself in Vijayawada, where he also opened an elementary school for the children from the orphanage, which was developed into a high school by 1968. In the later 1970s, P. M. Samuel broke with Christian Mission Service. The orphanage was maintained with help from Compassion International, and the teachers were paid by the state. In the 1970s, with help from World Wide Mission, Amsterdam, a school for blind children was set up in Vijayawada. Another orphanage was instituted in Gudivada, at the beginning of the 1980s, with the support of the International Gospel Centre, Canada. In 1995 Noel Samuel, who

---

19. The posts of T. K. Thomas (d. 1989) in Warangal, of P. T. Chacko (d. 1990) in Secunderabad, and of Philip Abraham in Hyderabad went to Telugu-speaking pastors.

had taken over the Vijayawada center after the death of his father Abraham Samuel in 1993, opened a new orphanage for girls in Surampalem.

The successful recruitment campaign of World Missionary Evangelism in the 1960s was of doubtful outcome, as the organization was shaken by repeated internal crises and never came to a settled condition. World Missionary Evangelism was registered in India in 1969, and the Englishman R. Courts, a resident in north India, named as president. However, the financial resources came directly from the USA, and all Indian representatives of the organization received their pay directly from America. The committee headed by Courts was more of a supervisory authority and was scarcely capable of effective oversight. As the work was extended and the flow of money was hardly under control, somewhat uncontrollable and chaotic situations arose in the course of time. In 1977 Courts was removed and Godi Samuel from Andhra Pradesh was chosen as president. Immediately, together with the representative sent from the American headquarters, he initiated a complete restructuring of the organization. All financial contributions from the USA were to be shared through Indian administration, and all representatives were required to register themselves as members of World Missionary Evangelism. In contrast to Tamil Nadu, where almost all the work of World Missionary Evangelism came to a halt as a result of these changes, the reorganization in Andhra Pradesh led to a remarkable consolidation. However, apparently there was also a growing undercurrent of rivalry among the representatives. Decisive change came when John E. Douglas died in 1988 and the direction of the organization was taken over by his daughter Yvonne. For reasons that are not completely clear, Yvonne arranged for the dismissal of Godi Samuel in 1990. This was handled in such an inept manner that it caused serious harm to the work. When Isaac Komanapalli took over the succession from Godi Samuel, he had to contend with significant problems. Reluctant acceptance among the organization's workers, an outbreak of the undercurrent of rivalry, the departure of important representatives, judicial confrontation, Godi Samuel's unwillingness to leave his post — all these conjured up a delicate situation of crisis. Isaac Komanapalli reacted to these problems in an extremely authoritarian style of leadership that, in spite of undoubtedly good intentions, only served to worsen the situation. By the 1990s, World Missionary Evangelism had plenty of money but showed little evangelical dynamism.

New Churches

By the end of the 1960s, many more Pentecostal churches were established in Andhra Pradesh. The Indian Pentecostal Church and World Missionary Evangelism, which so far had dominated the scene, lost their significance. Among the new churches there were significant differences. The missionary success of the classical Pentecostal churches proved to be comparatively modest. Since the mid-1950s, the Church of God had some mission work in Andhra Pradesh worthy of mention, but it contained more or less of uncoordinated aid offered to particular pastors from Kerala. Some of these, originally sent by the Indian Pentecostal Church, later joined the Church of God.[20] Systematic mission work only began in 1963 when the American Harold L. Turner, who had been stationed in Kerala, moved with his family to Kakinada. With foresight, he took care to arrange opportunity for study in America for his Telugu-speaking coworkers, so that soon he would have a well-educated succession of Indian workers. Thus Reddi Stephen in Kakinada, converted by the Church of God to Christianity and the first Telugu pastor sent to study in America, was called in 1970 to be State Overseer for Andhra Pradesh, replacing not without controversy his predecessor from Kerala, P. E. Verghese.[21] In this way continuity was secured when Turner left India in 1974. Under the family-based leadership style of Reddi Stephen, the church revealed a modest capacity for growth in the following decades, without, however, any vibrancy within the Pentecostal movement in Andhra Pradesh. The Church of God of Prophecy, Cleveland, came into Andhra Pradesh, after K. Vijayaratnam left the Bible Mission following long-lasting confrontation at the beginning of the 1960s, and he joined this church which, until then, had exercised no missionary activity in India. However, it seems that his work was not very successful; for this reason his son D. Joseph took over the leadership in 1969. Joseph set about the missionary work in quite a new way and acquired a site in Rajahmundry in 1970 in order to build a large church from which he began systematic outreach. Up to the 1990s, with generous financial support from American headquarters, he achieved modest, continual growth. For a long time the Assemblies of God had completely neglected Andra Pradesh. Hence, apart from some independent churches that joined the organization, there was no mission activity until the 1970s. This situation changed gradually after

20. See Varghese & George 1973: 37; Cook 1955: 145. Also see McLeish & Watts 1951: 135, 53 (here only I. C. Mathew is mentioned as pastor of the Church of God in Kovur.); Hugh Warren 1959: 38.
21. Varghese & George 1973: 52.

Gera Peter started a Telugu-speaking Bible school in 1978. In 1979 the American Earl Stubbs left Kerala on account of internal strife and moved to Hyderabad.[22] It was especially Peter and Stubbs who gave a new impulse to the work in Andhra Pradesh. In 1983 Stubbs began an English-speaking ministry in Hyderabad, and in 1984 Peter began a systematic initiative toward founding new congregations. To further this enterprise it was decided that Andhra Pradesh should be made an independent district, because until then Karnataka and Andhra Pradesh formed an administrative unit within the South Indian Assemblies of God. Peter was named as the first District Superintendent. However, at first there were setbacks to note in the work of the new district. Several of the independent churches that had joined the Assemblies of God soon left again. In spite of great efforts, few new congregations were founded before the 1990s. The English-language ministry of Stubbs stands out in this scene. His congregations count among the three largest in Hyderabad.

It is a notable phenomenon that new Pentecostal churches were also founded by expatriate Indians (in India called Non Resident Indians/NRIs) in Andhra Pradesh. This ministry was conducted by Indians who had migrated to the USA and later returned to India to begin their own missions. In 1971 Ernest Komanapalli came to India to take the leadership in projects he had already started in the USA. The main focus of these projects was missionary activities leading to the foundation of a new independent church called Manna. Good relations with American and European partners and the help of his father-in-law P. L. Paramjothi ensured his success. A further development of the work occurred with the buying of a building plot in Hyderabad. For formal reasons the church in Hyderabad was not called Manna but was separately registered as Rock Church. Komanapalli gradually freed himself from direct administrative work. Spurgeon Raja succeeded him as president of Manna, and his wife became president of Rock Church Ministries. Though Komanapalli now concentrated successfully on gaining overseas sponsors, he kept control over the two organizations. In spite of the difference in registration, Komanapalli was behind both. The organizations led by him are marked by professional and effective administration and show little internal conflict. All the same, they depend to a large extent on money from overseas. By the 1990s Komanapalli had become the most influential Pentecostal leader in

22. Gera Peter (b. 1944) came from a Lutheran family in a village twenty-five kilometers south of Guntur. In 1964-1967 he studied in Andhra Pradesh Christian College, Guntur, and finished with a B.Sc. In 1972-1974 he studied in Southern Asia Bible College, Bangalore. After finishing his studies he began to work as a pastor of the Assemblies of God among the Telugu-speaking population in Bellary. In 1987 he came to Hyderabad.

Andhra Pradesh. Manna is particularly distinguished by the great number and variety of organizations through which they work. The three most important associations founded and controlled by Komanapalli are: Miriam Children's Homes (registered 1969), Manna Full Gospel Ministries (registered 1974?), and Rock Church Ministries (registered 1979). An extraordinarily large proportion of the work is devoted to social work. A brochure of 1990 reports, among others, forty-five orphanages, a center for lepers, ten schools, two junior colleges, and a fifty-bed hospital. Another important ministry founded by an expatriate Indian was started by P. J. Titus in 1982. Titus came to Vizag from the USA and, through the mediation of the pastor of the Indian Pentecostal Church in that place, who was also from Kerala, he obtained a large site in neighboring Bheemunipatnam. From the beginning there were enough overseas sponsors available to establish on this property, almost from nothing, a big institution for theological education, the Church on the Rock Theological Seminary. This quickly developed into one of the most important educational institutions for the Indian Pentecostal movement. Social projects were also realized on the site, including public schools. In the same year, 1982, Titus began with the founding of his own church, the New Testament Church, which, however, did not prove very successful and remained in the shadow of the theological seminary. As in the case of Ernest Komanapalli, Titus's organizations were distinguished by efficiency and professionalism. In order to ensure adequate finances, he registered his own missionary society, Christ for India, Inc. Ministries, in the USA; he acted as its president and extended its influence to England and Australia. The fact that expatriate Indians were well acquainted with the Indian as well as the American scene enabled them to show considerable results in a relatively short time. However, such crossing of cultural boundaries between India and America led some to adopt doubtful practices, as can be shown, for example, in The Ancient Pattern Pentecostal Church. The U.S.-based K. A. Paul, the youngest son of a Telugu-speaking pastor of the Indian Pentecostal Church, achieved an outstanding career in the south Indian Pentecostal movement in only a few years. After interrupting his Bible studies at the Church on the Rock Theological Seminary in Bheemunipatnam, he went to the USA and became a star in American televangelism. Scarcely into his thirties, at the beginning of the 1990s, Paul began a mission project for India under the name Gospel to the Unreached Millions. Owing to his successful career in the media, the project had considerable financial resources. In India the project went under the name The Ancient Pattern Pentecostal Church. In his efforts to secure the favor of American sponsors, he was not too scrupulous in his concern for the truth. He told stories of the fearful persecution he suffered for his missionary activity in India and reported fabulous church work and the many Bible schools he allegedly supported — experiences and deeds that existed only in his imagination. Equally alarming, however, was the inability of the leaders of the south Indian Pentecostal movement to hinder Paul in his multifarious schemes. Although they were unanimous without exception in their judgment concerning him, they apparently did not dare expose him, perhaps out of fear that the ensuing scandal would reduce the availability of resources from the USA and so would cause them more harm. In the mid-1990s Paul had recruited two well-regarded leaders of the Pentecostal movement in Andhra Pradesh,[23] men who happened to be in financial difficulties. From this he gained a certain increase in reputation, which made open criticism of his questionable activities even less possible.

New and interesting tendencies in the Pentecostal scene of Andhra Pradesh appeared in the big cities in the 1970s. In Vizag, for instance, there were two churches, independent of one another, whose leaders had never belonged to a Pentecostal congregation and who went their own ways in shaping the church work. At the beginning of the 1970s Pastor G. D. Poornachandra Rao of the Church of South India aroused keen evangelistic interest in Vizag. On his initiative a prayer circle was formed, consisting of young people from the established churches, especially the Baptists. It led, moreover, to a strengthening of missionary activity in the surrounding villages. When he moved from Vizag in 1972, he handed over the leadership of the prayer circle to the young N. Krupa Rao, who became the uncontested leading figure.[24] The group engaged with great commitment to evangelism in the villages, and their unity grew ever stronger. Young people from the established churches who had had Pentecostal experiences in other connections joined them. In the mid-1970s they made closer contact with a Pentecostal organization named Blessing Youth Mission in Vellore, North Arcot District, whose mission strategy they imitated.[25] Here a distinctly Pentecostal influence could be seen, and it is also reported that in the mid-1970s a woman evangelist of the Indian Pentecostal Church from Vijayawada set up a prayer circle in Vizag in which members of the group received Spirit baptism. However, the circle about Rao first took explicitly Charismatic form in the mid-1970s. Rao him-

23. These two leaders were K. P. Devasahayam from Eluru (Vice-President, Indian Pentecostal Church of Andhra Pradesh) and Godi Samuel from Srikakulam (until 1990 chairman of World Missionary Evangelism). Both were managing a Bible school and were financially supported by K. A. Paul.

24. N. Krupa Rao (b. 1946) came from the region of Kakinada and belonged at first to the Canadian Baptist Church.

25. On this style of mission see Pothen 1990: 195-214.

self received baptism in the Spirit in 1975. After the separate registration of the group in 1977 as Upper Room, the open break with the established churches resulted in 1978. Until then they had understood themselves as simply a prayer group, and members who mostly came from Baptist churches took part in worship and Holy Communion in their mother churches. Now the circle was organized as an independent church in which all offices were exclusively honorary. Since many members were in full employment, they could manage well on their own resources. In 1983 they erected a church building, and in 1984 one of its members was ready to give up his job and become full-time pastor, but without affecting the honorary leadership of Rao. But because of the latter's autocratic style of leadership, there was a confrontation that led to a split; in the event more than half of the families separated from Upper Room with Rao. Then, whereas Upper Room lost importance, Rao with the families that followed him founded Jesus Christ Prayer and Evangelistic Ministries, which soon developed into the fastest-growing Pentecostal church in Vizag. In spite of this success, it was only in December 1991 that Rao gave up his employment in public service in order to devote himself to full-time work in the church. In the following years a big church was built. A special characteristic of this church is its thoroughgoing independence of overseas aid. The church enjoys a substantial income and has the declared intention of being financed with its own money. The other big independent church in Vizag was led by M. A. Paul, who was converted to Pentecostal faith through a friend at work, and he shortly afterward left the Lutheran Church to which he had belonged until then.[26] Immediately after this, he set up his own group in 1973 for worship in his own house. It was probably soon after this that he gave up his job as a port employee. Thus, just like N. Krupa Rao, M. A. Paul founded his own church without having been an active member of any Pentecostal church. Already in 1976 the numbers at the Sunday worship necessitated the construction of a separate tent, and in 1982 he extended his own house to make room for worship. The church grew quickly and, since many members had a regular income, financial independence was secured. At the center of the church was an evangelization team grouped around M. A. Paul, which went to the surrounding villages and to neighboring districts where adivasis live. Thus a range of branch congregations was developed, supported by the main congregation. In the 1980s M. A. Paul made contact with overseas partners and visited the USA and Australia in connection with overseas finance. The registration of the church was effected in 1989 but, like

---

26. M. A. Paul (b. 1940) belonged to Trinity Lutheran Church (Andhra Evangelical Lutheran Church) in Vizag.

that of Rao, church work remained until the 1990s apparently largely independent of overseas help, depending in the first place on its own resources.

Other independent churches in Andhra Pradesh were the result of splitting, where financial help from overseas played a part, as is especially clear in the case of Sion Fellowship. In the 1980s Y. S. John Babu founded a big independent church at Hyderabad. Before that he had started a congregation for the Indian Pentecostal Church in Armoor in 1972. Having himself engaged in the search for overseas sponsors, he attended a conference in Bombay in 1979, where he met Alan Vincent of the West Herts Community Church, a representative of the British Restoration Movement who later moved to the USA.[27] Alan Vincent proposed himself to Babu as "apostle," which the latter accepted. Babu consequently left the Indian Pentecostal Church to make himself independent. Now with ready financial support he was able to extend his church work systematically. Congregations were called community churches, for example, Sion Community Church or Hyderabad Community Church. At the beginning of the 1980s he moved to Hyderabad and bought a large property on the outskirts of the city, where he erected, among other things, a school and a church. In the early 1980s there were further branch foundations, most often due to pastors moving with already-existing congregations. It was the founding of a Bible school in 1989 that made it possible to train pastors.[28] So by the 1990s Sion Fellowship had attained considerable size. Apart from establishing his own denomination, Babu tried to transpose the teaching of the British restoration movement for India, and he who recognized Alan Vincent as apostle, for his part, proposed himself as apostle for other Indian churches. In one journal published by him, we read: "Now he is received Apostalically [sic] by many Churches in South India."[29] But apparently apostolic recognition only occurred in the case of Prince of Peace, a Tamil church, led by James Santhosam, with whom he had established relations in 1987. On closer inspection it appears that this relation arose out of financial needs only. In the journal mentioned above Santhosam wrote:

> My early ministry although it was full of excitement followed by signs and wonders I still had problems in running the Churches, helping the workers and I was in a great financial stress having [been] involved in heavy debts. I was seeking the Lord to help me in this situation. The

27. On this movement see Hocken 2002a: 549-50.
28. See Sion Fellowship ca. 1990.
29. *Outpouring* Hyderabad, vol. 1, Mar./Apr. 1992: 15.

Lord was gracious to bring Pastor John Babu from Hyderabad into my situation and his Apostalic [*sic*] input brought a great relief to me.[30]

Apart from the financial help given to Santhosam by Babu and his influence resulting from this, there is hardly any indication of an "apostolic" relationship. The claim by Babu to be apostle to Prince of Peace remains unsubstantiated.[31]

Another, rather unique, independent church is the Maranatha Visvasa Samajam founded by Moses Choudary in Vijayawada. Moses Choudary, embodying the hopes of the Church of God in Andhra Pradesh, had returned to India in 1981 after successful postgraduate studies in the USA. He brought with him decisive proposals for reform aimed at strengthening the missionary capability of the Church of God. The proposals did not find much favor with the rather cautious Reddi Stephen. Consequently he left the Church of God and in 1982 founded his own independent church in Vijayawada. Since he had sufficient overseas support, he had scarcely any difficulties in the early stages. In the year of foundation he opened an orphanage and in 1984 a Bible school, and in 1994 a great multi-purpose building was erected in the heart of Vijayawada. Some branch congregations were initiated, although the numerical strength of the church remained comparatively meager until the 1990s. The specialty of the churches Cloudary founded consists in their mission strategy: the principal aim is conversion of high-caste Hindus. To this end he avoids all the traditional outward signs of Christianity, a practice exemplified in the use of the name Maranatha Visvasa Samajam. Hardly any Indian would right away suspect this to be the name of a church. His emphasis on contextualization goes so far as to encourage the high-caste members of his church to stand by their former caste practices. He places himself within a distinct tendency in the Indian church that understands the caste system as primarily socio-cultural. In his accommodation strategy for Christian mission, Choudary is strongly influenced by Donald McGavran of the Church Growth movement:[32]

---

30. *Outpouring* Hyderabad, vol. 1, Mar./Apr. 1992: 24.

31. In the contemporary journal *Prince of Peace* edited by James Santhosam, there is no mention of any relation with Y. S. John Babu. In the author's interview with him the supposed special relation did not come up. In his autobiography Babu is mentioned once only and casually as his "spiritual guide" (Santhosam 1990: 58f.). However, in an interview with the author Babu did speak of "his work" in Madras.

32. He put many of his ideas into a term paper at the Church of God School of Theology (Choudary, "Reaching and Discipling Caste Hindus in Andhra Pradesh, India," class term paper, Cleveland, Tennessee, 1980). For McGavran's views see McGavran 1979.

All I plead, here, for is that . . . she [the church] offers all communities the option of becoming Christian in their normal ethnic groupings. . . . I propose this along with the leaders of the Church Growth Movement . . . homogenous units or mono-ethnic congregations may be started in the caste Hindu localities.[33]

Thus he quite consciously places himself in a missionary tradition that treats caste as being in the first place a socio-cultural arrangement.[34] He is concerned above all with the problem that high-caste Hindus generally treat Christianity as a religion of the Dalits and consequently are not interested. For this reason, he wishes to found congregations in which high-caste Hindus can stay with their own people even after going over to Christianity. Hence he goes for a contextual form of missionary proclamation. For his mission to the high castes, he would use forms of religious drama, relying on scenic representations of the stories of Ramayana and the Mahabharata displayed at temple feasts. He would also like to provide Christian presentations in the form generally known as Katha,[35] especially Harikatha and Burra Katha, and make these part of the mission. What is noteworthy about Choudary's project is that it comes from an Indian Pentecostal. These views are anything but new, and one fails to see in Choudary any reflection on the painful experiences of caste discrimination suffered by Indian Christians. In consequence his ideas of contextualizing are rather naïve and take no account of the differentiated discussion on this matter, which has taken place in the established churches since the days of De Nobili. However, his approach indicates that the south Indian Pentecostal movement is gradually becoming aware of the problems of inculturation.

33. Choudary 1980: 28.
34. See Grafe 1990: 97-113.
35. See Choudary 1980: 21. For the use of Katha in Hinduism see Lutgendorf 1994: 115-17.

CHAPTER 6

Evangelists, Interchurch Fellowships, and Marginal Movements

Evangelists and Interchurch Fellowships

The Pentecostal movement in south India is marked by a profusion of churches independent of one another. The fragmentation of the movement is mainly attributable to splits, but there is also a concern to preserve a distinct awareness of the common Pentecostal identity. Evangelists are an important way to maintain a spiritual unity among Pentecostals as they overcome denominational boundaries and are invited by a wide range of different churches. The numerous church conventions and rallies arranged by Pentecostal churches make great demands on charismatic preachers. Many leading pastors are in fact impressive as revival preachers and faith evangelists.[1] Until the beginning of the 1960s, large Pentecostal rallies were only attempted by American healing evangelists.[2] But then there was notable development in south India with the appearance of important highly professional Indian evangelists. These were generally without a congregation to pastor or with a vanishingly small one, but by acting as chief speakers at rallies and conventions they gained such reputation and recognition that they could earn a good living. For the coordination of their evangelistic activities they founded their own organizations, often of considerable size. It began in 1960 with the young Tamil evangelist Paulaseer Lawrie. After a long trip to America, where

1. For the ministry of evangelists also see pp. 203-4.
2. See, e.g., pp. 50-51. A good survey of the American healing evangelist is given by Harrell 1975.

he came into close contact with W. M. Branham, he returned to India.[3] In the spring of 1961 he arranged his first big healing campaign in Madras, which proved to be the start of an extremely successful career that reached its highest point in 1966 when a big event in Madras drew an immense crowd and was spoken about throughout the city.[4] Even though Lawrie left the Pentecostal movement soon after this, he had established the pattern for many later evangelists. Many of them were clearly influenced by his activities in the 1960s: N. Jeevanandam received baptism in the Spirit at one of his rallies. John Joseph stayed with his parents for a long time in the Manujothi Ashram. It is credibly reported of D. G. S. Dhinakaran that he too was in some way influenced by Lawrie.

In the following decades there were some leading evangelists with worldwide reputation but whose popularity was often not very long-lived. A striking fact is that all the outstanding evangelists in these years were Tamil. At the end of the 1960s two women evangelists were especially well known: Pappa Shankar and Sarah Navroji. The latter was especially recognized for her composition of Tamil hymns in the style of popular film music. In the sequel it was mostly men who took the leading positions. In the 1970s the career of D. G. S. Dhinakaran rose like a comet, so that in the 1980s and 1990s he became the best-known and most successful evangelist in the whole of India. His outreach exceeded that of all his predecessors and his healing missions were attended, by his own report, by hundreds of thousands. Alongside the exceptional phenomenon of Dhinakaran, by the 1980s a whole range of important evangelists was established in Tamil Nadu, parallel to the rapid growth of the Tamil Pentecostal movement. N. Jeevanandam was famous for his All Night Prayers. Sadhu Chellappa created a sensation when he held rallies in which he read from classic Hindu scriptures and tried to convince Hindus that they had reference to Jesus Christ. Sam Jebadurai set up a printing press and in the first ten years published hundreds of edifying books. In addition, he edited a daily Bible reading that enjoyed extraordinary popularity among Tamil-speaking Christians. At the beginning of the 1990s another woman evangelist, Padma Mudaliar, entered the ranks of the most important evangelists. A new accent was heard in S. J. Berchmans, who had practiced as a Catholic village priest until he left his mother church in 1991 and turned to Pentecostalism. Like Sarah Navroji he gained a reputation though his modern hymns, which reached almost all Christian homes. All these evangelists un-

3. Similar to Branham, Lawrie did not emphasize Oneness teachings in public. For Lawrie see also the chapter on Manujothi Ashram, pp. 117ff.
4. See Hoerschelmann 1977: 317.

dertook numerous preaching tours outside India, usually through invitations from Tamil migrants.

Apart from the uniting impact of the evangelists there are also institutionalized efforts to make a common Pentecostal identity visible. Again and again there are attempts to reunite the south Indian Pentecostal movement in interchurch fellowships. Such fellowships are usually no more than regular monthly meetings of pastors in a particular region.[5] Participation together in arranging events with prominent evangelists will often provide the crystallization point that facilitates the formation of pastors' fellowships. Although the fellowships as a rule last only a few years and not infrequently break up because of internal conflict, they are regularly reinstituted after an interval.[6] Because they are so short-lived, there are hardly any historical sources on these regional fellowships.[7] There is also interchurch activity at the all-India level. In Madras in 1949 an all-India Pentecostal Fellowship was founded. This

---

5. See also pp. 236ff.

6. Often attempts are made to register the fellowship as an association, so as to create a lasting structure. But in the last analysis this only leads to more internal power struggles and proves to be an unsuitable step on the way to a more legalistic connection.

7. The following is a selective overview of important regional fellowships in south India in 1995. Where available, we give the foundation year and the name of the actual president. *South Tamilnadu:* Pentecostal Fellowship of Kanyakumari District, ca. 1989, led by Y. S. Devasundaram; Pentecostal Fellowship of Tirunelveli District, led by M. Rajendran. *Trichy:* Full Gospel Churches Association. *Coimbatore:* from 1969 to ca. 1984, there already existed a fellowship under the leadership of Job Gnanaprakasam (see Gnanaprakasam 1995: 4), who became again president of a new Pentecostal Pastors' Fellowship, started in 1993. *Madras:* in the 1950s there was a Pentecostal Fellowship Madras in which, however, after over two decades of existence, a serious conflict over leadership broke out between P. S. Chelladurai Sr. and Henry Joseph. In the 1980s a fellowship was called into life by Jochen Tewes in which it was mainly pastors from the organization supported by Intermission who met. In 1993 the organization of this fellowship was given into the hands of the younger pastors, under whose enthusiastic lead it gained acceptance among the pastors of Madras. It was then called Madras Pentecostal Fellowship and Charles Finney Joseph was the secretary; South Madras Pastors' Fellowship, 1987, with Dhayanandhan as convenor. *Kerala:* Pastors' Conference, Trivandrum; Kerala Pentecostal Fellowship Convention (a movement to promote unity among Pentecostal churches in Kerala), 1990, with P. J. Thomas as convenor. *Bangalore:* Pentecostal Pastors' Fellowship, Bangalore, ca. 1984, with K. V. Jeyavel (Full Gospel Fellowship) as president; *Hyderabad:* Pentecostal Pastors' Fellowship of Greater Hyderabad, 1995, with Ernest Komanapalli as chairman. *Vizag:* from 1984 to 1985 there already existed a Vishaka Christian Leaders Fellowship, and in 1987 the Evangelical Fellowship of Vishakapatnam was started with E. M. George Raju (Hebron House of Worship) as president. *Andhra Pradesh:* Full Gospel Leaders Fellowship of Andhra Pradesh, 1986, founded by Ernest Komanapalli and led by Spurgeon Raju.

happened on the initiative of John Vasu supported by the authoritative participation of Donald Gee, who was visiting India at the time.[8] The secretary was M. L. Ketcham, an American missionary of the North Indian Assemblies of God. However, this fellowship fell apart as early as 1951 when Ketcham left India.[9] It was apparently some decades before a similar far-reaching project could be undertaken. On the margins of the Pentecostal World Conference in Singapore in 1989, Thannickal invited Indian participants to a meeting where it was decided to call into life a Pentecostal Fellowship of India. A preparatory group met with Thannickal in Bangalore in 1990, and in 1991 an inaugural meeting took place in Madras and was well received by leading pastors. Although this fellowship was dominated by the south Indians, Pentecostals from north India also took part. Thannickal was chosen as first president and Henry Joseph as secretary.[10] The next meeting was arranged for Delhi in 1993, where leading representatives of the Pentecostal World Conference took part.[11] Ernest Komanapalli was chosen as the new president and Prabhudoss Vasu as secretary. During the Delhi meeting, P. J. Titus persuaded many participants to work out common accreditation for the various Bible schools in India.[12] At a meeting at the beginning of 1994 it was decided to found a National Association of Pentecostal Theological Institutions.[13] This initiative was understood to be closely dependent on the Pentecostal Fellowship of India: its president is an ex officio member of the national Association of Pentecostal Theological Institutions. In the late 1990s the Pentecostal Fellowship of India was still very loosely structured, and its main activity was to hold biannual meetings for pastors and engaged laity.

8. See Gee & Woodford 1948; Vasu ca. 1950: 17; Hollenweger 1965/1967: 03.07.049.

9. Ketcham 1973: 3; Shemeth 1990. The All-India Pentecostal Fellowship mentioned by Hollenweger (1965/1967: 03.07.049) is in fact the Pentecostal Fellowship Madras (see below).

10. See Pentecostal Fellowship of India 1991.

11. See Thannickal 1993; New Life Herald, Feb. 1994: 6, 11. Participants from the Pentecostal World Conference were: Ray H. Hughes, Jakob Zopfi, Raymond Carlson, Reinhold Ulonska, Cornelio Castello.

12. Until this point, Pentecostal Bible schools, in case of necessity, sought accreditation through the evangelical Asian Theological Association (ATA), whose president was Ken Gnanakan. Only the Faith Theological Seminary, Manakala (Kerala), had accreditation through Serampore University.

13. See P. J. Titus 1994; New Life Herald, Feb. 1994: 11. For the first two years the following executive committee was chosen: P. J. Titus (president), John Thannickal (vice-president), P. S. Philip, Bethel Bible College, Pulalar (secretary), David Prakasam (joint-secretary), Noel Samuel (treasurer), besides three members from north India and Ernest Komanapalli as ex officio member.

Marginal Movements

In south India there are many independent Christian communities that do not maintain contact with the Pentecostal movement but still stand in close, historically verifiable relation to the movement. In south India, so-called Jesus only or Oneness churches, generally known as Yesunamam churches, have a strong Pentecostal identity,[14] but at the same time, Indian Oneness Pentecostalism has hardly any established contacts with the mainstream Pentecostal movement, and it remains isolated with restricted outreach. However, the ministry of Paulaseer Lawrie and the Athmunasar at Thanjavur show that Yesunamam churches are potentially part of the wider Pentecostal network in India. Another interesting example is the Bible Mission, where in the beginning the founder had good contact with Pentecostalism before his community went its own way. Exemplary cases of the possible dangers for Pentecostals of personality cult are found in the Beginning Pentecostal Truth Church and the Manujothi Ashram. Both of these concern a former Pentecostal church from Tamil Nadu whose leader experienced an apotheosis. The following accounts are mainly concerned with describing the present relation of these groups to the Pentecostal movement.

Yesunamam Churches

At the end of the 1940s, Canadian missionaries of the Apostolic Church of Pentecost came to south India. George W. Neilson and three single women missionaries went to Kerala,[15] and George Shalm went to Kodaikanal, Dindigul District. At the beginning of the 1950s Neilson began a Bible school that in 1964 moved to Manarcad near Kottayam. This became the Indian headquarters of the church. Though Neilson left India in 1968, he kept in close contact with the small church he had founded. The members were overwhelmingly Dalit, while leadership was exercised by Thomas Christians. At the end of the 1940s, Ellis L. Scism, an American missionary of the United Pentecostal Church, came to Kerala. In 1942 an American woman missionary of the Pentecostal Assemblies of the World had already been in Adur, Pathanamthitta District, and had founded some small congregations there. Scism took over and made this the starting point of work by the United Pentecostal Church. He

---

14. For history and teachings of Oneness Pentecostalism in general see Reed 1978; Gill 1994; Faupel 1996: 270-306.

15. Mrs. J. Swannell, Miss J. Baker, and Miss L. I. L. Anderson (see Shalm 1954: 4).

bought a plot in Adur, and the headquarters of the church was erected there. In 1957 a Bible school was opened. In 1963, George Shalm went over to the United Pentecostal Church and brought with him some congregations from Tamil Nadu. The Apostolic Church of Pentecost thus lost its work in Tamil Nadu and remained restricted to Kerala. Ellis L. Scism's son, Henry, came at the beginning of the 1950s to support his father in Kerala but after a few years moved to north India. When Ellis Scism left India in 1965, the main interest of the church's work turned to north India. Consequently, two independent districts were formed — North India and India.[16] For the new India district, George Shalm remained general superintendent. In 1972 all western missionaries departed and the church was given into indigenous hands. The United Pentecostal Church supported by Dalits in the succeeding period developed a modest increase in Kerala and, to a lesser extent, in Tamil Nadu.[17] It is notable that there has never been a closer contact between the two big Oneness denominations in India. The Apostolic Church of Pentecost held to the doctrine of the eternal security of those once saved, but this doctrine was rejected by the United Pentecostal Church. In south India this difference in teaching was considered by both churches a reason for separation.

Besides the two big Oneness churches there are some other independent churches worth mentioning, which go back to Paulaseer Lawrie's activity. When he organized a rally in Trichy,[18] a small prayer group was formed that had as honorary leader the medical doctor S. S. S. Stephen. At his side was the engineer D. R. Jesudian, who gave up his post in 1967 to enter full-time ministry. Both were prominent as guest speakers at Lawrie's missions, but their collaboration ended in 1969 when Lawrie described himself as Son of Man. From then on, Stephen and Jesudian with their followers continued as an independent church called Assembly of Christ Jesus, but this church showed no increase and remained isolated. However, at the end of the 1970s, the Assembly of Christ Jesus sent D. Asirvatham as pastor to Thanjavur but, after a while, he left them and founded an independent church that he called Athumanesar.[19] He organized big healing services, clearly indicating the in-

---

16. In contrast to the situation in south India, in northeast India they (United Pentecostal Church in North East India) had more missionary success. So, for example, in 1974 up to 11 percent of all Christians in Mizoram were members of the United Pentecostal Church (Hminga 1987: 206, see also 198f., 206, 228, 339).

17. The following pastors were active as general superintendents of the United Pentecostal Church in India: 1972-1974 M. Joseph (Kerala); 1974-1985 Solomon Isaac (Indore, Madhya Pradesh); 1985-1989 Victor Hobday (Madras); from 1989 P. George (Kerala).

18. See Dale 1973: 64.

19. D. Asirvatham (b. 1948) came from Tirunelveli and grew up in the Church of South

fluence of Paulaseer Lawrie. In the 1990s his ministry showed spectacular success, and he was leading the largest Pentecostal congregation in Thanjavur at that time. In addition, he formed small prayer groups throughout Tamil Nadu and held rallies in various places with the support of the small independent Yesunamam churches in the localities. Through the latter activity, he helped to draw these churches to some extent out of their isolation, since his miracles and exorcisms attracted people from the established churches. When in the 1960s Lawrie became popular in Andhra Pradesh, Jonah from Rajahmundry joined him with his Yesunamam church, called the Independent Full Gospel Church. Jonah soon belonged to the inner-circled fellow workers with Lawrie and was a guest speaker at his rallies. In 1970 he married one of his daughters to Devaseer Lawrie, the second son of Paulaseer Lawrie. But at the beginning of the 1970s they separated, since Jonah would not go along with the new teachings of Paulaseer Lawrie. After Jonah's death in 1985, his son A. S. W. Jaikumar took up the leadership of the Independent Full Gospel Church, which also had some branches in Andhra Pradesh.

Bible Mission

For decades, M. Devadas was a prominent evangelist of the Andhra Evangelical Lutheran Church, until in 1938 he founded his own independent church, the Bible Mission.[20] It is clear that in the first half of the 1930s he had close relations with P. M. Samuel, although detailed information is not available. Up to this point, he worked as evangelist in a Lutheran sanatorium in Rajahmundry and, at the same time, was a welcome guest speaker at church rallies. When in 1934 Samuel organized a mission in Rajahmundry, Devadas was with him to help.[21] On the margins of this event, there was a meeting between Samuel and a small prayer group led by Devadas in the house of a Charismatic Lutheran missionary from the USA.[22] Devadas was probably also en-

---

India. He experienced conversion at seventeen and a little later received baptism by immersion through Paulaseer Lawrie. After a short time as teacher in a state school, he received the call to ministry. He stayed for a time with the husband of his sister, a pastor in the Full Gospel Pentecostal Church, which is not a Yesunamam church. But then he joined Paulaseer Lawrie for two years. After leaving Lawrie, he worked under S. S. S. Stephen in Trichy.

20. The history of the Bible Mission is relatively well researched. See Devasahayam 1982: 55-101; Solomon Raj 1986b; Solomon Raj 1986a: 39-46; Solomon Raj 1995: 61-68.

21. Samuel 1980: 24f.; Devasahayam 1982: 61f. According to Samuel (1980: 63) the meeting had already taken place in 1932, but this seems rather unlikely.

22. Samuel 1980: 25. He is speaking of Miss Targin, an American Lutheran missionary,

gaged in organizing evangelical rallies for Samuel in other Lutheran churches in Andhra Pradesh.[23] In one of his writings, Devadas relates how he was present at a rally in Eluru, where a western preacher explained that he had seen in a vision that God would raise a prophet like Moses in India. Devadas related the vision to himself and to his own activity.[24]

The Bible Mission founded by Devadas follows the typical Pentecostal pattern, especially in its teaching on baptism in the Spirit, which seems to have been the main reason for separation from the Lutheran Church. So K. Vijayaratnam, one of Devadas's closest fellow workers, in an open letter to the leader of the Lutheran Bible school in Rajahmundry and to the president of the Andhra Pradesh Evangelical Lutheran Church, demanded that future pastors should not be admitted until they had received Spirit baptism.[25] In relation to gifts of the Spirit too, the teaching of the Bible Mission corresponded to that of the Pentecostal movement. But there were considerable differences. Infant baptism was recognized by the Bible Mission and rebaptism was not required.[26] Tongues, apparently, did not count as initial evidence of baptism in the Spirit.[27] The emphasis on dreams and visions, as the means by which God speaks directly to people, went much further than is usual in Pentecostal communities. According to the teaching of the Bible Mission, only those would be raptured before the tribulation who had received Spirit baptism, kept themselves pure, and waited in expectation for the Lord.[28] Besides this, in the Bible Mission there was a very strong reverence for their founder. After his death in 1960 they even expected his resurrection in three days, since they saw in him the beloved disciple who was not to die until the return of the Lord. However,

---

who received Spirit baptism during furlough in the USA and was in close contact with M. Devadas. According to P. M. Paramjothi (interview with the author) Devadas received baptism in the Spirit in the 1920s (?) in the hill station of Kodaikal, Dindigul District, where the overseas missionaries retired in the hot season. There some western women missionaries had formed a Charismatic prayer group in which Devadas had taken part. It was mentioned that Devadas had said, in connection with Samuel's evangelistic work, that he had experienced it all before (see Devasahayam 1982: 62).

23. See Samuel 1989: 25.

24. See Devasahayam 1982: 73; Solomon Raj 1986b: 48. The date and circumstances of this rally are unknown to the author. But, since up to this time P. M. Samuel had never invited any western preacher to Eluru, it could have been a rally organized by Lam Jeevaratnam at which a missionary of the British Assemblies of God spoke.

25. See Solomon Raj 1986b: 61, 78.

26. See Devasahayam 1982: 76; Solomon Raj 1986b: 55.

27. See Solomon Raj 1986b: 133.

28. Solomon Raj 1986b: 112-14. In this the Bible Mission is close to the eschatological teaching of the Ceylon Pentecostal Mission (see pp. 64-65).

all the evidence suggests that such thinking does not go back to the founder himself. His followers believe that, even after his death, he continues to have some share of his spiritual leadership. So there exists a collection of messages that he is supposed to have given through a human medium.[29] During prayer meetings, an empty chair covered with a white cloth is placed in a prominent position. Some consider that by this practice the spirit of Devadas is invited, others that the Lord Himself will take the place as invisible guest.[30] This ambiguity means that special reverence is observed in the Bible Mission toward the founder, but there is no agreement on the manner and content of this reverence. The Bible Mission has no ecumenical contact with the Pentecostal movement or with any other church. Even in the lifetime of the founder, there were sharp internal conflicts and splits.[31] In consequence of these, after the death of Devadas, K. Vijayaratnam left the Bible Mission and joined the Church of God of Prophecy.[32] This is an indication of how near the Bible Mission is to Pentecostalism.

Beginning Pentecostal Truth Church

Sadhu G. Devanesan was originally a pastor in Kirubasanam before he made himself independent and founded the Beginning Pentecostal Truth Church.[33] The independent Christian community he founded lost all contact with the Pentecostal movement and with any other church in the course of time. It understood itself as the "first true Pentecostal church" and severely criticized the existing Pentecostal movement.[34] Devanesan had a radical teaching on healing and forbade any medicinal treatment for his followers. One of his points of criticism against other churches was that women were too influential in them. He introduced the practice of dividing men and women at worship by a curtain.[35] The field of activity of the church was concentrated around the

---

29. See Solomon Raj 1995: 65.

30. See Solomon Raj 1995: 67.

31. See Devasahayam 1982: 67-71.

32. See p. 99.

33. Sadhu G. Devanesan (1915-1983) came from a Hindu family. At the age of thirty-one, he was converted through Sadhu Yesudhason, the founder of Kirubasanam. He left his wife and children and became a pastor in Kirubasanam. It is not known when he founded his own church. In 1980 he undertook a pilgrimage to Jerusalem (Selva Raj ca. 1986). But the background remains obscure.

34. See Hoerschelmann 1977: 285.

35. See Hoerschelmann 1977: 284.

headquarters in Kulasekaram, Kanyakumari District, where in the 1970s Devanesan resided with about a thousand fellow workers. For these workers, the majority of them women, celibacy was desirable, and at their entry into the ashram they had to give over their property to the church.[36] In the course of time, the church concentrated more and more on the person of the founder. Already at the beginning of the 1970s, Devanesan was spoken of as "extraordinary apostle," blessed with "higher qualities than other people."[37] In the second half of the 1970s these tendencies were strengthened, and he seems to have begun to concentrate the community on his own personality. Before his death in 1983 he had already described C. Selva Raj as his successor.[38] His followers believed he would soon rise from the dead. His body, according to Raj, was left out in the open without any signs of decay.[39] On the fourth day it was sealed by the workers so that no more sight was had of it. His followers hold that in the future it will not decay until his resurrection. According to Raj, Devanesan is the "righteous man from the east" of Isaiah 41:2-4.[40] He will soon be brought to life through the Lord Jesus Christ to work many wonders, and then the Beginning Pentecostal Truth Church will spread throughout the whole world. Raj writes as follows:

> When the Lord Jesus Christ rises up Aiya Esq. [= Sadhu G. Devanesan] from the dead; and when performing his great and wonderful miraculous deeds through Aiya Esq., India will become a glorious holy country; and Malavilai, a place in Kanniyakumari District (place from which the righteous man Aiya Esq. is going to rise up) will become a glorious holy place next to Jerusalem.[41]

---

36. See Hoerschelmann 1977: 284. Hoerschelmann visited the ashram in 1972 where at the time one hundred workers were living. When we visited the ashram in 1994 a similar number of workers were there. The ashram corresponds in many respects to the Faith Homes in the Ceylon Pentecostal Mission.

37. Hoerschelmann 1977: 286. However, we do not find in this author clear reference to divinization of Sadhu Devanesan.

38. C. Selva Raj (b. 1947) comes from a village only three kilometers from Malavilai. He previously belonged to the Church of South India. At Madras Christian College he finished with an M.Sc. in mathematics. In 1973 he was converted by Sadhu G. Devanesan and became a member of the church. He worked for more than three years as a tax inspector until he left the service and entered the ashram.

39. See Selva Raj ca. 1986: 6.

40. This, the translation of the King James Bible, is also in accord with the Tamil Bible translation in common use (kiḻakkiliruntu nītimanāṉ).

41. Selva Raj ca. 1986: 13.

So the church teaches that before the actual return of Jesus Christ, Devanesan will rise and assist his small church toward a worldwide breakthrough.

Manujothi Ashram

In the 1960s, Paulaseer Lawrie was the most important healing evangelist in India.[42] The fact that, under the influence of W. M. Branham,[43] he held to Oneness doctrines does not seem to have been a significant factor. He did not explicitly plan his own church foundation. But certain small congregations existed that later were to become independent Yesunamam churches.[44] The real separation from mainstream Pentecostalism began in 1967 when, at the invitation of Ewald Frank, a German follower of Branham, he undertook an extended preaching tour through Germany, Switzerland, and Austria, which eventually also brought him to the USA. There he impressed Branham's followers, who up to this point had been very unsure. In 1965 Branham unexpectedly died, shortly after having unmistakably indicated that he was the eschatological prophet-messenger.[45] Many of his followers were convinced that in the very near future he would rise again and that then he would make ready the bride of Christ for the end of the world, which he had predicted for 1967. After this expectation of an immediate rising of Branham within a few months had not been fulfilled, hopes were transferred to 1969 as a possible end of the world.[46] In that year Lawrie undertook another tour in the USA, again mostly to followers of Branham. In the hopeful atmosphere of 1969, some American audiences suddenly saw miraculous light phenomena around Lawrie as he preached. Lawrie welcomed these observations and explained, during his visit to Chicago, that they were signs of the coming of the Son of Man; he connected them with the American moon landing, which happened

---

42. For a more detailed account on the life and teachings of Paulaseer Lawrie see Bergunder 2003.

43. W. M. Branham, also, was a healing evangelist recognized in all Pentecostal circles until the beginning of the 1960s (see Harrell 1975: 159-65; Weaver 1987: 107-40).

44. In a newssheet published by Paulaseer Lawrie, we read: "Bro. Lawrie is not building any denomination as [is] commonly misunderstood by so many. The numerous prayer groups and few assemblies which are functioning in various centres are simply the meeting places of people who have been touched by God. . . . No material help is given to these prayer groups and assemblies by Bro. Lawrie and no control over them is exercised by him" (The Eleventh Hour, Jan.-Apr. 1964, vol. 2, no. 1: 3).

45. See Weaver 1987: 126-39.

46. See Hutten 1989: 209.

at the same time. God Himself was coming to earth to collect the bridal community and prepare the rapture, which he predicted for 1973 in India. In 1971, following this promise, many visitors, especially from Germany and the USA, came and settled with Lawrie in India. First they resided in Gandhinagar, a suburb of Tirunelveli, and then in 1972 moved fifteen kilometers west to the Manujothi Ashram. This was a plot that had long been in Lawrie's possession and became the headquarters of the movement. Lawrie now modified his prediction of the rapture, and explained that in 1973 the gathering of the bride would be completed and the age of the Son of God was to begin. Relying on Branham, he predicted the destruction of the world and beginning of the thousand-year reign for 1977. Then the Son of God would be changed into the Son of David and, together with the glorified bride, would appear on the Mount of Olives in Jerusalem. The end of the world failed to happen, but Lawrie denied having made a false prediction and taught that in 1977 a progressive revelation of his own person took place. Because of visa problems, but also because many had lost faith in Lawrie's predictions, all the foreign visitors of the ashram had returned home by 1977 at the latest. Although some remained true to him, by the end of the 1970s he had lost a large part of his original followers.

By the mid-1970s he had begun to prove his divine calling from the Hindu scriptures too.[47] In the 1980s he began to develop this in various forms. He related his Christian-messianic claim to Hindu predictions, claiming they were fulfilled in him and that he was the divine savior of the Kaliyuga. For proof he quoted especially the prophetic books of Swami Muthukutty,[48] the Bhagavata Purana, and the Bhagavad Gita. This led to many Hindus, including Indians from overseas, turning to Lawrie whom they venerated as Gurudev Shri Lahari Krishna. When he died in 1989 this did not mean for his new followers any contradiction of the promise that he would be the divine savior of the Kaliyuga. An Indian from Bihar living in the USA, who joined him in 1986 and was a very influential follower, wrote:

> Now, after preaching this doctrine for the past twenty years (hidden since the foundation of the world) and revealing the deep hidden truths

47. Hoerschelmann 1977: 384-85.
48. Swami Muthukutty (1809-1850) worked hard in south Tamil Nadu for the emancipation of the Nadars who, in his time, suffered extreme discrimination. He was revered by his followers as an avatar of the Kaliyuga. He was considerably influenced in his teaching by Christianity. There is still today a small religious community near Nagercoil, Kanyakumari District, whose origins go back to him. See Hoerschelmann 1977: 125-31; Rajamani 1981.

(secrets) from all the Scriptures, Shri Lahari Krishna ascended to Heaven on February 24, 1989, without our knowledge, yet fulfilling the Scriptural prophecies of Kalki Maha Purana. Now, we are awaiting eagerly His glorious return to earth as the King of Heaven and Earth for the purpose of judgement.[49]

After his death there was a leadership struggle between his three sons. For the time being, his second son, Devaseer Lawrie, was successful. The mainly Hindu adherents in India and abroad formed local gatherings and were regularly visited by Devaseer Lawrie. Some Christian adherents from the 1960s and 1970s also still kept in touch with Manujothi Ashram. On special feasts, like the yearly memorials of the moon landing, in the 1990s, hundreds of adherents from all parts of India and from abroad streamed to the Manujothi Ashram.

49. Prasad 1990: 9-10.

Public advertisement for a "Miracle Festival" in the New Life Assembly, Madurai

Public advertisement for a Gospel Meeting with evangelist G. P. S. Robinson, Madras

Public advertisement of the Indian Pentecostal Church, Hyderabad

Public advertisement for the Reinhard Bonnke campaign at Secunderabad

Full Gospel Pentecostal Church, Kattathurai

Church of God, Madurai

First Assembly of God, Madurai

Zion Assemblies of God, Coimbatore

New Life Assembly of God, Chennai

Church of M. O. John, T. Kalupatti

Rhema Church, Madurai

Indian Pentecostal Assemblies, Coimbatore

Rock Church, Hyderabad

Full Gospel Church in India, Bangalore

BELIEFS AND PRACTICES

The south Indian Pentecostal movement consists of a number of churches independent of one another, but on central issues there is widespread agreement and there is a common Pentecostal identity. This is not changed by the
fact that some churches prefer to call themselves "Charismatic" rather than
"Pentecostal," because no fundamental difference between the two can be observed in south India.[1] As a rule, the Charismatic churches, just like the Pentecostals stand by the doctrine of speaking in tongues as the initial evidence
of baptism in the Spirit. Criticism by the Charismatics is restricted entirely to
some radical Pentecostal teachings on holiness, which they treat as antiquated
"Pentecostal tradition" and will not accept as binding.[2] However, since in
south India classical Pentecostal churches like the Assemblies of God also
characteristically stand for more moderate views on holiness, we can hardly
see the Charismatic and Pentecostal churches as two distinct tendencies. Furthermore, there are very few Charismatic churches whose founders had not
been members of Pentecostal churches before.[3] Most pastors of Charismatic
churches have a Pentecostal background and understand "Charismatic" as
not being in opposition to "Pentecostal." Church fellowships are formed
without problem with definitely Pentecostal designations, like the many Pen-

1. On the distinction, see Hocken 2002c: 515-17. Charismatic movements within the
Protestant mainline churches are beyond the scope of this study. For the Catholic Charismatic movement, however, see p. 240 n. 35.

2. On the question of holiness see pp. 144-45.

3. For exceptions see the Christian Fellowship Centre Bangalore; Jesus Christ Prayer
and Evangelistic Ministries, Vizag; Christ's Church Vizag. The founders of these churches
were never members of a Pentecostal church.

tecostal Pastors' Fellowships, and there are no networks or fellowships considering themselves as definitely Charismatic. It is hard to avoid the impression that many churches fail to designate themselves as Pentecostal because their overseas partners understand themselves as Charismatic. Consequently, the following systematic presentation will not differentiate between Charismatic and Pentecostal churches at the outset. Only in particular cases will distinctions be made. The hesitant acceptance of certain spectacular practices and teachings from the western Charismatic movement fits well into this more uniform picture of the south Indian Pentecostal movement.[4] An exception is the Faith Movement, which could report considerable influence since the 1980s especially in Madras.[5] The arrival of the Faith Movement led to a certain polarization in south India, because it was decisively rejected by the Pentecostals but also by most of the Charismatics. Especially the prosperity gospel was generally rejected. The extremely sharp criticism by the classical Pentecostals led to the result that only a few churches showed themselves open to the Faith Movement.[6] These few consequently remain outside the inter-church unions of the south Indian Pentecostal movement.[7] However, some pastors admit in conversation to being influenced by the teachings of the Faith Movement, although outwardly they distance themselves. The books of Kenneth Hagin and Yonggi Cho, in particular, are read by many pastors. The author has the impression that above all it is the consequential this-worldliness of the Faith Movement that is positively received in south India. To assure oneself of God's blessing in this world is a general leitmotif of Pentecostal spirituality in south India.

4. In anticipation of the Benny Hinn rally, announced for the spring of 1995, for example, the author was aware of a general rejection of being "slain in the Spirit." Also the Toronto blessing, in spite of close contact with North America, was not discussed in the south Indian Pentecostal movement. On the restoration movement, see below. On Slain in the Spirit, see Alexander 1990. On the Toronto blessing, see Chevreau 1994; Hocken 1996; Poloma 1996.

5. On the Faith Movement and its position in the Pentecostal movement, see Horn 1989; McConnell 1990; Neuman 1990: 32-55; Smail et al. 1994: 57-75.

6. The Assemblies of God in Tamil Nadu, e.g., saw occasion in 1984 to translate a position document of their sister organization in the USA, against the Faith Movement, into Tamil (see Assemblies of God 1984).

7. Living Word Church, Madurai; Apostolic Fellowship Tabernacle, Madras; Rainbow Church, Madras.

CHAPTER 7

Context

The south Indian Pentecostal movement is no simple copy of western models, but shows many contextual approximations to elements of Hindu and Indian Christian popular spirituality. Such contextual interfaces are not in opposition to but run parallel to the religious practice of the American Pentecostal movement. This parallelism is a characteristic trait of Pentecostal spirituality in south India. It is preferable, therefore, first to determine phenomenological links and then to work out the contextual interfaces in order to propose a suitable framework for a comparative description of the spirituality of the south Indian Pentecostal movement.

Popular Hinduism

It is above all in their view of the causes of misfortune that south Indian Pentecostals come close to popular Hinduism. The following description relates especially to the situation in Tamil Nadu,[1] where these spirits are called pēy or picācu (Sanskrit piśāca). Popular Hinduism attributes to evil spirits illness and untimely death but also infertility, strife in the family, failure in professional career, material deprivation, etc., in short everything that is a threat in daily life or cause of severe insecurity. With regard to health and blessing, the Hindu popular religiosity of the Tamil people mostly pays attention to the fe-

---

1. The following especially depends on a study by Michael Moffatt (1979) on popular Hindu spirituality among the Tamil Dalits. Moffat claims that his findings are representative for popular Hinduism in south India (see Moffatt 1979: 223).

male deities like Māriyamman who have a low position in the divine hierarchy of Brahmanical Hinduism. While the gods of the Brahmanical traditions are mainly seen as beneficent, deities like Māriyamman, originally the goddess of smallpox, are more ambivalent.[2] Māriyamman can be the cause of blessing or of dreadful calamity, and the worship of her consists in averting the baleful side of the goddess and attracting her beneficent power.[3] Various spiritual beings, to whom no clear divine genealogy has been assigned, act as servants of Māriyamman. Her main distinguishing characteristic is her mastery over larger groups of evil spirits. The evil spirits that we mentioned at the beginning, the pēy and the picācu, are those really responsible for misfortune. They function exclusively as bearers of bad luck.[4] They are mainly spirits of those who have died "bad" deaths, that is, premature or unfortunate deaths. It belongs to the characteristic properties of the evil spirits that they possess people (Tamil pēykkōḷ, pēypiṭittal, or picācupiṭittal),[5] and if they take up their abode in people, they can be the cause of all kinds of misfortune but especially of diseases.[6] In many cases the evil spirits are summoned by means of black magic (Tamil cūṇiyam, pillicūṇiyam, ēval) to plague people.

Protection against the activity of these evil spirits is a burdensome problem in the daily practice of religion. If anyone is made sick by their hostile activity, there are various exorcizing rites available for relief. Here we mention only two examples.[7] The person in question may go to a Cāmiyāṭi, that is, to a human medium who at certain times is ritually possessed by goddesses like Māriyamman. Entering the medium, the goddess carries out an exorcism; if this succeeds, the evil spirit leaves the victim.[8] Such ecstatic possession phenomena in which gods come down on particular people are widespread in Hindu popular religiosity.[9] Besides the Cāmiyāṭi there is the Mantiravāti (Sanskrit Mantravādin), a specialist who offers his professional help for payment in the case of possession by evil spirits. Central to his practice as exor-

2. Moffatt 1979: 248f.; see also Whitehead 1988: 116-17. See also Masilamani-Meyer 2004: 55-58.

3. Moffatt 1979: 267.

4. Moffatt 1979: 233. See also Ziegenbalg 1867: 182-201; Meyer 1986a: esp. 206-8.

5. See University of Madras 1982: V, 2648, 2893-96; see also Caplan 1989: 57-58.

6. Besides the evil spirits, there is a range of explanations for illness and misfortune. According to Ayrookuzhiel 1983: 160, there would be also, for example, belief in karma and astrology to be considered as causes.

7. For descriptions of exorcisms in the popular Hinduism of south India, see also Elmore 1984: 47-53; Whitehead 1988: 161-64; Neill n.d.: 28-29; Masilamani-Meyer 2004: 188-92.

8. Moffatt 1979: 235-46.

9. See Ayrookuzhiel 1983: 66-70.

cist is a powerful incantation, called his mantra, which compels the spirit to
leave. But there is also a a dark side to him. According to many representations, he not only liberates people from evil spirits but also practices black
magic against the enemies of paying customers so as to cause *them* to be visited by evil spirits.[10] The various practices of exorcism are not mutually exclusive. On the contrary, those who seek healing follow an experimental strategy. Every possible remedy promising success will be tried one after the other
or even at the same time. Naturally, western medicine will also be employed,
if there is any access to it. As will be explained later, the Pentecostals have
taken over the demonology of popular Hinduism, with some slight differences. They work in competition with these exorcists and thereby have an effective contextual link. The experimental approach of Hindus to these services prepares the way for Christian healing to be accepted. Moreover, there
are parallels to the ecstatic elements of popular Hindu religiosity as it is expressed, for example, in the person of the Cāmiyāṭi. Pentecostal pastors and
evangelists most often speak in tongues when they are engaged in healing or
exorcism.

Indian Christian Popular Spirituality

Alongside Hindu religiosity, Indian Christian popular spirituality also pro-
vides a decisive background for the Pentecostal movement. By Christian popular spirituality we refer to the everyday religiosity of Christians in the established Protestant churches.[11] It is the Christian equivalent to Hindu popular
religiosity that arose independently of the practice of western missionaries
who, in the great majority, held to a kind of enlightened optimistic view of
progress and took belief in evil spirits for a superstitious error that would
quickly disappear with the increasing influence of western medicine and
education.[12] They did not accept the indigenous interpretation or, at most,
brought a folkloristic interest to it. Western missionaries in India were rather
more inclined to come to terms with high Brahmanical Hinduism. This
stance is also taken by many indigenous Indian theologians. However, recently, liberation theology projects, especially Dalit theology, have rediscov-

10. Moffatt gives no description of the Mantiravāti. But see e.g., Diehl 1956: 267-334;
Diehl 1965: 135-39.
11. Catholic popular religiosity in south India is distinguished in many points from
that of Protestants. Above all, the prominent veneration of Mary makes its mark; see
Rzepkowski 1991.
12. See Caplan 1989: 45-48.

ered the everyday experience of simple people as a theological reference point.[13]

After their conversion to Protestant Christianity most Indians still attributed any illness or mishap that visited them to the activity of evil spirits. Only a minority of them could be convinced in the mission schools of the non-existence of evil spirits. The majority of newly converted Indians thus being left to themselves experimented with various strategies.[14] The simplest and most common was to continue seeking the counsel of the Hindu specialists in exorcism. Though this was officially forbidden, most went as usual to specialists like the Cāmiyāṭi or Mantiravāti and made use of their capabilities in exorcism. However, they also tried to find Christian substitutes. An invaluable help was surely found in the fact that the Bible was available in the vernacular. Reading of the miracles in the gospels or of the anointing in James 5 often served as guidance. They prayed to Christ for healing and protection from evil spirits, they anointed the sick with oil, or they often put a Bible under the pillow of the one lying sick. In short, answers were sought to threats experienced within a worldview that was not recognized by the western missionaries. Of course, they in turn proclaimed in their preaching that Jesus had mastered the evil spirits and this promise also found acceptance.[15] However, they apparently were also of the opinion that, with the defeat of the evil spirits, they also ceased to exist. It is precisely here that the Indian Christians have a different experience: the evil spirits remain. Indian Christians have therefore developed an indigenous subculture, hidden from the critical eyes of the missionary, which offers help: in cases of illness and other misfortunes that are attributed to the activity of evil spirits. In this subculture, Christian prayer and Hindu practices go together.[16] This Indian Christian religiosity cannot be set within precise sociological limits. It is to be found in the city as well as the country, and equally among the educated and the uneducated. However, among the educated who have the experience of western education we may find more persons with an enlightened worldview. In the author's opinion, it is this religious subculture that helped the Pentecostal movement to its great success because it brought with it an explicitly Christian resource to deal effectively with the problem of evil spirits, without denying their existence.

Moreover, it should be specially noticed that even phenomena that are

13. See Wilfred 1992: 309; Clarke 1998.
14. See Estborn 1958: 22-24; Diehl 1965: 135-39; Luke & Carman 1968: 165, 177, 184.
15. See Neill n.d.: 51.
16. See Estborn 1958: 22-24.

thought to be characteristic for the Pentecostal movement, such as speaking in tongues, are also found in popular Indian Christian spirituality in the nineteenth century. They are reported as accompanying phenomena in certain revivals or eschatological movements and show that most charismatic phenomena, introduced by the Pentecostal movement, have strong phenomenological parallels in popular Indian Christian spirituality of the nineteenth century.[17]

Spirituality of the American Pentecostal Movement

Though the worldwide Pentecostal movement was a global movement right from its beginning in the twentieth century, it was considerably shaped in its spirituality by American Pentecostalism. However, this is not to be misunderstood for an "Americanization" because American Pentecostal spirituality managed successfully to connect with conceptions from local popular religiosity in Africa, Asia, and Latin America not least due to the fact that the spirituality of the American Pentecostal movement is strongly marked with elements of folk religion. A theory of secularization developed by David Martin is helpful in understanding the full significance of this. He argues that in America there was a way out for religion that prevented urban development reaching the crystallization point of secularism, as it did in Europe. He justifies this as follows:

> Because America lacked the association of a major religious institution with a class culture or cultures it was able to engender religious forms that could adapt to and reverse the anomic conditions of the city. Religion did not have to cope with a combination of anomic personal chaos and class alienation. To have reversed or at least nullified a major secularizing tendency in this way suggests that tendency is contingent on certain circumstances, not a necessary aspect of universal processes. The reversal is important because the adaptations have been passed on to the varieties of Pentecostal and evangelical religions now expanding (for example) in the megacities of São Paulo and Seoul.[18]

17. See Hoerschelmann 1977: 83; McGee 1996a; McGee 1999. However, according to the definitions suggested in the beginning of this study it makes little sense to call these occurrences in nineteenth-century India "Pentecostal" because there are no historical links to the Pentecostal movement. Moreover, they lasted only for a short time and it was the Pentecostal movement that first made these phenomena part and parcel of their day-to-day religion.
18. Martin 1990: 274-75 (emphasis deleted — M.B.).

This means that the American Pentecostal movement is part of a process of religious adaptation, in which the traditional religiosity of people is tuned to the demands of modernity, surviving in new forms. Thus American Pentecostalism is not simply "pre-modern" or "pre-Enlightenment" but rather a response to the pressure of secularization, as expressed, above all but not exclusively, in urbanization. Pentecostal spirituality is "the union of the very old and very modern."[19] The survival of traditional folk-religion elements in the American Pentecostal movement is most evident when its African American roots are examined.[20] Similarly, the first white members of the movement came from quite simple circumstances and brought with them their everyday religious piety. Moreover, it is a spirituality guided by experience that is characteristic for the American Pentecostal movement. This is not to deny that the theology practiced by Pentecostals follows the pattern of the fundamentalist-evangelical doctrinal structure. However, this seems to be a secondary alliance, as present-day Pentecostal theologians emphasize. Russell Spittler writes: "There is a profound difference between the cognitive fundamentalist and the experiential Pentecostal."[21] Cheryl Bridges Johns explains that, on the basis of their folk-religion characteristics and of their social origins, the Pentecostal movement never gained full recognition by the Evangelicals: "There was always the hidden, and sometimes not so hidden, message that Pentecostals were the stepchildren in the Evangelical family."[22] Therefore, the "Evangelicalization" of the Pentecostal movement should be understood as a secondary process.[23] This will allow a clearer look at Pentecostal spirituality, which is directed by experience and informed by many elements of folk religion. It is this combination which helped the south Indian Pentecostal movement to its success, and resulted in the blending of Indian Christian, American Pentecostal, and Hindu popular religiosity. This is also indicated by the fact that the non-Pentecostal, Evangelical missions in India have hardly played a noteworthy role and have even been displaced by Pentecostal missions in places.

Contextual Interfaces

The folk religiosity of Hindus and Indian Christians is phenomenologically related to American Pentecostal spirituality. Insofar as the latter already implies a

19. Martin 1990: 282; see also Martin 2002.
20. See Synan 1971: 76-78; MacRobert 1992; Hollenweger 1993: 267f.
21. Spittler 1994: 108.
22. Johns 1995: 7; see also Wacker 1993.
23. See Robeck 1990; Ellington 1996: 16-38.

response to modernity, it is of particular interest for the Indian side. The missionary strength of the south Indian Pentecostal movement is thus to be understood from two angles. First, it is connected to a lived popular spirituality. Its orientation to experience and its ecstatic elements have much correspondence with the Indian context. Its theological views are to a large extent shared orally, they are communicated less through books than in Bible hours, prayer meetings, and conventions. Secondly, the Pentecostal movement incorporates a very modern variant of the Christian witness. This already finds expression in the fact that the western origin and international relations are often strongly emphasized. One leader of the South Indian Assemblies of God, for example, in an interview expressly emphasized the attraction that the American origin of his church exercised on many Indians. A similar point is to be made about the numerous western guest preachers. They are not, it seems, an irritating foreign body but make an important contribution to missionary success, because they indicate that Pentecostal spirituality is firmly set in western culture and so might serve as a gateway to the scientific-technical age with western culture as its guarantor. In the Pentecostal movement, then, there is a connection between the old piety and new western modernity. This results in certain tendencies to westernizing worship and community life which we can observe especially but not only in congregations dominated by English-speaking and western-oriented elites.

The observation that certain beliefs and practices of the south Indian Pentecostal movement have parallels both in Indian folk religion and in American Pentecostalism is a difficulty the following descriptions have to wrestle with. As a result, it is not easy to identify typical Indian elements, despite the many parallels to the Indian context. However, as will be shown, miracle healing and exorcisms, but also holiness, have distinct expressions in the Indian context.

CHAPTER 8

Themes

In an analysis of south Indian Pentecostal spirituality certain leitmotifs can be identified as being of decisive importance in the whole of religious practice. They form a frame in which Pentecostal spirituality moves. Religious experience, prayer, and blessings are surely the themes that contribute in no small way to the attractiveness of Pentecostal spirituality. Intense expectation of the return of Christ is commonly regarded as another central theme in Pentecostal spirituality. However, at least in the south Indian Pentecostal movement in the 1990s, this expectation remained rather theoretical and was neutralized by a strong this-worldliness.

Religious Experience

The experiential spirituality of Pentecostalism, also in south India, stands out most evidently in the phenomenon of tongues, which is closely connected with the baptism in the Spirit and will be discussed in the following chapter. However, direct experience is not limited to speaking in tongues, but God also regularly imparts Himself in direct manner to believers with visions, dreams, and prophecy. Such manifestations of God are largely found in testimonies concerning key religious occurrences such as conversion, Spirit baptism, or call to ministry.[1] Visions, dreams, and prophecies are also strongly confirmed constituents of Pentecostal everyday religion. In this, three aspects are of special interest. First, unmediated experience plays an important role in the life of many laypeople.

---

1. On the role of visions in connection with the call to full-time ministry see pp. 194ff.

Secondly, through such experiences pastors and evangelists often claim legitimacy. Finally, modes of experience have been largely formalized. The first aspect, the unmediated experience of God by many congregational members, is closely related to the active participation of laypeople in worship life. The intensity of this lay participation is evident in the internal Pentecostal criticism that warns not to overemphasize this element. A good example is the following statement by an independent Pentecostal pastor from Andhra Pradesh:

> I tell them: "Don't get carried away with the visions and dreams." . . . that is *the* major thing in any [worship] service in some places. For everything, they relate it to the dream they have, they relate it to the prophecy they have . . . they relate it to the vision they have. . . . If you get carried away, yes, it is wrong. It is wrong. You can't just get carried away by that. You can't be washed away by those dreams. Not that I have no experience of receiving dreams and visions and prophecies. Yes, I did, and I still do. Not only me, but the church folks still do. But don't [make too] major dreams and visions and prophecies.[2]

With regard to the second aspect, it is notable that pastors and evangelists claim especially intense experiences of God. This may be some quite spontaneous inspiration suddenly coming upon them, as in the following report of an evangelist who anticipated a dreadful marriage drama through a direct order from God:

> One day, one o'clock in the night, God told me: "Go and ring a number." . . . So, I simply took that number. . . . At that particular moment, husband and wife were fighting, they wanted to kill each other.[3]

Even with regard to theological doctrines spiritual leaders may claim to have received a direct revelation from God. A Tamil pastor reports:

> So, I decided, myself, to follow the word of God. I took fasting for forty days, and, learnt the word of God from the voice of God. I studied the Bible, I never went to the Bible college. I studied the Bible and took notes from that. I heard some voice from above in my prayer room, that is asking me, teaching me, and revealing me the thoughts from the Bible. . . . In this way, I studied the Bible.[4]

2. Interview.
3. Interview.
4. Interview.

It is not uncommon for the content of preaching to be attributed to direct inspiration by God. Thus, an evangelist from Madras fasts before every meeting to obtain God's direct guidance for his sermon:

The Holy Spirit tells me what message I have to speak: what message, what the problems within the church, what the problems of those who come. . . . A lot of people they are coming for the crusade. So [I ask God:] what message I have to speak among them, tell me. . . . I am very particular about the leading of the Holy Spirit. Not only during preaching time, not only during praying time, even when we are walking and traveling, all the time, I believe, can the Lord speak in unknown tongues through the Holy Spirit. So I believe, I am fully confident about this anointing. So, every Wednesday, we are fasting for the next crusade. Then the Lord speaks to me: "You should speak about this."[5]

The claim to gain important revelations directly from God that is apparent in these examples is related to almost all circumstances. A Tamil pastor who was seeking sponsors for students in his Bible school reported the following experience:

[O]ne night, God told me: "Rise up and write!" I rose from my bed and wrote. I thought: "The letter is to whom?" I had one friend. I remembered the name and address. . . . He is a believer, a member, he is not a pastor, or anything. So, I wrote him: "This is the time, 12:30 a.m., in the midnight, I am writing this letter because somebody has asked me to rise up and write. . . . We are conducting the Bible school. . . ." In those days we had fifteen students. "So, you please pray for this school, I do not know what God is going to tell you." In this way, I wrote a letter and sent it. He sent a reply: "On the time you were awake, God told me to take care of fifteen students of India to train them for the ministry."[6]

From the reports, one cannot avoid the impression that the experience of God is presented in a very formal way. This brings out the third important aspect with regard to religious experience. D. G. S. Dhinakaran, for instance, claims direct instruction from God for all the projects undertaken by Jesus Calls, but the instructions come in stereotyped form and with all the clarity one could wish for, as the following typical example shows:

5. Interview.
6. Interview.

At 4 o'clock in the morning of 25th July 1985 the presence of Jesus filled my room. He said: "My son, I am in great agony when I see how children and youngsters below 25 years of age go astray. I want you to enrol them in a Young Partners' Plan and pray for them tearfully each day. I shall take them into my safe keeping, bless their studies, keep them above want and ensure for them a blessed future."[7]

This formal justification of decisions as the unquestionable will of God is characteristic for large part of the south Indian Pentecostal movement. Conclusions reached were often supported by "God has told me" or similar expressions. In this way the Pentecostal concern to be led by the Spirit can become a formalized ritual or even a caricature of religious experience. Any human behavior may be so spiritualized and withdrawn from rational critique that even conflict and scandal is masked by the formula "God has told me this." Thus, for instance, a pastor who had to leave his congregation after a legal dispute with the elders was able to justify his departure with a divine command: "God spoke to me that my ministry is over there and that I must leave that place and go and start my own independent faith ministry." Apparently the claim of an unmediated experience of God in certain cases represents hardly more than a conventional expression. The stereotyped usage "God has told me" is indeed a reflection of the desire to follow God's will in everything, but, semantically, it is often a synonym for "I have made up my mind." How this is to be distinguished from genuine expressions of experience is still an unsolved problem in the Pentecostal movement.[8]

Prayer and Blessing

Prayer and blessing are a further central theme in everyday Pentecostal spirituality, although here no fundamental distinction can be made between Pentecostals and Christians in the established Indian churches. The particularity of the Pentecostal spirituality lies more in the intensity and high expectations of the real power of prayer. Pentecostals feel that, by the virtue of the Holy Spirit as manifested in Spirit baptism and the gifts of the Spirit, prayer also gains a new dimension full of power. The more spectacular claims on the power of prayer are found in miracles and exorcism, which we deal with else-

---

7. Dhinakaran 1987: 23-24.

8. Here we are concerned with a universal problem for Pentecostal theology; see Stephen E. Parker 1996.

where.[9] In their normal daily life, prayer serves believers as protection and blessing. A Tamil evangelist, for example, writes on the necessity of morning prayer:

> We need God's grace for our survival every day. The devil attacks us in different ways. . . . Cleanse yourself in the blood of Jesus every morning. You shall remain holy throughout the day. Begin the day with Jesus and you will close the day with Jesus. We are in the battlefield always. The spirits fight against us. It is essential that we seek His protection every morning.[10]

Pentecostal Christians assure themselves in nearly all living relationships with the protective power of God in prayer. Hence great importance is attributed to intercession by other fellow Christians. The numerous house prayer groups and congregational prayer meetings, which form part of everyday activity in all the congregations, are above all services of intercession. Much sought after is the intercession of pastors and evangelists, since special power of blessing is attributed to their prayers, and it is customary, on any given occasion, to seek their personal intercession. For example, a student before handing in her dissertation took it to an evangelist so that he could pray over it; also a member of the congregation late one evening sought her pastor to pray so that she would have a good start in her new employment the next day. The pastor's visits and the intercessory prayer associated with it are also treated as an especially effective blessing. Belief in the power of blessing attributed to intercession through charismatically distinguished persons explains the popularity of the Young Partners' Plan in Jesus Calls. Parents are offered to register their children as "young partners" against a certain contribution. For these children, then, there will special prayers. A leaflet reads:

> Their photographs, along with their bio-data shall be placed in the "Prayer Tower" and intercession on their behalf shall be made continuously before the throne of our Lord round the clock. Added to this Bro. D. G. S. Dhinakaran and Dr. Paul Dhinakaran will pray for each Partner every day. The Prayer will be three-fold: 1. That the holy hands of the Lord Jesus Christ may rest upon, bless and protect each Partner from evils of this world. 2. That the Lord may undertake complete responsibility for the Young Partner's education and grant the Partner the re-

9. See pp. 155ff.
10. Francis 1990: 65.

quired wisdom, knowledge and a retentive memory. 3. That the Lord may grant the Partner, a life free from poverty and disease, so that the life of the Partner may ever be bright and prosperous. The Lord has also commanded Bro. Dhinakaran to meet these Partners at least once in their life time personally and to pray for them. They can also write about their life's problems for which Bro. Dhinakaran and Dr. Paul Dhinakaran will offer counsel and pray with a great burden.[11]

This "Young Partners' Plan" well illustrates how concrete the connection between prayer and blessing is seen to be. Concerning prayer, there are other practices that are seen as bestowing blessing. This is especially the case with tithes and with participation in the Lord's Supper. But much more than this is entrusted to prayer. Even political events can be influenced by intensive intercession. For instance, the author was assured by several pastors and evangelists that prayer by Indian Pentecostals played a considerable part in the fall of the Berlin wall. In many Pentecostal churches concrete political issues are brought into the intercessions, but this is on condition that they concern the lives of Christians or could be favorable to revival in India. Intercession about general social and political grievances does not occur. Trust in the power of prayer can in extreme cases lead to all active participation in social affairs being explicitly renounced and, in its place, social and political change being sought by prayer alone. Zac Poonen is one of the few who take this attitude to its ultimate consequences. He said of himself, "I never voted in my life. I vote in the prayer meeting."[12] He is quoted in a Christian periodical in the following terms:

A few years back the so-called Freedom of Religion Bill [i.e., a law restricting the change of religion] passed in Parliament and caused an uproar among Christians in the country. But while many Christians were busy taking out processions, holding public meetings, presenting memorandums, dashing off letters to newspapers etc., others, like Mr Zac Poonen's fellowship in the city reacted in a different way. They prayed. And as Mr Poonen justifiably says, "I believe it was the result of God stopping it from heaven. I don't believe it was the result of processions."[13]

11. Leaflet of Jesus Calls International Ministry, Madras, ca. 1992.
12. Interview.
13. *The Forerunner*, Bangalore, vol. 1, no. 4 (1982). The factual correctness of this news report was confirmed to the author by Zac Poonen.

This extreme example shows how far Pentecostal spirituality can go in its reliance on prayer. In general, the reluctance to engage in politics is based on "holiness" ideas.[14] The examples presented here show that Pentecostal understanding of prayer also plays its part.

End-Time Expectations

Intense eschatological expectation is abundantly found in theoretical teaching but, at least to the observation of the author, scarcely in lived experience.[15] In their eschatological conceptions, south Indian Pentecostals follow the prevailing dispensationalist teaching such as premillennialism and pretribulationism.[16] Particularly influential are the writings of Clarence Larkin, whose books are even available in Tamil translation. In the numerous publications and in the frequent preaching on eschatological themes, two points are heavily emphasized.[17] On the one hand, the events that will be set in train by the return of Christ and the rapture of the faithful are elaborated in detail; on the other hand, the present condition of the world is investigated to see how far prophecies of the end-time are being fulfilled so as to indicate the imminent coming of Christ. This encourages wide-ranging intellectual speculation.[18] However, the question of the timing of the Second Coming is answered with reservations. Job Gnanaprakasam, for example, writes: "The time of His coming is unknown to anyone except God the father (Mark 13:32). We are not date setters. Many date setters have failed in their calculations and many were deceived."[19] In many interviews, the author received answers such as the following: "He will come soon. No doubt about it. Whether we are then alive or not makes no difference."[20] In general, we should be cautious in understanding south Indian Pentecostalism as consolation for eternity. The the-

14. See p. 190.

15. On eschatology in the Pentecostal movement in general see Land 1993; Dempster 1993: 51-64; Horton 1995: 597ff.

16. On the problem of dispensational eschatology taking over the Pentecostal movement, see Sheppard 1984: 5-33.

17. See e.g., Abraham 1976; Ratnasingam 1985; Geevargheese 1987; Stanley 1988; Gnanaprakasam 1987/1993; Gnanaprakasam 1990.

18. So, for example, in 1994 in the headquarters of an independent Tamil Pentecostal church, the author witnessed a vigorous discussion of press reports on the ultra-nationalist Russian leader Zhirinovsky, concerning his Jewish provenance. It was thought he could possibly be the Antichrist.

19. Gnanaprakasam 1993: 70.

20. Interview.

oretically cherished belief in the imminent return of Christ is to a large extent without practical significance for Pentecostal spirituality. It should be set against the intense practice of prayer described above, through which God's blessing is sought in daily life and which gives evidence of a strong this-worldliness.

CHAPTER 9

Ordo Salutis

Pentecostal teaching usually contains some kind of an order of salvation. It comprises mostly two stages (conversion and baptism in the Spirit), but there are also churches that allow for three stages (conversion, sanctification, and baptism in the Spirit). In the USA, there was much controversy in the early years of Pentecostalism about the difference between two and three stages;[1] later the two-stage way to salvation became the majority view.[2] The south Indian Pentecostals in general hold to a two-stage ordo salutis, comprising conversion and baptism in the Spirit; sanctification is only rarely viewed as a distinct stage, and there is substantial agreement that only conversion is really necessary for salvation.

Conversion

The conception of conversion follows in principle evangelical teaching according to which conviction of sin and individual experience of rebirth are essential. The awareness of sin is often articulated in testimonies as descriptions of the sinful life before conversion. However, this is mostly a matter of a very restricted register of sins: special mention is made of smoking, drinking, visits to the cinema, and similar habits. Another frequent motif is the intention of

---

1. On the history of the ordo salutis and its contents, see Robert Mapes Anderson 1979: 153-75; Schmieder 1982: 142-236, 309-58; Fee 1985; Leggett 1989: 113-22; Faupel 1996: 229-70.

2. The main representative of the three-stage teaching is the Church of God, and of the two-stage teaching the Assemblies of God.

committing suicide, which is prevented by conversion.[3] Only in a very few cases was the author informed of a really rowdy life before conversion. In most cases the informants had some difficulty in naming serious sins, as the following example illustrates:

> And, the Lord showed me my sins. I have not tasted the cigarette, I did not taste the alcohol, but, because I was working in the factory with the uneducated people, the vulgar verses will come out of my mouth. They will ask: "You are a Christian, how can you speak the vulgar words?" . . . In Ephesians 4:29 it says: "Do not speak any vulgar. Speak the word, that will edify others." My sins are mentioned in the scripture. The Lord showed me this. So, I confessed my sin, and accepted Jesus.[4]

As is usual among Evangelicals, south Indian Pentecostals are able to date their conversion experience precisely, and an altar call at evangelical rallies is often the occasion reported. The Pentecostal emphasis on experiencing God is reflected in accounts of conversion. Often they tell of special visions accompanying the experience of rebirth:

> Then, I saw, one light was coming toward me. . . . That light came into my room. . . . Such a big light, a fluorescent light. In that light, in that vision only, I saw a man was hanging on the cross. And, I was looking, and I was so surprised, and I was afraid to see. I heard the voice from the cross: "My son, my son. I am Jesus. I am the power that you have been seeking." I was so afraid, and I fell on the floor, and I was rolling on the floor like a baby. I cried: "Help me, help me, help me!" But, no one was there to help me. But this mighty voice, this voice was ringing in my ear: "I am Jesus." . . . Then, I opened my eyes, no one was there, but the voice was ringing. The sound was ringing in my ears. Then, I got up, and then, I knelt down, and that was the first time in my life to kneel down before God. And, I confessed all my sins, the holy Spirit did help me to confess. . . . Then, I asked God: "Come into my heart!" Then, immediately, my heart was so happy.[5]

The experience of rebirth effects a real and outwardly visible transformation in people. It is often related that the born-again Christians devote them-

---

3. Suicide is also an important topic in the conversion narrative of Sadhu Sundar Singh (see Biehl 1990: 139-43).

4. Interview.

5. Interview.

selves to regular Bible reading right away. Already connected with the conversion is the first turning away from sins. Suddenly cigárettes lose their attraction, there is an aversion to alcohol, or the use of vulgar expressions ceases, as in the following example:

> The next morning [after my conversion] I went to the office. I am a very big joker, and I just told filthy words so that people laugh. The next day I was in the office, it didn't come. And, some of the fellows were waiting for me to start. They found nothing coming from me, they asked: "Are you sick?" Then, I thought: "Well that is the first day, I am not sick."[6]

Christian rebirth must be publicly attested by immersion baptism. In general, infant baptism is not awarded the slightest validity. In any case, most south Indian Pentecostals treat baptism as merely an outward sign of inner change.[7] Only the Ceylon Pentecostal Mission and churches close to it teach a sacramental saving work in baptism itself.[8] The actual baptismal practice will be dealt with elsewhere.[9]

Baptism in the Spirit

The Pentecostals in south India generally agree with the western Pentecostal movement in their views on baptism in the Spirit.[10] Spirit baptism is not seen as necessary for salvation, except in the Ceylon Pentecostal Mission and related churches.[11] It may follow conversion at any point in time and does not presuppose baptism by immersion. However, it should be observed that a large proportion of Pentecostals have no experience of baptism in the Spirit, even if reliable statistics are difficult to obtain.[12] On the other hand, there are even cases where children of leading pastors have received the Spirit baptism at the age of seven or under, before receiving water baptism. Very widespread

---

6. Interview.

7. See e.g., Assemblies of God 1994: 5; Easow 1991: 60; Poonen 1990: 27-31. This is also the majority opinion among all Pentecostals (see Dusing 1995: 559).

8. See The Pentecostal Mission 1987b: 26-31.

9. See pp. 223-24.

10. On this understanding see Lederle 1988; Wyckoff 1995; Bush 1992: 24-41.

11. See Easow 1991: 77-79.

12. The South India Assemblies of God are the only churches to give figures. According to statistics for the year 1993, about 40 percent of their members have experienced baptism in the Spirit.

are special prayer meetings, called tarrying meetings, which are dedicated to the prayer for Spirit baptism. Such meetings are regularly offered in some congregations. A pastor from Madras describes how he received the baptism in such a meeting:

> [T]here was a meeting specifically for receiving the Holy Spirit. So, I was sitting there, actually watching: "What are these people doing?" . . . Of course, there was a lot of shouting and other things going on. So, I was a little bit, probably annoyed. And, then, I was rather a spectator to look what was going on. Immediately, that pastor came close to me and said: "S., please close your eyes!" . . . Then, I closed my eyes. Then, just I noticed the filling with the Holy Spirit. And something happened, and, I do not know, for the next couple of hours I was full of the Holy Spirit and I was speaking in tongues, jumping and I received real joy of my life.[13]

It is widespread practice for a pastor or evangelist to lay hands on someone and pray for the person to receive the Holy Spirit. Certain pastors and evangelists are seen as specially capable of dispensing Spirit baptism by laying on of hands. An evangelist of Andhra Pradesh relates how the gift of leading people to the baptism was conferred on him when the whole congregation to which he belonged laid hands on him. This was promised him through a prophetess:

> She was prophesying in a meeting, and she came and laid her hands on me and said as prophecy: "I am going to use you, as I used Paul . . . and, whomever you lay hands on, they will be filled with the Holy Spirit." That is what she said. So, I took this as a challenge and as a great promise of the Lord, and, I submitted myself to the prophecy to be fulfilled in my life. . . . So, I was praising the Lord in tongues, and suddenly, I was moving on my knees from my position, and I didn't know where I was going. Suddenly, I went to one person, and I was laying my hands on him. Immediately that fellow fell down, and he started praising God in tongues. That was the day, he was filled with the Holy Spirit. . . . So, this continued for several years, till all the members in our fellowship came into this experience.[14]

13. Interview.
14. Interview.

Baptism in the Spirit can also occur in private prayer; its reception is not bound up with public meetings. In such cases it is often said to be accompanied by extraordinary phenomena. N. Jeevanandam (Dr. J.), in his detailed life testimony, relates how he received baptism in the Spirit:

> There was no one to guide Dr. J. properly, but he sincerely prayed for the Holy Spirit. Dr. J. always used to pray every day in the morning from 3:30 to 9:30. After a month, one morning, as Dr. J. was crying for the anointing of the Holy Spirit, a bright light focussed on his mouth, he then felt that he was eating butter mixed with sugar, it was very tasty. Dr. J. couldn't stop eating, more than three hours passed, his whole body was sweating. Dr. J. spoke in new tongues as the Spirit of God was anointing him. Someone knocked at Dr. J.['s] door, he got up and opened the door with shivering hands, his whole body was shaking. Dr. J. couldn't speak even one word to them in his mother tongue.[15]

The great majority of the south Indian Pentecostal movement holds to the position that tongues should be seen as initial evidence for baptism in the Spirit.[16] Even among churches calling themselves Charismatic, the author has not yet encountered anyone taking the position that there can be a separation between baptism in the Spirit and tongues as initial evidence. Nevertheless, a prominent Pentecostal leader in an interview expressly explained that, in his opinion, Spirit baptism can take place without speaking in tongues. He qualified this as follows:

> Baptism in the Holy Spirit means not necessarily speaking in tongues. Without speaking in tongues a believer can be baptised by the Holy Spirit. . . . I used to say to them: "As you are baptized with the Holy Spirit, God has given you the ability to speak in tongues, but you are not using it. You can use it." When they understand, then they begin to pray and then they use to speak in tongues.[17]

15. Jeevanandam ca. 1993: 14.

16. On tongues understood as initial evidence in Pentecostal theology, see McGee 1991.

17. Interview. See also the opinion of a pastor of the Indian Pentecostal Church in Bombay who is not known to the author, who writes: "Though there are three clear cases in the book of 'Acts' where Spirit-baptism was accompanied by 'speaking in tongues,' there are umpteen cases where this 'sign' did not accompany Spirit-baptism. . . . Let us therefore understand that the gift of tongues is not the only sign of either Spirit-baptism or Spirit-filling" (Koshy 1989: 92f.). The relevance of this statement is hard to assess.

In south Indian Pentecostalism, the gift of tongues is taken principally as a personal, experientially directed practice of prayer. It is more a stammering praise than a distinct recognizable speech in a foreign language, even if this claim is formally made on the Pentecostal side. This kind of prayer has its special place in worship when believers in an emotion-laden, ecstatic atmosphere pray in tongues individually and simultaneously.[18] This use in worship is justified biblically as follows:[19]

> Paul says about "Prayer in the Spirit" (1 Cor. 14:15). By "Prayer in the Spirit" he means "Prayer in tongues." Nobody can, therefore, understand what such a person (the speaker in tongues) speaks though he may speak great mysteries with God (14:2). In the church, however, he is to speak "silently" to himself and to God if his tongues are not interpreted (14:28). "Silently" means without disturbance to others or to the general procedure of the church. Paul says such a speaker in tongues edifies himself (14:4). Hence, nobody should forbid him (14:39). Paul was often a speaker in tongues, for which he thanked God (14:18). . . . he permitted the speaker in tongues in the Church to speak silently to himself and to God, when there is no interpreter for him (14:28).[20]

Besides the use of tongues for praise in worship, they are used by pastors and evangelists when they pray for someone for God's blessing or when they are practicing healing or exorcism. A pastor will pray for the congregation alternately in tongues and in normal speech, which may sometimes be understood as an interpretation of his own tongues speech. But most would criticize this on the ground that the gift of interpretation should be practiced by a person different from the tongues speaker. This form of the gift of interpretation is rarely used in south Indian worship. After receiving the gifts of Spirit baptism and speaking in tongues, believers can receive further gifts, which will be treated below.

---

18. See also p. 220.

19. The question to what extent Indian Pentecostals practice tongues-speaking when alone needs further investigation. Findings by Sundara Rao (1990: 44) suggest that this is not necessarily the case.

20. Easow 1991: 75-77. See also The Pentecostal Mission 1987a: 36-37.

Sanctification

As was mentioned above, the south Indian Pentecostal movement generally represents a two-stage ordo salutis. Accordingly, sanctification is hardly ever seen as a second experience, distinct from conversion. In general, one cannot escape the impression that the question much discussed in America and Europe, whether the two-stage or the three-stage way of salvation is right, plays no role in south India. At all events, no open controversy is reported. Naturally, the Indian branch of the Church of God, in their statutes, publish a confession of faith exactly as it was expressed by the American mother church,[21] but in many interviews and conversations, the author never came across any cases of Church of God members justifying their distinctiveness as against other Pentecostal churches with a three-stage way of salvation. This is all the more remarkable in that the Church of God in Tamil Nadu and in Kerala expressly stands for ethical rigorism. It should be noted in this connection that Robert F. Cook, before he founded the Church of God in India, worked as a missionary for the two-stage Assemblies of God. Moreover, a glance at confessions of faith of south Indian independent churches, as they appear in constitutions and in periodicals, reveals that they do indeed have a passage on sanctification but never mention a three-stage way of salvation.[22] Also all the written theological statements of south Indian Pentecostals known to the author without exception agree that sanctification begins with the Christian new birth and has the character of a process.[23] The two following quotations can be taken as representative of the majority opinion. The first comes from a catechism that a teacher in the Southern Asian Bible College composed for a congregation of the Assemblies of God in Bangalore:

> Holiness is the outstanding mark of God's moral character, and the Holy Spirit works in our lives to free us from the power of sin and to make us pure like Jesus (Ex. 15:11; Heb. 10:14; Rom. 12:1). Some believe in "instant" and complete sanctification [as, for example, representatives of the three-stage order teaching], but the New Testament seems to indicate that sanctification, is a process. While sin should no longer be the master of a Spirit-filled believer, we never come to a point in the Chris-

21. Church of God 1976: 1-2. An identical Declaration of Faith published by the mother church is reprinted in Hollenweger 1988: 517.

22. See The Pentecostal Mission 1984, The Voice of Pentecost, Feb. 1994: 15-16, Indian Pentecostal Church 1991, Apostolic Christian Assembly 1957.

23. See Poonen n.d.: 4-5; Easow 1991: 48; The Pentecostal Mission ca. 1985: 5; Apostolic Christian Assembly n.d.: 28-32.

tian life when we can say that we have reached sinless perfection (Rom. 8:2-6; 1 John 1:8; 1 Thess. 4:3-7).[24]

The second quotation is taken from a short presentation of Pentecostal theology by an author close to the Indian Pentecostal Church in Kerala:

> The word sanctify (Gk. hagiazo) means to make holy. From the time of our repentance and adoption the Holy Spirit undertakes a work of sanctification in us (Rom. 15:16; 2 Thess. 2:13 & 1 Pet. 1:2). It is a gradual process by which we become more and more Christ-like. God demands us to be holy, for He is holy (Lev. 19:2). While Justification implies deliverance from the penalty of sin, Sanctification implies deliverance from the pollutions and potency of sin.[25]

It is the very pragmatic approach to theological questions within the south Indian Pentecostal movement that prevents the laying down of dogmatic statements on sanctification in the framework of an ordo salutis. The author received the following typical answer from a prominent leader of an independent church in Kerala:

> It [sanctification] is a progressing [thing]. Doctrinally, it is progressing. But, in practice, we should emphasize it as finished work. Entire sanctification. . . . Perfection, all those things, we emphasize. But, also at the same time, it is progressive because man has to grow [spiritually].[26]

This position indicates that the idea of holiness, even if not distinctly placed in an ordo salutis, is something highly valued. Important impulses to ethical behavior follow from it.

---

24. Satyavrata ca. 1994: 30-31.
25. Easow 1991: 48.
26. Interview.

CHAPTER 10

Gifts of the Spirit

The view, widespread among Pentecostals and Charismatics, that according to 1 Corinthians 12:8-10 there are nine distinguishable gifts of the Spirit, is also held by the majority of the south Indian Pentecostals.[1] But in practice, special consideration is only given to five of these gifts.[2] These are: 1.-2. the gift of tongues-speaking together with the gift of its interpretation as was already discussed in connection with baptism of the Spirit; 3. healing; 4.-5. prophecy with the word of knowledge as a special case.[3]

Healing

Healing is one of the most important themes in the south Indian Pentecostal movement. The underlying etiology differs considerably from the traditional understanding of western medicine and requires special consideration. A further distinction is necessary between miracle healing (and exorcism) for all people and divine healing for born-again Christians. It is especially to miracle

---

1. The gifts, in particular, are 1. Word of knowledge, 2. Word of wisdom, 3. Discernment of spirits, 4. Faith, 5. Healing, 6. Working of miracles, 7. Prophecy, 8. Various kinds of speech (tongues), and 9. Interpretation of tongues (see Horton 1976: 31-32). Many Pentecostal-Charismatic descriptions favor a more comprehensive understanding of gifts of the Spirit (see Grossmann 1990; Lim 1995).

2. You won't find a devotional practice regarding the "word of knowledge," the "word of wisdom," the "discernment of spirits," and "working of miracles" comparable to that of the other gifts. However, regarding discernment of spirits see also p. 151.

3. See also Martin 1990: 529.

healing and to exorcism that the south Indian Pentecostal movement owes a great part of its appeal. This is probably also the reason why it has such a close connection with Hindu and Indian Christian popular religiosity.

Causes of Disease and Misfortune

The etiology of the south Indian Pentecostal movement is characteristically determined by the demonology of Hindu and Indian Christian folk religiosity. The consequence of this is that illness and misfortune are attributed to the same causes and that traditional western diagnostics will only be partially used.[4] The causes of sickness and misfortune are treated in close connection with sin, so that the associated themes are influenced by the demonological basis of the etiology. A special case of this is the model of divine punishment by sickness brought in to explain certain testing situations for believers, seeing in illness a particular warning from God. The belief in the existence and activities of evil spirits, as well as the possibility of recourse to black magic through their agency, is widespread in south India among Christians of all confessions. But we hardly ever find such ideas among pastors and theologians of established Protestant churches who have been educated in theological colleges. Also, among Hindus in comparable levels of society such ideas are less pronounced or else completely rejected. However, reliable data in this matter are hardly available since definite answers are hard to get. Within the south Indian Pentecostal movement the existence of evil spirits is uncontested, and exorcism is an essential part of pastoral and evangelistic practice. But it is noteworthy that we rarely get independent statements about the nature and appearance of evil spirits: rather, it becomes clear from the usual practice of exorcism by south Indian Pentecostals that they have taken over the demonology of Hindu popular religiosity. The British anthropologist Lionel Caplan has made express reference to this.[5] It is not at all the case that the whole of Hindu religion is taken as demonic by the Pentecostals, but rather there is clear distinction made between evil spirits and the world of Hindu gods.[6] This approach is also that of the Bible translations. As already

---

4. There has been little research so far on the cultural dependency of diagnoses (see Sich et al. 1993).

5. Caplan 1989: 32-71.

6. See, however, Caplan 1989: 65. Caplan indicates that many Pentecostal healers admit the possibility that one of the higher gods, as for example Murugan or Ganesh, could on occasion possess people like evil spirits. But, as far as the author knows, in the overwhelming majority of cases, exorcism is concerned with evil spirits.

mentioned, evil spirits in Tamil are usually rendered as pēy or picācu In the commonly used Tamil Bible translation, picācu (occasionally pēy) is used for "demon" (Greek daimónion) as also for "devil" (Greek "diábolos"), but "Satan" is used as a loan word.[7] With this, the translators have theologically anchored the evil spirits of popular Hinduism in the Christian conception of "devil," since pēy and picācu become underlings to Satan.[8] Precisely this position is taken by the south Indian Pentecostal movement. In their views on the origin of evil spirits, then, many south Indian Pentecostals agree with the conceptions of popular Hinduism. Only a few interviewees took the position that they were fallen angels. They rather presumed, in common with the Hindu view, that it was a matter of those deceased persons who had died a bad death, that is, a premature or unlucky death.[9] Evil spirits can be responsible for all conceivable sicknesses, calamities, and misfortunes. In such a conceptual framework, bodily illnesses are only one among many possibilities in which possession by spirits can be realized. For example, possession can be the cause of marital problems, as in the following testimony from an evangelical rally of Jesus Calls:

I was convulsed very much in the clutches of the devil for the past four months. I used to beat and drive my husband out of the house. Today my elder brother brought me here. During Brother Dhinakaran's prayer, the devil departed from me. I am now very happy.[10]

Illnesses, interpersonal conflict, personal misfortune, failure in family life or in profession, etc. all fall in one and the same category insofar as they are attributed to possession and black magic. Evil spirits who visit whole families through black magic are capable of completely ruining them. A pastor from Madras related the following case of a Hindu family obsessed by black magic:

The owner of this house is a Hindu man. He was affected by witchcraft. He lost his third daughter. He lost one daughter. Then, he lost his second daughter. So, two sons. One son is insane, mental disorder. . . . So, he was completely affected. One by one the children were collapsing. At

7. See Asirvatham 1994: 467f., 505f. It should be noted in this connection that in the revision, the so-called Revised Version, picācu is almost everywhere replaced by pēy. Also the Catholic Tamil Bible (TNBCLC 3rd edition 1986) has pēy throughout. See also Bergunder 2002a.
8. Mark 3:22-27 and parallels.
9. Caplan 1989: 54f.
10. Jesus Calls, Apr. 1995: 30.

that time, one doctor, who used to attend our worship, he said: "Pastor, there is a family who is coming [in my practice] for treatment. I gave lot of treatment, nothing has happened. Why not you go and visit?" At the time they had kept their house locked up for seven years. Because there was some devil, witchcraft going on. So, they were staying far away, around forty miles away from city. They were staying in a separate house. Then, at the time, they were in the hands of a Hindu magician, a Mantiravāti. . . . Totally, they were committed to him, and they were well off. So, the Mantiravāti was getting a lot of money to help them. The Mantiravāti said that he will make them free, and that he will do this and that.[11]

As mentioned elsewhere, religious specialists like the Mantiravāti are twilight figures who perform exorcisms but also may offer black magic for payment. This double role of the Mantiravāti is recognized by the south Indian Pentecostals. So, on the Pentecostal side, it is often reported that it was a Mantiravāti who caused an illness or misfortune by black magic but, at the same time, the Mantiravāti is in competition with the Pentecostal exorcist. However, in the south Indian Pentecostal movement there is also general agreement that illnesses are caused by sins:[12]

Sickness is in the world because God has allowed sickness to enter the world as a curse on the disobedient human race. Exodus 4:11 states, "The Lord said to him, 'Who gave man his mouth? Who makes him blind? Is it not I the Lord?'" Sickness is in the world for people to experience the consequences of sin with which they are born.[13]

Here the causal connection between sin and illness is not abstract theological speculation but is understood in a quite concrete way: "Most of the sickness seen among people are the direct result of sin."[14] This conception stands in close connection with the demonology we have described; for each sin there is a different evil spirit. Ziegenbalg, in his research on popular Hinduism, finally after enumerating sixty-nine distinct pēys stated, "In summa, there are specifically just as many devils as there are sins."[15] Such a close rela-

---

11. Interview.
12. See, for instance, The Pentecostal Mission 1986; The Pentecostal Mission 1994; Apostolic Christian Assembly n.d.; Dhinakaran 1979; Job 1989 (Job is close to the Assemblies of God).
13. Job 1989: 37.
14. Job 1989: 36.

tionship between evil spirits and sins is quite consonant with the thinking in the Pentecostal movement and, in fact, there are lists that relate demons to particular sins.[16] On this demonological basis, accidents also are placed like sickness within the explanatory context of sin. It is also not unusual for the sins of ancestors to bear upon their descendants, as the following example shows:

> A sister once told me: "Sir, our home is a veritable place. All who see us say that we are very much blessed. But we do not get a square meal every day. However much the income may be, it vanishes without a trace." When I made enquiries about her forefathers I came to know that they had acquired all that wealth unlawfully by ruining many others.[17]

Such an extended chain of causality, establishing collective guilt, is also associated with the work of evil spirits. However, it is not in every case that the committing of a sin is explicitly related to the work of an evil spirit. In practice, also, natural causes for the onset of a disease will be unreservedly recognized without drawing theological consequences. For example, the most successful Indian healing evangelist gives the following explanation:

> There are countless such microscopic beings which are beneficial to us. There are again microscopic beings in their teeming millions which are injurious and produce disease. These bacteria and viruses bring harm to our bodies. When infection spreads due to the infestation of theses harmful bacteria, physicians inject healing drugs into our system to destroy them, and our bodies are restored to health. At this point some may naturally raise a doubt. The Bible says: "God is Love" (I John 4:8, 16). Why then did He create these harmful bacteria? Friend, it is indeed God who created the world and all its inhabitants. . . . Can you ask Him why? Can we plumb the depths of His great wisdom? . . . (Romans 11:33-36).[18]

Such an interpretation prevents the notion that every illness must be caused by some concrete sins; in its vagueness it is typical for low speculative interest in such questions. It is not so much the causation of sickness that arouses interest but rather the promise that Jesus, the healer, can cure all diseases and all suffer-

15. Ziegenbalg 1867: 186.
16. E.g., Gnaniah 1994: 50-57.
17. Dhinakaran 1979: 16.
18. Dhinakaran 1979: 5.

ing. In concrete cases, it so often remains unclear whether, for example, illness and misfortune derive from natural causes, evil spirits, or black magic. In some cases, they are not held to be connected with sins but are given natural explanations. There are cases of sickness and accidents that are attributed to concrete sins but not explicitly related to possession by evil spirits. Certain sins could also facilitate possession by evil spirits and so cause illness or misfortune without black magic playing any part in it. As Caplan observed, there is also in popular Hinduism the conception that evil spirits can visit people without any practice of black magic.[19] If black magic is suspected, this does not necessarily mean that the perpetrator will be sought out. All these differentiations may be found in practice. The determination of each case is a matter of judgment and often there are different diagnoses of one and the same case. In many cases, the gift of discerning the spirits will be referred to in this regard, as the following statement by a Tamil pastor and evangelist illustrates:

> Some sickness by Satan, some sickness due to ill physical power. . . . In the Charismatic movement there may be some people who think that every sickness is spiritual, but we have to find out, to discern what the problem is. When I'm dealing with sick people I'm always careful [and I ask]: "Is it a spiritual problem or a physical problem?"[20]

The majority opinion in the south Indian Pentecostal movement would support this kind of pragmatic and balanced approach. At the same time it is obvious that clear criteria for diagnoses are lacking, and the Pentecostal movement is always in danger of attributing everything to the activity of evil spirits.

Divine Punishment Through Sickness

In many testimonies, pastors and evangelists report that their devotion to full-time ministry was caused by an illness. "Divine punishment" is an established motive but it comes primarily from oral tradition. Only the writings of the Ceylon Pentecostal Mission go into this question and refer to particular texts in the Bible.[21] In the oral testimonies available to the author, two types

19. See Caplan 1989: 44.
20. Interview.
21. Texts given in The Pentecostal Mission (1994: 20-30) are: Numbers 12:1-15; 2 Samuel 12:15-19; 2 Kings 5:27; 2 Chronicles 16:12-13; 21:4, 13-20; 26:16-21; Daniel 4:30-37; Revelation 5:1-10; 12:20-23; 13:6-12; 1 Corinthians 5:5.

may be distinguished. In one type the sick person gives God the promise that in case of healing he will go into full-time ministry, as can be shown from two examples, the first coming from the leader of a big Tamil Pentecostal church and the other from a prominent Tamil evangelist:

[I]n 1964, I got another disease, that is hernia attack. For four days, I was suffering. . . . So, I was suffering a lot, but we had complete faith in the Lord's healing, that is faith healing. So, I was in the church . . . and the workers there, they prayed for me. Then, in the last day, I told the Lord: If He heals me, and gives me another time of life in this world, then I will give myself completely to His hands, and no one in the world will have any claim on my life. So, the Lord healed me instantly. On the fourth day, He healed me instantly.[22]

In the year 1968, I had a sickness called microstenosis in the heart. . . . When I went to the doctor he diagnosed that my valves were not functioning properly. The doctor said it was very serious. So, they sent me to a hospital in Madras. . . . They said I am going to live just four hours, it is very critical. In those days, I didn't receive the baptism of the Holy Spirit. But, still I had a faith that He is not only my saviour, He is my healer also. So, I said: "Lord, if You heal me, I will resign my job, and I will step out for the ministry." So, two hours passed, four hours passed. After six hours, the same doctor came and examined me and said: "Boy, not through the medicine but through the God whom you are worshipping, you are healed." So, they kept me for ten days under observation and then discharged me.[23]

In this type the stress is laid on free consecration to ministry, where one is apparently drawn by the hope that thereby God will be especially gracious and will send healing. This type, then, represents only a special case of the more general promise of consecration in case of illness and misfortune and is not so often reported.[24] More often pastors and evangelists report that God called them to full-time ministry and that they did not follow the call immediately since they shrank from the associated material insecurity. Subsequently they became ill and took this as a sign from God who was laying special emphasis on His call. In testimonies two respected pastors from Bangalore reported:

22. Interview.
23. Interview.
24. See also the consecration of children to full-time service, pp. 192-93.

152

So, I was hesitating to resign my job. I thought, I can earn and also do this ministry, but the Lord did never intend that. So, I felt sick, and, you know, I was in such a condition, that I did not get sleep, no other problem. I did not get sleep. Night and day, no sleep, even with sleeping pills. Then, I went to the hospital, got myself hospitalized. But they found nothing. Then, I thought, this is God. So, I knelt down, and committed my heart: "God, I serve You, please leave me alive. Whatever may happen, I will resign my job, and serve Thee full time." On the very day, instantaneously, God did a miracle, and healed me completely. I could sleep again.[25]

At the beginning of 1979 the Lord started to speak to me about my calling. Many times and strongly came the call: "Resign the job!" But, I did not because the family had a lot of financial problems. . . . But, anyhow, by September, God's dealing became heavier and heavier. And, September end I was in hospital, October sixth, being on the threshold of death, I made a decision, a covenant with the Lord: "I know that You call me, and I am running away from Your call like Jonah, but I will surrender my life now, and, I will not go back in any kind of trade or business, making money. I will serve You full time." When I made that decision on October sixth, the Lord healed me. The doctors kept me a few days more in the hospital just to make sure, that I am alright.[26]

Sickness as a form of punishment by God for disobedience is widely recognized. It results from prophecies calling particular people to full-time ministry. Here it is quite possible that a Pentecostal prophet may, in a case of disobedience, threaten an illness sent by God. In the following example such a prophecy was made when, after the sudden death of a leader, his son hesitated to give up his job and assume the leadership of an independent church. As soon as he decided for full-time ministry, he was healthy again:

So, what happened, one man, a prophet, he came and prophesied like this to my wife: "If your husband doesn't resign his job, and come for full time ministry, he will go through a very difficult time in his life." Within months, this happened in my life. I cannot sleep in the night, I cannot eat, I cannot stay in one place, and it became a very big problem. And I consulted the number one heart specialist in Madurai, because I

25. Interview.
26. Interview.

used to get chest pains, and I used to have a fear 24 hours a day, a nagging fear that I will die and this fear used to tell me that if I die I will go to hell also. . . . I hadn't baptism by the Holy Spirit then. On November 26th, the day when my dad started this ministry, there was a special meeting going on here. In that meeting another prophet came, and he was revealing all my problems. On this day I said: "God, I serve You." I resigned my job and come for full-time ministry.[27]

Besides this strongly stereotyped motivation, the conception of divine punishment can also play a role in other less clearly defined connections. For a pastor or evangelist in active healing ministry it can be a great advantage to have experienced a healing himself, as is explained for instance in a booklet by the Ceylon Pentecostal Mission: "Divine healing being preached by a servant of God who had been healed for the glory of God carries more weight, conviction and confidence in them that hear him, than it being preached by a man who never knows what divine healing is in his own personal experience."[28] In the same way, a Tamil healing evangelist is interpreting a disease he had suffered from:

Then, in 1969, I had a terrible sickness with my lungs. Both my lungs had gone. So, I was very rejected by my friends and depressed and whatever. So, one day, Jesus appeared, and said: "I love you. I want you to know . . . unless you go through sickness yourself, you will never know the agony of My people. Then only, you can really pray with compassion. So, this is the truth, you should know. Now, rise up. And you will carry My love and compassion."[29]

The theme of divine punishment is very extensive. As an explanation for sickness and bad luck it often goes along with the general view that sickness is a consequence of sin, bringing out the pedagogical aspect of divine punishment. An outstanding example of this combination is reported by D. G. S. Dhinakaran:

On the 1st day of April 1961, I lost my first child. My parents and all our relatives wept bitterly. I myself cried bitterly: "O Lord I am serving Thee. I am preaching Thy Gospel to hundreds. Why have you dealt with me

27. Interview.
28. The Pentecostal Mission 1994: 17.
29. Interview.

thus?" The Lord spoke to me in the depths of my being. I had a mistaken idea that the paths I was pursuing were the only right ones. I had mistaken impressions about God's anointed servants. I confessed this sin to God. He absolved me. In the years that followed He blessed me with two other children.[30]

Miracle Healing and Exorcism

It has already been said that Pentecostal etiology does not basically distinguish between sickness and unfortunate accidents and that there is no clarity concerning the place and extent of the activities of evil spirits. The consequence is that miracle healing and exorcism must be treated together. In the present study "miracle healing" will be used as a generic concept that can include exorcism while "exorcism" will be used in a specific sense. Strictly speaking, miracle healing should not happen to born-again Christians, since for these the promise of "divine healing" stands. But in practice the distinction is not clear, since born-again Christians often seek the prayers of pastors and evangelists with recognized gifts of healing. The practice of miracle healing as a rule consists of a prayer with the laying on of hands, often no more than the short sentence, "In the name of Jesus, be healed!" In addition, quite often the sick person is anointed with oil. Fasting in preparation for the prayer lends greater power. In big rallies, but less often in ordinary worship, the healing will be announced through prophetic gifts. In all this, the practices associated with prayer for healing are not spectacular. The case of exorcism is somewhat more complicated, and here elements from popular Hinduism are most influential. The Pentecostal exorcist and Hindu specialists like the Mantiravāti claim the same professional competence, as shown in the following testimony from an evangelistic rally of Jesus Calls:

> My husband drank too much and was breaking up the family. I used all my money on a Mantiravāti to bring him to his senses. There are no bounds to what I have suffered in the last 16 years. Will the Lord not bring a freeing to my husband? With this wish I came to the rally. As brother Paul Dhinakaran prayed for me, implored the Lord with tears. I was amazed to see Jesus with his crown of thorns close to me. He said to me: "Since you have truly sought me during your time of anxiety, I will change your husband's life." Then I had a good feeling in my heart. I

30. Dhinakaran 1979: 18-19.

came to believe that Jesus would change my husband. With that I was filled with a happiness I had never known.[31]

Between specialists like the Mantiravāti and Pentecostal exorcists there are striking phenomenological parallels. The former seeks to influence the world of evil spirits by means of an effective incantation, called a mantra; this influence can be greater or lesser according to his capability. The calling on Jesus, e.g., "In the name of Jesus, come out!" has certain external similarities to a mantra.

There is no lack of impressive phenomena associated with Pentecostal exorcism. Thus, a recognized exorcist, a well-known Tamil Pentecostal leader's wife, says that she requests a visible sign from the evil spirit that it has really gone out. Such a sign could be, for instance, that the branch of a tree breaks off of its own accord.[32] In popular Hinduism, when spirits are driven out they often pass into trees.[33] Furthermore, a person from whom an evil spirit has been expelled by calling on the name of Jesus with the laying on of hands often falls immediately to the ground in a kind of faint and then revives after a little while. This also has parallels in Hindu popular religiosity.[34] Apparitions are rarely objects of exorcism in the south Indian Pentecostal movement. A notable exception is found in impressive accounts of the expulsion of evil spirits from haunted houses. A prominent Tamil healing evangelist gives an example:

There was a house which was not sold for about five years. Frankly, they wanted to sell it. It was whitewashed, everything was beautiful, when we went inside. And, they said: "Please, pray uncle, that this house should be sold." With a glass of water, I prayed over it, I started sprinkling. When I came to the four corners, you won't believe, there were four [limes] on four corners which were covered in a white paper, and it was stuck over there. From outside, even the man who whitewashed it, did not notice it. So, once that was removed, the house was sold.[35]

If a sickness or misfortune is traced to black magic, then special exorcizing rituals contain the visible elimination of the presumed tools of sorcery. One who has been attacked by black magic would spit them out during exorcism.

31. *Iyēcu alaikkiṟār,* March 1995: 34.
32. Interview.
33. See Moffatt 1979: 244f.
34. See Caldwell 1869: 165; Moffatt 1979: 242.
35. Interview.

A Tamil evangelist related how she encountered this phenomenon for the first time:

> I saw in Kolhapur in Maharashtra, one particular person spew out that witchcraft medicine. Thick colour, jelly-like thing. The moment he spew out, he was cured. So far, even I couldn't believe in what pastors told me. But I saw it with my own eyes.[36]

The prominent leader of a Pentecostal Yesunamam church in Kerala bears witness that black magic was practiced on him by means of such sorcerer's medicine:

> I had a nervous problem on account of witchcraft. This spoiled my education. I was a good youth and studied well but these things happened just before leaving high school. Do you know why I believe it was witchcraft? As the pastor was praying for me, I felt something coming out of my stomach. It was a lemon, a big lemon. While he prayed, I felt I ought to vomit it out. As they prayed, it came out. Then they prayed and controlled the evil power.[37]

The author was informed that some Pentecostal pastors, during exorcisms they carried out in the houses of families visited by black magic, had discovered little metal tablets (Tamil takaṭu) on which curses had been written.[38] Closer investigation, however, revealed that this practice within the south Indian Pentecostal movement is unacceptable to the majority, since they suspect fraud. How dramatic an exorcism can turn out in cases of black magic is illustrated by the following example related by a Tamil pastor in Bangalore:

> One lady's husband had spent ten thousand rupees to kill her by witchcraft. This was revealed to me [by the Lord]. I said: "Who is that lady here? Your husband has spent ten thousand rupees to kill you. Come forward." So, nobody came. I called three times and then I left it. Then, this lady got up and she came. [She said:] "I am the one . . . that is the first time, I am meeting pastor T. and he told everything about me." From that distance I looked at her and said: "In the name of Jesus!" She fell flat by the power of God. . . . And, then, she got up. She was having

---

36. Interview.
37. Interview.
38. This form of black magic is mentioned also by Frölich 1915: 15.

this demon and evil spirits. Three times, she had planned to kill herself. From all those powers of the enemy, she was released completely, with the anointing of God. And her husband was totally shocked. Three months [and] she was still alive. So, again he went to that witchcraft fellow, because he had promised that she would die. When the man came back to him, he said: "I am chanting the maximum evil on her, but something powerful is stopping it."[39]

In view of the situation of rivalry between Hindu specialists like the Mantiravāti and the Pentecostal exorcist, a well-known healing evangelist's declaration that he had received threatening letters from an angry Mantiravāti with the request to refrain from certain particular cases of black magic is not altogether implausible.

In general it can be said that in the practice of exorcism, a whole range of phenomenological parallels can be discerned between popular Hinduism and the south Indian Pentecostal movement. Nevertheless, the basic particularity of Pentecostal exorcism should not be overlooked. A not unimportant fact is that, unlike in the case of specialists like the Mantiravāti, no payment is taken. In Pentecostal exorcism, the evil spirit is identified only in rare cases, and the ritual is comparatively simpler than in Hinduism. But the essential difference lies in that whereas specialists like the Mantiravāti or Cāmiyāti make use of small divinities or spirits for exorcisms, Pentecostal exorcists call upon the direct power of the one God or rely on the exorcizing power of Jesus, whose supreme authority no evil spirit can withstand. Thereby, the traditional Hindu system of references is decisively broken and recentered on the Christian God.

A special role is played by the persons who heal and perform exorcisms, although it is always emphasized that it is God who works the healing. Yet, since God has granted them the gift of healing, an exalted status is automatically given to the ministers as the ones who have received this spiritual gift. In the form in which the gift of healing is taught and practiced in the south Indian Pentecostal movement, abuses are inevitable. Nevertheless it should be noted that also within Pentecostalism there is a sharp critique of any kind of personality cult. A brochure of the Apostolic Christian Assembly relates:

A lady gave a short witness about the healing that she received from God. The pastor who conducted the meeting asked her to give the witness more clearly. The lady stood up again and gave a few more details about the disease and sat down saying, "I gave all the glory to God, who

39. Interview.

healed me." The pastor was still not satisfied. He asked her a few questions and made her confess that it was the pastor's prayers which were responsible for the healing she received. This attitude is yet another reason for discord and strife in the Christian church.[40]

This sharp critique already shows in practice how much pastors and evangelists can bring their own personality into play. For pastors as much as evangelists, a successful ministry is closely connected with the recognized possession of an extraordinary gift of healing. This again leads to testimonies in which the hearer is made to forget that essentially God is the healer. The following event recounted by a founder of the Madras Pentecostal Assembly is not at all untypical of the charismatic claims of many Pentecostal pastors:

> During my itinerary work, I took up a small room in a village and stayed there for more than a year. . . . There was a Christian in that village whose wife was demon possessed. It is regretful to note the Christians adhering to the customs and manners of heathenism even though they have come out of it. The husband of this woman instead of asking the children of God to pray for her he went after sorcerers to drive out the devil from his wife. All his efforts were futile, incurring a good lot of expenses. After trying all other ways, he thought of me and asked his brother to fetch me to pray for his wife. The moment he mentioned my name the devil began to tremble and say, "Do not send for the preacher, I shall leave her." The husband was aware that as soon as he mentioned my name the devil was afraid. So he insisted upon calling me. Immediately the devil shouted, saying, "Don't bring him, don't bring him. I'll go away," and after showing signs of departure, left the woman.[41]

Although celibacy is only made obligatory in the Ceylon Pentecostal Mission and in a few small churches, the concept that spiritual power can be increased by celibacy is widespread in the south Indian Pentecostal movement. In many Pentecostal churches there are pastors and evangelists who remain single deliberately. They reckon this as a special strength, as the following account by a Tamil evangelist shows:

> I was praying for a demon-possessed person. Witchcraft. It was a very [poisonous] one [demon]. So, I . . . just standing and all of the people

40. Apostolic Christian Assembly n.d.: appendix, 6-7.
41. Vasu ca. 1950: 12.

are around me. So, [I said:] "Let us start praying!" This person who was possessed was very quiet for some time. The demon possession came and [the demon said]: "Have you come, have you come to torture us? . . . Yes, yes, I know, you are a chap who is not married, no woman has touched your body, that's why you are able to stand before me. No one else yet has been able to do it."[42]

Apparently, numerous stories have been passed down in Pentecostal oral traditions that depict Pentecostal healers and exorcists as charismatic wonder workers, even though it is always emphasized that only Jesus is the healer. D. G. S. Dhinakaran distributes prayer oil, with a label in Tamil saying: "This is oil which Brother Dhinakaran has blessed with his prayer."[43] A drop of this oil is to be applied to the body of a sick person, thereby praying to Jesus for help. A special healing power thus is attributed to oil blessed by a Pentecostal wonder worker. Moreover, successful Pentecostal healers and exorcists have their counterparts not only in specialists like the Mantiravāti but also in the powerful, popular Hindu gurus who, as a rule, perform similar healing miracles. To illustrate, a report of three healings by the popular Hindu guru Ramsurat Kumar in Tamil Nadu:

[1] Thiru Kanakavel Raj of Aruppukottai, an ardent devotee of Bhagwan [Ramsurat Kumar] had chronic back pain. He was put to great agony, because of this disease. When Bhagwan's Holy Hands touched his back, he was relieved of the pain and is now leading a healthy life. . . . [2] A father was filled with anxiety finding that his only son was unable to talk. He placed the boy at the feet of Bhagwan. By the Grace of Bhagwan the child started talking. . . . [3] A girl of eight was suffering from cancer and even doctors from America had lost all hope. With the Grace of Bhagwan the child was cured of the disease. This was related by Dr. M. S. Udayamurthy in "Kumudam," a Tamil weekly magazine.[44]

A story by Pastor K. R. Paul from Bangalore related in his autobiography is relevant in this connection. According to this, an Australian came to Bangalore to the well-known Hindu guru, Sai Baba, to be freed from chronic demon possession. There he met K. R. Paul, who prevented him from going to Sai Baba and took him to himself. Through his prayer, the Australian was

---

42. Interview.
43. "Āttuma, carīra, piṇi nīkkum jeba eṉṉey," Jesus Calls Ministry, Madras, n.d.
44. Srinivasan 1991: 24.

healed.[45] Moreover, it is well known that Hindu gurus are often venerated by their followers as avatāras ("divine incarnations"). In south India, this is the case, for instance, with Ramsurat Kumar and Sai Baba.[46] D. G. S. Dhinakaran, by far the most successful Pentecostal healing evangelist, is treated by the Hindus, among whom he has a great following, as an avatāra. This was not a mere misunderstanding, as the case of another famous healer prophet proves. During the 1960s, Paulaseer Lawrie had acted as an extremely successful Pentecostal healing evangelist. He broke with the Pentecostals at the beginning of the 1970s and was thereafter venerated as a Hindu guru and avatāra.[47] This shows that, similar to the corresponding phenomena in popular Hinduism, the south Indian Pentecostal practice of healing and exorcism is much centered on the personality of the miracle worker.

Of great importance in judging Pentecostal healing and exorcism is the question of its effect on congregational practice and on the lives of individual believers. Evangelistic rallies and conventions play a particularly distinctive role here, with their spectacular healing events. Without any kind of qualification, participants are promised that "all," "here and now," will experience healing. There is no doubt that at such events several visitors experience some healing, proved by the numerous testimonies published in the periodicals of the healing evangelists. The author has the impression that in essence these are quite authentic. This means that, as a rule, healings that are not falsified or fantasized are interpreted by both healer and healed as miracle healings and are so described. Nevertheless, there are also enormous exaggerations and even false reports. But unfortunately, there is a lack of critical research into the reliability and veracity of healing testimonies. Such an investigation is extremely difficult in the Indian situation. Many cases would be assessed by scholars of classical medicine as within the range of psychosomatic diseases or spontaneous cures, and would be explained in that way. But healings do occur that are difficult to explain by the scientific means at present available to us.[48] However, a problem the south Indian Pentecostal movement clearly does not see at all is that of only apparent cures. In the extraordinarily stressed situation of the thaumaturgical drama and the apodictic affirmation of the healer, an emotional tension is produced that gives some sick people the feeling that they are healed. But in many such cases, no real healing has actually taken place. This false awareness of being cured by God leads these people, presuming full health, to

45. Paul & Paul 1977: 29-30.
46. See Srinivasan 1991; Gokak 1989. On divine veneration of the gurus see also Mlecko 1982: 33-61, 50-56.
47. See pp. 117ff.
48. See the cases described by Hoerschelmann 1977: 244, 268, 270, 349.

put medicines aside all too easily, which can be dangerous to health. The author has become familiar with such cases. Even if it only occasionally comes to such serious consequences, it was distressing for the author to observe how, in a big rally, an old handicapped man was prayed for. Through the suggestive power of the event, the old man was brought onto the stage, walked a few steps without crutches, and acknowledged his cure at the microphone. However, the author also saw how, after the supposed cure, the man was carried from the backstage by two strong men and, overtired by the whole effort, finally could no longer move at all. There was no cure to observe — and this was not an isolated case. Critics complain that at such rallies all the sick people present are promised healing but many go home unhealed. The charge is that expectations of the unattainable are aroused, which leads to disappointment.[49] Such criticism is only partly justified, since there is much to indicate that visitors to these rallies are implicitly quite clear that not all will be cured. This is expressed in a testimony of healing from a Jesus Calls rally:

> I brought my younger sister Maragadam from far away and with much labour and difficulty. For three years she was bound by black magic (pillicūṉiyam) and she did not know who she was. There was no place we would not go, no gods [teyvaṅkaḷ] we would not implore to make her well. They all let her down. Out of the belief that she would be cured if she came here, we brought her with great difficulty. When it was time for prayer, . . . a power came down on her. Now she knows who she is and she has a complete cure.[50]

From this typical testimony it is clear that, even before visiting the rally, many other ways had been tried to obtain a cure. This rather sober and pragmatic approach is often overlooked. People who hope for a miracle healing are at the same time acting experimentally. If they are not healed at this rally, they will, as a rule, try other events. Though somewhat frustrated, they will not give up hope in spite of the disappointment in once again finding no cure. In the author's estimate, real frustration occurs only in isolated cases. However, the big rallies of which we have spoken are not the only forums where prayer healing occurs. It also has its place in the daily life of the congregation. After each worship service, the pastor lays hands on all who ask for it and prays for their concerns, often with the assistance of elders. Where healings result, this will be presented as testimony at the following Sunday's worship. An extremely popu-

49. E.g., Schäfer 1993: 40.
50. *Iyēcu aḻaikkiṟār*, July 1995: 32.

lar event is the weekly fasting prayer organized within the congregation. In general, power to reinforce the gift of healing is attributed to fasting. All the sick come to this fast and prayer is offered for their healing. Many of the sick also go straight to the pastor so that he may pray for them individually. The author can scarcely remember one interview period with a pastor that was not interrupted by a member of the congregation coming to seek prayer for healing or blessing. An important part of the personal care that a pastor exercises in a congregation consists of prayer for healing. Moreover, a large proportion of members also practice prayer for healing. The big rallies divert our attention from the fact that a great part of prayer for healing goes on rather unspectacularly in the daily practice of the congregation.

If an Indian attributes his healing to the prayers of a particular pastor or evangelist, he will often draw the most practical conclusion and will become a member or adherent of the corresponding Pentecostal congregation. Miracle healings contribute to a considerable extent to the numerical growth of the Pentecostal movement It is remarkable how readily healing is attributed to the prayer of a pastor or evangelist as the case of the twenty-five-year-old student A., well known to the author, clearly shows. A. suffered from slight pains that occurred during urination. By chance he attended a Pentecostal rally where the following word of knowledge was spoken: "A., you will be cured of an abscess." Next morning he perceived that the pain had ceased. As he reflected on it, he came to the conclusion that the healing had taken place the day before through prayer at the rally. On the basis of this insight, he left the Catholic Church and became a member of the Pentecostal church that had led the rally. This readiness to attribute healing to a particular prayer leads to many church plantings through miracle healing and exorcisms. A successful Tamil pastor from Bangalore relates how he gathered his first church members through a successful healing:

> Then, one day, I was praying, and the Lord told me. He said: "I have anointed you to pray for the people, and to heal them. Why don't you do it?" . . . So, I printed some notices, and distributed them. They said: "If the doctors have given up, contact pastor T." So, I was in the room, praying, in my house. Suddenly, one man came and knocked at the door. He said: "I want to meet Rev. T." I said: "Yes, please come inside." Then, he said: "I got this notice. My mummy has something with cancer, what can you do?" I said: "I can come and pray." So, I told him, "You give me one hour's time, I will come to your house." . . . So, I went to this house. I sat there. All the people were standing. And, I asked them one question: "How many of you believe that Jesus Christ can heal this lady? And, all

those who don't believe," I said, "go out of this room." And, I closed my eyes [to pray]. When I opened my eyes, nobody was there. Then, I prayed for this lady, and within four days, this man came and said: "The Lord touched her and healed her." And, the church slowly started to grow. Seven people, eight people, [were there at the beginning].[51]

A leading Pentecostal pastor from Madras gives an impressive description of the role played by miracle healing in the founding of his independent church. At the beginning, for months he had no one attending his services except his own family. Then by chance on New Year's Eve at the midnight service, he found that a family living in the same quarter could not get an auto-rickshaw (taxi) to go to their home congregation, which was quite distant:

The very first soul that we received came to us at the 1st January in '81. On 31 December it was watch night service with no one except my family and me. And, the Lord gave me a scripture: "Behold I do a new thing and it shall happen now" (Isaiah 49:19). So, while I was preaching this, a family, husband, wife and daughter came in. . . . Then, while I was preaching the Holy Spirit led me to go and pray for this man, laying my hands on him. But, I said: "Lord, in my twenty years of my ministry, I have never done that during the preaching." Now, I was being led to go and do this, and then also, there was a fear. This is the first time I had some people come in, and if I lay my hands upon him, I [may] drive him away, I feared. . . . But, without my knowledge I went and laid my hands on him, and said: "The Lord is doing a new thing in your life." Just the way that I had preached. And [I said]: "Receive it now!" So, I came back and finished the service and prayed. At the last prayer when I opened my eyes, they had already left. I was totally disappointed. I could not even get their addresses. I was not able to sleep that night. Then 1 January, 1981, around ten o'clock . . . all the three of them came to our house. . . . Immediately, I knew that something had happened to them. So, that man expressed his happiness, and then, he said, he had not gone for work for four and a half years, because he had a nervous breakdown. Not even able to hold a glass of water. . . . And, so he said: "By the time you laid hands on me, I felt heat going through my head. And, by the time you left, my shaking was gone." He went home without the help of his wife or anybody, he tried to sign his name. He was able to sign it. . . . And, next morning, they went to the company doctor. Because, they

51. Interview.

164

were going to put him out of the service on medical grounds on 14 January, completing four and a half years. . . . Here, he was okay. So, the company doctor signed his papers, saying that he is quite fit to join duty. So, on the 15th January he joined duty. But, in the meantime, he saw quite number of people. They asked him: "What happened?" And, he said: "This church." That's all he said. So, that [next] Sunday morning, we had about thirty-five people for the first time.[52]

Without doubt, miracle healings and exorcisms are one of the main attractions of the Pentecostal movement, but they are not the basis on which Pentecostal congregations are built. They just represent the contact point for winning church members and, through testimonies of healing, they provide confirming evidence of God's power in the life of the congregation. The south Indian Pentecostals refer to this strongly, as the following assertions from pastors in Madras show:

If they experience a healing they stay a while in the congregation but if there is no system [to hold them] they go away again. If they have no system, their church never grows. They come just to be healed and then they go. Once they have come to church they must really see the presence of God. That is our strong point.[53]

So, some people, they just come for healing. After the healing is over they again they are back in their own temples. So, like that, many people. So, after I came here, I can say: about . . . no less than two hundred, two hundred and fifty people I have baptized. And, only seventy people are with me. The problem is: they used to come. They used to get healing, and they used to be faithful for two or three months, but when they are persecuted in their own families, they run back. Like that, many people have gone.[54]

Miracle healing and exorcism play a prominent role in the congregational practice of the south Indian Pentecostal movement. But by themselves they are scarcely responsible for its missionary success, which is rather due to the interplay of various factors. Much of the missionary activity takes place on the personal level in families, in the neighborhood, or among workmates or

52. Interview.
53. Interview.
54. Interview.

fellow students, usually without the direct invention by the pastors. For the pastors, important opportunities for mission occur on house visitations. The spectacular nature of miracle healing and exorcism must not overshadow the fact that the missionary success of the Pentecostal movement in south India is also very much based on individual communication and intensive pastoral care. Nevertheless, it is particularly miracle healing and exorcism that establish a strong phenomenological connection with traditional Indian popular religion, and it is here where one can most convincingly show that the south Indian Pentecostal movement is a quite indigenous version of Indian Christianity.

Divine Healing for Born-Again Christians

In the Pentecostal movement there is generally a promise of healing for born-again Christians that should be distinguished from the miracle healing of which we have been speaking.[55] In south India, the Ceylon Pentecostal Mission expresses the teaching on divine healing with great emphasis. This is how they put it in one of their publications:

> Jesus came to abolish all causes of death, such as sin unto death or death caused by sin, and sickness unto death; . . . a Spirit-led life delivers us from the law of sin and death; . . . physical death need not necessarily happen through some incurable sickness; . . . a Christian can continue to live overcoming sin, sickness, death through Christ, and to serve Him until he is called Home like some of the saints in the Bible. . . . God has promised to grant us length of life preserving us from sickness and death.[56]

These general and cautious formulations would probably find agreement among most south Indian Pentecostals. But they are complemented in the Ceylon Pentecostal Mission by a radical oral tradition. By this the true believer has the promise that he will be healed solely through faith in Christ and that consequently he need take no medicine. Furthermore, the Ceylon Pentecostal Mission forbids its members to undergo any medicinal treatment. Often enough this has led and still leads to fatal cases or to lasting harm that could easily have been avoided by medical treatment. The founding father of

55. See Purdy 1995: 489-525.
56. The Pentecostal Mission 1986: 61, 64-65.

the Ceylon Pentecostal mission, P. Paul, died as a result of a serious untreated carbuncle on his back.[57] A well-known Tamil healing evangelist suffers from a lame foot that was caused by an illness contracted in childhood and not treated, because his parents were true followers of the Ceylon Pentecostal Mission. Many similar cases could be adduced. In the background of this radical rejection of medical treatment lies the view that medical healing is not real healing: "Medical and surgical healings cannot cure the mind and soul, while divine healing heals not only the body, but also the mind and soul."[58] A specially problematic consequence of this way of viewing things is the tendency to explain a sickness by saying one's faith is not strong enough. Strong faith means:

> Confess that Jesus has already borne your sickness and carried your pain, and therefore provision is already made for your healing. It is up to you to claim it by faith . . . claim your healing. You are sure to be healed. Although your symptoms may say that you are still sick, stand on the word of God firmly, without wavering, and praise God for healing you. God's word says, "With his stripes you are healed."[59] What His word says, God will surely confirm. Keep praising God for your healing, until He accomplishes what He has promised you.[60]

Firm, confident faith in divine healing must not be disturbed by doubts. The conviction that doubt is one of the greatest hindrances to divine healing is stated with heavy emphasis:

> Incomplete knowledge of God's will might give way to unbelief, doubt and fear. That was the reason why he continued to be sick. He always believed that Jesus could heal anyone, *only if it was the will of God.* Millions of sincere Christians and preachers all over the world dwell on the same thought, letting sickness have a great hold on their body. . . . We must claim our healing against all doubts, fears and symptoms.[61]

The Ceylon Pentecostal Mission is sharply criticized for its radical rejection of all medicinal treatment by almost all the other Pentecostal churches. Zac Poonen writes:

57. It is most likely that the carbuncle was aggravated by diabetes.
58. The Pentecostal Mission 1994: 40.
59. See Isaiah 53:5.
60. The Pentecostal Mission 1986: 82.
61. The Pentecostal Mission 1994: 86.

[T]here are believers who do not take any medicine when they are sick. They do not have any Scripture to base their so-called "faith" on. But they imagine that they are "trusting" God. That is exactly like jumping down from the temple, expecting the angels to provide supernatural protection! [see Luke 4:9-10] Many of them finally die of their sickness — and the Name of Jesus Christ is dishonoured among the heathen, who get the idea that Christianity is the religion of foolish fanaticism.[62]

Of especial paradigmatic interest is the detailed critique prepared by E. J. C. Job, a doctor who is close to the Assemblies of God.[63] He had himself belonged to the Ceylon Pentecostal Mission and, at that time, had renounced medicinal treatment for himself and his family, although he was practicing as a doctor. After his wife fell ill and no divine healing was available for her, her condition became life-threatening and he decided, in a quandary, to put her in the hospital. There she was successfully operated on and restored to health. On the basis of this key experience he reflected on the question of divine healing and medical treatment and came to the following conclusion:

[E]ven though the promise of divine healing is available for every child of God . . . the comfort of medical science need not be withheld from them when they are sick and seeking divine healing. God will provide divine healing even when a person is taking medical treatment. They need not fear any judgement from God for using medical treatment.[64]

This standpoint, that belief in divine healing is simply to be combined with medical treatment, is today, with the exception of the Ceylon Pentecostal Mission and churches close to it in teaching, the general and official understanding in the south Indian Pentecostal movement. At a closer look, however, some problematic indications appear. In each of the interviews conducted by the author, wherever possible, the question was raised of the place of medical treatment; although in almost all cases the coexistence of divine healing and medicine was asserted, often there was a carefully considered theological statement of position. To the question on this point, answers like the following were not rare:

62. Poonen 1994: 26.
63. Job 1989.
64. Job 1989: 115.

If you have strong faith, God can heal you. If you have little faith, go to a doctor, no problem.[65]

[I]f we have faith, why can't God hear our prayers? You increase your faith, then it is not necessary to take medicine. . . . If there is no faith, and you are not taking medicine, what will happen? Understand? You need faith. If you have faith, you don't need to take any medicine. Without faith not taking medicine is meaningless.[66]

Such forms of argumentation imply that, with the presence of sufficiently strong faith, taking medicine would be unnecessary. The informants most often admitted candidly that they themselves would have recourse to medical treatment. In these cases, their statements serve to establish that they hold to the theoretical possibility that faith in Jesus can be healing for all illnesses. It is another matter if they do not admit to needing medical treatment for themselves. Such claims were made by some leading pastors and evangelists. Statements by a prominent healing evangelist and two pastors will illustrate this:

I believe God keeps disease away from me. So, I am not against people who take medicine, but for me no need. So far, God has kept me. . . . Even the doctor will never give a guarantee for your life. When you go for the operation he will tell you, to sign [a document], afraid if you die that nobody should blame him. So, who gives the guarantee? Only Jesus. So, I strongly believe, He is the healer. But I am not against people who take medicine. That's all a matter of faith. And according to the faith I have, I take [or don't take]. So, I won't judge anybody.[67]

I don't take [medicine], that is personally. I don't insist that others should not take medicine. My children, my daughter takes medicine. . . . I don't take medicine, and God has been my healer, I know it's a personal thing. I cannot force you. See, it has some personal faith also involved. When you are not well, you have also to claim your healing. When the man thinks: "I must take medicine," I tell him: "You go ahead, I will pray for you."[68]

65. Interview.
66. Interview.
67. Interview.
68. Interview.

I haven't taken any treatment for the past twenty-four years [the time of his conversion]. I believe in divine healing. But, people who are taking medicine, I am not condemning them. It is up to their level of faith.[69]

The positions taken by these individuals show that it is not only in the Ceylon Pentecostal Mission such attitudes to medical treatment exist, but generally in the south Indian Pentecostal movement the same theological view continues.

In congregational practice, thinking about divine healing reaches the most spectacular form in the Ceylon Pentecostal Mission and related churches, in that here any medical treatment is forbidden. In qualification, however, it must be said that a great number of laypeople and pastors informed the author they gave up their belief in divine healing without medicine the moment they became seriously ill. A good example is that of E. J. C. Job, which was already mentioned. The author has the impression that this pragmatic attitude is the rule. Moreover, there are a good number of laypeople in the Ceylon Pentecostal Mission who, despite official teaching, accept medical treatment in cases of illness. When there was a tragic accident on an excursion for the Sunday school of the Ceylon Pentecostal Mission in May 1994, the congregation prayed for God's help and undertook nothing to take the seriously injured to hospital. In the Tamil weekly that commented in detail on the accident, it was noted in this connection that First Aid is unknown in India and that, even after they reached a state hospital through the generous offer of helpful witnesses of the accident, in the end no emergency medical help was available.[70] Such events point to a further aspect worth considering in this connection. As a rule, no medical treatment that deserves the name is open to the poorest levels of Indian society. Consequently, the rejection of medicine for these people is only a theoretical affair without practical effect. State hospitals where they are available are often in a catastrophic condition. So the rejection of medical treatment, which was formerly widespread in the other Pentecostal churches too, was given up by a large proportion of the Pentecostals who have risen into the more prosperous levels of society and for whom medical treatment in expensive private clinics has suddenly become a genuine alternative. Nevertheless, it remains beyond doubt that the lack of clarity in the south Indian Pentecostal movement with regard to the connection between sickness and sins often leads to serious consequences. If a born-again Christian contracts an illness or suffers some misfortune, some

69. Interview.
70. *Jūniyar*, Madras 11 May 1994; *Nakkīran*, Madras 14 May 1994.

ostensible sins will be brought up in explanation. The pastoral consequences
are often hair-raising. The author knows a Pentecostal family whose youngest
daughter died very young, and where the father was seriously reproached by
his relatives as being to blame because of his alleged sins for the death of the
child. But belief in divine healing can also be expressed in unproblematic
ways. The moving witness of a woman from Kerala, who died of cancer and
believed to the end in divine healing, is an example. The stations of her incur-
able illness were impressively marked out by her husband and published in a
book. He writes of his wife Grace's way of suffering:[71]

> Grace read many books on "healing"[;] she held the view that God
> would heal her completely in spite of the medical verdict. One of the
> first things she mentioned to me, as soon as the diagnosis of cancer was
> conveyed to her, was that we pray only positively for healing and not
> negatively at all. At times when friends prayed for her in a doubting
> manner by saying "if it is God's will, let her be healed completely," she
> took objections to such prayers and told me to inform such friends to
> change their attitude to pray only in a positive way. . . . It became a fact
> that her physical condition deteriorated very rapidly; we had to stop
> further chemotherapy; she was unable to take solid food, even liquid
> food only in very small quantities and that too not very frequent, unable
> to sit up. For all intent and purpose one finds it difficult to see complete
> physical healing.[72]

Out of Grace's faith in divine healing arose an unshakeable will to live.
Although she received the treatment of the best hospital in south India in
vain, she hoped to the end that God would heal her. When in face of her
death there was no more hope, it was clear that her faith in divine healing
was only the consequence of an iron-hard confidence in God. Her husband
wrote:

> Therefore it became necessary to prepare Grace for a change of attitude
> towards the whole question of complete physical healing. . . . On the
> night of March 8th, Grace raised the question of her complete healing
> again. I took the opportunity to lead her to a change of attitude by ex-
> plaining once more what I had told her a few time before, the three lev-

71. The couple belonging to the Church of South India were influenced by a Charismatic circle of St Andrew's Cathedral in Sydney (see George 1991: 36).
72. George 1991: 36.

els of healing — physical, mental, spiritual. She agreed with me that she had already obtained complete spiritual healing as she had reconciled completely with God and with man thus establishing a perfect vertical and horizontal relationship. . . . At this stage Grace said: "Yes, Lord, whether we live or whether we die, we belong to the Lord. I don't make any demands on you. I obey you completely. I completely surrender to you, Lord. Use me as you like. I am just clay and you are the potter. Mould me as a potter would mould the clay. Let your will be done on me."[73]

The fate of Grace proves that faith in divine healing can be preserved in sickness and death. Seen from the medical point of view, the unshakeable will to live coming to expression there is a positive factor promoting healing. Moreover, from this factor, Grace was able to accept her death with deeper composure and to clarify her faith in divine healing.

Prophecy

While nearly every pastor and evangelist will automatically claim the gift of healing, such a claim is not taken for granted in the case of the prophetic gift. This gift is exercised to a large extent by laypeople, especially women. Many women have a recognized and established position in the congregation as prophets. Most prophecies are directed to individual persons. Rather rare are prophecies that go beyond the horizon of private problematic situations. When this extension does take place it is most often a message of woe.

Prophecies for Individuals

Prophecies for individuals are dominated by the "word of knowledge," where the so-called naming plays a particularly spectacular part. The contents of the word of knowledge are closely tailored to needs of the one addressed and are thematically limited. Mostly it is a matter of encouragement toward miracle healing or a call to conversion or to ministry.[74] Apart from prophecies by the "word of knowledge" there are tendencies to predict the future of individuals,

73. George 1991: 36-37.
74. Here also we have the prophetic warning of divine punishment in the case of one seeking to escape the call to ministry (see pp. 194-95).

i.e., prophecy in the form of fortune-telling. The word of knowledge makes public the inner thoughts and feeling of a stranger. Mostly, it is bound up with general prophetic appeal to God's help. This second component, however, may be strongly subordinated to the first or even quite neglected. The word of knowledge is held in high esteem in congregational practice. An evangelist describes how he practiced the word of knowledge for the first time:

> One time, three Lutheran Bible women came to visit my house. . . . They visited me, and I asked them: "Do you believe in the baptism of the Holy Spirit?" One said: "It is all humbug. I don't believe in any such experience. It's all hypocrisy what the Pentecostals claim." She was so angry with me. Then, I was very jealous, brother. I was sixteen years old. I just ran outside, I said: "Holy Spirit, tell me something about that lady. I want to show that you are real." I heard a voice inside me: "She has three daughters, and the middle one is demon possessed." Then, I went inside. It is a matter of two, three or five minutes. I said: "Sister, how many daughters do you have?" She said: "Why do you want to know that?" I said: "How old is your middle daughter?" Immediately, she screamed and said: "The Holy Spirit is real, real." She started crying. . . . She said: "My middle daughter, I got her married, and she was demon possessed, and she began to act like a mad person. And, the husband said that he don't need my daughter anymore. He left the wife in my house. And, I didn't tell this to anybody, because a Bible woman's daughter, if she has a demon, nobody will believe her." . . . And, she has come thirty kilometers from her house to my place. I don't know nothing about her. So, she said: "Oh, the Holy Spirit revealed that to you."[75]

Spectacular happenings of this kind are frequently related in the oral tradition but are exceptional in actual congregational practice. It is mostly general allusions to problematic situations in which people find themselves and decisions they have to make that find expression in words of knowledge. It is also often reported of the wives of pastors that they have the faculty of opening up the problems and cares of newcomers to the congregation. Joint prayer is also often the place for a word of knowledge. This indicates that such prophecy belongs rather to pastoral practice. All too often a newcomer is hoping for help in a distressing crisis. The word of knowledge allows direct approach to the unknown stranger who is thereby enabled to share his needs

75. Interview.

with the congregation to seek their prayers. The author has the impression that the one to whom the word is directed is normally not exposed. Usually the word of knowledge is bound up with prophecy only to the extent of a general promise of God's help. A typical prophecy would be: "Sister, you see no way out of your problems, your relatives oppress you. But fear not, the Lord is with you." However, the most spectacular form of prophecy for individuals, reckoned to belong to the word of knowledge, is the so-called naming or calling by name. It is not at all prevalent in the south Indian Pentecostal movement but is practiced mostly by those evangelists and pastors who are active in a marked thaumaturgical way. For an illustration we can take a typical example of a large-scale rally in Hyderabad in 1995. It was organized by the evangelist D. G. S. Dhinakaran of Jesus Calls, who is a leading proponent of "naming":

[1] Mohana! God's power is descending on you right now. The problem you have in your stomach and uterus is leaving you now. Glorify Jesus Christ! . . . [2] My dear brother Sekhar, you are praying like this: "Lord! My whole family is under the grip of the powers of darkness. Deliver us completely." Sekhar, the power of God is descending on you right now. You could see a bright light on you. The power of God is descending on you and your family members. . . . [3] Peter! You are faithful in your ministry. You are an ordinary person. You are ministering in villages and on streets for God. You could see the power of God descending on you. . . . [4] There is a sister by name Glory here. Sister! God wants to heal you. I do not want to mention your disease. The Lord will use you in the healing ministry mightily, in the days to come. Jesus Christ is waiting for you.[76]

This selection of namings from the account of an evangelical rally can be taken as representative. Other evangelists and pastors treat naming in the same way. The generalized and unspecific statements in the word of knowledge make this form of prophecy remarkably close to prophetic preaching. If preaching is understood as a prophetic message, it has exactly the same function as prophecy for the individual. The following account of a Tamil pastor from Madras illustrates this similarity:

When we preach people must be blessed, not in the sense, just be happy, just receive the word which they are looking for. One man came and

76. Jesus Calls, Nov. 1995: 28-29.

asked me, a few weeks ago: "Who told you about me?" I said: "Nobody. What's the matter?" He said: "You were preaching just exactly as if somebody told you about me."[77]

The word of knowledge becomes significant when the person addressed is open to the prophet and bears witness that his personal problems have been addressed. It is the witness of the person concerned, describing his own situation, that gives evidence to the prophecy. The two following examples illustrate this. The first was given by an evangelist, the second by a pastor in Madras:

One young man came, I forgot his name. . . . He said: "Aṇṇanē, that is, older brother. You don't know me, but I was in your meeting where I surrendered my life to the Lord." It seems that I had given a revelation: "Young man, you are a graduate, standing there, thinking of doing a postgraduation or doctorate, or something. Your father is saying that you should do theology, you are tossed in between to do master's or to do theology. The eternal father says: 'Obey your father, because it is the will of God.'" That day was the day of salvation for him.[78]

I gave a prophecy sometime: "A person is here and she is trying to end her life. You trust on Jesus, Jesus will save you, He will help you." And, all the congregation left, and one girl was just there. And, she came weeping, and she said: "I was the one, and I was thinking of committing suicide." And, I gave her the gospel, and she was saved.[79]

These prophecies attain significance through the one addressed finding in them an authentic answer from God to the problems oppressing him or her. It should be realized in this connection how seldom personal problems are spoken of openly in Indian culture. In such a context, it is easy to explain the great readiness to recognize a personal concern in generalized allusions. They open up the possibility of verbalizing problems that normally one would not dare to confess to others. This openness is only possible because the challenge comes from a divine prophecy and hence is above human curiosity and the connected danger of envy. Often the prophecy is addressed to one who comes with a predetermined attitude of expectation. Usually the person, before

77. Interview.
78. Interview.
79. Interview.

coming to the rally, will have formulated quite concrete questions for which he or she expects a concrete answer. In the context of healings, no further explanation is needed. But, in prophecies that contain a call to conversion or to ministry, the context contains preparation for a decision. An example is an account of conversion from the rally in Hyderabad:

> I had been praying in this meeting, for the many problems in my life. It was then, brother Paul Dhinakaran called out my name and said: "Sister Juliet, you are lamenting, 'I have committed all the sins under the sun. Will the Lord forgive me?'" I was wondering within me, whether it is me that he is calling. I have committed many sins against Him. I was praying for the Lord's forgiveness and brother Paul Dhinakaran to call my name. The Lord heard my supplication and revealed to brother Paul Dhinakaran to call my name first and foremost. Hallelujah! I saw a bright light at that time. Joy unspeakable welled up in my heart. I submit my life to God. Praise the Lord.[80]

The prophetic message will be seen by the one addressed as the answer to a prayer. The prophet is the appropriate medium to give the message expected from God. All that is desired of the contents is that they should be valid as an answer in the broadest sense. This explains why a completely generalized statement, saying nothing precise, which may even appear relevant to several different people, can be so readily accepted as a life-changing prophecy from God for oneself. This viewpoint is especially well expressed in the following testimony of a pastor from Coimbatore who was seeking a word from God in a difficult life decision:

> So, I went to the church and told the Lord: "You must speak to me." . . . The pastor said [in the worship service]: "Let's pray. Let's see what God wants." . . . As I closed my eyes to pray, the pastor called out my name. . . . He said: "Victor, the Lord calls you to be a shepherd." We specifically [had] told the Lord [before]: "You have to tell us, either what you want us to do, or we will start a business." So, the Lord told me on that particular day: "I have called you to be a shepherd." That was July 1st. I went and borrowed money from a brother, took up a house, started a Sunday service on July 8th. That is the following Sunday. Because, I knew that the Lord had told me very clearly what is the gift.[81]

80. Jesus Calls, Nov. 1995: 23-24.
81. Interview.

If nobody is there who feels that the prophecy addresses his situation, then no consequences follow. But if someone has related the prophecy to himself, the desire is great to make it known in public, as the following testimony from the Hyderabad rally shows:

> My name is Rachel. Bro. Dhinakaran called me by my name day before yesterday. . . . When I made an attempt to come to the dais and testify, I was prevented because of the large crowd. Hence, I went back home. The Lord spoke to me that night: "Why didn't you glorify My name?" When I came to this meeting today, I felt a hand pulling me toward the dais. . . . That hand brought me to the dais to share my testimony. Glory be to God.[82]

Critical thought on this theme among Pentecostals is interesting. For example, a Tamil pastor from Madras says that such prophecy is not very spectacular:

> I believe in prophecy, but not [in statements like:] "Fear not!" Specific prophecy should be there. Nowadays, it is not a prophecy in the churches, it is an exhortation. But, in the name of the prophecies, they are not doing prophecy, but exhortations. Prophecy must be a specific message for a specific person. Nowadays: "Fear not, I am with you. Fear not!" These are all not prophecies. Prophecies should be something supernatural.[83]

But others demand on theological grounds a restriction of prophecy to this very way of proceeding, as can be seen from a position taken by another Tamil pastor:

> In the way I understand prophecy in the New Testament it is for exhortation, edification and comfort [see 1 Cor. 14:3]. In that way, it is most generally instructed: exhorting, encouraging, saying: "Oh, the Lord is here, don't be afraid. Praise the Lord. . . ." That type of thing. That is what I consider to be exhortation, edification. General words spoken to uplift the people in a congregation. . . . Prophecy as in the Old Testament, it was a prophecy that was used mainly to guide people because the Holy Spirit was not given to everyone. The Holy Spirit was working

82. Interview.
83. Interview.

only through certain anointed ones, like prophets or priests. . . . In the New Testament, prophecy can be used in guidance, but only as a matter of confirmation, never as a direct guidance.[84]

However, such theological arguments are rare. Usually, it is simply maintained that the word of knowledge is a matter of genuine, free prophecy, without expounding on the actual realization. In general it can be established that the forms of Pentecostal prophecy we have mentioned are more or less a stereotyped role-play. The contents are largely confined to a complex of themes around healing, conversion, and call to ministry. Prophecies proclaiming such contents will surely find recipients. Conversely, those who are seeking answers within the same range of themes expect to receive an appropriate prophecy. This kind of prophecy for individual persons is consequently a spiritual institution where, in ritualized form, answers from God are sought to closely defined questions.

There are also forms of prophecy for individuals that aim rather at predicting the future. Thus a Tamil healing evangelist prophesied the death of a seriously ill child. This prophecy served as starting point for a greater outcome:

From Vellore, one family wrote to me for prayer, saying, that their son, eldest son, is dying of kidney failure. So, I wrote to them: Your son will not live. But, when he dies, this will happen: He will suddenly say: "I see an angel of God, coming to take me." And, he will request you not to cry. But to sing this particular song, which he likes. That should be the sign to you that he is going to God. Don't cry. So, he died exactly like that. And, the angel of God came, and he said: "I see an angel of God. Daddy now, don't cry, sing that song," and as they were singing, he closed his eyes.[85]

Apparently there is more need of prediction in the cases of planned marriages. Although the author seldom observed such prophesying, since such prophecies happen mainly in the private domain, it can be gathered from reports that here genuine predictions take place. This is not surprising if one thinks how, in popular Hinduism, complicated astrological constellations are observed on the occasion of a marriage and how strongly influential this heritage is even in the established churches.[86] Proof that this is a widespread prac-

84. Interview.
85. Interview.
86. See Diehl 1965: 139-52.

tice in Pentecostal churches is provided by frequent warnings to the congregations. Thus a Tamil pastor said: "I also warn my church simply to go to some men of God, saying: 'Pray and tell us what God is saying.' [I say to my congregation that in this case] I would rather for you to go to an astrologer."[87] Unfortunately, there are scarcely any reliable sources about this kind of Pentecostal prophecy.

Prophecy of Future Events

Prophecies of future events not directly related to individual persons and going beyond the horizon of the congregation are rare. If such prophecies remain bound up with the churchly domain, they are usually promises of greater inter-regional spiritual awakenings to be expected in the near future. But prophecies of misfortune also occur. A Tamil evangelist claimed to have foreseen the unexpected death of Justin Prabakaran:

A prophecy comes definite. You know before that man, Dr. Justin Prabakaran, died. Before that, in December, we prayed that All Night Prayer. There, the Lord showed me that there is a great man of God who will die.[88]

If prophecies are about greater events beyond the horizon of the church, they will only be foretelling misfortunes or catastrophes. There was a prophet, for example, who claimed to have foretold the severe earthquake in Maharashtra in 1993. In the history of the south Indian Pentecostal movement, at least one such prophecy of evil has left deeper traces. P. Rajaratnam, who lived in Rangoon in 1942, prophesied the destruction of the city by the Japanese. In P. M. Samuel's autobiography there is the following note:

Seeing the situation of the war Bro P. Rajaratnam prophesied that the city of Rangoon was going to be destroyed with bombs and other plagues. He was ridiculed by a Pentecostal pastor and some church men. They condemned it as a false prophecy. This news was published in our Suvartha Prakashini (Gospel Illuminator) too. Bro. Rajaratnam laughed at their poor understanding and stubbornness.[89]

87. Interview.
88. Interview.
89. Samuel 1980: 53.

This prophecy, which apparently caused a sensation in Rangoon at the time, became known in India when in 1942 more Indian Pentecostals, among them P. Rajaratnam, returned from Rangoon to Andhra Pradesh to escape the Japanese occupation. They saw to it that the prophecies of the fall of Rangoon would get wide currency. However, such a prophecy remained an exception and the author is unaware of anything comparable. Noteworthy in this connection are some letters written by evangelist Pappa Shankar to Rajiv Gandhi.[90] In the last letter of 17 May 1991, that is, five days before the murder of Rajiv Gandhi by LTTE terrorists, she wrote:

> I would like to write briefly some important matter that my Lord revealed to me during my fasting prayer. I would like to advise you as a mother. When you come down to Tamil Nadu, never ever speak about the LTTE in your speeches and campaigns. Let others speak about this. Kindly avoid coming to Tamil Nadu very often. The reason why I am writing this is that my desire that you should have a long life and your family likewise also.[91]

As described by Pappa Shankar, this is a matter of a concrete prophetic warning to Rajiv Gandhi, which, according to Pappa Shankar, unfortunately did not reach him in time. But, apart from such individual cases, prophecy in the south Indian Pentecostal movement is restricted to the interpersonal and congregational domain and is consequently ritualized to a great degree.

---

90. Shankar 1990/1991: seven letters dated 20.7.90; 20.11.90; 15.4.91; 10.5.91; 17.5.91; two formal acknowledgments of reception by Rajiv Gandhi 26.7.90; 30.11.90.
    91. Shankar 1990/1991.

CHAPTER 11

Ethics

Different conceptions of the ethical standards to which a born-again Christian should hold divide the south Indian Pentecostal movement into several layers. The discussion of ethical norms, with their differences, offers the most explosive matter for conflict and is raised by pastors and laity alike. At first sight it seems a rather superficial affair since in practice the confrontation focuses mostly on the question whether the born-again Christian should wear jewelry. But closer examination shows that it concerns much more serious questions. It has been shown above that sanctification is treated by the majority of the south Indian Pentecostal movement as a process, beginning with justification and not forming the second stage of an ordo salutis, in which people can experience their complete purification from sins.[1] Nevertheless, in the oral tradition there is a widespread view that the true Christian lives without sins after conversion. Throughout the south Indian Pentecostal movement there is de facto the idea of holiness as complete purification from sins, even if this does not find expression in any stage theory. There is scarcely any reflection on the theological problems connected with this idea of holiness. The author only knows a few published discussions of this theme. One of them comes from Zac Poonen, who goes back to the distinction used by John Wesley between conscious and unconscious sins.

> There is also a difference between *falling* into sin and *having* sin. To have sin is to have unconscious sin in our personality — sin that we ourselves are unaware of, even though others who are more mature

1. See pp. 144-45.

than us may be able to notice it in us. But such unconscious sin need never make us feel guilty. For God's Word says, "Sin is not imputed when there is no law" (Rom. 5:13). (This also means that God does not impute sin to us when there is no awareness of sin in our conscious mind).[2]

In view of the high expectations of the life of the believer, much hangs on the way that sins are defined. In the first half of the twentieth century, there was general agreement in defining the exterior signs of a holy life in the south Indian Pentecostal movement as also in the western Pentecostal movement. Sins and worldliness were seen in close connection and sin included everything that stood for a worldly attitude. Holy conduct of life depends, in no small degree, on whether one was "separated" from the world.[3] In the writings of the Ceylon Pentecostal Mission we still find views that must have enjoyed universal currency in the early Indian Pentecostal movement:

The world is in the hands of Satan who has filled it with sin, corruption and vanity. . . . Satan rules the world which he has deceived. . . . Satan captivates man through his physical instincts and senses. Man has three realms within him: (i) The realm of physical desires; (ii) The realm of imagination; (iii) The realm of earthly desires. When Satan captures these realms the outcome is: (i) The lust of the flesh — All sinful, physical desires and appetites which include desire for alcohol, gluttony, lust for clothes, make-up, uncontrolled sex appetite, desire to be attractive and beautiful etc. (ii) The lust of the eyes — The eyes are drawn away by the worldly things, and the heart follows the eyes (Job 31:1, 9; Matt. 5:28). (iii) The pride of life — An earthly ambitious life, to be very great in the world in the way of education, position, wealth, fame and name etc. (1 Jn. 2:16) . . . Worldliness is an enemy to spiritual progress hindering one from doing the will of God. . . . Those who love the world will be judged with the world.[4]

The separation from the world, as it is propagated here, makes for the rejection of every kind of leisure, enjoyment, and sensual pleasure. In the booklet we have just quoted from the Ceylon Pentecostal Mission, among

2. Poonen 1990: 41. See also Hollenweger 1988: 328.
3. Separation is expressly mentioned by the Indian Pentecostal Church 1991 and *The Voice of Pentecost*, Feb. 1994: 15f.
4. The Pentecostal Mission 1989: 6-10.

the things forbidden the following points are especially emphasized: cinema, television, fashionable clothes, cosmetics, jewelry, smoking, alcohol, confidence in scientific education, depending on material riches, and sexual relations outside marriage.[5] Separation from the "world" should serve as a guarantee that believers will not be prevented or diverted from serving God. Believers are urged to attend meetings several times a week and to practice an intensive prayer life with Bible study at home. However, it is not only that true worship of God must be protected from other exterior attraction, it is often also pointed out that the born-again Christian has become the temple of God and this temple must not be defiled.[6] Only separation from the potentially impure world can assure a holy life. This starkly dualistic tendency leads to a certain ethical legalism. Separation is the "external sign of the internal change."[7] "The Holiness, always, it starts from our heart. So, when your heart is pure, your outward appearance also is pure."[8] Although outer behavior is not regarded as an indicator of purity of heart, conversely, every form of worldliness is seen as a clear indicator of sinfulness. As long as the south Indian Pentecostal movement represented a small radical minority, whose members kept apart from the "world" in a self-evident way on account both of their lowly social origin and of their wholehearted devotion, this ethical conception raised no questions. But already in the first generation this comprehensive rejection of the world was given up by many. Here even leaders often played a leading role. We may recall the example of K. E. Abraham as a case in point, who came from a situation of poverty. As leader and cofounder of the Indian Pentecostal Church, a church that saw itself as committed to radical holiness, he soon acquired the lifestyle of the upper middle class and gave his son a theological education in the USA. However, at the time a holy life actually required a distancing from riches and worldly education. This example shows that in south India, within the first generation, in many places the original contents of the holiness concept were implicitly given up and in practice declared as adiaphora. This weakening of the separation from the world from the start naturally threatened to put the whole system in question. Consequently, quite early a vigorous discussion began about which worldly amusements must definitely not fall into the category of adiaphora. Hence a casuistic treatment developed that resulted in a reversal of the whole argumentation.

5. See The Pentecostal Mission 1989.
6. See 1 Corinthians 5:16
7. Interview.
8. Interview.

This complexity will become especially clear in attitudes to the question of jewelry.

In the south Indian Pentecostal movement a vigorous discussion broke out, some decades ago, about whether it was permissible for believers to wear jewelry. Many south Indian Pentecostals saw in this a status confessionis. This had the result that nearly all pastors had to take an explicit stand on the question and that current attitudes to wearing jewelry form an important indicator to distinguish different streams in the south Indian Pentecostal movement. That the controversy over ethical norms should concentrate on the question of jewelry is perfectly understandable. In south India, jewelry, always made from gold, silver, or precious stone, is above all a status symbol. Still at the present day, acquiring jewelry is the most widely used form of saving. A richly jeweled wife puts on display not inconsiderable riches and thus marks the social status of the family.[9] It is therefore quite understandable if Pentecostals see a special threat to holiness here, since wearing jewelry strongly suggests consideration of status and, with it, worldliness. Pentecostals also draw attention to the fact that jewelry has religious significance for Hindus. Even if this is not always the case, at least the bridal necklace, the so-called thali, has in fact clear religious connotations. Besides, there will often be decorations on the jewelry drawn from Hindu symbolism, and particular pieces of jewelry function explicitly as amulets. But this argument is only of limited validity since Pentecostals also reject jewelry worn by Christians of the mainline churches. These have no Hindu elements in them: bridal necklaces in the established churches have Christian symbols — doves and crosses. Moreover, the ban on jewelry has also a biblical argument. Three texts especially are referred to: Genesis 35:4 where, before breaking camp, besides changing clothes, Jacob buried the earrings; also 1 Timothy 4:9 and 1 Peter 3:4, where it says women should not wear expensive jewelry.[10] The attitudes of particular Pentecostal churches on the jewelry question vary considerably. It can be said in general that within the whole south Indian Pentecostal movement there are strong reservations. In the rare cases where a positive attitude is observed it is a matter, as a rule, of the Faith Movement. In current attitudes to wearing jewelry we also see regional variations. Nearly all Pentecostal churches in Kerala categorically reject it. In Tamil Nadu there is embittered controversy on the subject: in southern Tamil Nadu the majority is for rejec-

---

9. In south India jewelry is traditionally worn not only by women but also by men. But, under western influence, this custom is becoming less common. There is a list of traditional kinds of jewelry, as used for example in Tamil Nadu, in Chitty 1992: 74-80.

10. The Pentecostal Mission 1989: 40f.

tion while in the north, especially in Madras, there is a more liberal attitude. In Andhra Pradesh there is hardly any rejection. In Karnataka it depends on the ethnic composition of the congregations and corresponds to present attitudes in Kerala, Tamil Nadu, or Andhra Pradesh.[11] These regional variations can at best find a historical justification. When the Pentecostal movement came to Kerala in the first half of this century, the idea of radical holiness was taken for granted. In addition, at this time, many Brethren, known to represent especially radical separation, joined the movement. In Tamil Nadu and Andhra Pradesh, on the contrary, Pentecostalism gained a footing only after the Second World War. The American missionaries brought with them a much more moderate attitude to ethical norms. Tamil Nadu differs from Andhra Pradesh, especially in the south under the influence of Kerala: here the rejection of jewelry prevails much more strongly than in Andhra Pradesh. Only the two larger, trans-regional churches have a uniform attitude to the question: the Ceylon Pentecostal Mission and the Church of God reject the wearing of jewelry. The other churches reflect the regional variations. So, for example, the Indian Pentecostal Church in Kerala and Tamil Nadu are rejecting but not in Andhra Pradesh.[12] So it is too with the Assemblies of God, who in Tamil Nadu are protagonists of the moderate tendency but in Kerala incline to the majority rejectionist view. The question of jewelry is closely related to the baptism question. Apart from Kerala, most churches, with the exception of the Ceylon Pentecostal Mission, take the position that it is allowable to baptize with jewelry.[13] But, at the same time, it is still decided as before that wearing jewels is not up to the standard of a Christian lifestyle. The debate about jewelry is a good example of how Pentecostal theology, being experientially guided, is capable of such unconventional argumentation. This orientation by practical experience is a resource, not to be underestimated, for breaking deadlocks. The founder of the Apostolic Christian Assembly, G. Sunderam, went in at an early stage for baptism with jewelry, although he himself was strongly stamped by the radical teaching of the Ceylon Pentecostal Mission. According to a well-publicized version, his view was justified as follows:

11. In the case of the few Kannada-speaking congregations in Karnataka, the author has no information concerning their attitudes on the jewelry question.

12. Against the general trend, in 1995, Isaac Komanapalli for World Missionary Evangelism put a clause in the constitutions providing that baptism is not to be conferred with jewelry.

13. There are indications that now even in the Ceylon Pentecostal Mission there are cases of getting baptized while wearing jewelry. If this proves to be the case, it is exceptional.

Once, he [G. Sunderam] gave the baptism for one sister, that time, she is having jewels and everything. Some people came and told: "Pastor, why are you giving baptism, because she is wearing jewels and all?" Pastor told them: "Why? Already, she received the anointing. When she received the anointing while she was having this jewels. That time, she is receiving. So, why you ask what this is? I am just an ordinary man. So, already, she is having this experience with jewels. So, there is no obstacle, I have to do this, to give the immersion baptism. So, that is not a problem." So, he told the congregation.[14]

In another case, a pastor from Bangalore explained his change of opinion by the fact that God had spoken to him:

So, the leader of the church, he insisted that we have to baptize without jewels, and give communion without jewels. So, I was practicing it. I was, one day, having this communion service. There was a lady with jewels. I did not give communion to this sister, I bypassed her, because she was wearing jewels. When I did that, the Holy Spirit stopped me. He said: "Who gave you authority to bypass her?" I heard it from the Lord. So, I came back and gave her the communion. So, that afternoon, I came back and I closed my room. I said: "Lord, I want to know about this from You, not from what men would say, or what men's opinion would say, but what You would say to me." . . . God told me that nowhere it is written that you should not baptize [with jewels] or force people to do this. Or that you should exercise communion service with this kind of doctrine. I felt it is not really from God. It is somewhere opinion of a man, in the name of separation.[15]

This example shows clearly that the Pentecostal emphasis on experience of God can be an aid to reinterpreting a biblical text in an altered situation and to breaking through rigid biblicism. To a considerable extent, successful mission activity prevents the refusal to baptize with jewelry. Since there is often competition for the same target group, the congregations whose pastors refuse to baptize people with jewelry fall behind the moderates in their rate of growth. The following example is illuminating. An independent Tamil pastor relates how he came, through a decisive experience, to the conviction that baptism can be administered to people with jewelry:

14. Interview.
15. Interview.

I baptize with jewels, I give communion. . . . I think, I got the reason for that when I was pastor in the Church of God in Madras. My wife's college mate. She was a Master's degree holder. She was a lecturer. She and her mother, they both used to come to our church. And, during one baptismal service, I gave them all the lessons and everything, and I mentioned to them: "Next Sunday, if you want, come prepared for baptism, those of you, who are wearing jewels, please remove them." So, I said, that is a routine announcement that you make in the Church of God. So, I did that. And, the next week, out of ten people to be baptized these two ladies didn't show up. And, I know, how much I have prayed for them, how much I have visited. And, we did a very hard work to get them to the Lord. Of course, God saved them, but we really worked hard, and then, they did not turn up to the baptism service. Of course, I thought, maybe, they had changed their minds or were hindered in some way. And, next week they also didn't show up. So, I was really wondering. And, during that week, after the second Sunday, I saw them on the road walking. So, I stopped my scooter and I said: "Why don't you come to the church on Sunday anymore?" So, she said: "Well, pastor, we wanted to be baptized, we wanted to be baptized in our church only. But, you mentioned about the jewels. My husband is quite against removing it. But, I wanted to obey the Lord either. Someone told me that Pastor [G.] Sunderam is baptizing with jewels. So, we went there and got baptized." So, I said: "Okay, why didn't you come to the church?" They said: "Well, we got baptized, so we started to continue there." So, we lost two of them. And, not even three month later, again, we saw them on the road, on Sunday afternoon, after coming from the service. And, there was nothing on them [no jewels]. And her husband was walking along with them. And I stopped and said: "Praise the Lord." And, she said: "Pastor, I have a joyful news, my husband also got saved. We removed all the jewels, just two weeks ago." And, she also told me: "We would have stayed in the church where we got saved, but for this [jewels] only we left it." So, I thought about it very deeply.[16]

The case described here contains the justification most often used for the possibility of baptizing even with jewelry: holiness is a process the beginning of which does not require putting jewelry away. In the course of time, the believer, if growing in faith, will see that it is better not to wear jewelry. To the question of the connection between holiness and jewelry which the author

16. Interview.

put forward in nearly all interviews, it was often emphasized that it should be left to the decision of the believer if and when jewelry should be put aside. The following position taken by two pastors from Thanjavur and Bangalore can stand as representations of this more moderate opinion:

> Jewels, we leave it to the congregation. If you really want to remove, you can remove. But it is not a strict order. . . . We tell them, but we don't force them.[17]

> But, we have had a sister coming into our Assembly with jewels. I never tell them to take it off. I say: "If you take it off because I tell you, it doesn't work. You must be convinced about it yourself. So, if you want to sit here, sit here ten years. I will not treat you like a second-class believer if you love the Lord."[18]

The Assemblies of God, which were growing rapidly in Tamil Nadu in the 1970s, played a leading role in the liberalization of the jewelry question. There were many pastors who attributed no importance to the rejection of jewelry, although officially there remained a whole range of restrictions. For pastors in the Assemblies of God and their wives it is strictly forbidden to wear jewelry themselves. The marriage celebration, as formerly, must be without bridal necklaces but privately after the church ceremony, there is nothing against giving the bride the necklace. So there is an undeniable tendency to put the wearing of jewelry in the range of adiaphora.

Originally, practically every secular tendency is under suspicion of aiding and abetting worldliness. Strict separation from the world is to be taken for granted for the born-again Christian. Right up to the beginning of the 1990s, every development started from the assumption that only a few clearly defined forms of behavior could be taken as the external signs of a holy life; anything that could not be counted among these signs was implicitly left in the domain of the adiaphora. Thus in practice not much remained of the formerly radical idea of holiness. These decisive changes are well known to representatives of the south Indian Pentecostal movement and cause some unease. In innumerable interviews with the author, members deplored the decline of ethical standards and of clear teaching relating to standards. Since now wearing jewelry is often reckoned to belong to the sphere of the adiaphora, there is no longer much that could be taken as external evidence

17. Interview.
18. Interview.

188

of holiness. Separation from the world now is limited to abstention from smoking, drinking, cinema viewing, and any form of sexual promiscuity. So Pentecostal ethics comes to be restricted to private matters, and the social implications of holiness, which undoubtedly were given with its radical hostility to the world, are neutralized. Moreover, the south Indian Pentecostal movement does share the remaining ethical minimal standards with the majority of the Indian population: in India smoking is generally considered to be in bad taste, and calls for prohibition of alcohol are winning political support.[19] As always, the majority of marriages in India are still arranged by the parents,[20] and in Indian society strict separation of the sexes still prevails. In spite of the fact that the cinema represents by far the most popular leisure activity, it is not highly regarded from the moral point of view in conservative Hindu circles; in established Protestant churches an inquiry showed that over two-thirds held that going to the cinema was a sin.[21] With this turning away from hostility to the world, the Pentecostal movement has shown considerable flexibility and has managed to face the demands of modernity. Even the radical Ceylon Pentecostal Mission has not set itself completely against possessing a television set. Hostility to technical things is quite alien to the south Indian Pentecostal movement. In addition, it should not be overlooked that ethical rigorism is affected by congregations' general economic rise into the middle classes. It remains to be seen how ethical norms will develop. In spite of all weakening, the demand that the Christian should live a life that is visibly without reproach remains fixed in the thinking of the south Indian Pentecostal movement. The connection between holiness and unworldliness has long kept the south Indian Pentecostal movement from preaching a prosperity gospel. The appearance of the Faith Movement in the 1980s and the propagation of the "financial aspects of the gospel" went parallel with an increasing turn away from the original separation. Indeed, it was only then that the idea of a prosperity gospel struck a chord with many south Indian Pentecostal congregations.

The strict hostility to the world in the early period, as well as the increasing restriction of holiness to individual taboos, were factors preventing the south Indian Pentecostal movement from bringing holiness and social engagement into close connection. The social engagement of particular Pentecostal churches, which was sometimes not inconsiderable, served as a rule as a

19. According to a representative questionnaire of Indian voters from 1996, 86 percent supported a countrywide ban of alcohol; see Yadav 1996: 43.

20. According to a questionnaire in 1996, even in the urban middle class 81 percent are still arranged marriages; see Jain 1996: 78-85.

21. See Gnanasekar 1994.

means toward mission and usually arose through the initiative of overseas partners. This is treated elsewhere.[22] In attitudes to politics, holiness thinking still plays a significant role. Although south Indian Pentecostals in the 1990s were politically concerned contemporaries, they showed a thoroughly distanced relation to politics. The author put questions about politics in nearly every interview. The majority could not understand that a Christian in India could combine active involvement in politics and a holy life. But apparently many Pentecostals vote in political elections.[23]

22. See pp. 212ff.
23. See also Augustine 1993: 152. On the relationship between Pentecostalism and politics in general, see Freston 2001.

CHAPTER 12

Ministry

The life of the south Indian Pentecostal movement depends on strong participation by the laity. However, there is also a pronounced, almost sacramental conception of the ministry. The ministry of the pastor is defined relatively clearly. It is distinguished in practice from that of the evangelist, but the latter is less clearly comprehended. Other ministries play no role worth mentioning.[1] There is strong reserve against allowing women into church ministry.

Pastors

Divine Calling

For a pastor in the south Indian Pentecostal movement, it is generally desirable that he should have a direct calling from God and be in full-time minis-

---

1. On the question of ministries, the author was repeatedly referred to texts like Ephesians 4:11 where, alongside pastor and evangelist, other ministries were distinguished, but in practice no use was found for the text. When some older Pentecostal leaders like K. E. Abraham and P. M. Samuel claimed the title of apostle for themselves, it was a matter of a purely honorary title not connected with any special understanding of ministry. It is only in connection with the Restoration Movement that the idea of the ministry of the apostle caught on. But this did not lead to any wider acceptance. If the leader of the Church of God of Prophecy in India took the title of bishop, this was according to the worldwide rule of this particular church and has no further parallels in the south Indian Pentecostal movement. For a general treatment of ministry in the Pentecostal movement, see Dusing 1995.

try. The experience of a calling is strongly stamped by the pattern of the Old Testament prophets. The south Indian Pentecostal pastor sees himself as a charismatic leader rather than as a priest. The following explanation from a Tamil pastor expresses this attitude:

> I believe, that for a preacher the basic requirement is that he must be saved, and the second, most important requirement is, that he must be called by God. Not just university education or seminary education, it is not enough. You must be called by God, because Moses was, Joshua was, David was called. . . . God calls people.[2]

The similarity to charismatic patterns of leadership in the Old Testament is clear. Likewise, the call to ministry frequently finds its pattern in Old Testament accounts, as the following example from Tamil Nadu shows:

> [T]hat night I was sleeping and I saw words of the book of Jeremiah, chapter one, verses five to ten, written on the wall. The Lord said that as you are a child I have put my word in your mouth. So, get up and speak. So, when I explained it to the pastor he said: "That is what God wants you to do. You have to go into the ministry."[3]

Strong dependence on Old Testament patterns appears also in the following complex of themes. In stories about a call there will often be a reference to a vow taken by parents who have no male progeny, promising God that, if a son is born, they will dedicate him to church ministry. This is a practice quite widespread among Christians of the established churches in south India. The following example from the autobiography of P. M. Samuel illustrates elements typical of such dedication:

> Like Hannah in the Old Testament my parents had no sons but had seven daughters. They poured out their heart before God. My mother took an oath that she would dedicate her son if the Lord grants her heart's desire. God heard her prayer and granted her desire. Since they took an oath they dedicated me for Christ's service and named me Samuel.[4]

2. Interview.
3. Interview.
4. Samuel 1980: 3.

This kind of dedication is recognized by the south Indian Pentecostal movement. Many pastors and evangelists treasure the fact that they were already dedicated to service for the Lord before they were born. This strengthens in a certain way the credibility of their later call to ministry. But the call to ministry remains the decisive fact, as shown by the following example from south Tamil Nadu:

> When I was eighteen years old, God met me and called me for this ministry. Before that, before my birth, my parents had a vow upon me. They prayed to God: "Oh God, if You give us one male child, we will give him to your work," they said to themselves. When I was eighteen years old, they told me about that, but I asked me, if there is not any call or any vision of the Lord, I will never accept that vow. So, I prayed very much. One day, when I was praying, in a meeting, I heard a voice from above: "My son, I forgive your sins, and I clean your heart by my blood which is shed for you. Your name is written in the book. You follow me and do my work." . . . I was full of joy.[5]

The dedication before birth serves some pastors and evangelists to emphasize their special election by God. They interpret the dedication carried out by their parents, generally based on 1 Samuel 1, in the sense of being chosen by God before birth, as they find it in the prophetic tradition of Jeremiah 1:5 and Isaiah 49:1 and also in the mission consciousness of Paul (Gal. 1:15). Thus, a Tamil pastor reports:

> I was the first born. When I was in the mother's womb just before my birth, the Lord visited my mother in a vision, and said: "This birth is in your womb, some boy, and he shall serve me." So, that is the calling, revealed to [my mother].[6]

Besides this dependence on Old Testament themes, there are many other kinds of calling to ministry. There is great variation in the way a call is received and all recognized forms of communication with God occur. Often it is just that a Bible text becomes clear before the eyes of the one called:

5. Interview.
6. Interview. On the question of Pentecostal tradition formation, it is not without interest that in the written autobiographical draft left by the same pastor it just says: ". . . my parents dedicated me for God's work when I was still in my mother's womb . . ." (Chelladurai 1995).

[O]ne day, Sunday service, I attended, and I prayed and I opened my Bible, and my eyes fell on a verse. Matthew, sixteenth chapter, sixteenth verse. And, my eyes fell on that one. Suddenly the letters became alive, you know, and those verses spoke to me. Those verses are like: Peter, I will build my church on your rock. When I read that, suddenly I knew. . . . You know, I read many times those scriptures. I read the New Testament, many times. On that day, it is something. God is speaking that he wants me to be a full-time minister. So, I felt the call of God after I read that word. And, you know the word Peter. So, my name is Peter. God is calling me by my name and asking me to build a church, to establish churches.[7]

Many who are thinking of going into full-time ministry seek clearer guidance through prophecy. We have already dealt with this possibility of being called through prophetic promise.[8] In rallies there are often special altar calls challenging people to openly announce a decision for full-time service. Very widespread are accounts of visions through which people are called in this way:

So, in that prayer meeting, the Lord gave me a vision. That vision lasted for three hours, or so. . . . It was my sister who died that I saw. And she showed me the horrors of hell, and the beauty of heaven. And she asked me: "Do you want the people to go to hell?" I said: "No." She went on: "But, brother, will you preach the gospel?" I said: "Daddy is preaching. That is alright, he suffered enough." She said: "But, this is a beautiful place, I am not suffering, I am here with God." And then I said: "Yes, I will do God's work."[9]

There is no withdrawing from the divine call. Many testify that they try to reject the call and discover that God is not to be bargained with. This motif is closely related to the conception of divine punishment through illness.[10] A typical example is the following case in which one vainly attempts to offer a great part of one's earnings to church work, if only he could continue in a secular calling:

7. Interview.
8. See pp. 176ff.
9. Interview.
10. See pp. 151ff.

Usually, after I received the baptism of the Holy Spirit, I would pray three hours a day. One day, I am praying, six o'clock, and had a big light around me. From the right side I heard a voice: "My son, carry my work and follow." Again and again, I am hearing the same voice. When I heard the voice, I understood that it was a call to ministry. I said: "Oh Lord, raise some other people. I am educated. I will give a good part of my salary to those men that you are going to raise." Then, again and again I was hearing this voice. My heart was broken. Then, I said: "Oh Lord, if it is your will, I will do your job."[11]

The strong emphasis on direct divine calling to ministry corresponds to the idea that a pastor must be in full-time ministry. Part-time congregational leaders are not thought of as of equal status. Anyone who has a secular job and at the same time is leading a congregation independently will normally call a full-time pastor for celebrating baptism and Holy Communion. It also appears that part-time ministry amounts to lack of trust in God. If God calls one to his service, he will care for his minister. This view represents a particular motif in testimonies:

In the middle of the night, God spoke to me. I had a vision. In the vision, Jesus appeared to me and He said: "Son, you must come and follow Me to do My ministry." Then, I said: "Lord, I suffered a lot, I was hungry, I know the starvation [from my childhood]. So, I don't want to go to the same experience in my life. So, I will make money, I will give You more than a half." But, God spoke to me: "I don't want your money, I just want you. I will give you money."[12]

The conviction that a pastor should be engaged in full-time ministry is not based so much on practical necessities but rather on the idea that one called by God "lives by faith", which invokes the "faith principle," as worked out in detail in the worldwide "faith missions."[13] This reference is explicitly made by the south Indian Pentecostal movement. George Müller is especially honored here. It is said concerning K. E. Abraham: "The faith life of George Muller and of other faith heroes inspired Pastor Abraham."[14] "Living by faith" means the radical intent to expect help from God alone and is highly

---

11. Interview.
12. Interview.
13. See Fiedler 1992: 100f.; Franz 1993: 1-28.
14. Verghese 1974: 79.

appreciated in the south Indian Pentecostal movement. The faith principle, put briefly, is: "Never to tell man his needs; Never to borrow; But to depend entirely on God."[15] Both oral and written accounts are full of examples of how situations of need were marvelously brought to an end. An example from the autobiography of Abraham, which has been a model for following generations to large extent, will provide some insight into this theme, so important for the self-identity of the south Indian Pentecostal movement:

> Including the Bible School students we were fifty. From Monday to Wednesday none of us had any food. All became exhausted. I was lying down. Unable to get up, I prayed on my bed. "Lord, haven't I started this school with your guidance? If it is without your approval, tell me, I shall close it immediately; otherwise send thy help." In reply, God spoke to my heart. "Son, I wanted the young evangelists to be trained to depend upon me in their life of ministry. Therefore, call them together and ask them to pray. I shall send food." Soon I rang the bell. When assembled, I asked them to stand in a circle, holding each other's hand and to pray thus: "Lord, we thank thee for the food." This was in line with Jesus' teaching: "When you pray believe that you receive them and you shall have them." [See Mark 11:24.] At the end of the prayer I asked my wife to put water to boil as the rice and provisions were on their way. Nothing was in sight. I said this only on faith. Immediately Satan whispered in my ears: "What a fool are you? Where will you hide your face if the food doesn't come?" I rebuked Satan. What a wonder! While we were looking through the window one of the brothers living two miles away came in with a basket full of foodstuff. We could not believe our eyes. The man had no notion of our situation whatsoever.[16]

This typical account shows that the "life of faith" is often exaggerated and embellished in the telling. With closer analysis, the faith principle proves to be part of a well-functioning financial system of distribution, which we will describe later.[17] The principle was often useful to south Indian pastors to free themselves from dependence on foreign missionary undertakings, because it is a complete contradiction to the life of faith to receive a regular salary as most western missionaries paid to their coworkers. In contradistinction to the faith principle, which emphasizes God's care for his own, there is a phenome-

---

15. Verghese 1974: 77.
16. Verghese 1974: 79-80. This is an English translation from Abraham 1983.
17. See pp. 215ff.

nologically related complex of ideas, though less widespread: Any opponent who sets himself against the servant of God or wishes to harm him will have to reckon with direct punishment from God. It is not unusual for mishaps that come upon the adversary to be interpreted as direct divine punishment. This is the case in the following account by a leader in the Pentecostal movement of the fate about a fellow worker who tried to split the congregation:

> They started another church. The foreign mission money, dividing the national churches. . . . This fellow was a lecturer, a member of my church. . . . And, that fellow, when he divided my church, that fellow, [and] another elder. . . . This fellow after constructing Douglas church buildings he died. Young fellow, the lecturer died. . . . The elder also, after two years, he died. Another family joined with him, they died. This fellow took my work, really, I told you, this is a deceit. . . . He took his relatives and heathens and Hindus as pastors . . . his relatives and all he wrote as pastors, and deceitfully, he got money [for them]. And, God punished him, and he died. He died as a young fellow when he was thirty-five.[18]

This interpretation of a directly punishing God is often used to prove that one side in a controversial encounter is right. The following argument was delivered to the author by a member of A. Jacob's family to show that God was on the side of Siloam:[19]

> But, God's grace was also with us. See, the main key persons, even some police officers, some three police officers, who were the key reason for raiding and all this, they died actually. And, even this Job's elder son [Job was an investigating tax inspector], he was a very boy, he got some kind of attack and he died. So, like that, I am not happy about it, but at the same time, what I can say. Those who raised against God's work and God's ministry, God teaches them some lesson also, while proving that God is with us.[20]

Such narrations are taken quite seriously in the Indian context. The Pentecostal pastor as a charismatic man of God, who cannot be withstood without punishment, corresponds to the Hindu image of the holy man who is ca-

18. Interview.
19. On Siloam see pp. 76-77.
20. Interview.

pable, through supernatural power, of harming those who oppose him. Thus reports about Hindu adversaries to the Pentecostal movement interpreting potential misfortunes as punishment for their actions do not seem all that incredible. The author was repeatedly told of non-Christian house owners who had first been reluctant to let their premises to a Pentecostal congregation. When they experienced misfortune they attributed this to the supernatural power of the pastor and gave in.[21] Pentecostal conceptions of a vengeful God can, in consequence, go as far as bloodthirsty *schadenfreude*. Nowadays this appears only occasionally, such as in the event described by G. Nickelson:

[M]y Second Son-in-Law Rev. Y. D. Jayaseelan was conducting the Sunday morning service in the city of Agra, the R. S. S. fellows waited till the Church service was over and waited that all the people in the Church to go away. They went inside the Church while he was alone and dragged my Son-in-Law Rev. Y. D. Jayaseelan and began to beat him and assault him. No one came to rescue him[;] they attacked him severely. After this incident one day while my daughter Mrs. Lizzy Jayaseelan while she was washing the dishes began to cry and pray[: "]God, Lord is it not that we came here to this City of Agra according to your call? Then why did you allow us to suffer in the hands of these religious fanatics? If no one comes to our aid, the heathen will rage and take upper hand and persecute, thy children more and more["];] while she was crying and praying like this, she heard a very big sound as if a big bomb exploded. It was very near to their house, what had happened, four of the R. S. S. people they were making country bombs and keeping them on the table. Accidentally one bomb rolled and fell from the table and exploded, just to the heat all the bombs which they were making got exploded. It appears these four people became the victims of the bombs burst, and four of them were reduced to pieces and their bodily flesh was sticking on the walls. Then the people were exclaiming[, "]these four people were the cause for beating the servant of God Rev. Y. D. Jayaseelan some days before[.] How wonderfully God meets his children's need and encourages them.["][22]

21. Hoerschelmann 1977: 182 tells similar stories.
22. Nickelson 1993: 9.

Human Confirmation

What we have related so far shows that the ministry of the Pentecostal pastor is understood as depending on divine calling. But in contrast to this radically charismatic self-understanding, a thorough human confirmation of the divine calling is also required. Although it is theoretically possible and occasionally happens, there are hardly any pastors who have not been ordained by another acknowledged church leader. As a leading pastor from Tamil Nadu emphasized:

> God has already ordained, but we make it open to church. We lay hands and pray and bless them. . . . We acknowledge that God has ordained them and lay our hands on them.[23]

Thus ordination is expressly distinguished from divine calling. However, in practice it entails a not insignificant control over new pastors. In the case of smaller organizations, the presence of recognized and established leaders is greatly valued at ordination celebrations. In the classical Pentecostal churches and in the larger independent churches a yearly renewal of ordination vows is requested. A further regulatory factor is pastoral education, undergone in the 1990s by the majority of ministers, which makes an important contribution to doctrinal consistency in the south Indian Pentecostal movement. However, there seems to be a wide range of form and content in the formation of pastors. The reason for this probably lies in two opposing tendencies that come into play. On the one hand, the idea of radical holiness brings with it an anti-intellectualism that distrusts all worldly knowledge and finds no value in theoretical education. For a long time this anti-intellectualism had great influence within the south Indian Pentecostal movement. A younger Tamil pastor with several academic degrees from American universities, looking back on his early life, reflects critically:

> [A] lot of these Pentecostal pastors . . . none of them are able to read books. I tell you that much . . . they never read any book. If they read one book in a whole lifetime [then that is a great deal]. It is not because they can't read. Some of them are educated enough to read a book, but they don't read, because, they think reading a book is unspiritual. They think the way you get a message is you get it straight from above. You know [everything simply from the] Bible. These are the same people

23. Interview.

they taught me when I was little, that I should never even read a news-paper. . . . They told me that I should not read a newspaper, or a maga-zine or anything.[24]

On the other hand, as opposed to such anti-intellectualism, there is an enormous hunger for education. This is the case in all layers of society in In-dia, and Pentecostals form no exception. A long-serving American mission-ary has a very concise expression for this: "They are mad for education, will do anything or, go anywhere to get education."[25] This zeal for learning is due to the simple fact that in India education is almost the only way to social mo-bility. Anti-intellectualism and the hunger for education must somehow come to terms with this situation. Therefore pastors of the first generation, who would forbid their children to read books etc. at home, were nonetheless eager to let the same children have access to higher education. The social sta-tus conferred by formal educational qualifications explains why pastors and evangelists, who did not hold it necessary to attend a Bible school themselves, decorate themselves publicly with dubious honorary doctorates and titles. If we then take anti-intellectualism and hunger for education as the two guiding influences in the development of Pentecostal training for pastors, the follow-ing picture emerges: in the 1920s and 1930s, leading pastors gathered round them young people who thought of going into full-time ministry or already had a definite call. The young people lived in the pastor's house, helped in the congregation, and received special biblical instruction from time to time. A formal education, as was usual in the seminaries of the established churches, was rejected on the basis of anti-intellectualism. Even in many institutions known as Bible schools, all that happened was that for a few months in the year intensive knowledge of the Bible was imparted. The famous Hebron Bi-ble School, founded by K. E. Abraham in 1930, for example, worked in its first decades entirely according to this principle. But this was nothing other than an adaptation of the Indian model of the guru-shishya relation. This fact has already been noted by Indian Pentecostal theologians themselves:

The teaching style is typically Indian. For two months the College gives an intensive Bible course and then the student works with an experi-enced pastor according to the ancient Indian *Guru-shishya* relationship. During this period the student (disciple) would learn the doctrines, the traits and qualities of the *Guru* (experienced Pastor). The disciple goes

24. Interview.
25. Rajamoni n.d.: 5, p. 1.

through this process for a year or two. When the *Guru* considers him capable of taking up a new work on his own, he encourages the student to open a new preaching point and plant a new Church. In the beginning the organisation will give moral and financial support to start work. When the new pastor rises to the status of his master, he takes disciples and gives them the same practical training.[26]

Formal education for new pastors was first brought in by American missionaries of the classical Pentecostal churches, especially the Assemblies of God. They instituted intensive Bible learning according to the American model, ending with a certificate and organized in a comparatively professional way. The training was generally free or at a quite modest charge for board and lodging. The fact that the school was run by American missionaries made it quite attractive, and these training institutions soon experienced rapid increase since they were seen as a good opportunity to get an education. It is clearly not an exceptional case when, in the present day, a leading member of the Assemblies of God describes his motivation for attending the Bethel Bible School in Punalur as follows:

After I finished my high school, I just wanted to join the Bible School, for the purpose of studies, not for the ministry.[27]

The option of getting a western-style education at an affordable price together with the hope of making western contacts also constituted a significant factor in the success of these Bible schools. This is especially true of the Southern Asian Bible College in Bangalore. However, there were great difficulties in using these Bible schools effectively for training pastors. In 1975, T. C. George wrote concerning the situation in the Bible schools of the Assemblies of God:

Usually after graduation each one goes away on his own. . . . The A. G. Mission [Assemblies of God missionary board in the USA] grants full subsidy to the Bible Schools, but has no program to make use of their graduates. As a result the Bible Schools tend to become an end in themselves rather than a means of multiplying churches.[28]

26. George 1975: 23-24.
27. Interview.
28. George 1975: 27-28.

A glance at the typical career of pastors in the Assemblies of God shows that, as a rule, it is less the Bible school that leaves a lasting mark on the new pastor than the "spiritual father" whom he adopts as a role model. The formal certification of education from the school is seen as a personal status symbol rather than a helpful qualification for pastoral training. Anti-intellectualism continues to bear on this contrast.

However, in the 1970s a new generation arose for whom anti-intellectualism was no longer a constituent part of holiness. An intellectual preparation was gradually recognized as useful for new pastors, and the motivation for entering formal education was no longer exhausted by the acquisition of a paper qualification. Against this background the conviction grew, at least among the Assemblies of God, that a formal education for new Pentecostal pastors was quite necessary. By the middle of the 1990s, in the Assemblies of God of south India, attending a regular Bible school was a condition for ordination or else, in the case of a more experienced candidate, at least the completion of a correspondence course was expected.[29] Such an unequivocal ruling, which is also well observed in practice, makes the Assemblies of God an exception in the south Indian Pentecostal movement. But the tendency is that in the bigger churches, which already have at their disposal bigger Bible schools in the western style, similar rulings will soon be found. Many independent churches too had already taken over some elements of formal training by the 1970s at the latest. In the course of time, they had adopted in many ways a certain minimum of theological instruction. With the help of powerful foreign sponsors, Bible schools were being established, professionally organized and with a western-style curriculum. But, in contrast to the arrangements of the classical Pentecostal churches, these Bible schools held on to many elements of the guru-shishya system. In this way, some of the difficulties mentioned above were avoided in this hybrid form of education, because the head pastor was the one who shaped the character of the work while a somewhat western form of education was offered. So it can be said that in most south Indian Pentecostal churches new pastors now receive a certain formal education. With this general readiness to accept such training methods, the south Indian Pentecostal movement shows considerable flexibility; this is made especially clear by the comparison with the Ceylon Pentecostal Mission. This church is the only notable Pentecostal organization that still in the 1990s held strongly to the guru-shishya system and cherished the old anti-intellectualism, and any kind of formalized education with its western

29. See Assemblies of God 1994: 45-46. Earlier rules contain no such passage (see Assemblies of God 1962: 21).

influence was rejected. The Ceylon Pentecostal Mission, consequently, finds it increasingly difficult to develop its own leadership, which is surely one reason for the stagnation observed in this church. To sum up, it can be observed that direct calling by God is most highly valued. On the other hand, most Pentecostal pastors now serving in south India are subject to considerable human control mechanisms, if only through the training courses they attend. This is certainly one reason why the south Indian Pentecostal movement presents quite a homogeneous face in respect to doctrine.

Evangelists

The ministry of an evangelist is distinguished from that of the pastor in the south Indian Pentecostal movement, as is also the case elsewhere.[30] The boundaries are fluid, however. The ministry of the Evangelist is much less clearly laid down than that of the pastor. The typical evangelist claims a divine calling just like the pastor. But it is not equally clear that he ought to be in full-time ministry. He does not have the care of a congregation and is not considered to be ordained and so cannot administer baptism. He devotes himself principally to the ministry of proclamation, that is, he goes mainly as guest preacher to congregations and church conventions or to organized evangelical rallies. His preaching concentrates on conversion and healing; most often he is a recognized prophet. He crosses church boundaries and often his influence extends to the established churches. However, in reality there is considerable digression from this ideal type of the evangelist. In the first place, many pastors are also active as evangelists. It is easy to understand that a pastor with a special gift for preaching or healing will receive invitations from other congregations. But one can only speak of a "double calling" to be "pastor cum evangelist"[31] when the evangelical activity undertaken is ranked equally with work for the congregation. It is rare for successful evangelists to found their own congregation. The reason is that their acceptance depends to a considerable extent on the fact that the pastors inviting them do not see them as rivals. Competitiveness plays a part in the fact that evangelists in general do not have the undisputed right to administer baptism. On the other hand, Sam Jebadurai was scarcely bothered for having laid claim to this right as evangelist. Some Pentecostal evangelists, like D. G. S. Dhinakaran, John

---

30. On the ministry of evangelists in the Pentecostal movement generally, see McClung 1990.
31. Interview.

Solomon, and John Joseph have official recognition as members of the Church of South India, which facilitates their invitations to established churches. Most evangelists put their church allegiance in the background and would rather be called interdenominational. With respect to teaching, the evangelist has more freedom than a pastor. For example, Justin Prabakaran, as an evangelist of the Assemblies of God, could present the peculiar teachings of the Faith Movement at some length, which could scarcely have been allowed for a pastor in this church.

Women

Leaders and pastors in the south Indian Pentecostal movement are almost exclusively men, as is the case in most Protestant mainline churches in India. Whereas, at least theologically and theoretically, many Indian mainline churches promote the ordination of women, the overwhelming majority of south Indian Pentecostal leaders and pastors, when directly questioned by the author, denied the permissibility of ordained women pastors on theological grounds. Even preaching before Christian believers is generally not allowed. As a rule, reference is made to the New Testament house tables (Col. 3:18–4:1; Eph. 5:22–6:9), and it is argued that a woman should not exercise mastery of any kind over a man. This would exclude a woman giving doctrinal instruction to men; hence, it is not allowed for a woman to preach in church services. Some also refer to the fact that all twelve apostles were men. Nevertheless, it is the activities of the women that contribute to a large extent to the growth of the south Indian Pentecostal movement. Apart from these restrictions, women have the freedom to engage in many authoritative ways in the congregations. For instance, the gift of prophecy is exercised especially by women. Moreover, women have complete freedom to lead a circle of women and to preach there. Also, preaching to those who are not born-again Christians is allowed. So the whole field of mission is open to them, and in fact they play a decisive role in it. Furthermore, practice reveals that not a few women have succeeded in overcoming the restrictions laid on them and have assumed leading roles in the south Indian Pentecostal movement.

Pastors are often married to women who are spiritually gifted. This is not accidental. Women who feel that they have received a call to ministry often quite deliberately seek marriage to a pastor. Such a choice often means a conscious break with the traditional role their family has intended for them. This is expressed quite explicitly in the account of a Tamil pastor's wife who received a call to ministry and was quite ready to reject an arranged marriage with a member of an established church in order to marry a Pentecostal pastor:

> My family arranged a marriage to a Lutheran man. . . . At that time, Pastor S. [the pastor of a Pentecostal congregation which she attended], had a vision that: "If she rejects, I will give her a pastor [as a husband]." Like that the word of God came to his vision. Then he revealed [to me]: "If you reject the marriage, God will give you a pastor [as a husband]." The same word he told me. Then I had the clear-cut idea, that this [arranged marriage] is not the will of God. Then, I started to resist the marriage. The bridegroom party printed the wedding cards. My brother printed the wedding cards for me. . . . Only ten days [until the marriage] . . . I came to my sister's house: "Please call the bridegroom party, I am going to stop the marriage." . . . So, everything was confused like anything. I stubbornly stood alone. . . . So, then I told: "Now, I am going to follow Jesus. I have taken the cross, I took the narrow path, I have to go alone." Then, all my brothers were shouting like: "Such a mad idea!" I said: "No, I am telling the truth. I am going alone." [The pastor then arranged a new suitable bridegroom who was a Pentecostal pastor.][32]

In practice, pastors' wives overcome the restrictions theoretically laid on them and de facto undertake leading roles in the congregations. They preach before the congregation and on particular occasions, such as house prayer groups, fasting vigils, and other smaller events; they even stand in for their husbands.

The whole congregational life in general is also strongly shaped and influenced by women. Their manifold and wide congregational engagements lead very often to their overcoming the theoretical limitations. For lack of engaged and gifted men, many women are leaders in house groups where members from the neighborhood meet weekly. In that way, women do exercise a leading and educational role over men. Still more significant are the women who have a special gift for healing. As a rule they are recognized as prophets and they are popular. Often they go so far as to found their own congregations with the single restriction that they must get a male pastor for baptism and Holy Communion. It is especially easy for groups led by women when there is a spiritual revival, but especially difficult in the move toward establishment. This appears to be the reason why significant limits are set to their growth. At any rate, in the history of the south Indian Pente-

32. Interview.

costal movement, there have been no large-scale or trans-regional churches
led by a woman so far. However, reference should at least be made to Sarah
Navaroji's Zion Gospel Prayer Fellowship in this context. Congregations
founded by women and growing rapidly would often be taken over later by a
man.[33] When questioning this development critically, the author often heard
the following justification:

> Nowadays, we don't allow them to conduct the church services and
> other things. Because, in the beginning, lady workers did a lot, a lot of
> Christian work. Now we have enough men workers. That's why that
> problem doesn't arise.[34]

In spite of this, some women have managed to establish themselves as recognized evangelists. This is facilitated by the fact that the ministry of evangelists is less clearly defined and is not connected with ordination. Well-known
women evangelists like Padma Mudaliar are readily invited even by the Pentecostal churches that generally deny women the right to preach. These contradictions do not necessarily lead to theological reconsideration. Indian Pentecostals, with their practical orientation, can quite easily live with exceptions.
When asking about the inconsistency between theory and practice on the position of women leadership, the author was often answered in ways such as
the following:

> [I]f God calls them [the women] who am I to say they cannot do it?[35]
> When God has appointed. . . . He is almighty, omnipotent, all-perfect
> God, He can use anyone to any place, that's what I believe.[36]

However, certain changes are happening. They go back to the influence of
the American Pentecostal movement,[37] although such influences toward
change should not be overestimated. The many female American missionaries, from Mary Chapman to Dora P. Myers, who formed hundreds of Indian
pastors by their direction of Bible schools in Kerala and Tamil Nadu, and who
exercised considerable theological and administrative control, had no impact

---

33. For a typical example of a small congregation led by a woman, see Hoerschelmann's account of Rachel Devadasan in Hoerschelmann 1977: 396-415.
34. Interview.
35. Interview.
36. Interview.
37. On historical developments in the role of women in the American Pentecostal
movement, see Riss 1990; Poloma 1995: 245-52; Griffith & Roebuck 2002.

on a more tolerant approach to the role of women in leadership positions within south Indian Pentecostalism. It seems that these women were always perceived as westerners, governed by different principles from those valid for Indians. There was no impulse from them on the question of women, as was repeatedly confirmed to the author. With some qualifications, this is true today. The American missionary Naomi Dowdy is senior pastor of the Trinity Christian Centre, one of the largest Pentecostal congregations in Singapore, and she also serves as Founder-President of the Theological Centre for Asia, a graduate and postgraduate training school for both ministerial students and laymen. Dowdy holds intensive contacts with the Assemblies of God congregation New Life Assembly at Madras. When she visits the New Life Assembly, she will be fully accepted as an ordained Pentecostal pastor there, even though the leader of that congregation, D. Mohan, holds it to be impossible for *Indian* women to be ordained as pastors. After all, the South India Assemblies of God, in 1994, have at least decided to institute a "Bible Women's Certificate."[38] This may be seen as a small step on the way to women's ordination. In the meantime, among Indian women active in the ministry of proclamation, decisive arguments are being brought forward against the limitations laid on them. Thus, a well-known evangelist who also directs a successful Bible school for women comes out decidedly and in all clarity against restrictions on the right to preach:

> See, when I started to preach, people said, "You should not preach doctrines. You only simply say, Jesus loves and heals, and saves. That's all." Then I started to cry to Jesus: "If I preach I preach the Full Gospel . . . I will tell the truth and liberate the people. So, give me a verse which will support my call." Then God gave me three Bible verses. God gave me the following foundational teaching. Number One: Those who worship Him, must worship Him in truth [John 4:24]. Like as a doctrine of worship. Number Two: The truth about resurrection and life. Paul says without resurrection there is no preaching [1 Cor. 15:14]. Number Three: On the day of resurrection Jesus said, he is inaugurating a new and living way by which we can call God "Abba, Father." Through the blood of the new covenant [apparently referring to John 20:17-18]. All the three doctrines were given to a woman. Number One: The doctrine of worship is given to a Samaritan woman. Number Two: The doctrine of resurrection is given to Mary. Number Three [John 20:17-18 is also directed to Mary]. All the three doctrines . . . why Jesus told [them to] women?

38. Assemblies of God 1994: 47 (art. x, p. 2).

The moment God told to the Samaritan woman, she went straight away into the village and gave the gospel and brought the people [to Jesus]. Jesus never rebuked her, rather he accused the people to accuse her. And, also on the day of resurrection Jesus told: "Mary, go and tell my disciples. That is a command, Go and tell." So, who can stop me from going and telling? When God gives me a command who is there to stop me?[39]

To the question whether she believed a woman could become a pastor, she answered, at first evasively, "Not in Indian culture." To further questioning, even on this point, she came out clearly:

Yes, they can, because in the Bible there were churches, gathered in the houses, where the church worker was a woman. I can give you the reference. But in the Indian culture. If anything hinders . . . you should not do it [Romans 14]. So, if a lady pastor is hindering some people I won't do it. . . . If I start a church, they throw me out. Then, all the doors will close for the propagation of the Gospel.[40]

Such expressions of opinion make clear the growing self-awareness in south Indian Pentecostal women, who are no longer ready to accept the traditional theological arguments by which women are excluded from the ministry of pastor as self-evident. Women's acceptance as pastors in the south Indian Pentecostal movement may be closer at hand than might be expected.

39. Interview.
40. Interview. It is noteworthy that the Indian Pentecostal theologian M. Stephen also supports the ordination of women; see Stephen 1999: 50-56.

CHAPTER 13

Church Life

Ecclesiastical Landscape

The south Indian Pentecostal movement is largely made up of various independent regional churches. At the same time there are five large, inter-regional
denominations active in the four southern states (Ceylon Pentecostal Mission,
Indian Pentecostal Church, Assemblies of God, Church of God, World Missionary Evangelism). The many independent churches testify that an ecclesi-
ology with extreme congregational elements is widespread. Individual congregations can see themselves as fully independent "churches," and the existence
of such small independent churches is acceptable on all sides in the south Indian Pentecostal movement.[1] The genesis of a small church, in the ideal type,
can be described as follows: a pastor settles in a particular place in order to
found a church; after hard times, in the beginning, he succeeds in collecting a
small congregation around him that grows steadily and guarantees him a certain income. Representatives of this conception of church will explicitly reject
democratic structures of leadership as, for example, the following explanation
by a pastor of a Tamil independent church makes clear:

> God always calls one man. That's the Bible. He never called a committee.
> He called one Moses, one Joshua, one David, one Gideon. See, that's the
> Bible, he calls one man, imparts his dreams and visions into his soul and
> spirit. And, he gives thousands of people to help him to fulfil his call and
> his vision. So, if the whole power is given in the hands of a committee

1. On Pentecostal understanding of church in general, see Dusing 1995; Hunter 1996.

. . . God doesn't give important visions to a committee. The quality is not there.[2]

The pastor treats the small church over which he presides as "his" church; he has founded it and claims autocratic right of leadership. This right includes that of appointing a successor, which in the majority of cases means a son or a son-in-law. This dynastic principle has no theological justification but is never subjected to criticism within the south Indian Pentecostal movement. It is merely expected that the son or son-in-law designated for the succession should be able to refer to some special divine calling. In cases where the pastor has an outstanding charismatic personality, the church has a considerable growth potential, for example the Living Word Church of J. Harris (Madurai) or the Apostolic Christian Assembly of G. Sunderam (Madras), where the principal congregations number more than a thousand. Under the pastor of some small churches, besides the main congregation, there are small branches. Often this is because a member has moved to another place and founded a prayer group there, which, in effect, becomes a branch. The leader of the main congregation then appoints a pastor for this branch so that it remains directly under him. Such branch congregations are strictly subordinate to the main church.

Often small denominations will evolve from such small churches with miniscule dependent groups, with a larger number of congregations under the oversight of the pastor of the main congregation.[3] The founding of a small denomination will be an objective for most south Indian Pentecostal pastors, although few will attain it. Small denominations develop in various ways. New congregations may be founded by direct mission. Not uncommonly a small Bible school is maintained in the headquarters and the graduates will be helped to found new congregations which will then be subordinate to the main congregation. This missionary method contributes considerably to the growth of the south Indian Pentecostal movement. Small denominations have to struggle with special problems. The loyalty of the branches is often not great because there is a strong tendency of the pastors to set themselves up as independent small churches. If these pastors are to maintain fellowship with the principal congregation, usually financial support for the branches is required. For a small denomination to hold together, signifi-

2. Interview.

3. The distinction between small church and small denomination used here represents only a gradual difference. We speak of a small church as long as there are few or no branches that remain insignificant in comparison with the principal congregation.

cant financial means will be necessary for the headquarters; this, as a rule, is only available with foreign sponsors. Small denominations that grow by missionary methods have only a slow rate of growth. It will be decades before a larger alliance of groups evolves in this way. Hence, a considerable number of leading pastors, who have good relations with overseas supporters, try to get around the labor of fostering missionary growth by taking over small churches into their organization or, put bluntly, by buying them. They take advantage of the fact that the leaders of most small churches are not very well cared for by their congregation and will be thankful for a modest financial backing. In this way, there appears to be an enormous rate of growth, which encourages the foreign sponsors to even greater financial support. But such bought denominations are for structural reasons of only slight constancy. Small churches cobbled together in this way as a rule preserve considerable autonomy: they will make themselves autonomous again or join another denomination with better financial subsidies when financial support dries up — or also in cases where the headquarters tries to influence them too much. It is no exaggeration to say there is a kind of market in which pastors of small churches make bids to join small denominations. The phenomenon certainly brings discredit to the south Indian Pentecostal movement, but foreign sponsors are not without blame for investing so much money in these failing enterprises.

The large inter-regional denominations distinguish themselves from the small denominations especially through a collective leadership and strong administrative structures. Whereas in the small denominations succession as a rule goes by dynasty, the inter-regional denominations have electoral bodies to determine succession. However, regarding administration, the inter-regional denominations differ considerably. The Ceylon Pentecostal Mission is extremely centrally organized. The Church of God also has a very centralized leadership with strong communications through the American headquarters. World Missionary Evangelism is completely controlled by the American headquarters. In the 1990s, the Assemblies of God had the most democratic form of organization within south Indian Pentecostalism, and the Indian Pentecostal Church developed into a union of small denominations. In spite of these differences in administration, harsh internal disputes and confrontations, often conducted with great passion, are characteristic of all of these inter-regional denominations, which is a serious problem. Not a few conflicts have been dragged out into years of legal dispute.

Social Work

A whole range of social projects, especially orphanages, are managed by south Indian Pentecostal churches. But this is not at all an expression of a general awareness of social responsibility on the part of the churches. On the contrary, the south Indian Pentecostal movement maintains a traditional attitude of rejecting social engagement.[4] The following statement from a Tamil pastor could be seen as typical:

> I have found out, wherever the social institutions are, there the church is not growing, because people get help and they demand more. . . . See, my purpose is that everything we do should have eternal value. If they accept Christ, it will help them eternally. . . . Once you help, then they continuously want help. That is not really helping these people.[5]

The strong reservation against church social work was especially pronounced in the early stages but in the course of time it has weakened. It also varies according to region and theological training and goes along with the prevailing conception of holiness. Where the more radical view of holiness is taken, the rejection of social work is strongest. So, for example, in the middle of the 1990s the least social involvement in all the south Indian Pentecostal movement was found in Kerala. A not unessential reason for the extreme rejection of church social work in the beginning must have been conscious distancing from the established churches with their manifold social engagements. But in the 1990s there was an explicit change of position as a leader in the Tamil Assemblies of God explained:

> Social work is good, we need that. But, two things are there. Catholic, Lutheran, CSI [Church of South India]. . . . They do good social work. Number one in India. But, they lost evangelism and church planting. I talked to some Catholic fathers. Practically, no evangelism at all. Null, zero. But, they do tremendous social work. Other the side, Pentecostal, nothing: "No. Go to heaven. No social work. What is this nonsense? . . . Anybody can have a school. Let us preach the gospel." Okay, this is the other extreme. One side is no evangelism. Other side is only evangelism,

---

4. On the position toward social engagement in the Pentecostal movement in general see Snell 1992; Robeck 1992; Dempster 1993; Alexander 1996; and Bergunder 2002b.
5. Interview.

we don't need anything else. . . . We have to find the middle way. And, if there is a need, we can have social work.[6]

But to take such a balanced position does not mean that social engagement in the church has attained real theological significance. The same church leader goes on: "Anything we do. . . . If it is not going to have the result of bringing people to Christ. . . . all that we do must have the result of bringing people to Christ."[7] This means that social work in the church is not explicitly rejected but it does not cease to be treated as a potential danger for mission. Such thinking suggests that those Pentecostals who engage in church social work are motivated by the advantage this brings to church mission. At first, it was western missionaries who initiated social projects and apparently had not merely charitable intentions. Since Indian independence there is difficulty in sending Christian missionaries to India, but for sponsors of charitable institutions this is less of a problem. The Assemblies of God, for example, used the trade school in K. P. Valasai as a way of getting visas for American missionaries.[8] For Scandinavian Pentecostal missionaries, also, it was possible to get residential permits through managing social institutions. This instrumentalization of social work for the Christian mission is in consequence devastating and can go so far as making "rice Christians." Although it is in complete contradiction to Pentecostal self-understanding, some churches use social work as direct incitement for obtaining new members. As to be expected, the results are of a doubtful nature. This is illustrated by the following account of the experience of a Tamil pastor whose congregation completely broke up when the foreign help with which he did social work ceased:

Sunday congregation, we used to have about 200 people. . . . I used to help some people also that they get money. I used to help some poor people, widows, and aged people, and some neglected people. So, they were also coming. But, when they saw that the help is stopped. Naturally, many people left slowly. So, one after the other. But, I told them: "When I was getting, I gave you, but now, you have to trust in the Lord. But, I can't press you on that. But, if you are for the word of God, you come. If you can get some help somewhere and if you want to go after help, you can go, it's left to you." So, many people went away. So, with

6. Interview.
7. Interview.
8. See Rajamoni n.d.: 1, 6.

some, about 20 people, maximum, we can say, we started this work
[without foreign help].[9]

Often western visitors, during their short stay in India, are so struck by the
poverty that they cause their Indian partners to open orphanages financed by
them. A typical example is Thomas Wyatt, who helped to start an orphanage
at Antarvedipalem in 1956.[10] John E. Douglas must also be mentioned in this
context, although he represents an exceptional case insofar as he called into
life, with World Missionary Evangelism, a big organization with strong social
commitment that in the course of time developed into an independent Pentecostal church. Indian pastors are ready to manage these orphanages and other
social institutions since they can provide a considerable additional source of
income. Personnel, facilities, and materials for such institutions can have parallel use for church work. Such a pragmatic view is thoroughly approved of
and supported by the foreign sponsors. Here the line to open abuse is blurred.
Apart from the fact that most pastors already find the task of managing an orphanage in an appropriate way too much of a challenge, not a few succumb to
the temptation to put aside part of the money for private ends. This is quite
proverbial in the south Indian Pentecostal movement. Through this, social
work is further discredited by those who would have nothing to do with such
malpractices. A Tamil pastor from Madras explains:

> I think, I will not do it [social work], unless I can do it like the Catholics,
> or the Lutherans. You go, look at it. You look at Catholic orphanages,
> and, you know, look at the Pentecostal orphanages. Immediately, you
> will see that. Immediately. You will see, the standard of living, every-
> thing, there will be a big difference in the two. Because, these Pentecostal
> orphanages, mostly are run by pastors who find it as a real living for
> them. . . . This is the thing that support is from. It puts petrol in the car,
> it buys the car for them, pays the rent for them, sends their children to
> college . . . whatever is left over goes to it [the orphanage].[11]

Such doubtful practice is the consequence of insufficient theological reflection about the social responsibility of the church. Social work is seen as a
means to other ends. Unfortunately, notorious abuses in social work on the
part of some in the south Indian Pentecostal movement have not led to new

9. Interview.
10. See p. 285.
11. Interview.

theological thinking but rather to an even more critical attitude to church social work in general. However, there are numerous exceptions where church
social work is neither an instrument to mission nor begun only at the wish of
foreign partners nor used for personal enrichment. There certainly are Pentecostal pastors who, within the means of their own congregation and without
foreign sponsors, have established a small orphanage and have given it a simple foundation:

> I believe that by charity God is pleased. Every church should do. So I be-
> lieve not only CSI [Church of South India], but every Church should
> do. They should look after widows, orphans, poor people. So, God is
> pleased by that.[12]

It should also be mentioned that social projects such as those carried
through by representatives of the younger generation, P. J. Titus especially
(Church on the Rock Theological Seminary, Bheemunipatnam, A.P.), show a
new quality and are of such potential that the south Indian Pentecostal movement in the not-too-distant future might become conscious of its social responsibility in a suitable way.

Finances

As is usual in the Pentecostal movement in general, also in India the giving of
tithes is expected.[13] The contributions vary greatly. Not all members actually
pay tithes. But we can assume that in most of the churches at least a kernel of
the congregation will be giving tithes. A notable exception is Zac Poonen,
who is against the practice of expecting tithes:

> I have always preached, all my life, that tithing is a commandment under
> the law, and I openly, publicly, preached, that there is no commandment
> after Acts chapter two, the day of Pentecost, in the new covenant to tithe.
> And, therefore, I talk to all the people: "You don't have to tithe. But, that
> doesn't mean that you don't have to give. There is a difference between
> tithing and giving." So, I don't preach tithing, I preach giving. And, I say,
> first of all, you must give your whole life to the Lord, and, then, [give]

12. Interview.
13. See Mahoney 1993: Ch. 8, pp. 67-69, where the most important Bible texts are gathered.

your money as God has prospered you, and cheerfully, whatever you feel like. That is the New Testament principle. That is 1 Corinthians 16 and 2 Corinthians 9 [1 Cor. 16:2; 2 Cor. 9:7]. It is scriptural. There it is said: "as God has prospered you, and cheerfully."[14]

In this opinion Zac Poonen is quite isolated — moreover, the report that he is against tithes brings him under suspicion of preaching false doctrine. Such a strong reaction of one criticizing the giving of tithes is quite understandable, since tithes form the core of the financial system of the Pentecostal movement. This system, however, includes much more than giving of tithes. It is a matter of an extensive system of distribution based on the idea that through spending on God's work, one can be sure of God's blessing. The following story from a Tamil pastor from Madras may illustrate this:

> [O]ne lady, she is working here nearby. She used to go and wash vessels for every house. She used to earn at most 350 Rupees altogether. But, the tithe which she was giving actually shocked me. She started with 25 Rupees, and 50 Rupees. One day, she came and gave me 100 Rupees. And I was thrilled, and didn't like to take it, because I did know her poverty. I didn't like to take it. Anyway, then I prayed and gave it back to her, saying that: "I know your situation sister, I don't want to take so much from you." Then, immediately, she asked one question which actually slapped me on my face. She asked me: "Pastor, do you stop the blessing which God gives me?" Then, I couldn't answer. But, accordingly, God blesses her in some way or other, and she is much blessed now. God has touched her husband, and he is doing some business, in coconut. Every time it was loss, but when she started giving to the Lord liberally, God started blessing his business.[15]

The motivation to spend arises from the wish to remain under God's permanent blessing. In this system of reimbursement, God is treated as receiver of gifts brought to Him as thanksgiving for blessings already experienced or expected. The pastor or evangelist is only the mediator who takes the gifts in God's name to use in God's work. This recognized mediating role is what enables the full-time minister to live according to the faith principle.[16] A contribution must be made to him, if God has sent a blessing or is to send a bless-

14. Interview.
15. Interview.
16. See pp. 195-96.

ing. So it is customary for an offering to go to the pastor or evangelist as thanksgiving, whenever he prays for someone.

There is a fixed ritual on the occasion of such giving. The money is pressed into the right hand of the full-time minister on departure. While the hands of giver and receiver are in contact, the receiver says a short prayer of thanks in a low voice and takes the money without looking at it. The contribution is understood less as a payment to the one praying than as a gift to God for the blessing imparted through the prayer. Of course, the boundaries here are fluid and it remains an open question how often the gift is rather to the pastor as wonder worker. Still it should not be overlooked that, through the faith principle (that help is from God alone), the relation between giver and receiver is defined in a particular way and is transcended. If the pastor or evangelist receives the money spent for God, it is God who lets him receive it and not simply a member of the congregation. Interpreting it as a miraculous transaction, therefore, transforms the human act of contributing into a divine act. Thus the pastor or evangelist is prevented from falling into a dependent situation, which would be a necessary result of the logic of reimbursement. For this reason it is important for the faith principle that one's needs are presented only to God and not to a human. If a person was directly addressed, then one would be in a relation of human dependency.[17] Many prominent Pentecostal pastors, who have a number of influential foreign sponsors, emphasize vehemently with regard to their preaching tours of the USA that they never tell anyone of their needs or directly ask for support. Literally, this is quite true. Appeals for contributions are presented as prayer intentions ("Please pray for me about these matters"), where it is rather clear on all sides what is really at issue. Pertinently, Zac Poonen criticizes such "prayer letters" as often being another name for "begging letters" relating precisely to financial needs.[18] However, the formal assumption of not having directly asked for support is quite significant in that it tries to prevent a relation of dependence to the giver. This financial system contains a whole range of ritual elements. A pastor or evangelist, when accommodated by a family, will rarely leave the house without some small contribution. In the same way, pastors and evangelists also share gifts among themselves, a fact that should not be overlooked. Furthermore, there is a rich tradition of spontaneous gifts. They are presented with the justification: God has told me to give this money. Such

---

17. There is a comparison in this connection with Marcel Mauss's reference, in his famous treatment of the logic of giving, to complicated rules in classical Hindu law for Brahmins that prevent them incurring dependence on almsgivers. This has a certain phenomenological analogy to the faith principle (see Mauss 1990: 145-47).

18. See Poonen 1982: 33.

spontaneous giving is far from rare. Often, they are claimed by the pastors and evangelists as marvelous proofs of the faith principle. This will be illustrated in the following account by a Tamil pastor:

> Last week, when I left Madras, I took thirty thousand Rupees with me, for all these eight pastors' meetings. But, when I came to Coimbatore, my budget came to two thousand Rupees. There is no money for the pastors' meeting [in Coimbatore left]. . . . Sunday, I can take rest. . . . I decided on Sunday, I must go to some church. So, I went to pastor Arumanaiyakam's church: Zion Assemblies of God. When he [Arumanaiyakam] saw me, he said: "Pastor, the Lord only brought you, you are going to preach." . . . So, by the grace of God, I preached. Then came a lady from Abu Dhabi. She missed her flight, because of the plague. She doesn't know where to go for the service. So, she came to that church Sunday service. And, the Lord spoke to her. She came and said: "Pastor, the Lord has brought you from Madras to Coimbatore, just to speak to me. I want to come and meet you." I said: "Okay, tomorrow morning, before ten thirty, you can come and meet me." . . . There she said: "Pastor, I appreciate your humility and humbleness. . . . Here is an offering." And, she gave an offering. When I saw it, it was ten thousand Rupees. So, likewise, the Lord is meeting the need.[19]

How firmly this financial system is based on the associated faith principle is made clear by the realization that it only functions where there are Christians who are accustomed to make contributions to full-time ministers, whether in the form of tithes or at house visits or as spontaneous giving. This ritualized character of the faith principle is clearly acknowledged by some indigenous Pentecostal missionary societies. They learn by experience that the faith principle will hardly work in non-Christian situations. Accordingly, in one of their publications it says:

> The misconception about "faith living": There are an increasing number of "faith missions" in India for which we thank the Lord. They pay their staff only a small part and expect them to meet the rest of their needs by "faith living." While we greatly respect this concept of dependence on the Lord for one's personal needs, in practice this has an adverse effect on the willingness of persons to go to the unreached areas. It is relatively much easier to "live by faith" in Kottayam or Madras be-

19. Interview.

cause of the concentration of Christian communities there. Therefore most evangelists stay there.[20]

The south Indian Pentecostal movement from the beginning relied on state registration to be able to manage their finances and land holdings in a regular manner. The Indian Pentecostal Church had already registered in 1935. Most small denominations and even many small churches are state registered. As history has proved, this is no protection against abuse. For example, the "trust" as a form of organization has earned a bad reputation since, in contrast to the more democratically structured "society," it allows the founder and his family absolute control of the business of the trust.[21] But even societies are not in practice completely immune from autocratic leadership and misappropriation. In addition, many Pentecostal pastors hold that the faith principle is incompatible with formal and orderly bookkeeping; consequently they insist on managing their financial affairs informally. In the 1990s, however, this attitude was subject to stronger critique within the movement opposing the fact that "'Faith living' in India is too often made synonymous with handling money without an account book."[22] The financial administration of the Pentecostal movement is structurally extremely susceptible to almost any kind of abuse, but there is no reason for universally negative judgments. A certain help in judging the economic relations of a congregation is to be found in the way it was founded. Almost every Pentecostal pastor dreams of having his own church building. In the best case, the building grows with the congregation, that is to say, the congregation is always a little bigger than the building and the latter is steadily enlarged on the basis of a growing congregation. Such church building reflects many stages of expansion and it may be assumed that, in addition to contributions from abroad, considerable local effort has been included. Certainly, the most successful and fastest-growing Pentecostal congregations in south India have built their churches in this way. If the church building is much larger than the congregation and constructed all at once, then it is usually a case of complete financing by overseas sponsors, without notable contributions from the members of the congregation. Such completely sponsored church buildings have as a rule congregations that show no signs of growth. So the way in which churches are built is a good criterion for assessing the actual situation of a congregation.

20. India Missions Association 1994: 8.
21. On the distinction between trust and society, see Sunder Raj et al. 1992: 11-12.
22. Sunder Raj et al. 1992: 168.

Worship and Rites

Sunday worship is the center of Pentecostal piety; by and large, the simple ground pattern is the same as is typical for the movement worldwide.[23] Typically, worship begins with several hymns while the church is filling. Then the pastor greets the congregation. After the hymns there are common prayers of thanksgiving and praise. This will include intercessions and simultaneous prayer by individuals, that is to say, all praying loudly their different prayers together and partly in tongues.[24] At this point, prophecies may be given. In between further hymn singing, Bible passages will be read by members of the congregation and personal testimonies offered to the meeting. Then the collection is taken and the preaching begins. After the preaching there will be some mostly short prayer in common.[25] Worship finishes with a blessing. Then the people stream forward so that hands may be laid on them for their individual needs by the pastor or by elders appointed for this purpose. Such a typical order of service can be subjected to many variations and can be adapted to the actual situation: in fact, in a certain sense it is a characteristic mark of Pentecostal worship throughout the world that the leader may alter the course of things just as he wishes.[26] Thus, a pastor in Coimbatore began his service with the following announcement: "Today I have not brought my message, I don't have a message, I have just come to church, because this is a tenth anniversary of this church. The Lord told me to come in and see, so I have come."[27] Such "free" worship happens not at all infrequently and it can diverge considerably from the basic pattern. Sunday worship has great power for attracting people, and it is to this that the south Indian Pentecostal movement owes its success. Though the manner of south Indian Pentecostal worship is in general agreement with the international basic patterns, it also displays many interesting contextual aspects. Paul Younger, an American Indologist, after he had made a visit to the Apostolic Christian Assembly in Madras, said: "There are, however, many features of the worship Hindus and former Hindus find familiar and in harmony with Tamil

23. See Bloch-Hoell (1964: 162-63) for a general Pentecostal order of worship and Cherian (1995) for a typical agenda in south Indian Pentecostal churches.

24. This also is a general Pentecostal practice; see Parker 1996: 95 n. 9.

25. In contrast to the practice in established churches, Cherian (1995) understands the prayers after the entry hymns as thanksgiving and the prayers after the sermon as intercession. This distinction hardly corresponds to practice in the south Indian churches.

26. See S. Parker 1996: 94-103, where he discusses this phenomenon in some North American Pentecostal communities.

27. Interview.

religious tradition."[28] In particular, he refers to public testimonies and to church songs. But there are also a few congregations in the metropolis in which worship is strongly committed to the American style. Whereas in the more traditional churches people sit on the floor and the sexes are separated, here they sit on chairs without sex discrimination. The language is English, the music American. Such congregations are particularly attractive to English speakers and to the western-oriented elite; in some states they are growing strongly. Typical examples are the Full Gospel Assembly in Bangalore and the New Life Assembly of God in Hyderabad.

Some elements of ministry deserve special consideration. In the first place, we mention the singing in church. Popular film music plays an outstanding role in Indian culture, and Pentecostal hymns are a successful Christian response insofar as they adapt many elements of the culture. It is not surprising that Sarah Navroji and S. J. Berchmans, who have ventured far in such adaptation, are the most famous Pentecostal composers. Pentecostal music is modern and responds to present-day tastes. Moreover, this brings them immense popularity among Christians of the established churches. Cassettes with Pentecostal music have a growing circulation among all Christians. It can be said without exaggeration that the south Indian Pentecostal movement with its music has reached almost every Christian home. The hymns by themselves make Pentecostal worship attractive.

Great significance is also attributed to thanksgiving and praise. This is the part in worship where free rein is given to emotions, where people go into ecstasy and sense the nearness of God. Open emotional devotion is something extraordinary in Indian society, maybe except for the bhakti traditions. In a restrictive society like the Indian, emotion-laden praying may have a liberating effect. A leading pastor from Andhra Pradesh describes the lasting impression that was left in him from Pentecostal worship when he was still a Hindu:

> One man, he was crying and weeping like a woman. And, I saw him. Why this man was weeping? Ladies' weeping is different. Why this man was weeping? So, I was surprised. . . . Then, I looked at the women's side, and the ladies were crying like him. . . . Then, immediately, I got up and went out and told my friends. Friends, this was a confusing place. Nothing, no one was there to hurt them, but they were crying and weeping.[29]

28. Younger 1989: 195.
29. Interview.

Although the prayer is very heartfelt and loud, the members of the congregation do not make themselves very conspicuous. Hardly any of those praying will leave their places or expose themselves in any other way. In many churches believers sitting on the ground maintain a prayerful attitude throughout the intercessions. In other churches, there is standing during prayer with raised hands. It was only when demonic possession was manifested during part of the service that the author was able to observe women creating a chaotic situation with wild gesticulations and jumping about.

Another fixed part of the Pentecostal service is the giving of testimonies. Here members relate their experiences of healing or the situations of need from which they have been miraculously delivered. Also, the intercessions of the congregation for particular intentions can be requested. This giving of testimonies ensures the active participation of the laity and facilitates mutual interest in each other's lot. In this connection really astonishing things may happen. The author, for instance, witnessed the case of an impoverished, illiterate slum dweller speaking for five minutes at a microphone in front of six hundred people, telling how she was nearly bitten by a snake in her house but was delivered by God. One may estimate how this woman from the margins of society would experience a sense of her dignity when she was allowed to speak before so many people and to feel their sympathy.

The sermon is highly valued and can take up half the time of the service. In a certain sense, it represents the rational bit in the emotion-laden course of prayers. All the same it is marked by elements of empathy and rhetoric; a man can be a good pastor only if he is also a capable and exciting orator. A moving sermon is greatly appreciated and is expected to be of appropriate length. It is worth mentioning in this connection that, in south India and especially in Tamil Nadu, public speaking plays an important role, and crowds will assemble to hear a "platform speaker" of repute. Many Tamil preachers, therefore, try to let high Tamil influence their sermons stylistically. In respect of content, the sermons have little originality and vary in quality; they range from randomly aligned explanations of several Bible passages to elaborate, typed scripts that are read in their entirety. Some pastors assert that the content of their sermons comes directly from God, but many others admit that they make use of edifying books in their preparation. In all cases they are confident that it can provide prophetic messages for particular hearers, as explained elsewhere.[30]

The Holy Communion is generally celebrated once in a month at the Sunday service. As in the established churches of India, fruit juice is minis-

30. See pp. 174-75.

tered in place of wine. Any born-again Christian who has received baptism by immersion will be admitted to Holy Communion, but hardly any actual control is exercised in the big congregations of the cities. When directly questioned by the author, most would explain the Lord's Supper as a mere commemorative act. At the same time, there is the idea of a real blessing — as was stated, during Holy Communion in the Apostolic Christian Assembly, that its consumption affects bodily healing. In the big urban congregations, as in the established churches, the attendance at Holy Communion services is up to twice that at regular services. Until the 1950s, the opinion was widespread, especially in the Pentecostal churches of south Kerala and south Tamil Nadu, that Holy Communion should always be celebrated at night and always accompanied by a general washing of feet. This custom, the origin of which cannot be determined with certainty,[31] was the occasion of vigorous controversy. But in the 1990s there are only a few who insist on this particular tradition and even these tolerate celebration on Sunday morning. Not a few churches in these regions leave their pastors free to celebrate morning or evening, and this parallel observance of both practices goes on without conflict. It may be seen as a result of this special tradition that in some churches the foot-washing is observed on special occasions.

Baptism is usually not connected with a Sunday service but constitutes a separate church event. Valid baptism, for the majority of the south Indian Pentecostal movement, is always believers' baptism by immersion. This means that those who were baptized as infants in the established churches must, after conversion, be baptized again. For children of members of the congregation, a kind of substitute for infant baptism is offered in the form of a blessing ceremony.[32] Since baptism is seen as closely connected with conversion, it is rather an individual affair of the one baptized than a matter for the congregation. This is shown in the readiness of most Pentecostal pastors to rebaptize members of the established churches even when these do not belong to their own congregations. Moreover, Pentecostal rebaptism of at least one ordained pastor of the Church of South India has been known to occur, though privately and individually conferred by a leading Pentecostal pastor in Madras. The decision for baptism is almost entirely the responsibility of the one baptized. If a person claims to have experienced the Christian rebirth, a pastor hardly refuses baptism. Regular instruction before baptism is only rarely practiced. In some churches the only impediment to baptism is wearing jewelry.[33] As a rule

31. See also Saju 1994: 173.
32. See also Titus 1995: 5-8, discussing such blessing ceremonies.
33. See pp. 185ff.

baptism takes place after the Sunday service. Usually the only persons present are the pastor, the elders, the candidate, and perhaps a few friends and relatives. The ceremony is short and simple, reduced to essentials. Baptism is conferred by the Trinitarian formula with single immersion. The larger congregations, however, may try to turn it into a celebration of the whole community, in which candidates are assembled at regular intervals for mass baptisms.

A great weakness of south Indian Pentecostalism has been in conducting marriages. Though it is true that many Pentecostal pastors have the necessary official authorization to perform marriages (the marriage license),[34] those who have a double membership marry as a rule in the established church. Then the Pentecostal pastor is only a marriage guest. This is because in India marriage is a matter for the whole family, and the marriage partner is chosen by the parents or elder siblings. As long as the greater part of the family and relatives belong to the established churches, the tendency is particularly strong to marry there, not least because the Pentecostal rejection of the bridal necklace (thali) is scarcely acceptable for Christians of the established churches.[35] However, the traditional form of arranged marriages is expressly welcomed by all the south Indian Pentecostal churches. In the Ceylon Pentecostal Mission, love marriages even lead to automatic exclusion from the church.[36] For a long time Pentecostal marriages in south India were limited to those directly converted from Hinduism and for marriages between young pastors and evangelists. In these cases, the leading pastors acted as marriage brokers. But, after the strong growth of the Pentecostal movement in the 1980s, Pentecostal marriage gains a growing recognition by former members of the established churches.

Funerals, in the early years, seemed a rather distant problem in Pentecostal thinking. There are many accounts that show that the first deaths in the newly founded congregations presented a sudden new problem. The established churches, which had experienced great hostility, refused a burial in their cemeteries. In the 1990s the situation became considerably less tense since in many places regular arrangements for burial are available, either in state cemeteries or through unions of Pentecostal churches who have acquired their own plots. Still, among many pastors, above all, those in small

34. Note that the legal requirements are not uniform in south India. The Indian Christian Marriage Act (ICMA) has no validity in the former Travancore. In its place is the Cochin Christian Civil Marriage Act (CCCMA) under which de facto no special authorization is needed for Christian marriage. Otherwise under ICMA officially recognized marriage registrars are needed. See Rao 1991: esp. 8-14, 132.

35. See pp. 184, 188.

36. The Pentecostal Mission 1984: 16.

denominations, there is great uncertainty in the liturgical handling of funeral ceremonies. This is P. J. Titus's criticism:

On a number of occasions I have noticed that independent Pentecostal pastors are confused, not knowing what to do next. E.g. You take a casket to the burial ground and do not know what to do with it, or you lower a casket not knowing how to finish the Service. Sometimes I have seen people conducting a revival meeting at the eulogy service.[37]

As with marriages, there is an increasing acceptance of Pentecostal burials, although in the 1990s marriage and burials still belonged to the neglected problems of the south Indian Pentecostal movement.

Organized Events and Festivals

Besides the Sunday worship, congregations as a rule have a full weekly program. The form and contents are remarkably uniform within the south Indian Pentecostal movement. As in the established churches, there is usually a special Sunday school for the religious instruction of children. Many Hindus readily send their children, since they recognize great competence in ethical training. Consequently some Pentecostal churches have a much greater attendance at Sunday school than the number of members in the congregation would lead one to expect. Once a week there is a Bible hour, usually on Wednesday. It is significantly less well attended than the Sunday school. Some churches have regular tarrying meetings in which there is special prayer for the participants to receive Spirit baptism. A prominent place in the life of the congregation is taken by the fasting vigil usually every Friday morning and mostly attended by women. Fasting here means taking no meal until the end of the event in the early afternoon. It is the established place for intercession. There is prayer for written petitions and for the participants present. As an inter-regional event, in many states there is a so-called All Night Fasting Prayer. It is assembled in the late evening and often lasts to the next morning. As with the fasting vigil, this night prayer is mainly focused on intercession. By far the best-known organizer of these events in south India is N. Jeevanandam in Madras. Easter and Christmas are celebrated either not at all or with much reserve. The reasons brought up for this are usually either a lack of biblical basis or the festival's pagan origins. However, since they are

37. Titus 1995: 4.

national holidays, many Pentecostal congregations meet for vigil or worship on these days. Yet, emphasis is laid on the fact that these customs have nothing to do with the Easter and Christmas celebrations of the established churches. Only the Assemblies of God and the independent churches influenced by them celebrate Easter and Christmas as the established churches do.

The really central annual festivals, however, are the conventions. These are the high point and center of the Pentecostal church year. They are organized evangelistic rallies lasting several days, usually from Thursday to Sunday. Each evening, there will be a mass event of several hours on an open-air stage, to which the most prominent evangelist available will be invited. The convention is open to anyone and will by preference be in a public place. Traditionally, the four days are given to fixed themes, with variations as a rule. The first day is on conversion, the second on baptism, the third on Spirit baptism or call to ministry, and the last day on holiness. As the contents of the sermon show, the convention progresses from day to day. In addition, at the evening meetings, daily worship services are celebrated as well as Bible hours and special prayer meetings. Besides the conventions of the local congregations, the bigger churches hold regional and central conventions. In procedure they are like the local conventions, except that adherents from all associated congregations are brought together and attendance registered. These church conventions are an important means of strengthening unity among the churches. Rallies are closely related to conventions in their way of proceeding. The difference lies in the fact they are tailored to the work of a particular evangelist. Either they are entirely managed by the evangelist's organization or they are set up in cooperation with a local congregation that has decided to invite this evangelist to a particular meeting. The most prominent evangelists, especially D. G. S. Dhinakaran, prefer all the churches of the neighborhood to jointly organize an invitation.

Pastoral Care

The pastor of a Pentecostal congregation devotes a good deal of his time to house visiting. In small congregations he will visit at least once a month to pray for the family. Hospital visits and special individual care in cases of need are taken for granted. In cases of special concern, the pastor can always be called upon. The course of a home visit is arranged in such a way that any problem or need in the family can be verbalized. Requests are brought to the pastor so that he can express them in his prayer at the end of the visit. Personal conflicts and problems are brought out as prayer concerns. The pastor, of course, will not hesitate to give his advice. But really all that is expected of him is that he listens and at the end brings the problems before God in prayer. Since a special blessing is attributed to this prayer by the pastor, there is great interest in bringing out all problems in explicit words so that they can be rightly expressed in the prayer. The home visit by the Pentecostal pastor is thus an important occasion for open communication. Therefore, the pastor exercises good pastoral care in this, especially for women, who as a rule bear all the burdens of the family but are hardly ever listened to in their needs.[38] In the larger congregations where the pastor himself cannot regularly pay visits to all the families, there are assistant pastors or elders who give themselves to this visiting ministry. In many congregations, there are house prayer groups in which members from the neighborhood meet weekly and through which additional pastoral care is exercised. These groups are to a large extent led by women. A special form of these is the so-called prayer cells patterned on those of Yonggi Cho.[39] This system of prayer cells is practiced most successfully by the New Life Assembly of God in Madras.[40]

Mission

The south Indian Pentecostal movement is strongly oriented toward mission.[41] A good part of this effort is concentrated on winning members of the established churches, but it also recruits a qualified minority of Hindus for the movement.[42] Most of the missionary activity takes place on the personal level in families, in the neighborhood, or among workmates and companions in study — usually without direct intervention by the pastors. The author was quite amazed by the number of cases where the wife first converted

38. If the pastor visits a female member of the congregation when her husband or father is not present, then it is expected that he will come accompanied by his wife. Neglecting this unwritten rule would quickly bring a pastor into disrepute.

39. See Vaughan 1984: 44-47; Maier 1995: 124.

40. See p. 70.

41. In what follows we are concerned with Pentecostal missionary activities in south India only. Many Pentecostal congregations in the south also support, financially and partly by personnel, indigenous missionary societies that operate principally in north India; many of these are Pentecostal oriented in spite of their interdenominational character (e.g., Blessing Youth Mission, Gospel Echoing Missionary Society). Since the situation in north India is not the subject of this book, we cannot go into this any further. An overview of the indigenous missionary society active in north India can be found in Pothen 1990; Lazarus 1992; Sargunam 1992.

42. See also the statistical analysis in the following chapter.

to the Pentecostal faith and then in the course of time brought her family to do the same.[43] An important missionary task, then, is exercised by the house prayer groups led by congregation members. A leading pastor from Madras explains:

> We have prayer groups all over, and every prayer group invites people in their group, and they pray for the problems and pray for the sick. . . . And, when they get an answer to prayer, they know that something has happened to them, then they open themselves to God and come to church.[44]

For pastors on home visits good opportunities for mission may occur as the wife of a young pastor relates:

> We do house visiting. So, when we go house visiting, sometimes, people will take us, saying: "Pastor please, we have a new friend please come and pray for the family." So, when we go to the house and pray, we sit there, at least just half an hour, and say: "Please come to our church." So, we invite them.[45]

Special attention is given to welcoming people on their first visit for Sunday worship. They are cared for in a special way. The leader of a big church in Hyderabad gave out the following maxims:

> [When] visitors come, I ask my associate pastors and the elders: "When they come on Sunday, Monday and Tuesday, before Wednesday, they must be visited. Before Wednesday, they must be visited. Then, from Wednesday on, you visit the old members. But, all the new ones you must visit before. And, when visitors come, greet them, make them feel at home, talk to them about the Lord. When you visit, don't make that just a social visit. When you go, make sure, you leave the word with them, and present the gospel to them." And, people are touched when they go and visit, and they come. And, one of the secrets of growth in the church is that.[46]

---

43. Something similar is reported by Wingate concerning conversions of Hindus to the Church of South India (see Wingate 1986; Wingate 1997).

44. Interview.

45. Interview.

46. Interview.

We have already written elsewhere of Pentecostal power evangelism through signs and wonders in relation to mission.[47] In this connection, we would like to make reference to mission methods used in the big rallies. Printed forms are distributed on which addresses may be given together with prayer requests; these also contain points to be ticked, such as:

- I have accepted Jesus as my Lord.
- I have been healed of an illness.
- I will permanently accept God's guidance.
- You may visit me at home.[48]

In this way at big rallies a whole number of addresses will be collected. The persons so identified may then be contacted by the local pastor so as to win them for his congregation. Especially people who have experienced a healing are then ready to join a congregation. Often such collected addresses are the starting point for a new congregation, where it is hoped, with the addresses, to have enough contacts for a Sunday worship service. D. Mohan, founder of the New Life Assembly of God in Madras, relates that he collected 150 addresses at a rally. He then visited 125 houses in a short time and began a Sunday worship with seven people.[49] The numbers suggest that at any rally there will be many people who react positively, but we must reckon with the fact that only a few will be won as members of a congregation.

There is considerable influence on the south Indian Pentecostal movement from the "church growth" movement;[50] this school of thought is always in danger of making "numerical growth into a *nota ecclesiae*."[51] From the 1980s, a kind of growth hysteria could be recognized, leading a large number of pastors to a complete overestimation of themselves. The most extreme example is Justin Prabakaran, who set himself the target of winning ten million members in Madras within ten years.[52] The pressure to present oneself as a rapidly growing church brings with it many faulty developments. It begins in

---

47. See pp. 163ff.

48. From a Tamil handout at a David Terrell rally under the leadership of the Assemblies of God from 1 to 6 Feb. 1994 on the TELC playground, Madurai.

49. See Mohan 1989: 4.

50. On the theological and historical background of the "church growth" movement, see Maier 1995. On the relationship between "church growth" movement and Pentecostalism, see McClung 1985.

51. See Maier 1995: 150.

52. See Rajendran 1992: 72. For comparison, in 1995, Madras had about 6 million inhabitants of whom around 7.5 percent were Christian.

a small way when, on inquiry about Sunday attendance figures, completely exaggerated figures are given, since one dare not admit that one is responsible only for a small congregation. It goes further with the leader of a larger church who systematically divides his congregation so that on paper an exorbitant statistical growth will be displayed. Finally, it can go so far that many leaders are led to buying the pastors of independent churches. These actions are only intended to prove outstanding growth. Such tendencies also bring the suspicion that, in not a few cases, small denominations may be successful in gaining overseas sponsorship with exaggerated statistics and fictional accounts of growth. Actual experience has shown that small denominations, on account of their centralizing structures and their fixation on one leading personality, have definite limitations on growth. It is scarcely possible to manage successfully more than one hundred congregations in such organizations. Further long-term sustainable growth is only to be observed where there is decentralized and at least inchoately democratic leadership present and where the pastors are trained in well-organized Bible schools. But above all it is clear that much time is needed to achieve real growth.

CHAPTER 14

Social Structure and Ecumenical Relations

Social Structure

Reliable data on the social structure of the south Indian Pentecostal movement are difficult to obtain since there is a lack of empirical studies. However,
some basic findings are available at this time. Various research findings have
consistently shown that about 15 to 20 percent of the members of south Indian Pentecostal churches are former Hindus.[1] These statistics, which were in
line with the author's experiences, show considerable Pentecostal missionary
outreach among Hindus. Yet at the same time they make clear that a majority
of their adherents come from the ranks of established Protestantism or Syrian
Orthodoxy. Former members of the Catholic Church are conspicuous by
their absence: scarcely more than 5 percent of the whole total are former
Catholics.[2] The strong Catholic Charismatic movement, then, has not led to

---

1. See Bergunder 1999: appendix 2, table 6. Persons there indicated as directly converted
are almost exclusively former Hindus. Conversions from Islam, according to the author's
experience, are extremely rare exceptions (see also Hoerschelmann 1977: 426f.). Churches
dominated by the Thomas Christians, however (e.g., Church of God Kerala State, Indian
Pentecostal Church in Kerala, Assemblies of God in Kerala), probably have hardly any directly converted non-Christians. But empirical findings on this are not available.

2. See Bergunder 1999: appendix 2, table 7. It should be noted that there are findings
opposed to this. In a study conducted by students of the Catholic Jnana-Deepa Vidyapeeth
(Pontifical Athenaeum) in Poona on "Neo-Pentecostalism in India," 41 percent of those interviewed were former Catholics, 31 percent former members of other churches, and 28
percent former non-Christians. But the group was not statistically representative, since the
method of recruiting automatically favored former Catholics, as Catholic students made
their first contact there. See Parathazham 1996: 81-101.

any greater movement toward the Pentecostal churches, a surmise that was repeatedly affirmed to the author from the Catholic side.[3] The question is much debated how many members of the Pentecostal churches retain formal membership in their mother church. Two inquiries gave 14 percent and 29 percent as possessing continued membership in an established church.[4] Hence, one could argue that a majority of Christians converting to Pentecostalism have found themselves at home there. Caste membership apparently corresponds to what is usual in non-Catholic churches.[5] So the Pentecostal movement has reached only those population groups that are already reached by the established churches. From various sides the justified suspicion is expressed that, in the Pentecostal congregations of Madras, the Nadars are represented disproportionately, but this is not statistically verified so far.[6] It is especially difficult to estimate the economic situation of the members. The author's experience indicates that they come predominantly from the "lower middle class"[7] and in smaller numbers from the "middle class."[8] But also in nearly every congregation there are many who are quite poor, and, in urban congregations, there are some representatives of the "upper middle class" too. Thus the congregations are not as a rule uniform but are mostly drawn from people who have hardly escaped poverty and are rising to real "middle-class" conditions. A separate phenomenon is represented by the elite English-speaking congregations in the metropolis, which contain many of the "upper middle class."

The outstanding part played by healing and exorcism in ensuring the success of the Pentecostal movement is supported by the statistics. In 1980, of

3. For the Catholic Charismatic movement see p. 240 n. 35.

4. See Bergunder 1999: appendix 2, table 8.

5. See Hoerschelmann 1977: 432; Zechariah 1981: 112-15; Augustine 1993: 140, 109-80.

6. Research by Zechariah in 1980 showed a slightly higher proportion of Nadars (Nadars 48 percent, Dalits 31 percent) in the congregations of the Assemblies of God on Madras (1981: 112-15). But these figures are of less significance, since the Assemblies of God only set foot in Madras in the 1980s. In the author's experience, since the time Bishop M. Azariah (Church of South India, Madras diocese) took office, conflicts between the disadvantaged Dalits and the privileged Nadars have led to a considerable movement of Nadars from the Church of South India to the Pentecostal movement. This observation has been explicitly confirmed by leading Pentecostal pastors.

7. Generally, the term "lower middle class" is used when in some way there is assured employment and income, as is already the case with street sweepers appointed by the magistrate. With the exception of Kerala, in south India 30 percent of the population live below the poverty line (see Rothermund 1995: 66).

8. See also Hoerschelmann (1977: 465) and Augustine (1993: 140), who come to a similar assessment.

ninety-six members of the Assemblies of God directly converted from Hinduism in Tamil Nadu, eighty-one reported that the Pentecostal practice of healing and exorcism had drawn them to Christianity.[9] In this connection, the well-known study of Herbert E. Hoefer is relevant.[10] According to this study, in 1981, 10 percent of the non-Christian population of Madras had experienced an important cure through prayer to Jesus and 21 percent were aware of the healing power of prayer to Jesus.[11] Of the group classified by Hoefer as non-baptized believers, 52 percent had experienced healing through prayer to Jesus.[12] From such research we know that Pentecostal healing practice has the potential to speak to Hindus. The further conclusion that healing and exorcism also play a central part, not only for Hindus but also for Christians of the established churches, in their conversion to Pentecostalism is statistically supported by Hoerschelmann's data. The interviewees, of whom about 80 percent came from Christian families, when asked what they saw as the attractiveness of the Pentecostal movement, gave the practice of healing and exorcism as by far the most common answer.[13]

Sociological findings on the social profile of Pentecostal pastors are still completely lacking. In the first place, there is a clear distinction to be made between Pentecostal leaders and the many pastors of small congregations living in very simple conditions. The latter mostly depend on material support from their church headquarters. In most cases, they receive a monthly subsidy of 200 to 600 rupees (1994 rates). This money, together with the contribution of the congregation, enables them to lead a "lower-middle-class" life; without such support, these pastors would usually be in real need. This situation is due to the fact that, according to the Pentecostal understanding, one commits oneself to full-time ministry and then founds a congregation. The many small Bible schools and also the altar calls bring ever more people to this way of life. But not all succeed in founding a congregation that in the short term could earn them a living. The self-understanding of the full-time ministry is contradicted by the labor market. Most candidates for full-time ministry start very young; they have no other qualifications and have not practiced any

---

9. Zechariah 1981: 208, 273-76.
10. See Hoefer 1991.
11. Hoefer 1991: 86; see also pp. 59-60.
12. Hoefer 1991: 288.
13. Hoerschelmann 1977: 451f. Apparently this point is not sufficiently appreciated by Indian theologians of the established churches. It is difficult to explain why, in John S. Augustine's sociological findings on Pentecostal-Evangelical groups in Madras, under the rubric "first priority for joining the group," there is no mention of healing and exorcism (see Augustine 1993: 143, 169).

trade. In practice, therefore, it is difficult to bring a failed career as pastor to an end by returning to a worldly calling. On the social profile of the Pentecostal leadership, there are some definite findings in an empirical investigation by the author.[14] The leadership consists of relatively young people compared to the Indian background. Sixty-three percent are under fifty-six and only 14 percent older than sixty-five.[15] Although nearly 90 percent live in the city now, over 64 percent originally come from rural areas.[16] The living standard of the Pentecostal leadership corresponds largely to that of the "upper middle class." This is revealed in the fact that at least 66 percent have spacious private houses with modern equipment and that 80 percent of the interviewees used a car. By a rough estimate, 60 percent had a living standard in proportion to their own church's income. Conversely, that means that 40 percent owe their living standard to powerful overseas sponsors only.[17] It is the author's impression that this 40 percent exercises considerable influence as a role model by showing the possibility, through foreign aid, to get rich quickly and to disconnect living standards from the church's revenue. Origins by caste correspond largely to those of the established churches. But representation among the Dalits deserves closer attention. Of the total of Pentecostal leaders interviewed, 19 percent were Dalits.[18] In Madras only 16 percent were Dalits and 33 percent Nadars.[19] In all cases, the Dalits are under-represented in the leadership.[20] The leaders interviewed had a notably higher level of education. About 61 percent had college or university education and almost 39 percent a degree.[21] Not one Pentecostal pastor was previously a pastor in an established church. A good half went into full-time ministry directly from school, or at most with two or three years in between in a secular job.[22] In 16 percent of cases, it was a matter of direct conversion from Hinduism and only 5 percent were former Catholics.[23] A good 32 percent come from a Pentecostal house-

14. See Bergunder 1999: appendix 2, tables 9-18.
15. See Bergunder 1999: appendix 2, table 9.
16. See Bergunder 1999: appendix 2, table 10.
17. See Bergunder 1999: appendix 2, table 11.
18. See Bergunder 1999: appendix 2, table 12.
19. See Bergunder 1999: appendix 2, table 13.
20. There is no research on the percentage of Dalits in south Indian Pentecostal congregations, but it is certainly well over 20 percent.
21. See Bergunder 1999: appendix 2, table 14.
22. See Bergunder 1999: appendix 2, table 15. See also Hollenweger 1988: 474-77, where he researched 400 leaders worldwide. At least 26 percent were formerly pastors in established churches. Unfortunately he says nothing about those who come directly from studies into pastoral ministry.
23. Bergunder 1999: appendix 2, table 16.

hold. In Pentecostal churches that have existed for more than thirty-five years this figure becomes 52 percent.[24] However, 47 percent on average have attended a Bible school.[25] Conversely, this also means that half of the leaders have no theological education. This can be a reason why also in the leadership, to a great extent, theological teaching is still handed on orally.

Ecumenical Relations

The south Indian Pentecostal movement is organized as a multiplicity of independent churches completely independent of one another and finding themselves, to some extent, in a situation of competition with one another. This is a big obstacle to fruitful cooperation within the movement since it leads to serious mutual accusations and to hostility. The charge of proselytism is often brought up in this connection by the smaller churches against those that are bigger and growing more rapidly. Where jealousy is aroused by greater material wealth, in extreme cases there will be no shrinking from denunciation. A leading Tamil evangelist told of the time when he was working as a tax collector: a Pentecostal pastor came into his office to inform on another pastor for tax avoidance. The author is aware of at least one similar case. The charge of sexual misbehavior is also often brought up against other pastors. The bitterness worked up in mutual confrontation can be quite surprising.[26] Against these destructive tendencies, some distinct initiatives in cooperation stand out and serve not least in facilitating better understanding between churches. This cooperation is based on the fact that within the individual churches there is a clear awareness of a common Pentecostal identity. This has created the possibility that in many places an extensive informal network exists of different relationships between the individual churches. Pastors invite one another to preach in their churches, and the ordination of future pastors takes place usually in the presence of befriended pastors. But it is above all the conventions and rallies to which faithful and pastors of all Pentecostal churches in the region are invited. Many churches have compiled address lists of local congregations for sending invitations to special meetings. Invitations and leaflets for such events are then displayed at the corresponding churches. These close interchurch contacts bring about in no small degree a better understanding among the churches; they also help develop a rela-

24. Bergunder 1999: appendix 2, table 17.
25. Bergunder 1999: appendix 2, table 18.
26. See also Caplan (1989: 110) for similar accounts.

tively uniform theological style. In this way, theologoumena can be subjected to comparative control and be mutually adjusted. This process appears to function quite well because there is a considerable degree of agreement in Pentecostal interpretation concerning the distinctive doctrinal issues. There is strong agreement not to see their different standpoints on certain controversial themes, especially in the question of ethical norms, as issues dividing churches. The Yesunamam churches have found no acceptance in the interchurch network of the south Indian Pentecostal movement. On the question of baptism they are irreconcilably opposed and no change in the positions is foreseen. More complicated is the situation concerning relations with the Ceylon Pentecostal Mission, which refuses contact with other Pentecostal churches and has a whole range of church-dividing doctrines.[27] But still there are good reasons for placing it in the mainstream of the south Indian Pentecostal movement. Numerous Pentecostal pastors were formerly members or even pastors in the Ceylon Pentecostal Mission. Amazingly, they base their leaving the Ceylon Pentecostal Mission mostly on the strict ban on marriage for pastors, and they seldom mention theological differences. The very distinctive doctrines of the Ceylon Pentecostal Mission are scarcely a matter of general concern. On the contrary, many pastors and evangelists greatly value the teaching of the Mission. This is connected with the fact that they are the only south Indian Pentecostal church to have published on all important theological subjects in detailed but easily understood publications. Thus, it is reported about a certain well-known Tamil evangelist:

[H]e always says: "I go to all the Pentecostal churches, but for real teachings to get, I go to CPM [Ceylon Pentecostal Mission]." I used to wonder about this man, the way he thought. But still, he continues, whenever he goes for morning service, he goes for CPM to learn something.[28]

This evangelist would not be an isolated case, to go by the author's experience. Many members of other churches take part in the conventions of the Ceylon Pentecostal Mission and, conversely, their members (and even some of their pastors) attend these churches' conventions. So, in spite of its strong separatism, the Ceylon Pentecostal Mission has not entirely lost its connection to the mainstream of the south Indian Pentecostal movement.

This interchurch network of the south Indian Pentecostal movement derives in a decisive way from the various interchurch unions such as the so-

27. See pp. 64ff.
28. Interview.

called Pentecostal Pastors' Fellowships.[29] These unions, in which the pastors of a particular region regularly meet for common prayer and exchange of views, are especially suited to relieve the latent tension between individual churches. But the Pastors' Fellowships also reveal the limits of Pentecostal collaboration. They are usually short-lived and break up as a rule due to internal power struggles, broken friendship, and distinct interest groups. The bigger inter-regional denominations usually have little interest in such unions while the small churches and small denominations have a great interest since they are given more significance thereby. Although these unions individually last only a few years, each breakup is followed, after a certain time, with a new foundation so that the idea of interchurch cooperation through Pastors' Fellowships is kept continually alive. It remains to be seen whether the south Indian Pentecostal movement in the future will find more binding and lasting interchurch structures.

Overseas partners give much material support. But in many interviews it was repeatedly explained to the author that foreign money does much harm to the south Indian Pentecostal movement and corrupts pastors. Paradoxically, it was precisely those who made such complaints who were themselves the greatest exploiters of the aid programs. This contradiction finds expression in the fact that among many south Indian Pentecostals there is a deep and genuine unease about the negative aspects of overseas support, but a real self-critical working out of the problem does not take place. At the same time, it must be recognized that only a few south Indian Pentecostal churches will admit that overseas sponsors have influence in the administration of churches. There are historical causes for this awareness.[30] So, although overseas aid is not as a rule tied to direct administrative influence, it does in many cases cause problematic tension and splitting. This tendency has increased with Indian independence; there are numerous examples in the historical part of this study. The most spectacular case must be the work of World Missionary Evangelism in Andhra Pradesh. Many western Pentecostal and Charismatic churches as well as numerous independent missionary associations, especially those from the USA, were apparently very interested to find independent partners in India whom they could advertise as their own overseas mission. With this, they were at least indirectly responsible in part for splitting in the Pentecostal landscape, since not a few independent churches were constituted from the start with this partnership in view; as a rule this meant that they separated from other churches. It should be added that the overseas

---

29. See pp. 109ff.

30. See the confrontation with World Missionary Evangelism in Tamil Nadu on pp. 76-77.

sponsors usually knew nothing of this and so were not in a position to judge the eventual results of their commitment.[31] On the other hand, there are many thoroughly positive examples in which overseas partners have contributed something to strengthening interchurch cooperation in the Indian Pentecostal movement. Often foreign evangelists, when they came to India, insisted that local Pentecostal congregations should work with them in organizing their rallies. This was often taken by the Indians as an opportunity to call into life Pentecostal Pastors' Fellowships or to reactivate them. This move by a neutral third party often brought together pastors in a state of conflict and reconciled them. Usually foreign evangelists offered special morning meetings for pastors, which also served to bring them closer. Moreover, the many contacts with overseas partners helped Indian Pentecostals to become conscious of being part of a worldwide movement.

In south India there is little contact between Evangelical organizations and Pentecostals. The reason is not only the small numbers of Evangelicals but also their unfriendly attitude to the Pentecostal movement. The Brethren, the Anderson Church of God, and also both of the indigenous organizations, the Laymen's Evangelical Fellowship and Jehovah Shammah were decidedly anti-Pentecostal. It was the same with the mission of the fundamentalist Churches of Christ, developed with considerable financial aid from the USA in the 1970s and 1980s.[32] There was hardly any contact, either, for the south

---

31. See also the impressions of Glen Stout (1994: 21-27), an American Charismatic who stayed in Vishakapatnam as an independent missionary at the beginning of the 1990s. Very critically he declares that overseas sponsors give insufficient attention to the work of their partners in India.

32. The Open Plymouth Brethren, who carried out their Indian mission from the nineteenth century, had a special center in Kerala where, however, in the first half of this century many Brethren converted to Pentecostalism. They are distinguished from the Brethren Mission in Rajahmundry. Here it is a matter of the "Dunkers" (Brethren Church, Ashland, Ohio), which undertook a mission in Andhra Pradesh from 1969 (see Mar Aprem 1984: 140ff.). The Anderson Church of God was founded in India by the north Indian A. D. Khan, who was converted from Islam to Christianity and was especially active as an evangelist. In south India this church is only in Kerala, where Khan often spoke at rallies. The church resulting from this rejected the teaching of tongues as initial evidence of Spirit baptism and in Kerala is partly decidedly anti-Pentecostal (see Hollenweger 1965/1967: 03.07.002; Mar Aprem 1984: 135f.; Saju 1994: 210f.). The Churches of Christ belong to the fundamentalist wing of the movement, which has no fellowship with the Disciples of Christ. By the 1990s it had lost all significance in the south Indian religious landscape. Jehovah Shammah was founded by Bakht Singh. He was a former Indian Sikh who converted to Christianity in Canada and was active in evangelism in India from the 1940s to the 1960s. The church he founded is especially active in Tamil Nadu and Andhra Pradesh. The name was originally only given to the first church in Madras founded in 1941. The

Indian Pentecostal movement with the Evangelical Church of India (formerly the Oriental Missionary Society).[33] An exception is the South Asia Institute of Advanced Christian Studies, founded in 1981 by the New Zealander Graham Houghton, who had been active for more than ten years for the Oriental Missionary Society. This institution offered incontestably the best theological training outside the educational institutions of the established churches; it was built up with active participation by Pentecostal theologians, especially John Thannickal. However, such cooperation between Evangelicals and Pentecostals was still an exception in the 1990s. Occasional meetings have become more frequent, for example, where leading Pentecostal pastors speak at the consultations set up by Evangelicals on church growth and mission.[34]

There are relations at many levels between the south Indian Pentecostal movement and the established Protestant churches out of which a great part of the Pentecostal membership is recruited. The relations are naturally very tense because of accusations of proselytism and because of the increasing rather than decreasing attraction of Pentecostal Christianity. Dialogue is not made easier by the aggressive and dogmatic way the Pentecostals behave toward the established churches. One can detect on the Pentecostal side, so far, only a little openness and tolerance. They charge the members of established churches with nominal Christianity, lack of holiness, lack of the Spirit, lack of missionary endeavor, and theological liberalism. On the other hand, they attribute little significance to church membership. If anyone has experienced Christian rebirth, received baptism by immersion, and now follows the norms of Christian holiness, he will be recognized by Pentecostals without further ado, even if he is officially a member of an established church. It is thus the Evangelical teaching rather than spiritual gifts that is the cause of division in the church. For this reason Charismatic Christianity that does not follow the basic principles

---

teaching and form of worship are closely related to that of the Brethren but in many respects much freer; for example, women may pray aloud during services. On this interesting indigenous church, little is known so far. There are some autobiographical details in Bakht Singh's writings (see Bakht Singh n.d.; Bakht Singh 1968). There is also a B.D. thesis (see Samuel 1971). The Layman's Evangelical Fellowship was founded by N. Daniel (1897-1963) and continued by his son Joe Daniel. This was a decidedly Evangelical organization with many contacts in Germany and England (see Hoerschelmann 1977: 198-222).

33. The Evangelical Church of India derives from the work of the Oriental Missionary Society founded in 1901 by Charles Cowman and in 1993 was led by an indigenous bishop from Tamil Nadu, Ezra Sargunam (b. 1938). The church publishes statistics that show an exorbitant growth. But in the author's opinion there are doubts about the reliability of the data. As yet, there is no critical history but there are historical data in individual reports: especially Sargunam 1974; Sargunam 1994: 50-61; Sargunam ca. 1994.

34. See Sargunam 1992.

of Evangelicalism — such as the Catholic Charismatic movement[35] — has not so far been recognized by the south Indian Pentecostal movement. Thus, baptism represents the most public theme of controversy, since most Pentecostals will in no circumstances recognize infant baptism. The Pentecostal practice of (re-)baptizing those who were baptized as small children is a weighty challenge to the established churches. The latter treat the matter very pragmatically and avoid open confrontation. Little remained in the 1990s of the earlier attempts to keep their members from attending Pentecostal events by effective church discipline.[36] The members of the Protestant churches are now too strongly influenced by Pentecostal views for them to react in a purely negative way. Consequently, Pentecostal spirituality is allowed into the established churches. Pentecostal evangelists are invited to church events with the condition, however, not to preach against the host church or to raise the question of baptism. There are some special cases of evangelists who preserve their formal membership in established churches and are promoted by well-disposed bishops. Prominent examples are D. G. S. Dhinakaran, John Solomon, and John Joseph. This represents a delicate crossing of boundaries since it offers an additional platform for disseminating the Pentecostal views and thus risks the departure of even more members for the Pentecostal churches. The pragmatic laissez-faire attitude in the established churches goes so far as to accept that Charismatic-minded members could, by their own private decision, receive baptism by immersion from a Pentecostal pastor and yet remain members of their mother church. This attitude to the baptismal question witnesses also to

35. On the Catholic Charismatic movement there is not yet much research. But see Mascarenhas 1977: 78-80; Jacob 1995: 43f.; Plakkottam 1995. The Catholic Charismatic movement started in 1972 in Bombay, which continued to be the center of the movement. Influenced by the worldwide Catholic Charismatic movement, Charismatic prayer groups were formed in India. Three priests, Fio Mascarenhas S.J., James D'Souza, and Rufus Pereira, shaped the character of the new movement. They organized frequent retreats through which lay people were reached. In 1974, it published its own journal, *Charisindia*. In the 1980s the Catholic Charismatic College was opened in Bombay, offering two-month Bible courses. In Kerala, at the end of the 1980s, Charismatic healing services experienced massive growth. Especially successful was the Vincentian Mathew Naickomparambil in Potta near Chalakudy, Thrissur District. Over a hundred thousand people streamed to his retreats, which were comparable to Pentecostal healing rallies. In Tamil Nadu the movement was led by the Jesuit A. J. Thamburaj. The active kernel of the movement was estimated by Rufus Pereira in 1995 as 50,000 (see Jacob 1995: 44). There are no ecumenical relations with the Pentecostal movement (see Saju 1994: 294). Since the sensational conversion of S. J. Berchmans to the Pentecostal movement, relations have become even worse. However, some Malayali Pentecostals study in Catholic theological institutions (see Stephen 1995: 274-81).

36. See Caplan 1989: 33.

the firm determination of members to live their Charismatic spirituality within the established churches. So far in none of the established Protestant churches has an inter-regional Charismatic movement been formed, but there are many Charismatic prayer groups led by laypeople and also by some pastors.[37] These groups maintain lively contacts with the Pentecostal movement and so practice a basic ecumenism.[38]

Similar to their church leaders and pastors, who stick to a purely pragmatic approach, mainline church theologians have not entered into any academic exchange with the Pentecostal movement yet. This would seem to be needed since in fact a large proportion of the students in the educational institutions of the established churches relate to Pentecostal spirituality in a positive and uncritical way. Furthermore, Pentecostal students are now studying in these institutions.[39] Teachers of theology tend to respond with a sharp and mostly undifferentiated rejection rather than facing up to the ecumenical challenge. They are satisfied with simple answers to the complex phenomenon of the Pentecostal movement.[40] So it was repeatedly explained to the author that the best recourse against Pentecostal influence would be more basic instruction for the congregations in Christian doctrine because the Pentecostals were leading members of the established churches astray through their excessive emotionalism. They explained also that the Pentecostals were so successful because of American money. An essay by Franklyn J. Balasundaram, who was professor of systematic theology at the United College in Bangalore, can serve as a typical example of this attitude.[41] In his exposition he comes to the following conclusion:

37. See, e.g., the testimonies of Charismatically committed women published by the Women's Fellowship of the Church of South India (see Dharmagnani 1990).

38. It is not easy, however, to find a Charismatic identity without taking over the evangelical views of the south Indian Pentecostal movement, especially concerning baptism.

39. In 1994 there was one M.Th. student in Tamil Nadu Theological College, Madurai; one B.D. student in Gurukul, Madras; two M.Th. students; three B.D. students; two students in special courses; and two external B.D. students in the United Theological College, Bangalore. During the second half of the 1990s this figure increased rapidly.

40. There are, however, notable exceptions: A. C. Mathew, a pastor of the Mar Thoma Church, discusses in detail and in a neutral manner the justification of infant baptism, and he refutes the position that only immersion baptism is scriptural (Mathew 1992: esp. 56-77, 93-103). Some theologians of the United Theological College, Bangalore, deal impartially with the question of rebaptism (Chandran et al. 1985: 56-59). Surya Prakash (1993) expresses a critical but thoroughly differentiated view on revival preaching. Sundara Rao (1990) offers an interesting sociological interpretation of tongues.

41. See Balasundaram 1990. See also the polemical open letter of the teaching body of the Tamil Nadu Theological College to D. G. S. Dhinakaran (see Tamil Nadu Theological College 1989) as well as the abrupt rejection of Pentecostal views in two dissertations from the same institution (see Jeyachandran 1991; Wilson 1994).

How can suffering men and women be ecstatic and blissful when they reel under the manmade forced poverty and oppression? . . . Thus, the gospel is used as an agency to suppress men and women who seek liberation from the clutches of oppression and exploitation. It is in this sense the Charismatic movement serves as an opium and a tranquilizer! . . . the Charismatic movement is the organized religion exported to the Third World by the centres of power and capitalism. . . . An organized powerful business stalwarts' community in Europe and North Atlantic countries is interested in spreading Charismatic/Pentecostal religious experience in the Third World.[42]

But besides such sweeping judgments, there are increasingly earnest attempts to find a theological place for Charismatic spirituality within the established churches. Such an attempt is that of Victor Paul of the Andhra Christian Theological College in Hyderabad, who in his reflection on the social reality of his church gave this theological assessment:

In the midst of leadership crisis, institutionalism, materialism, corruption and spiritual Lethargy, there shines a ray of hope in the form of charismatic lay movement. . . . Today in almost all congregations of AELC [Andhra Evangelical Lutheran Church] charismatic groups are evident and are begging for recognition. . . . AELC is faced with two options: One is to reject them totally as a religiously and emotionally perverted group or to recognize this lay charismatic movement as a natural reaction and a mute protest against evils and secularism existing in AELC. It is time now to own and recognise these charismatics. . . . With proper investigation, study and reflection on the charismatic Lay Movement within the established churches, one may help the traditional churches to re-discover their identity and relevancy of their faith and service in today's world.[43]

The growing tendency in the established churches to take over elements of Charismatic spirituality is illustrated in the following example: M. Azariah is generally regarded as a critic of the Pentecostal movement and is a declared supporter of the liberation theology movement in working for the political and social bettering of the condition of the Dalits.[44] So it is all the more re-

42. Balasundaram 1990: 244-45.
43. Paul 1990: 106-7.
44. Azariah 1983.

markable that, in an article in the middle of the 1990s when he was bishop of Madras diocese of the Church of South India, he should write that he is convinced that healing and exorcisms belong to the tasks of the established churches also:

> [P]art of my holiday, I was privileged to spend at SAIACS [South Asia Institute of Advanced Christian Studies, Bangalore] and had the opportunity of reading certain good books, one of them was called "Healing From the Inside Out" by Tom Marshall. . . . After reading this book, I was deeply convinced that our Christian faith and practice has become a mostly verbal religion since we concentrate only on preaching and practically neglect totally the other important tasks of healing and casting out demons. It is my hope and prayer that all of us at least those who are called to be in full time Ministry will soon realise this great lacuna and take up the courage of spirit to engage in faith action Ministries of healing and casting of demonic forces as well.[45]

This recent development allows for the hope that soon an altogether different approach to the Pentecostal movement will be developed through the theologians of the south Indian mainline churches. With their difficulties in reacting creatively to the movement, the south Indian theologians are not exceptional, as theologians of the established churches in Europe have also made few substantial contributions to understanding the Pentecostal movement so far.

45. Azariah 1995: 13.

PROSPECTS

CHAPTER 15

Pentecostalism and Contextualization of Christianity

Pentecostalism has been a global endeavor right from its beginning. No country or place can claim the origin of Pentecostalism. Nevertheless, many Pentecostal and Charismatic churches in Africa, Asia, and Latin America (and also in Europe!) display quite a strong white North American evangelical flavor, which has its source in the huge missionary activities undertaken by Pentecostals from the United States. Theological statements of faith are copied from American Pentecostal originals, vernacular theological literature is translated from American sources, and in many cases, even worship service and style are shaped by American cultural patterns. This easily gives the impression that being Pentecostal — wherever it might be — means practicing an American Pentecostal way of spiritual life; and this opinion would even be backed by the popular self-understanding in quite a lot of Pentecostal circles all over the globe. And it is this observation that called many critics to the scene who designated Pentecostalism as an American religion that was exported from the United States to the Third World as a means of ideological control.[1]

Though this critical view is still popular in certain circles, recent anthropological and sociological research, including this study on south Indian Pentecostalism, paints a differentiated picture. Especially in the last two decades, anthropologists and sociologists have become interested in non-western Pentecostal communities and started to do field work among them; as a result, a

---

1. See Brouwer 1996.

247

vast scope of research has been done that has deepened the academic knowledge of the worldwide Pentecostal movement tremendously.[2] As the most amazing finding, anthropological research shows the Pentecostal movement as a contextual phenomenon and hardly as something destructive, foreign, or alien to existing societies. Interestingly, this factual contextualization can be found in both independent churches and churches with established organizational links to North American denominations. However, what anthropologists observe is not the result of a conscious contextual Pentecostal theological agenda, which is, as a rule, absent or even categorically rejected by the respective leaders and theological spokespersons. It is rather an unreflected and paradoxical contextualization shaped by different contextual interfaces, one that counteracts and sometimes even caricatures explicitly American evangelical representations by its implicit theology.

However, Pentecostal theologians are slowly starting to cope with that situation, and they are trying to make theological sense out of the anthropological data. It was first Walter Hollenweger who showed that there are many other variants of Pentecostalism that are different from American models but can claim the same representational right for being Pentecostal.[3] Hollenweger's insights (and to some extent a recent study by Harvey Cox)[4] have shaped a whole generation of new and critical Pentecostal theologians.[5] They are now in the lead of Pentecostal scholarship and have caught up with the academic theology of the established churches.[6] Among them it goes without saying that Pentecostalism must not be defined by North American evangelical standards only. At present, Pentecostal theologians based in North America and Europe are in the forefront of this discussion,[7] and as a result, the white North American evangelical type is regarded as just one variety of the Pentecostal movement, as can best be seen from the fact that there are

2. For an overview of anthropological literature on Latin America see Bergunder 2002b: 163-86; for Africa see Anderson 2000.

3. See Hollenweger 1988.

4. See Cox 1996.

5. See Jongeneel 1992.

6. See the judgment of Jürgen Moltmann and Karl-Josef Kuschel: ". . . but today a generation of Pentecostals has grown up which need not be afraid of comparison with the old churches either in scientific discourse or in the exegesis and systematic development of their faith" (Moltmann & Kuschel 1996: 208). Regular information on the current state of the discussion in Pentecostal and Charismatic theology is provided by the three journals: *Pneuma, Journal of Pentecostal Theology,* and *Journal of the European Pentecostal Theological Association.* An excellent introduction to state of Pentecostal theology in North America is offered by Burgess & van der Maas 2002.

7. See, e.g., Petersen 1996; Yong 2000; Anderson 2000.

now several acknowledged Pentecostal perspectives in the West, such as Hispanic-American and African American ("black") Pentecostalism.[8] Gradually, Pentecostal theologians from Asia, Africa, and Latin America are joining into this venture,[9] and it is certainly vital that they take the lead in future. But, of course, this new Pentecostal theology meets opposition from more conservative congregations and denominations, who see Pentecostalism simply as a version of Evangelicalism plus tongues-speaking, and it is far too early to say which side will dominate Pentecostal theology in the long run. By their own admission, for these theologians with their original views it is not a simple matter to receive a hearing in their churches. All too often there is tension with the church leadership circles. Nevertheless nearly all are active as pastors in their churches and as a rule they are not hesitant in bringing their theological convictions to the congregations and in discussing them there. Not a few are employed as teachers in the official theological institutions of the bigger Pentecostal churches, and their influence in the formation of future pastors is not to be underestimated. Moreover, it should be noted that the Pentecostal movement is often judged on the basis of the lived reality of the congregation, whereas the established churches set themselves against the background of their theological reflection which in turn is mostly concerned with what ought to be rather than with what is. For a suitable comparison the theologies on both sides need to be equated as well as, in a separate process, the sociological realities.

The theological challenge that contemporary Pentecostal theology faces is curiously similar to that in the mainline churches, where over the last decades concepts of inculturation and contextualization have been hotly discussed.[10] So, it is not surprising that Pentecostal theologians sometimes use words like "contextualization" or "inculturation" when they go into the issue. But they rarely deal with the philosophical and theological concepts behind these terms.[11] At present one can observe some uncertainty among Pentecostals on how to deal hermeneutically with the question of contextualization. That has certainly something to do with widespread reservations against ecumenical theology in general but probably more with the intrinsic difficulties: how to relate contextualization to a meaningful Pentecostal theology of mission (which is still missing too); or how to relate actual contextual performance to often explicit anti-contextual attitudes among the persons involved, and so

8. See, e.g., Gerloff 1992; Solivan 1998; Daniels 1999.
9. But see Kim 1999: 123-39; Sepúlveda 1999: 111-34.
10. See e.g., Collet 1990; Bosch 1991: 420-57; Bevans 1992.
11. But see Yong 2000: 206-19.

on. Pentecostal theology can't avoid these fundamental questions, but if it tackles these issues it will probably have to do so in a heated debate.

Nevertheless, there is some tendency to avoid this delicate debate by using a much older concept that still has some credit within evangelical circles: indigenization.[12] The concept of indigenization stems from Rufus Anderson and Henry Venn, who in the nineteenth century propagated as the aim of mission the "three selfs": self-government, self-support, and self-propagation.[13] This concept avoids a clear attitude toward inculturation or contextualization. It only emphasizes organizational independence from "western" Pentecostalism but implies that this would also mean independence from western dominance. Nevertheless, one should be careful not to fall prey to a wrong postcolonial reading of "indigenous" as free from western domination. The ongoing academic discussion on postcolonial theory has shown that the simple binary code "western/indigenous" does not help to decipher dominant colonial and postcolonial discourses, because the colonial encounter was quite complex and produced diverse, hybrid, and fluid configurations.[14]

It is too simple to suggest that western denominations like the Assemblies of God try to dominate their non-western sister churches, whereas Pentecostal churches in Africa, Asia, and Latin America that are without established institutional ties to any western organization or church would be more free, even if both have indigenous leadership. Oppression must not be narrowed down to the western/non-western antithesis. This would be misleading and would underestimate the effect of dominant discursive practices that work beyond established institutional links. Many independent Pentecostal churches get quite a lot of money from western partners, their leaders have studied at western Bible schools, and they regularly entertain westerners as guests or missionaries at gospel campaigns, and so on. Moreover, beliefs and rituals in indigenous churches are not necessarily more contextualized than in the churches that have official ties to western denominations. Even if one would add a fourth, "theological" dimension to the above given three aspects of indigenization, one would not get satisfying results, because according to this logic churches would be most indigenized when they hold the most non-western set of doctrines and practices. But without discussing criteria for relating that to the universal claim of the Christian message and for determining an authentic Christian witness, this

12. For a critique see Bosch 1991: 448-50.

13. Through Melvin Hodges (1999) this concept became well known in Pentecostal circles too.

14. See, e.g., Moore-Gilbert 1997; Young 2001.

theological dimension remains meaningless. If one analyzes leadership, corruption, nepotism, and similar phenomena, then the line is not at all between western and "indigenous" Pentecostalism, but spans this dichotomy. Indigenous churches are not simply a benefit in themselves, because independence does not necessarily mean good governance. Furthermore, the growth rate of independent churches is not inevitably better than that of western denominations. In many regions of Africa, Asia, and Latin America, the Assemblies of God are the fastest-growing Pentecostal church.

Hence, tendencies to look at Indian Pentecostalism within the straightforward antithesis of "indigenous" versus "western" must be looked at very critically. Roger Hedlund initiated a project on Indian "Churches of Indigenous Origin," identifying independent Pentecostal churches as the most important representatives.[15] Hedlund, a long-time missionary to India who has a decidedly American evangelical background, shows a genuine openness and appreciation for the disparate Indian church landscape. His intentions are certainly laudable, especially in the context of a rising Hindu nationalism that despises Islam and Christianity as foreign, western, non-indigenous religions. Nevertheless, if "indigenous" only means "under the control of Indians, guided by Indian leaders,"[16] then it is not clear why mainline denominations like the Church of South India and the Church of North India are not covered by that term. Accordingly, the assignments of respective churches are vague and inconsistent,[17] and "indigenous" remains nothing else but a synonym for "non-western" or "native." A similar example is Indian Pentecostal theologian Paulson Pulikottil, who refers to the independent Indian Pentecostal Church as an example of "indigenous Pentecostalism" as against what he calls "Western Pentecostalism."[18] He is certainly right when he claims an emancipatory, anti-colonial stance among the leaders of the Indian Pentecostal Church, who successfully resisted any domination by western Pentecostal missionaries. Nevertheless, the postcolonial debate, which

15. See Hedlund 1999: 26-42; Hedlund 2000a; Hedlund 2000b; Hedlund 2002c.
16. Hedlund 2000a: 81-82.
17. The Syrian Orthodox Church, though it uses a "foreign" (Syrian) liturgy, can at the same time serve as the "Original Indigenous Paradigm" (Hedlund 2000a: 23). Likewise, for instance, it is not clear why Pentecostal churches like the Tamil branch of the Church of God (Cleveland) or World Missionary Evangelism (Dallas, Texas) should be good examples for indigenous Pentecostalism (see Hedlund 2000a: 82, 198). Similarly, Stanley Burgess knows of "Indian Neocharismatics," which he explicitly considers as part of Hedlund's indigenous Christian movements; but as the most important example, he refers to the New Apostolic Church, which is actually a Swiss-based centrally organized church of German-speaking origin with no Pentecostal ties so far (see Burgess 2001: 95-96).
18. See Pulikottil 2001.

Pulikottil is explicitly referring to, goes much further. The subaltern studies project has shown that the anti-colonial national movement was mainly in the interest of the largely Hindu high-caste elites, whereas the subalterns ("untouchables," "tribals," and so on) didn't benefit likewise.[19] In the same way, because the leadership of the Indian Pentecostal Church was dominated by Thomas Christians, who consider themselves as an ethnically defined caste group of very high social status comparable to Brahmins, the perpetuation of an oppressive structure by the exclusion of subaltern groups from leadership positions took place despite indigenous leadership. And it was not only the Indian Pentecostal Church that was at fault. All major Pentecostal (and most of the mainline) denominations in Kerala have Thomas Christian leadership, and this Thomas Christian domination goes back as far as to the 1920s. As a reaction to that situation Pentecostal churches arose that are based on homogeneous Dalit congregations with Dalit leadership (e.g., World Missionary Evangelism, Kerala Division of the Church of God) but still, they are all at a disadvantage against the other denominations dominated by Thomas Christians (whether financially, or regarding access to foreign contacts and foreign funds, and so on). These internal oppressive structures of Indian Pentecostalism can't be named within a hermeneutical framework that is limited to the antithesis of "indigenous" versus "western," yet one of the most important contexts for contextual Pentecostal theology lies just here. So, for the hermeneutical task that lies ahead of Pentecostal theology, the concept of indigenization is hardly suitable, because it falls short of expectations. On the other hand, as the so-called ecumenical theology is still struggling for meaningful concepts of inculturation and contextualization, a distinctive Pentecostal voice within that debate might have a stimulating effect on academic theology in general.

At present, there is no such thing as contextual theology within Indian Pentecostalism, though there have been some rare examples that somewhat headed in that direction, but were rather motivated by the search for immediately effective missionary tools than by seeking new ways of theologizing.[20]

19. See Chaturvedi 2000.

20. In 1975, John Thannickal wrote a dissertation in which he researched Hindu and Christian ashrams to find some stimulation for a contextual proclamation of the Christian message; see Thannickal 1975. For information on John Thannickal see pp. 88, 296-97. In the 1980s Sadhu Chellappa started to go to the Hindu scriptures to prove Christ (see pp. 261-62). Moses Choudary — strongly influenced by Donald McGavran's church growth movement — promotes an accommodation strategy for Christian mission among high-caste Hindus so that they can stay with their own people even after going over to Christianity (see Choudary 1980, and pp. 105-6, 263).

Nevertheless, things are changing fast, and there are quite a few young Pentecostal Indian scholars who seem to be taking up the challenge.[21]

21. For instance, V. V. Thomas (United Biblical Seminary, Poona) is working on a Ph.D. thesis on "Pentecostalism Among Dalits in Kerala," and he explicitly relates this research to the concept of "Dalit theology," which is the Indian variant of liberation theology. Others, like M. Stephen (Faith Theological Seminary, Manakala; see also Stephen 1999) or Isaac V. Mathew (Bethel Bible College, Punalur), are trying to make theological sense out of the encounter between Indian Pentecostalism and popular Hindu religiosity.

Selected Biographies

Abraham, K. E. (1899-1974)

K. E. Abraham hailed from Puttenkavu near Chengannur, Alappuzha District. His parents belonged to the Syrian Orthodox Church. According to his own statements, he experienced his conversion at the age of seven, but he had a second conversion when he was fourteen years old.[1] After attending school for eight years, he became a teacher in a primary school. During that time, he came in contact with the Brethren and received baptism by immersion in 1916 from K. V. Simon, who was at that time one of the most influential indigenous leaders of the Brethren. After his baptism by immersion, Abraham became an active evangelist of the Brethren. In the 1920s, he heard about the Pentecostal movement and read two tracts published by George E. Berg.[2] In his prayer with C. Manasse, who was the indigenous coworker of Mary Chapman, he received the baptism of the Spirit in 1923. Probably thereafter, he gave up his job as a teacher and founded a Pentecostal congregation in Mulakuzha near Chengannur in 1924 with financial support from the Assemblies of God.[3] After his separation from Robert F. Cook in 1930, he settled down in Kumbanadu, which was not far from Mulakuzha. Perhaps during his collaboration with the Ceylon Pentecostal Mission in the beginning of the 1930s, Abraham, who was married at the time and had two children, made a vow of voluntary "celibacy."[4]

1. See Verghese 1974: 8, 15, 21; see also Varghese 1999.
2. See Indian Pentecostal Church 1974: 95.
3. Abraham always maintained that the congregation in Mulakuzha was started fully independently (see India Pentecostal Church 1974: 95), but this is highly improbable.
4. See Verghese 1974: 114. However, Abraham always lived together under the same roof with his wife and children.

Abraham, T. S. (b. 1925)

T. S. Abraham grew up as the son of K. E. Abraham in a Pentecostal home, was converted in 1937, and was baptized by K. C. Cherian in 1938. He studied in Alwaye College, Kerala, and finished his studies in 1949 with the B.A. degree. During the period of his study, he was active in the youth ministry of his church and he was the cofounder of the Pentecostal Young People's Association in 1947, which later on developed into the youth organization of the Indian Pentecostal Church. In 1950 he married a daughter of P. T. Chacko and went to Secunderabad to help his father-in-law. In the same year, he received the baptism of the Spirit there. Between 1952 and 1954 he studied at Elim Bible Institute, New York. Afterward, he shuttled between Secunderabad and Kumbanadu in order to support his father as well as his father-in-law in their ministries. Since 1956 he taught in Hebron Bible College, Kumbanadu, and became its principal in 1970. When his father became seriously ill in 1973, he took over his position with the intention of becoming his successor in Kumbanadu, after the death of K. E. Abraham. From 1973 to 1989, he was Secretary for the Kerala State. In 1990 he became the General Secretary of the Indian Pentecostal Church, and in 2002 he became General President. His son, Valson Abraham (born in 1952), studied at Fuller Theological Seminary, Pasadena, and completed his studies with a M.Th. In 1984, Valson founded an independent mission society by the name India Gospel Outreach based at Rancho Cucamonga, California. He works closely together with his father and supports his ministry.

Alwis, Alwin R. De (ca. 1901-1967)

Little is known about Alwin, the cofounder of the Ceylon Pentecostal Mission. His full name was Alwin R. De Alwis, and he hailed from an influential Singhalese family and was comparatively well educated. He was not married, and it is said that he had been converted to Christianity from Buddhism. In any case, he probably belonged to the Baptist Mission in Ceylon before he became Pentecostal. His sister Freda also had taken a prominent position in the church. Later, a brother of Alwin, Clement de Alwis, also joined the Ceylon Pentecostal Mission.[5]

Arumainayakam, Peter (b. 1939)

Peter Arumainayakam comes from a Hindu family in Rajapalaiyam. On completing grade ten in school, he found employment in Coimbatore. Here he contacted the nearby church of the British Assemblies of God and was converted in 1961 through the influence of the Liveseys. After the departure of the Liveseys, various pastors were active but without success until Peter Arumainayakam, who had been chairman of the council of elders, took over the pastorate. He has three sons.

---

5. See Williams 1962: 33.

The oldest, Lawrence Arumainayakam (b. 1965), graduated with a B.A. and studied at the Assemblies of God Bible college in Mattersey. Later he earned an M.Div. at the ACM Theological Seminary in the Philippines. In 1993 he became associate pastor in the main church.

Balachandran, Joseph (b. 1947)

Joseph Balachandran comes from a Christian family. His father is Lutheran, and his mother belongs to the Church of South India; both worked as teachers in Tirunelveli District. Joseph was working as a mechanic in a private firm in Madras when he was converted in 1967 at a Youth for Christ evangelization. In the same year he received Spirit baptism and became a member of Maranatha. During his time in Madras he was influenced by N. Jeevanandam. In 1970 he went to Usilampatti, Madurai District, to found a congregation in the name of Maranatha. Parallel to his activity as pastor, he founded, independently of Maranatha, Jesus Lives Evangelistic Ministries to coordinate his numerous evangelistic activities. In 1981 he left Maranatha and moved to Madurai. Together with his long-time friend Owen Roberts, he founded an independent church, the Good Samaritan Fellowship. But the main emphasis of his work has remained evangelism.[6]

Berchmans, S. J. (b. 1949)

S. J. Berchmans comes from a Catholic family in the neighborhood of Paramakudi, Ramanathapuram District. At seventeen he went to the Catholic seminary in Trichy. After finishing his studies he was ordained in 1974. In 1980 he had his own congregation in a small locality near Sivaganga, Muthuramalingam District. During this time he came into contact with the Catholic Charismatic movement. At the same time a member of his congregation gave him a cassette with a sermon by Dhinakaran. Impressed by this, he wrote to the preacher, who sent him more cassettes and books and invited him to his Institute of Power Ministry. In 1982 Berchmans took part in this, received baptism in the Spirit, and so entered into closer relations with the Pentecostal movement. Following this, he introduced special healing services in his own congregation, which were well attended. He proved a gifted musician and composer of hymns, for which his musical training at the seminary had prepared him. In the second half of the 1980s he was a popular Catholic revival preacher. In 1988 he received baptism by immersion in private and this strengthened his contacts with the Pentecostal movement. A little later he provoked conflict with his bishop by going against Catholic teaching on the Eucharist. In 1991 he was suspended from ministry and thereafter left the Catholic Church. He was well prepared for this step, since in 1990 followers in

---

6. See also *The Elim Evangel* 52, no. 34, 21 Aug. 1971: 6.

Kalayarkoil, Muthuramalingam District, had presented him with a site on which a prayer center had been erected. Here he made his headquarters after leaving the Catholic Church and called his organization Prayer Garden Fellowship. Some followers came with him on his departure from the Catholic Church and a few congregations were formed in the fellowship. But the main emphasis of his activities lay elsewhere. In 1990 he began to distribute cassettes with the hymns he composed, together with a small hymnal. This proved a breakthrough. His simple and attractive Tamil songs, in the style of Indian film music, became hits. All Christians in Tamil Nadu know and appreciate them. The success of his cassettes soon proved profitable for him. He also gained renown as an evangelist. His popular preaching was interspersed with song and dance, to good effect. As a result, his style of evangelization was much spoken of. His reputation rose even higher when in 1995 he conducted evangelizations in Tamil Nadu together with the two influential Tamil evangelists Joseph Balachandran and P. S. Rajamoni.

Burgess, John H. (1903-2001)

John H. Burgess was born in Muskegon, Michigan.[7] He studied in the Rochester Bible Training School in New York from 1924 to 1925 and in the Bethel Bible Training School in Newark, New Jersey, from 1925 to 1926. In 1926 he was ordained by the Assemblies of God, and in the same year he left for India. His future wife, whom he had come to know during his studies in Rochester, followed him to India in 1927 and they got married there. He returned to the USA in 1950.[8] There he became first pastor of a congregation of the Assemblies of God in Flint, Michigan, and simultaneously obtained an M.A. degree at the University of Michigan. In 1965 he was invited to teach in the Central Bible College in Springfield, Missouri. He retired in 1972. His son Stanley M. Burgess, born in India in 1937, became an important Pentecostal scholar.

Chacko, P. T. (ca. 1902-1990)

The parents of P. T. Chacko belonged to the Mar Thoma Church and lived in Kumbanadu. According to his own account, he was converted at the age of six (!). He went to the high school in Tiruvalla and was married in 1920. Thereafter he studied in the newly opened Union Christian College, Alwaye. During this time he attended the Pentecostal mission rallies of Robert F. Cook and Robert W. Cummings.[9] He met K. E. Abraham when the latter held his first Pentecostal meeting in Kumbanadu. Abraham conferred baptism by immersion on him in

---

7. See McGee 1990b.

8. See p. 44.

9. See Pastor Chacko's Family Members 1980: 5, but it should be noted that the text speaks only of "Cummings an old missionary from Madras," and we cannot be certain that it is R. W. Cummings that is meant. For R. W. Cummings see also Robinson 1990b.

1925 and on the same day he received baptism in the Spirit at a Tarrying Meeting. From 1927 to 1930 he taught at the Alwaye Settlement School, a social institution of the Mar Thoma Church for children of Dalit families. From 1930 to 1934 he studied theology at Serampore College, West Bengal, and earned a B.D. At this time he was in close collaboration with K. E. Abraham. He taught for some time at Hebron Bible School in 1931 and 1932; he took part in forming the constitution of the Indian Pentecostal Church and was present at the registration in Eluru in 1935.[10] In 1936 he settled at Eluru and, together with P. M. Samuel, he founded the first church in Andhra Pradesh. In 1940 he moved to Secunderabad. In 1964 his wife and traveling companion of many years died. His only son, P. C. Thomas, studied until 1961 at Osmania University. When he finished with an M.A., he taught journalism there for some time and then migrated to the USA in 1967. In 1972 his daughter Mary married C. T. Cherian, who was then pursuing a secular career in the USA. Cherian was the son of V. T. Thomas, who belonged to the first generation of pastors in the Indian Pentecostal Church in Kerala. P. T. Chacko's youngest daughter married M. S. Samuel, who came from Kerala and worked in New York, leading a Malayali Pentecostal congregation there. In a sense, Chacko's family is typical of many families of Pentecostal pastors from Kerala, where the second generation has migrated to the USA.

Chapman, Mary (1857-1927)

Mary Chapman came to south India as a missionary of the Assemblies of God.[11] Before she went to India, she had already been a missionary in Africa.[12] First she settled down at Madras where she worked closely with the congregation of Benjamin Jacob. Simultaneously she undertook many journeys to south Kerala and to Tamil Nadu. After she had come back from her furlough in 1921, she changed her headquarters to Trivandrum, where she found in C. Manasse an important indigenous coworker. Miss Aldwinckle also helped Mary Chapman during this time. In 1926, Mary Chapman went to Mavelikara, Alappuzha District, where she died a year later.

Chelladurai, Sam, Jr. (b. 1953)

Sam Chelladurai Jr., the son of P. S. Chelladurai Sr., received baptism by immersion and baptism in the Spirit in 1969. In his youth, he was influenced especially by N. Jeevanandam. He studied for a short time at an Indian college, but in 1973 broke off these studies and, with the mediation of C. T. Buchanan, went to Elim Bible Institute, New York. He then studied psychology and earned an M.A. After

10. See Indian Pentecostal Church 1991: 4.
11. See Shinde 1974: 107. For the biography of Mary Chapman, see above all Saju 1994: 54-56, 60, 277.
12. See Reginald 1995: 26.

finishing his studies in 1980 he became pastor of a white congregation in Winston-Salem, North Carolina. Although he possessed a Green Card, he was active there as a pastor for only thirteen months and in 1981 he returned to India.[13] Here he organized seminaries for representatives of the Faith Movement, until he took over his father's main congregation. Sam Chelladurai Jr. is a forthright exponent of the Faith Movement and has strong appeal for the educated middle classes. This not least is due to his formidable intellectual form of preaching. He doesn't have close contacts to other Pentecostal pastors, nor does he participate in interchurch Pentecostal fellowships, but he maintains a close friendship with J. Harris.

Chelladurai, P. S., Sr. (b. 1922)

The family of P. S. Chelladurai Sr. came originally from Tirunelveli, where his mother had been in contact with a female missionary of the Dohnavur Fellowship, and had been converted from Hinduism to Christianity and baptized by immersion. His mother's deep spirituality strongly influenced him. He grew up in Coimbatore and belonged to the Church Missionary Society there until the age of seventeen years when he took part in an evangelical mission of the British Assemblies of God, where he was converted. Soon after, he received baptism in the Spirit together with his mother. In order to receive immersion baptism he contacted S. Ponraj in Trichy. The latter took him to the church convention of the Ceylon Pentecostal Mission in Madurai, where he was immersed. Strongly impressed by this convention, he returned to Coimbatore and initiated a Pentecostal prayer group in which his mother also played an active role. They had close contact with the woman evangelist Sannyasini Ponnammal, who came from Kerala and was then working in Coimbatore. In 1941 P. S. Chelladurai Sr. helped to set up a convention of the Ceylon Pentecostal Mission in Coimbatore as a result of which a congregation with S. Ponraj as pastor was founded. In 1943 he went to Madras, where he got a post in the public service. There he was a member of the Ceylon Pentecostal Mission, and after some time he decided to enter full-time ministry in this church. However, rumors about alleged abuses in Faith Homes were spread at this time and P. S. Chelladurai Sr.'s father, because he was concerned about his son's well-being, wanted to discuss this openly within the church. This caused a conflict with chief pastor Alwin and, as a result, the whole family was laid under interdict, so that they left the church and helped to found the Apostolic Christian Assembly. P. S. Chelladurai Sr. separated from G. Sunderam in 1951. He then took over the church of pastor M. Murugesan, who was looking for a successor because of his age. But soon after he decided to found his own congregation with himself as lay pastor. In the second half of the 1960s he established a

---

13. See Chelladurai Sr. 1995: 82.

small denomination when he came into contact with powerful overseas sponsors, among them C. T. Buchanan and John Osteen.[14] He then went into full-time ministry and committed himself strongly to Pentecostal cooperation. In the mid-1980s he gave full leadership of the main congregation to his son but in 1986 he founded a new branch in Coimbatore, where he continued as pastor. He also remained formally president of the whole organization.

Chellappa, Sadhu (b. 1934)

Sadhu Chellappa comes from Sankarankovil, Tirunelveli District. His parents belonged to the Baptists. He passed his time of schooling at Tirunchengode, Salem District, where his parents worked as teachers. Notwithstanding his Christian family background, he attended evening courses at a Vedic school and so gained a certain insight into Hindu scriptures and learned a little Sanskrit. In 1951 he began training in nursing at the Christian mission hospital in Ranipettai by Vellore, but on finishing this training he failed to find employment. For some time he co-operated in the Dravidic movement (D. K.) until in 1959 he found work as a postal worker in Bangalore. In the same year he married the daughter of T. Daniel, a pastor in the Tamil Evangelical Lutheran Church. In 1966 he moved to Madras; in the following year he experienced conversion at a rally organized by Joe Daniel. He stayed only half a year with the Layman's Evangelical Fellowship before joining the Pentecostal movement. He became a member of a branch congregation of the Apostolic Christian Assembly led by Freddy Macden(?) in East Tambaram, Madras. There he received baptism by immersion and Spirit baptism. Shortly after he went to another independent Pentecostal church in Tambaram, led by Basker Dawson. By his own reckoning it was there that he felt the decisive shaping of his spirituality. In 1973 he moved to Coimbatore and in 1976 gave up his employment and entered full-time ministry. First he worked under Job Gnanaprakasam but later took a post as pastor in an independent church in Coimbatore's Tatapad area led by Lily and J. C. Isaiah.[15] Again he stayed only a year and then in 1978 founded the Evangelical Team of India, which first functioned as a small church but later served only to coordinate evangelical activity. In the 1980s this activity proved sensational. Texts from Veda, Tirukkural, Tamil Sangam literature, Bhagavadgita, and Saiva Siddhanta were expounded, showing that they all refer to Jesus Christ. This led to riotous scenes and militant reactions from radical Hindu circles. All churches, including the Pentecostals, distanced themselves from Sadhu Chellappa since such aggressive mission strategy was decisively rejected. Sadhu Chellappa then gave up this strategy and limited the sharing of his views to the Christian public in seminars and conferences. In 1987 he moved from Coimbatore to Madras. In 1994 he founded his own independent

14. See Chelladurai Sr. 1995: 69, 83.
15. For the history of the Tatapad church also see pp. 61ff.

church, where he had been active as evangelist before. One of his daughters married David Manoraj and another S. Subramiam. Both were pastors of the Assemblies of God in Madras at the time. In 1990 his youngest daughter married the German Wolfgang Simson, who manages a Christian printing press in Lörrach near Basel. The specialty of Chellappa's position is that he goes to the Hindu scriptures to prove Christ. According to him, this is possible because the authors of Hindu scriptures were influenced by Jewish religion. This for the first time on the Pentecostal side allows room for finding spiritual relevance in Hindu scriptures, and it challenges Pentecostal Christians to be concerned with them. Sadhu Chellappa's argument suggests the potential for a differentiated Pentecostal view of Hinduism if it is possible to overcome the extreme inclusivism of his approach. Moreover, Sadhu Chellappa wants to introduce contextual features into the Pentecostal worship service. However, he remains isolated within Indian Pentecostalism.

Chellappa, S. (b. 1953)

S. Chellappa finished high school (S.S.L.C.) and immediately after that he started to work in the railways. In 1972 he was converted and baptized. He received the baptism of the Spirit in 1975. In 1977 he received the call for the ministry and gave up his post in the railways. He then worked as a pastor for a man named Tachinamurti(?), a rich Hindu from the neighborhood of Uthamapalayam, Madurai District, who was converted to Christianity by D. G. S. Dhinakaran and had put up a sort of private chapel on his piece of land.[16] From 1981 to 1986, he was the pastor for the Pentecostal Church of India in Perumalpuram, until he took over the leadership of the whole church after the death of S. B. Daniel in 1986. The eldest son of S. Chellappa studied at the Southern Asia Bible College, Bangalore. The number of followers of the church, which did not receive any assistance from abroad, have become few over the years.

Cherian, K. C. (1900-1954)

K. C. Cherian hailed from Meluveli, Pathanamthitta District.[17] His family belonged to the Syrian Orthodox Church. At the age of eighteen he was converted by Muttampackal Kochukunju, an evangelist of the Mar Thoma Church. In the subsequent period he joined the Brethren and in 1921 he received from K. E. Abraham the baptism of immersion. When Abraham joined the Pentecostal movement, K. C. Cherian followed him and received the baptism of Spirit in 1924. Afterward he was a close coworker of Abraham and worked as an evangelist in different places. He went to Kozhikode in 1930 and further to Mangalore in 1933. In Mangalore he met Carl Swahn and arranged for the decisive foreign

16. A short description of this man is found in Hoefer 1991: 31-33.
17. About K. C. Cherian see Saju 1994: 67, 130-31, 175, 177, 181, 278-81.

contact of his church. His work in Karnataka, however, brought him little success. Therefore, in 1950, he settled in his native place, Meluveli, which was not far from Kumbanadu. He then fell out with Abraham, whom he accused of betraying the congregational principle and ruling over the Indian Pentecostal Church in an autocratic manner. Therefore, in the course of that quarrel, Cherian was excommunicated from the Indian Pentecostal Church. In his accusation against Abraham, he received the support of numerous other pastors of the Indian Pentecostal Church. However, Cherian met with an early death, and did not live to see how that quarrel devolved into a long-term split of the church after his death.[18]

Choudary, G. Moses (b. 1946)

G. Moses Choudary comes from a village southeast of Vijayawada. His parents were Hindus and belonged to the Choudary caste. He lost his father when he was four. At about thirteen, he was very ill with inflammation of the lungs. His mother prayed to Jesus Christ to heal her son. Since he was in fact healed, she converted to Christianity and found a prayer group of higher-caste Christians in a congregation supported by the Church of God. There she was baptized. Moses was converted in 1962 in this congregation and was also baptized. He did not complete his college education and instead began training as a nurse but broke off this also. He married in 1965, received the call to ministry, and began studies in the Church of God Bible school in Kakinada. In 1971 he went to Eluru for a short time and established a small congregation. From 1972 to 1974 he studied, through Harold L. Turner's mediation, at Lee College, Cleveland. On his return he was made State Evangelism Director for the Church of God in Andhra Pradesh and at the same time teacher in the Bible school. In 1980-1981 he successfully attended a master's degree course at the Church of God School of Theology, Cleveland. A short time after coming back to India he left the Church of God. For the coordination of donations for his church from the USA, there was a special organization, Maranatha Faith Ministries in Ludowici, Georgia.

Cook, Robert F. (1879-1958)

Robert F. Cook hailed from a Baptist family in the USA. According to his own statement, he experienced his conversion at the age of seven and a renewed revival at the age of twelve when he became baptized.[19] In 1909, his father led him to the Upper Room Mission in Los Angeles that was run by Elmer Kirk Fisher, where he also received the baptism of Spirit. He was already married at that time. Though he had already received the call to the ministry at the age of fourteen,[20]

18. See p. 38.
19. See Cook 1955: 10.
20. See Cook 1955: 10.

he gave up his job only in 1911 in order to enter the ministry full time. However, immediately after that he had to struggle with financial difficulties, and started to work again to earn his livelihood. In such a desperate condition he took part in the First World Wide Pentecostal Camp that was organized by the Apostolic Faith Mission (Azusa Street, Los Angeles). There he came in contact with George E. Berg and decided to go with him as a missionary to India. In October 1913 he came to India with his wife, and after a short period of getting used to the country in Ooty, Nilgiris District, he went to Berg at Bangalore. In 1917 his wife died at Bangalore and Cook was left behind with two children. After a year he married the American missionary Bertha Fox, who was working in a home for the orphans and widows in Dodballapur, Bangalore District. After the marriage, Cook moved with his second wife to Dodballapur and they opened their own home for orphans there. In 1922, the family moved to Kottarakara and in 1927 the headquarters were shifted to Mulakuzha. During the whole time of his stay in India, Cook went only twice on furlough: 1924-1926 and 1939-1940. In 1950, he left India and spent the last days of his life in Cleveland, Tennessee.[21] There, K. E. Abraham visited him shortly before his death.[22] Though his mission work was marked by many splits, there is no doubt that Cook was one of the most important Pentecostal missionaries in India. It is characteristic for him that he always tried to work closely and on the same level together with Indian pastors. Cook can also be considered the founder of two big Indian Pentecostal churches, the Assemblies of God and the Church of God.

Daniel, S. B. (ca. 1896-1986)

S. B. Daniel remained a celibate even after he left the Ceylon Pentecostal Mission. In 1962, he established contacts with the Christian Mission Service, which supported him in starting an orphanage.[23] However, they separated in 1965, since the Christian Mission Service demanded a registration of the orphanage in its name. The orphanage was closed and the church remained without any support from abroad. The building that was put up for the orphanage was then used a worship place and as the pastor's house. After the death of Daniel, his nephew S. Chellappa took over the church.

21. See Cook 1955: 256-57. According to Conn 1959: 224A, Robert F. Cook left India in 1949.
22. See Verghese 1974: 59.
23. The Christian Mission Service is a interdenominational relief organization with an evangelical character. It was founded in north Germany by Emil Richter and Erwin Klinge in 1958 and has also been active in Switzerland since 1969. A focus of its work lies in India. See Reimer 1991: 114-15.

David, K. R. (1917-1992)

K. R. David came from the neighborhood of Warangal. His parents were Hindu. During his attendance at the American Baptist school he converted to Christianity. He was active for a time as a non-medical practitioner. At one of the rallies organized by the Indian Pentecostal Church in Warangal in 1939 he converted to the Pentecostal faith and was baptized. A short time later he experienced Spirit baptism and the call to ministry. He was sent by P. M. Samuel as an evangelist to various places in the Warangal District and Krishna District. In 1942 he was associated with P. L. Paramjothi's Bible school in Antarvedipalem. In 1945 he was established as pastor in Rajahmundry. However, the more his position was strengthened in Rajahmundry and the more important his share became in the work in Andhra Pradesh, the more he felt his lack of material resources. The consequent increase in conflict with Samuel finally led to his having recourse to World Missionary Evangelism, who supported him financially from 1962.[24] In 1969 he formally separated from the Indian Pentecostal Church and was a founding member of World Missionary Evangelism in India.[25] During his lifetime he was one of the most influential representatives of this Indian body. In 1968 his daughter married Isaac Komanapalli. After his death in 1992, his two sons, one of whom lived in the USA, left World Missionary Evangelism to found their own organization.[26]

Devasundaram, Y. S. (b. 1930)

Y. S. Devasundaram comes from a Christian family (London Missionary Society) in Manavalapuram, Kanyakumari District. His parents were already in close contact with the Pentecostals. At the age of eighteen, after he finished high school, he was converted and received the call to ministry. At the time he was in contact with Kirubasanam and the Ceylon Pentecostal Mission. He was baptized by immersion through Sadhu Kochukunju and joined a Charismatic prayer group in Allenkottai that was shaped by the young Soorna Packiam and family. Soon he became leader of this group, which separated from the Church of South India in 1949 under his leadership and was constituted an independent Pentecostal church. Pastor Thesaiyan and Pastor Yesunesan stood by him as well as Soorna Packiam.[27] All of them remained unmarried. In 1954 the organization was registered, and land from family estates given for church building. At the beginning of the 1960s the church had contact with Canadian partners without, however, gaining substantial financial aid. One of the partners mentioned in his autobiography,

---

24. According to Samuel (1980: 65) this was already the case in 1961.
25. See World Missionary Evangelism n.d.
26. It is said that the property on which K. R. David built his church still belongs, in theory, to the Indian Pentecostal Church (see Samuel 1980: 65).
27. Devasundaram 1981: 15.

Tom Tutyko, put him in contact with Jean Christensen.[28] In 1975 Devasundarams fell into deep conflict with his closest coworkers, Thesaiyan and Yesunesan. The circumstances are obscure. The visit of Jean Christensen and the consequent material help must have helped him decisively to resolve the conflict to his own advantage. In the 1990s he was a well-known Pentecostal leader in Kanyakumari District.

Dhinakaran, D. G. S. (b. 1935)

D. G. S. Dhinakaran was the only child of his parents. He hails from Surandai, Tirunelveli District,[29] where his paternal family lived. They belonged to the Society for the Propagation of the Gospel. His father, S. Duraiswamy, was a schoolteacher. In 1947 his parents moved to Cuddalore. Years later, Dhinakaran joined St. John's College, Palayankottai, where he attended higher secondary school and pursued a B.Sc. degree at the Government College in Kumbakonam. From there, he switched to the National College, Trichy. In 1955, he had an experience of salvation, and received immersion baptism from pastor S. B. Daniel of the Pentecostal Church of India. In the same year, he finished his B.Sc. degree and began working at St. David School in Cuddalore. It seems that from this time onward, he became involved in evangelistic activities.[30] In 1956, Dhinakaran managed to get a job with the State Bank of India. He began working at Kurnool, Andhra Pradesh, and by the end of 1958 managed a transfer to Pondicherry. In 1959, he married Stella and probably lived with his parents at Cuddalore. In the course of time Stella became the backbone of and coworker in Dhinakaran's evangelistic ministry. It was in October 1962 that Dhinakaran received the baptism in the Holy Spirit through the prayer of an Anglo-Indian pastor, J. S. Lemeor, incidentally a friend of the family, with a small Pentecostal church in Coimbatore. At about this time Dhinakaran got promoted to the level of a bank officer and ended up working at various places like Mangalore,[31] Bangalore, and Mettur Dam. This caused the family to move often. While at Bangalore in the late 1960s, Dhinakaran regularly attended the Gospel Prayer Hall of K. R. Paul.

In 1970, Dhinakaran made his debut with a large healing campaign at Vellore.[32] The campaign, which proved to be quite successful, marked the beginning of his present day ministry. In 1972, he was transferred to Madras, where he has lived since. By 1973 Dhinakaran registered a trust under the

28. Devasundaram 1981: 38. In his autobiography others mentioned are Lawrence Barbour, Max Solbrekken and Theresa Collins.
29. The actual place of birth is Pamban, Ramanathan District. According to Indian customs, the mother goes to her family's place to deliver her first child.
30. See Dhinakaran 1978: 45.
31. Jesus Calls, Feb. 1996: 19.
32. Jesus Calls, Dec. 1995: 6-7.

name Jesus Calls for the coordination of his evangelistic activities. That was not to imply that he had withdrawn his membership from the Church of South India, but he consciously retained ties, making his work truly interdenominational. However, through the 1970s, he maintained close fellowship with two of the most influential Pentecostal pastors of Madras: P. S. Chelladurai Sr. and G. Sunderam. As early as the 1970s, Dhinakaran began publishing a magazine and producing audiotapes. At the beginning of the 1980s, he began producing videocassettes as well.[33] He also initiated radio programs beginning in 1972, and, in the 1990s, TV shows as well, most of which are in Tamil with a few in other languages, including English.[34] In response to the letters he received, Dhinakaran started a systematic-correspondence ministry in 1973. In 1980 Dhinakaran started, in addition to his evangelistic activities, a twelve-day course called *Institute of Power Ministry*. This course helped participants to receive the baptism in the Spirit along with the various gifts of the Spirit. By 1985 Dhinakaran had taken voluntary retirement from the bank, where he had grown to a leading position, and entered full-time ministry. At this time he began to extend his activities in a way that showed a clear influence by Oral Robert's ministry.[35] The headquarters was shifted to a newly erected building at R. A. Puram, Madras — that was dedicated in 1986. There, a "Prayer Tower" was established where "Prayer Warriors" pray round the clock over special requests, sent over either personally or by telephone. A bookshop exclusively for Jesus Calls publications (books and cassettes) was also included. By 1995, the headquarters had grown, with 150 persons full time and other voluntary workers active as "Prayer Warriors." Planning for a private Christian University got underway in 1984. Initially this led to the founding of the Karunya Educational Trust. As an outcome of the activity of this trust, the Karunya Institute of Technology (an engineering college) was opened at Siruvani, near Coimbatore, in 1986.[36] By the end of 1996, the Institute offered seven undergraduate programs in engineering (B. E.) and two postgraduate-level programs (M.B.A., M.C.A., M.E. Thermal Engineering) through the Bharathiar University, Coimbatore. Plans

33. P. Jeyachandran 1991: 52-55, 62-63.

34. In the beginning of 1997, he had regular radio programs with Sri Lanka Broadcasting Corporation, FEBA, and Madras-FM, and TV programs in Tamil with Raj TV and Vijay TV, and in Telugu/English with Gemini TV. In addition to that, he was able to broadcast special Christmas TV programs through Raj TV, GEC TV, J.J.TV, and others. See e.g., Jesus Calls, Aug. 1996, 3, 36; Jesus Calls, Jan. 1997, 11-12. See also Jeyachandran 1991: 41-42.

35. On Oral Roberts see Harrell 1985.

36. See Jeyachandran 1991: 75-89.

for developing colleges that would offer theological and medical programs were designed, but these still remain for the future. The funding for the university project came in the guise of the Young Partners' Plan — a device that employed the pay-for-prayer/blessing method, inaugurated in 1985.[37] In 1993, the Bethesda Prayer Centre emerged near the campus of the Karunya Institute of Technology. The Prayer Centre is located adjacent to a pool, representing Bethesda (John 5), where construction is going on to developing seven stations that would describe the way of the Cross. Each station will have various statues depicting biblical scenes. Previously this had only been seen in Catholic Ways of the Cross and clearly went against the Protestant hostility to images that had been traditional among Indian Protestants. Judging from the developments in the past, Bethesda Prayer Garden won't be Dhinakaran's last project. He will probably continue to expand his fields of ministry in the future too.[38]

The fact that Dhinakaran had not given up his membership of the Church of South India enabled him to represent himself as an evangelist of the established churches. This strategy contributed in no small degree to the success of Jesus Calls, since he had their support in his rallies. On the other hand, the Pentecostals treated him as one of their own. In his healing missions, organized with the utmost professionalism,[39] he avoided theologically controversial themes. They were, rather, encouraging appeals to God's love and the power of Jesus to heal from all worries and sicknesses. He presented himself as one who with God's help had been healed of various weaknesses and had overcome personal misfortunes. One is tempted to say that Dhinakaran represents himself as a kind of "wounded healer" (C. G. Jung), who got his healing power out of his own sufferings.[40] In the 1990s Dhinakaran conducted all

37. See pp. 134-35.

38. In the beginning of 1997, "Jesus Calls" presented itself as a "20 faceted ministry" in this order: 1. "Public meetings," 2. "Special youth meetings," 3. "24 hours Prayer Tower," 4. "Young Partners' (prayer help) Plan," 5. "Bethesda Prayer Centre (Karunya Nagar)," 6. "Marriage bureau," 7. "Employment bureau," 8. "Karunya International School," 9. "Book publication," 10. "Karunya Rural Community Hospital," 11. "Audio, video cassettes," 12. "Radio programs," 13. "Television programs," 14. "Women's revival ministry," 15. "Reaching out individuals through letters," 16. "Karunya Institute of Technology and Educational Trust," 17. "Institute of Power Ministry," 18. "Jesus Calls, True Friend magazine (in many languages)," 19. "To render support to mission organisations," 20. "Jesus Calls Transformer Youth Club" (Jesus Calls, Dec. 1996, 15; True Friend, Jan. 1997, 32). Until June 1995, the ministry had only "15 facets" (see Jesus Calls, June 1995: 10).

39. See Jesus Calls ca. 1992.

40. In 1969, he had a severe disease of the lungs (or liver?, see D. G. S. Dhinakaran 1987: 52); in 1985, he stayed for seven months in the USA to get a special medical treatment for

his bigger rallies together with his wife Stella and with his son Paul. He was concerned about the rising generation of evangelists, and there is scarcely one of the younger evangelists who has not been favored through him by a prophetic promise of the future. Some evangelists like, for example, John Solomon and John Joseph, imitate him in presenting themselves as members of the Church of South India.

Dhinakaran, Paul (b. 1962)

Paul Dhinakaran, the son of D. G. S. Dhinakaran, was associated with the ministry from a very early stage.[41] He graduated with a B.Sc. from Loyola College, Madras. During this time, when he was about eighteen years of age, Paul seems to have entered into an experience of salvation.[42] From what we know, it was only then that he was baptized at the St. Thomas Anglican Church (Church of South India), Madras. From then on, he is said to have become part of the evangelistic ministry of his father. Later, he completed a postgraduate program in business management (M.B.A.) and is said to have been "awarded a doctorate in Advertising (Ph.D.) by the University of Madras, at the age 26."[43] In 1989, he married Evangeline. Paul Dhinakaran is the designated successor to his father.[44] He was conferred with the post of Chief Administrator of Jesus Calls and Karunya Educational Trust. He is leading the Jesus Calls ministry relating to the youth, and is the second main speaker on every Jesus Calls campaign. In 1996, in connection with his involvement with the Karunya Institute of Technology, he was nominated as a member of the Syndicate of Bharathiar University, Coimbatore.

---

his kidneys; in 1990, after a serious heart attack, he got a by-pass operation. However, he never seems to have made sufficiently clear that his own healings were in the first place due to the possibilities of modern biomedicine and that it was not a question of miracle healing. For D. G. S. Dhinakaran see also Bergunder 2000b.

41. Before the birth of Paul, Stella Dhinakaran had two miscarriages (see Dhinakaran n.d.: 35-36). After Paul, in 1968, Angel Dhinakaran was born as the second child of the family. She died in a car accident in 1986.

42. See Jesus Calls, Oct. 1996: 25-26. It seems that a Spirit baptism is also related to that date (see also Dhinakaran 1995: 31).

43. Jesus Calls, Oct. 1996: 26. D. G. S. Dhinakaran, who has no postgraduate degree, also claims a Ph.D. of unknown origin, which he got probably in 1986 (see Jeyachandran 1991: 40). According to our knowledge, this Ph.D. is an honorary degree (D.D.) from an academically non-accredited institution.

44. The 2nd of October 1994 is given as the date when God conferred all the gifts of the Holy Spirit to Paul Dhinakaran that his father had received before (see Dhinakaran ca. 1995: 31-32).

Edwards, Doris (1906-1991)

Doris Edwards, née Davison, was one of the most important Pentecostal missionaries in India. She hailed from a Methodist farmer family in Wisconsin and was the eldest child of the family. At the age of fourteen she was converted in a Methodist convention. When a female Pentecostal evangelist organized a program on her farm, many of her family members, herself among them, received the baptism of the Spirit. She finished her high school, attended teacher training, and worked as a teacher for four years, until she decided to take up a course in the Central Bible Institute, Springfield. There she met Clarence T. Maloney, her future husband. Influenced by a visit of John H. Burgess in the Bible school, they decided to go together to India. After finishing the three years of study, they married in 1933. First, they took over a small congregation in the eastern USA, but departed for Kerala in 1937 as missionaries of the Assemblies of God at the invitation of John H. Burgess. In India, they first learned Malayalam, but later on Tamil also, since they decided to go to Tamil Nadu. After five years of work in Kerala, they went on furlough in 1942 determined to go to Tamil Nadu after their return. Because of the sudden death of Clarence T. Maloney in 1943, all those plans fell through and she stayed in the USA. During a lecture tour in American Pentecostal churches, where she gave reports about the mission in India, she met Robert Edwards, whom she married eventually. He was ready to accompany her to Tamil Nadu. At the end of 1946, they reached India and went first to Kerala, where they among other things learned Tamil, and they settled in K. P. Valasai in 1948. Clarence Maloney Jr. (b. ca. 1935), her son from the first marriage, came with them. He was later likewise appointed as an Indian missionary of the Assemblies of God, but left India for good in 1965. Robert W. Edwards died unexpectedly in the USA during their furlough in 1961. However, Doris Edwards went back alone to K. P. Valasai in the same year, and she continued to shape the further development of the Assemblies of God in Tamil Nadu. In 1967-1968 and 1979-1980 she undertook lecture tours in the USA to raise help for the Assemblies of God in Tamil Nadu. In 1984 she met with a severe accident that left her housebound. She died highly honored in K. P. Valasai and was buried there.

Gnanaprakasam, Job (b. 1925)

Job Gnanaprakasam comes from a Hindu family in a village near Pollachi. On account of a healing experience, he was converted with his parents in 1943 and received baptism by immersion through the Liveseys, who were working as missionaries of the British Assemblies of God in Pollachi at that time. In 1945 he was called to ministry and went to a small Bible school managed by the Liveseys in Coimbatore. The Liveseys arranged a marriage for him in 1948. In the same year he was ordained pastor by Donald Gee, then on a visit to Coimbatore. He then became the most important Indian coworker with the Liveseys. As the Liveseys had left India in 1954, he founded an independent congregation shortly after, in 1957. When the Liveseys came back for another visit 1960-1963, he rejoined them. From 1963 to 1975, Gnanaprakasam was a pastor of the Pentecostal Church of India. In 1967 he started to work with World Missionary Evangelism, and because of this, he came gradually into tension with his congregation, which he had to leave as a result. He then founded an independent church, which until 1979 was supported by World Missionary Evangelism. Thereafter, he found a number of new sponsors, especially from England, Sweden, and Germany (Intermission), but also from the USA and South Africa.[45]

His eldest son, David Prakasam (b. 1954), studied until 1977 at the Assemblies of God Bible college, Mattersey and, in further studies, gained an M.Div. at the Asia Graduate School of Theology, Bangalore. David Prakasam managed to build up the Bible school of the Indian Pentecostal Assemblies into one of the biggest Pentecostal training institutes in south India. His younger brother Peter Prakasam also studied at the Mattersey college until 1982. He married a daughter of P. S. Chelladurai Sr. The youngest brother, Andrew Prakasam, was trained at Zion Bible Institute, Rhode Island. All three brothers work under their father's leadership in various spheres of church work.

Harris, J. (b. 1941)

J. Harris came from a Christian family (Church Missionary Society) in Megnanapuram near Nazareth. He graduated from St. John's College, Palayankottai, and from 1986 onward, he worked in a chemistry laboratory for an armaments factory in Kotagiri. In 1971 he began to suffer from sleeplessness and was plagued by an anxiety syndrome. In search of healing, he took part in an evangelical mission of the Church of God in Coonoor, where Robert J. Reesor spoke as a guest preacher. He was converted and became a member of the Church of God and gradually regained health. He received baptism in the Spirit in 1972 during a visit to his birthplace at a branch of the Jehovah Salvation Church.[46] In 1974 he left his job to enter full-time ministry. For six months he remained in the Jehovah Salvation Church in his hometown, but in the same year began studies at the Tamil Bible Institute of the Assemblies of God in Madurai. There, on account of his good education, he was soon the preferred interpreter for the American missionaries. He married at this time, a marriage arranged by the local pastor of the Assemblies of God, S. S. S. Stephen. When the missionaries wanted to arrange graduate studies for him in Springfield, Missouri, this met with resistance from the established Indian pastors, who were not ready to give the necessary recommendation. Thereupon he left the Assemblies of God and accepted an invitation

---

45. See Indian Pentecostal Assemblies 1991; Gnanaprakasam 1995: 3-7.
46. See Devasundaram 1981: 27-28, 39.

from Henry Joseph to found congregations for Maranatha in Madurai. In 1994 he left Maranatha with the express intention of founding his own denomination.

Jebadurai, Sam (b. 1948)

Sam Jebadurai comes from a Pentecostal family whose ancestors were from the Tirunelveli District. His father, who belonged to the Church Missionary Society, worked in Ceylon. There he was converted at the end of the 1930s after a healing experience at the Ceylon Pentecostal Mission. On account of the growing tension between the Singhalese and the Tamil, the father sent his family to India at the end of the 1940s. Sam studied in Palayankottai from 1963 to 1967 and finished with a B.Sc. He was a member of the local congregation of the Ceylon Pentecostal Mission, where he received baptism by immersion. He came to Madras in 1968 looking for work. His eldest sister was a nurse in the Faith Home of the Ceylon Pentecostal Mission in Madras and there he resided for a year. After he had worked for a year as a teacher, he got a post with the tax authorities in Madras. In the 1970s he began to work as an evangelist in his free time. He left the Ceylon Pentecostal Mission with its exclusivist position and he kept close contact with Charismatic-minded members of the established churches. In 1976 he undertook a one-month missionary trip to the Andaman Islands with two independent pastors. The following year he wrote three edifying books, which were well received. In 1981 he visited Sri Lanka and met people connected with *Back to the Bible,* who suggested he should write daily Bible reading sheets in Tamil. He acted on the inspiration and in time this also was a great success. He wrote more edifying literature and became a welcome guest speaker at rallies. In 1985 he was so well established that he could give up his employment. The publication work was significantly widened. By 1994 he had published over 300 books, many of them Tamil translations of foreign edifying literature. As time went on, he began to publish books in other Indian regional languages; some English works also belonged to his publications program. His Tamil Bible reading sheets, appearing once a month, in 1994 reached publication figures of 60,000. From 1990 he conducted fasting-prayer retreats twice a year on the property of the Christukula Ashram in Tirupattur, North Arcot District.[47] These were so enormously popular that the attendance had to be limited to 6,000.[48] In 1995 he established a Bible school for laypeople. His work remained centered on the printing business, which also provided the financial backing for his other activities. With his publications he met the greater part of the need for edifying literature in Tamil Christianity.

47. For the eventful history of Christukula Ashram see Melzer 1976: 25-40.

48. Regular guest speakers at these retreats were the evangelists Mohan C. Lazarus and Ebenezer Paul. Before his death in 1993, S. Shankar also took part.

Jeevanandam, N. (b. 1932)

N. Jeevanandam comes from a Hindu family. His father was the village teacher in Salayam Palayam, near Villupuram, South Arcot District. After eight years at school he underwent teacher training at a Catholic educational institution near Villupuram and in 1951 came to Madras, where he worked as a teacher. He engaged in political activity in the D.M.K. but was converted in 1957 under the influence of the Layman's Evangelical Fellowship. In the following year he was active in his free time as an evangelist. He came to Pentecostal faith in the first half of the 1960s through the influence of Lawrie's evangelism and in 1964(?) received baptism in the Spirit. In 1968 he left his employment and became an evangelist in full-time ministry. At the time he was close to the Apostolic Christian Assembly. His first overseas trip took him to Jaffna in 1975; this happened at the invitation of the Tamil pastor C. P. D. Arumainayakam, who was a former follower of Paulaseer Lawrie. In the 1970s he became a popular evangelist. Many of the All Night Prayers he initiated were in company with D. G. S. Dhinakaran. From 1983 to 1990 he was representative of World Missionary Evangelism in Madras. In 1990 he left the organization and founded a small independent church, the Delight Christian Assembly. All these years he was successful as an imaginative evangelist. Many younger pastors, like D. Mohan, admitted being influenced by him.

Jeevaratnam, Lam (1891-1960)

Lam Jeevaratnam was born in a Lutheran family in a village near Guntur. Already in early childhood he manifested an extraordinary talent for drawing. At the age of seventeen he became a drawing master in a Baptist high school. In the course of time he acquired extraordinary artistic drawing skills. Thus, among other things, he was able to draw with both hands simultaneously, also with his mouth, nose, or toes. As a consequence, he gave up his job as drawing master and exhibited his drawing skills openly for show. After he had become known in palaces of Indian princes, he received an invitation to go to England in the beginning of 1920, where, it is said, he was even allowed to introduce himself to the king. In England he seems to have lived rather well with his skill, until accidentally he came across an evangelization of the British Assemblies of God that was taking place in Leeds (perhaps in 1925). There he experienced his conversion and a call to ministry. As a result, he visited the Hampstead Bible School in London, where he received the baptism of the Spirit. In 1926 he left for India, arrived there in December of the same year, and founded the Eastern Full Gospel Mission as an independent church. The church was supported financially by the British Assemblies of God, in which Lam Jeevaratnam was working as a missionary (with an Associate Missionary Certificate). The headquarters of the church was in Gudivada, Krishna District. Lam Jeevaratnam was also running a home for the orphans there in the name of the Eastern Full Gospel Mission. While he was less successful in his church work, Lam Jeevaratnam acquired, however, recognition as evangelist and guest speaker in church conventions. In 1937-1938 and 1949-1950, he undertook extensive journeys to Europe and the USA. However, Lam Jeevaratnam had hardly any close contact with the new Pentecostal churches that took their origin in Andhra Pradesh after the 1940s. For the 1950s, however, there is proof of a close collaboration with K. Vijayaratnam of the Bible Mission, who was also quite isolated in his work at that time.[49]

Jeyaraj, Y. (b. 1928)

Y. Jeyaraj comes from Nazareth. His parents were originally members of the Society for the Propagation of the Gospel. His father worked in Ceylon and there was converted to Pentecostal faith through an experience of healing, and became a member of the Ceylon Pentecostal Mission. When he returned to India, his family joined the Nazareth branch of that church. In 1942 Jeyaraj experienced baptism in the Spirit. He finished high school and went to Ceylon to work as a bookkeeper but came back a year later. After remaining distant from the church for some time, he decided to be baptized in 1949. For this purpose, he approached Santhosam Philip, former pastor of the Ceylon Pentecostal Mission in Nazareth, who had left the C.P.M. and joined the Assemblies of God. He met Santhosam Philip in K. P. Valasai and was introduced by him to the Edwardses. After his baptism he became interpreter for the Edwardses and their closest indigenous coworker. In 1959 he was made superintendent of the Assemblies of God in Tamil Nadu and remained in this post almost without interruption. In 1961 he was made assistant superintendent, and in 1979 general superintendent of the South India Assemblies of God. In 1991, he was transferred to the chair of the planned union of the Assemblies of God in all India; in 1995 he was the first General Superintendent of the General Council of the Assemblies of God of India. He is undoubtedly one of the most prominent Pentecostal leaders in India.

John Babu, Y. S. (b. 1935)

Y. S. John Babu came from a Lutheran family in Bheemavaram, West Godavari District. While stationed as a sub-inspector of police in Nizamabad, he had a decisive conversion experience that brought him into contact with the pastor of the Indian Pentecostal Church at this place. He became a member of this church and shortly left the police to found a congregation in neighboring Armoor in 1972. In 1979 he joined Alan Vincent from the British restoration movement, moved to Hyderabad, and established his own denomination, the Sion Fellowship.

---

49. For K. Vijayaratnam see pp. 99, 114-15.

John, A. J. (1882-1973)

A. J. John hailed from Puttenkavu near Chengannur, Alappuzha District.[50] His family belonged to the Thomas Christians. When he received baptism by immersion in 1909 and joined the Brethren, he was a high school teacher in Kottarakara. In 1918, he gave up his job and entered full-time ministry. He led a small congregation of Brethren in Mavelikara. In 1923, he invited Robert F. Cook as a guest preacher, which raised some excitement, since John and his congregation had changed over to the Pentecostal movement.[51] Thanks to him, Mary Chapman and John H. Burgess could establish their headquarters in Mavelikara. In addition, John was a popular preacher and through his teaching in the Bethel Bible School influenced many later pastors of the Assemblies of God. However, at a time that could not be pointed out exactly, he left the Assemblies of God and joined the Indian Pentecostal Church, which he also left later on. From 1961 until his death he lived in Nilambur, Malappuram District.

John, M. O. (b. 1926)

M. O. John came from a Hindu family in Ammapatti, near Madurai. In 1942 he converted to Christianity and was baptized the same year by M. M. Thomas in Ilanthakulam. He came into contact with Robert F. Cook and his son George, who invited him to Kerala, since he faced hostility in his village because of his conversion. He remained an evangelist in the Church of God in Kerala until 1945. Then he stayed for a short time with an elder in Ammapatti until finally he went to Madurai, where for some time he was working as a casual laborer. In Madurai he became a member of the congregation led by M. Benjamin. In 1947 he went back to Kerala and came into contact with the Edwards family, who sent him to the Bethel Bible School in Kerala. During this period, in 1948, he was married in Punalur and accompanied the Edwardses in their journey to K. P. Valasai. After having finished the Bible school in 1949 he remained there until 1951. Apparently it was then that he experienced baptism in the Spirit.[52] When M. Benjamin left the Assemblies of God, it seems that M. O. John soon joined him. However, in the second half of the 1950s, he left the Church of God and lived for a little while with Victor P. D. Kay in Thanjavur. There he came into contact with P. M. Samuel. In 1959 he went to T. Kalupatti, which was near his birthplace. With the assistance of Samuel he founded a congregation there. Samuel enabled him to open an orphanage in T. Kalupatti with the support of the Christian Mission Service.[53] In 1969, he had his own church building, which, however, he did not register in the

---

50. See Saju 1994: 66, 76, 81.

51. See Cook 1955: 125-26.

52. See John n.d.: 7.

53. In 1988, after a court case, the orphanage reverted to Christian Mission Service (see Gabriel 1993: 100 n. 84).

name of the Indian Pentecostal Church. In the sequel he was Samuel's most important coworker in Tamil Nadu. In 1981, as he did not agree with the system of succession in the Indian Pentecostal Church in Tamil Nadu, he left the church and made his congregation independent. In 1994 he joined the Indian Pentecostal Assemblies. His eldest son Ebenezer John (b. 1953) studied in 1976-1977 at Elim Bible Institute, New York. In 1979 in Tirumangalam near Madurai, he founded his own organization, the Elim Church of God.

John, P. V. (1877-1946)

P. V. John (Ayyapillai) was converted around the turn of the century from Hinduism to Christianity by the evangelist Kapiarupadesi of the Mar Thoma Church. Later he came into contact with A. D. Khan of the Anderson Church of God. He gave up his job as an employee in the court in 1920 and became the coworker of Khan. He received Spirit baptism in 1924 and became pastor of the Assemblies of God in 1925. While he was pastor in Kayankulam, Alappuzha District, he played quite a significant role in founding the Bethel Bible School.[54] In 1938, he picked a quarrel with the Assemblies of God and as a result left the church and became pastor of the Indian Pentecostal Church.[55] P. V. John is father of P. J. Thomas.

Jonah, A. N. (1912-1985)

A. N. Jonah came from a Hindu family, originally of Andhra Pradesh, but living in Burma. At eighteen, after a healing experience, he converted to Pentecostalism in Rangoon. It seems he belonged to the same congregation as P. Rajaratnam and came back with him to India in 1942. He settled in Rajahmundry and became a businessman. When K. R. David came to Rajahmundry in 1949 he was in the same congregation. In 1953 he received the call to ministry, gave up his business, and founded an independent church, the Independent Full Gospel Church. With the profits of his business activity he built its headquarters, along with some other church buildings, in Rajahmundry. Apparently he was convinced in 1954 by an English Oneness preacher of the baptism in the name of Jesus. So he and his congregation were rebaptized in the name of Jesus. At the end of the 1950s he had the support of the International Ministerial Association with headquarters in St. Louis, Missouri. Still in the 1990s, this organization helped the International Full Gospel Church. One of his daughters is married to Paulaseer Lawrie, and some of A. N. Jonah's other children were also married to prominent Yesunamam pastors in close contact with Paulaseer Lawrie. His son and successor A. S. W. Jaikumar (b. 1942) married the daughter of G. V. Titus in Nagpur. Another son married the daughter of James Morar (principal of Bharoshagar Mission College, Uttar Pradesh). Another daughter was married to a certain Pastor Israel in Guntur.

54. See Assemblies of God 1977: 3.
55. See Mathew 1990: 73A; Saju 1994: 163.

Joseph, D. Henry (b. 1924)

D. Henry Joseph came from a Methodist family in Mannarkudi, Thanjavur District. After completing high school, he came to Madras in 1943 seeking work. He gained a post in the public service. Apparently he came into contact with Bakht Singh's community, which was the occasion of his conversion in 1945.[56] When a pastor of the Ceylon Pentecostal Mission convinced him of the necessity of baptism by immersion, he became a member of that church and was baptized there in 1946. Three years later he experienced baptism in the Spirit. He was an active member of the church and gained especial recognition as an interpreter. When his marriage was arranged in 1949 with a woman who also worked in the public sector, this led to a break with the Ceylon Pentecostal Mission. He was refused marriage in the church because his bride wore jewelry. Thereupon Henry Joseph made contact with G. Sunderam, of the newly founded Apostolic Assembly. The latter allowed marriage with jewelry, and Henry Joseph became a member of the Apostolic Christian Assembly. However, a few years later, his wife put her jewelry away. In the 1950s Henry Joseph was a committed lay evangelist and an important coworker with G. Sunderam. Together with three other laypeople he founded the Fourth Man Gospel Team, which also got invitations from the established churches. Moreover, he vigorously supported cooperation among the Pentecostal churches in Madras. In 1961 he gave up his job and, for a year, he went to the International Bible Training Institute, Sussex. When he returned from England, Sam Sunderam was already ordained as assistant pastor so that he had no chance of gaining that post. This led to him founding his own Bible school. For help in this he had already made the acquaintance in England of the young Irishman John A. Prentice, who came back with him to India. In 1965 Prentice was officially appointed missionary of the Elim Pentecostal Church and traveled first to north India. From 1970 until his return to England in 1974, he was again with Henry Joseph in Madras, where he established the special partnership between the Elim Pentecostal Church and Maranatha.[57] Henry Joseph is a notable leader in the Pentecostal movement in south India. He has the advantage of numerous overseas contacts, especially as a close partner of Intermission.

Joseph, John (b. 1953)

John Joseph comes from a Pentecostal family. His father came from Kerala and belonged originally to the Mar Thoma Church; his mother belonged to the Church of South India in Madras. But his parents soon joined Sadhu Kochukunju and later Paulaseer Lawrie when their son John Joseph was healed at one of the latter's missions. John Joseph was baptized by Paulaseer Lawrie and through him received baptism in the Spirit. He finished high school (S.S.L.C.) in

56. See Hoerschelmann 1972: 2.
57. *Elim Evangel,* London 54 (8), 24 Feb. 1973: 12-13.

1969 and then lived for three and a half years with his parents in the Manujothi Ashram. Since he did not wish to go along with Paulaseer Lawrie's new teaching, he came to Madras at the beginning of the 1970s and found work in a private hospital. At the end of the 1970s he worked for a longer period as secretary for Graham Houghton of the Oriental Missionary Society. At the beginning of the 1980s he began an independent missionary work under the name Christ for Every Soul. John Joseph lives in voluntary celibacy and is a member of the Church of South India.

Joseph, K. S. (1908-1972)

K. S. Joseph came from Narasapur and belonged to the Baptist Godavari Delta mission. He regularly undertook trips to northern India, selling handmade textiles. On one such journey, he met the Lindens, who were Swedish American Pentecostal missionaries.[58] In Mussoorie, Uttar Pradesh, he came to Pentecostal faith and received Spirit baptism. On his return to Narasapur he converted his extended family, especially all of his six brothers. Soon he made contact with the Indian Pentecostal Church and taught at their Bible school in Tadepalligudam. When in the mid-1950s the Lindens came for a longer stay in Narasapur, P. M. Samuel was not pleased. He who himself enjoyed innumerable overseas contacts, reproached Joseph for being dependent on an overseas mission. For Joseph, who revered these missionaries as his spiritual parents, such reproach must have been extremely wounding. So it is no wonder that the strife escalated and immediately led to an open breach. Shortly after his dispute with P. M. Samuel, the Lindens died in north India. In 1962 K. S. Joseph became a member of World Missionary Evangelism. His Bethel Church, although consecrated by P. M. Samuel, remained just an independent family church and after his death was in the charge of his brother Nehemiah. In the course of time the family broke up. His eldest son lives in the USA as a teacher. Two sons, Ernest Komanapalli and Isaac Komanapalli, are prominent pastors in Andhra Pradesh. Two other sons, Carl Komanapalli (Manna) and Benjamin Komanapalli (Ministry to the Interior), are also engaged in church ministry.

Kay, Victor P. D. (b. 1924)

Victor P. D. Kay grew up in Malaysia, and from there his father returned to Thanjavur in 1931. His family belonged to the Society for the Propagation of the Gospel. In the 1940s he came in contact with the Ceylon Pentecostal Mission, and, as a result he was converted in 1943. In 1944, he received immersion baptism in the Ceylon Pentecostal Mission in Trichy, and baptism of the Spirit in 1946. He came in contact with P. M. Samuel in the beginning of the 1950s and for some time he

---

58. Probably they were missionaries of the Open Bible Standard Church.

became his most important supporter in Tamil Nadu. His marriage in 1954 was arranged by Samuel. In 1968, with the assistance of Samuel, he put up a prayer house, although his relationship with Samuel and with the Indian Pentecostal Church seemed to have cooled down already. In 1971, Kay contacted World Missionary Evangelism through G. Sunderam and got its support for an orphanage in Thanjavur. In 1978, he absconded from the scene of a fatal accident caused by his official car but he was caught. That was the main reason why he took leave of the World Missionary Evangelism. His wife took over the orphanage until his younger son, V. Rowlands N. P. Kay (b. 1960), took charge in 1985. His eldest son, Stephen Kay, works likewise in Madurai for World Missionary Evangelism. Since 1978, Victor P. D. Kay has had only a tiny house of prayer and has been practically without followers. However, he is considered a pioneer of the Pentecostal movement in Tamil Nadu due to his activities in the 1940s and 1950s.

Kochukunju, Sadhu (Muttampackal) (d. 1957)

Sadhu (Muttampackal) Kochukunju hailed from Aramada, Trivandrum District. Originally, he belonged to the London Missionary Society, but later joined the Brethren. He was a teacher by profession, but became a full-time evangelist of the Brethren in 1922. He practiced voluntary celibacy. In 1928, he visited P. Paul in Ceylon and was converted to the Pentecostal faith. After that he became a famous Pentecostal evangelist and stood close to the Indian Pentecostal Church. His influence spread primarily to south Kerala and the Kanyakumari District. Sadhu Kochukunju was a staunch proponent of the idea that the Last Supper must be celebrated as an evening meal, and this led to severe discussions between him and the Indian Pentecostal Church though it was generally tolerant in this respect.[59]

Komanapalli, Ernest (b. 1937)

Ernest Komanapalli is the second son of K. S. Joseph. He was converted in 1949 and a year later received the call to ministry. From 1956 to 1960 he studied at the Southern Asia Bible Institute, Bangalore. He had spent some time as evangelist when he heard of the Pentecostal World Conference due to take place in Jerusalem in 1961. He resolved to take part. His father mortgaged the house to get the money for the airfare. In Jerusalem he made his first contact with England, where he went after the conference. His father then communicated an address in Switzerland, where he went next. He was based here for ten months and undertook preaching trips in many European countries. Soon he had received enough to pay his debts in India and in 1962 he went on to the USA. He studied at Barrington College, Rhode Island State University, and finished with a B.A. Then he gradu-

59. See Saju 1994: 104-6, 173; Samuel 1989: 68-69.

ated at Rhode Island University with an M.Ed. That year he got an appointment to a school for the mentally handicapped. All this time he maintained close contact with the south Indian Pentecostal movement. During his studies in the USA he married P. L. Paramjothi's eldest daughter. As soon as he found employment in 1966, he decided to devote a part of his salary to the support of pastors in Andhra Pradesh. This was arranged for him by his father-in-law. Two years later he also set up an orphanage, and church work quickly developed. In 1971 he gave up his employment, returned to India, and settled in Amalapuram, East Godavari District, to found Manna. In 1979, with the help of Rock Church, Virginia Beach, he bought a large plot in Hyderabad and moved there himself. His son Sudarshan J. Komanapalli studied at Fuller Theological Seminary, Pasadena, and in the 1990s he took a key position in the administration. Ernest Komanapalli is strongly involved in cooperative work between Pentecostal churches; he founded the Full Gospel Leaders Fellowship of Andhra Pradesh and in 1993 succeeded John Thannickal as leader of the Pentecostal Fellowship of India.

Kumar, T. Yeswanth (b. 1951)

T. Yeswanth Kumar comes allegedly from a Tamil Hindu family. When his sister at the end of the 1960s was mentally ill, his mother sought help first from Hindu gods and then, as this was no help, from Jesus Christ. (She was already familiar with Christianity since she had been to a mission school.) At the time, the family was living in Madras, and his mother came into contact with the Lutheran Charismatic Joel Joseph.[60] When the daughter's health was significantly improved through his prayers in 1970, the family became members of the Lutheran Church as followers of Joel Joseph, and both daughters were converted to Christianity. At the beginning of the 1970s, the family settled in Bangalore and were members of the Lutheran Church there. Through a Charismatic prayer group of this church, they soon came into contact with Robert Sandy and became members of the Shekinah Gospel Prayer Fellowship. T. Yeswanth Kumar, who was then working as a trader, and his brother were converted in 1973 under the influence of Robert Sandy. The family became active supporters of the church. By the mid-1970s they established their own small Tamil congregation, led at first by Robert Sandy, until in 1979 T. Yeswanth Kumar took over.

Kunjummen, C. (d. 1979)

C. Kunjummen hailed from a Thomas Christian family and came over to the Pentecostal faith along with his parents. The family became a member of the Assemblies of God congregation in Mavelikara, Alappuzha District. There Kunjummen had a lot of contacts with the American missionaries, and he be-

60. On Joel Joseph, see Hoerschelmann 1977: 222-31.

came a teacher in the Bethel Bible School in 1935. In 1947 he became the secretary cum treasurer of the newly established Southwest District.[61] From 1947 to 1948 he was on a preaching tour in the USA. In 1950 he was appointed the new director of the Bethel Bible School at Punalur and, in 1967, he also became Superintendent of the Malayalam District.

Lawrie, Paulaseer (1921-1989)

Paulaseer Lawrie grew up in Ceylon, where his father worked as secretary for a firm. There he had his first years of schooling. His mother very soon moved with the children to Nazareth; his father followed after a little time. In Nazareth, the family belonged to the Society for the Propagation of the Gospel. The family later returned to Ceylon and Paulaseer Lawrie attended the St. John's College in Palayankottai, where he completed the Intermediate Class. He then went to Ceylon and in Wesley College, Colombo, he gained the London matriculation certificate. He went to Madras Christian College, Tambaram, to study for a B.A. but soon broke off. He tried for the army but was prevented by his father. He began again to study, this time in St. Xavier's College, Palayankottai. He took part there in action against the colonial regime and consequently had to leave Palayankottai. He took refuge in Ceylon, where he found a clerical post in a tea plantation. Under the influence of a colleague at work, he had a conversion experience associated with healing in 1943. After that experience he changed his job and now worked as secretary for Harrison & Crossfield, Colombo. In 1947 he married a woman from India. At this time he and his family were members of the Anglican Church in Colombo.[62] In 1949 he went with his family to India looking for work. Finally, he obtained a post as administrative official in Christian Medical College, Vellore. Apparently it was at this time that he came into closer contact with the Pentecostal movement. He was probably in close contact with the Assemblies of God in the 1950s.[63] In 1952 he received baptism in the Spirit. After healing from a severe illness he entered full-time ministry in 1954. In 1954 he traveled to Bombay to take part in a rally by W. M. Branham, without actual contact between the two. After a little time, he established himself as a healing evangelist. He was a frequent visitor in congregations of the Church of South India; he made his membership of this church expressly clear and was in close

---

61. See Assemblies of God 1977; Saju 1994: 161; Reginald 1995: 39.

62. Dale 1973: 20.

63. This conjecture is supported by the fact that Lawrie had studied for a short time at Southern Asia Bible Institute, Bangalore (Hutten 1989: 219), and that his father was baptized by immersion by Robert Edwards (Dale 1973: picture caption, following 16). According to Hoerschelmann (1977: 312), his mother was close to the Pentecostal movement and it is reported of his father that he had close contact with the Salvation Army in Ceylon (Dale 1973: 14f.).

contact with particular bishops.[64] At this time he conducted also two preaching tours in Ceylon, but his work was centered on southern Tamil Nadu, especially Nagercoil and Nazareth. In 1959 an overseas journey became possible through an invitation to a healing conference in Glasgow arranged by the International Order of St. Luke.[65] In spite of considerable financial difficulties, he also managed to get from England to the USA, where he made intensive efforts to gain overseas sponsors for his work in India but without success.[66] He was generally abruptly rejected, except by W. M. Branham, who also convinced him of his special views, and who gave him "Jesus only" baptism.[67] In 1960, Lawrie returned to India as a follower of W. M. Branham, and this began his main period as healing evangelist. In 1962 he openly broke with the Church of South India, which in no way affected his popularity.[68] In that year he also acquired from his father the property that later became the Manujothi Ashram but where at first he only conducted a few retreats. Without doubt, Paulaseer Lawrie is the most colorful personality produced by the Indian Pentecostal movement. Deva Eevu Lawrie (b. 1948), the eldest son of Paulaseer Lawrie, broke off his studies in natural sciences at Madras Christian College and was in the closest confidence with his father although, astonishingly, he did not appear to be of one mind with his father in matters of doctrine. After the death of his father, he moved back to Gandhinagar, Tirunelveli, and sought to develop his father's heritage under the name Lawrie Ministries. The second son, Devaseer Lawrie (b. 1950), began studies in veterinary medicine in 1967. In 1970 he married a daughter of A. N. Jonah in Rajahmundry and broke off his studies. From then on, as both the other brothers, he was fellow worker with his father until, after his father's death, he successfully claimed the leadership of Manujothi Ashram. The youngest son, Devadayavu Lawrie (b. 1953), since 1983 has been in a second marriage with a Swiss woman who in the 1970s had lived with her parents in the ashram. Until 1992 Devadayavu Lawrie was living with his brother Devaseer Lawrie in the Manujothi ashram, but then he founded in a neighboring plot an ashram named Laharinagar. There he claims to maintain the authentic heritage of his father.

Manasse, C. (1877-1938)
C. Manasse hailed from a Hindu family in Paraniam, Trivandrum District. In 1896 he was converted to Christianity and became a catechist in the London

64. See Dale 1973: 27-40.
65. For the International Order of St. Luke, see Judah 1967: 300-301.
66. See Dale 1973: 40-46.
67. It is certain that Lawrie already had infant baptism and after conversion surely received baptism by immersion, although this is not mentioned anywhere. In this case, it was most likely a matter of a third baptism.
68. See Dale 1973: 29.

Missionary Society. He was brought into contact with the Pentecostal movement by Miss Aldwinckle. In the beginning of the 1920s, he stayed for a longer time in Madras with Benjamin Jacob and received the baptism of the Spirit in 1921. From that time onward, he worked in Trivandrum District. There he first worked together with Mary Chapman and then with A. C. Samuel and Martha Kuchera.[69]

Mathew, C. S. (1915-1985)

The parents of C. S. Mathew came from a Hindu background and joined the Brethren after their Christian conversion. They lived in Karamala, Kerala. C. S. Mathew went to school only until the fifth grade and then worked as a day laborer in agriculture. He experienced his conversion only after his marriage in 1936, and, shortly after that, he received baptism by immersion. In 1939, he studied for some time in the Bible school of the Brethren in Kottayam led by K. V. Simon. After a visit to an evangelization on a big plantation near Sabarimala, he was attracted to the Pentecostal faith. In 1946, he received the baptism of the Spirit and began to found his own church. In 1947, he started to build a prayer house in Kunnam. A member of the congregation donated the land for it. In 1950, he founded his own Bible school and called it Ebenezer Bible Institute. In 1952, he moved to Kariamplave near Rani, which became the new headquarters of the church. In 1962, he opened what is still the only orphanage of World Missionary Evangelism in Kerala. His successor was his son-in-law O. M. Rajakutty (b. 1957). Rajakutty was born in this church and in 1973, at the age of sixteen, he went into full-time ministry. He studied in the Bible school in Kariamplave and in the India Bible Institute, Delhi. In 1979, he married the youngest daughter of C. S. Mathew, and in the course of time, Rajakutty became a well-respected Pentecostal leader in Kerala.

Mattai, Pandalam (1877-1940)

Pandalam Mattai belonged to the Mar Thoma Church. He experienced his conversion at the age of eleven in 1888. At the age of eighteen, he became a freelance touring evangelist of the Mar Thoma Church. He then came in contact with George E. Berg and received baptism of the Spirit in 1912. Though later he worked closely with Robert F. Cook and K. E. Abraham, it is said that he always remained a freelance evangelist.[70]

Mudaliar, Nataraja (1939-1982)

Nataraja Mudaliar was a South African of Tamil origin. In South Africa he belonged to the Full Gospel Church of South Africa, led by J. F. Rowlands, who

---

69. See Saju 1994: 58-59; Reginald 1995: 23-24; the two, however, do not agree in all data.
70. See Saju 1994: 32-33.

maintained good relations with India.[71] In 1961 he came to India, where he was active in evangelism. He was a gifted musician and singer and was in close contact with G. Sunderam. In 1970 he worked with World Missionary Evangelism. When the independent churches in Tamil Nadu left World Missionary Evangelism in 1978, Nataraja was the most important representative of the organization for Tamil Nadu. He held these posts until his death. The ceremonies at his grave were conducted by Zac Poonen.

Mudaliar, Padma (b. 1949)

Padma Mudaliar came from a Hindu family. At fifteen she had a conversion experience in her hometown of Nagercoil, after attending the showing of a Jesus film by the Church of South India. She received baptism by immersion through a pastor who was close to Bakht Singh. Later she came into contact with the Pentecostal movement, and during her studies at college she received the baptism in the Spirit. She completed her studies in 1968 with a B.Sc. degree. In the same year she attended a big Pentecostal rally by the South African Nataraja Mudaliar and there received the call to ministry. At the time, Mudaliar wanted to get married in order to obtain permission to reside in India. Marriage with Padma was arranged and the wedding ceremonies in 1969 were conducted by G. Sunderam in the Apostolic Christian Assembly. When her husband, after working with her in the World Missionary Evangelism, died in 1982, Padma Mudaliar continued his activity. When World Missionary Evangelism suffered a leadership crisis in 1990, she left the organization and became an independent evangelist. She developed a Bible school in 1981 through World Missionary Evangelism, in which it was especially women who received training. After her husband's death, Padma Mudaliar was gradually established as an evangelist in popular demand. So it happened that, after a long break, once again a woman penetrated the circle of outstanding evangelists. At the start, her popularity was aided by being the widow of a well-known evangelist. However, today, her success is really based on the unmistakably individual style that she developed.

Navroji, Sarah (b. 1938)

Sarah Navroji came from a Christian family (Tamil Evangelical Lutheran Church) in Madras. Her father, a music teacher in the Lutheran Gurukul College in Madras, died when she was ten. At fifteen she had a conversion experience. In 1956 she received Spirit baptism and became a member of the Ceylon Pentecostal Mission. At that time she worked as an employee of the Madras electricity board. In 1959 she received the call to ministry and became a Sister in the Ceylon Pente-

71. J. F. Rowlands (d. 1981) worked among the Indians in Natal. He belonged to the Full Gospel Church of South Africa, which joined the Church of God in 1951 (see Conn 1959: 281-82; Oosthuizen 1975: 72-85).

costal Mission. For three years she lived in a Faith Home in Ceylon. In 1962 she left the church on account of the Alwin affair, and returned to Madras. In the time to follow, she gained great popularity through the spiritual songs she began to compose and sing. These earned her many invitations to be a guest speaker at rallies, and she became extremely famous all over south India. Theologically, however, she openly held to the beliefs of the radical Ceylon Pentecostal Mission. Thus, her views drove her more and more into isolation in the late 1960s, and her popularity started to fade away. Despite this lack of interest, she was still composing hymns in the 1990s.[72]

Paramjothi, P. L. (1921-1996)

P. L. Paramjothi grew up in Vuyyuru, Krishna District. His parents came from a nearby village and belonged to the Canadian Baptist Church. In Vuyyuru a Tamil woman doctor named Subramaniam was working, who came from Madras and had belonged there to a Pentecostal congregation pastored by M. Murugesan. Paramjothi's mother came into contact with her and received baptism in the Spirit. He himself was converted in 1933 in his parental home village when his mother formed a prayer group in the Baptist church. At his conversion he also received baptism in the Spirit. In 1936 he finished the eighth class and attended the one-year Bible course in Kakinada that was necessary for reception into the Baptist high school.[73] There he had fellowship in prayer with a Charismatic couple who lived near the school. During the Bible course he received the call to ministry. On completion of the year in Kakinada, he passed the summer of 1937 with relatives in Eluru who had originally come to the Pentecostal faith through Pastor M. Murugesan but had later joined P. T. Chacko and P. M. Samuel when the two established themselves in Eluru. During his stay in Eluru, Paramjothi received immersion baptism through Chacko and entered full-time ministry in the Indian Pentecostal Church. In 1938 he went to Vijayawada with T. K. Thomas. In the same year they also visited Warangal and founded a congregation there. From 1940 to 1942 he worked with Thomas in Warangal. While Thomas remained there as pastor, Paramjothi moved to Antarvedipalem in 1942, and in this region he soon became the most influential Pentecostal pastor and founded new congregations. His position was further strengthened when he founded an orphanage with the help of Thomas Wyatt of *Wings of Healing*.[74] Wyatt had come to India at the invitation of P. M. Samuel as guest preacher at the yearly church convention. As Paramjothi interpreted for him, this was a personal contact that led to cooperation in the future. His authority and influence over the Pentecostal movement in

72. See also Hoerschelmann 1977: 262-71.
73. See Komanapalli ca. 1991: 4.
74. See Komanapalli ca. 1991: 23. For the American radio-evangelist Thomas Wyatt see Hewett 1990b.

Andhra Pradesh owes in some measure to his sons and sons-in-law. His eldest daughter is married to Ernest Komanapalli. His eldest son, Spurgeon Raju, is president of Manna. One daughter married G. Rakshanandam, who in 1973 founded World Wide Faith Missions of India in Tadepalligudam, another married Charles Finney Joseph in Madras, another Carl Komanapalli, a brother of Ernest Komanapalli. Another daughter lives in the USA with her husband A. K. Murthy, a chaplain in the U.S. army. His younger son John Lazarus was in 1993 leader of Rock Ministries International, a missionary association affiliated with the Rock Church, Virginia Beach, led by John Gimenez.

Paul, K. R. (ca. 1918-1983)

K. R. Paul came from a Hindu family in the Kolar Gold Fields. He was employed in mining, when in 1942 together with his wife, whom he had married in 1939, he converted to Christianity. This happened under the influence of western missionaries whose names are unknown to us. Both were baptized immediately. Five years later, K. R. Paul went into full-time ministry and worked with Constance S. Eady. In January 1949 he went to Madurai to study at the newly opened Tamil Bible Institute of the Assemblies of God. After completing these studies in 1951 he went to Bangalore and was a pastor of the Assemblies of God for a year before he made himself independent. The official foundation date of the Gospel Prayer Hall is 1953. His wife Lydia Paul (d. 1977) is a good example of a pastor's wife, giving a clear profile to the church. She preached often even in her husband's presence and was famous for her healing prayer and her prophecies. After the death of K. R. Paul, their adopted child T. Daniel Paul (b. 1964) formally took over the church. However, he was first sent to study at Doon Bible College, Dehradun,[75] and during this time an elder of the congregation, a brother of Lydia Paul, ministered to the congregation. In 1987 T. Daniel Paul was married. His wife, who comes from a Catholic family and was converted to Pentecostal faith by Justin Prabhakaram, is, like Lydia Paul, a great support for the congregation.

Paul, P. (1881-1945)

P. Paul hailed from a Hindu Ezhava family in Engandiyur, Trichur District, and his birth name was Raman. At the age of fourteen he went to Ceylon, where he found a job with a Christian doctor, Aserappa by name, who took the boy into his family. P. Paul came to know Christianity in that family, which belonged to the Church Missionary Society. When he was eighteen years old, he saw Jesus Christ in a vision, was converted to the Christian faith, and was baptized in the Church Missionary Society. At the beginning of the new century, he went to Kerala for two years to study in the theological seminary of the Church Missionary Society

---

75. The Doon Bible College was founded in 1943 by Swedish Pentecostal missionaries (see Andreasson & Andreasson 1989: 31-32).

in Kottayam. When he went back to Ceylon, he was made a catechist for the Malayalam-speaking community in Colombo. Perhaps shortly after his appointment as a catechist he married. In Colombo, one of his friends was P. I. Jacob, a Baptist pastor who hailed from Kerala and whose children lived in Madras. In the early 1920s when Jacob went to visit his children in Madras, he became acquainted with two Australian Pentecostal missionaries[76] who were most probably guests in the congregation of Benjamin Jacob. Impressed by their teaching, he invited them to Colombo, where they held Tarrying Meetings in 1921. During that time P. Paul received the baptism of the Spirit, and eventually Ceylon Pentecostal Mission was started, in which he became the dominant figure. Later, his son Freddy Paul (1915-1973) became likewise a leading figure in the church.

Philip, Thomas (b. 1938)

Thomas Philip hailed from Paippad near Changanacherry. His parents belonged to the Mar Thoma Church. He graduated with a B.A. in 1963 and ran an evening school, founded by him, from 1964 to 1969. His conversion to the Pentecostal faith happened through the Ceylon Pentecostal Mission, and immediately after that he became a member of this church for some time. In 1972, he founded his own Pentecostal church as New India Bible Church. Philip was a committed and active defender of close collaboration among the Pentecostal churches. He played an active role in founding the Kerala Pentecostal Fellowship Convention in 1990. His brother Abraham Philip (1932-1992) was much less clear in his understanding as a Pentecostal.[77] He took an M.A. degree at Bombay University and worked afterward as a teacher in Nigeria and Ethiopia. Most probably, toward the end of the 1960s, he went to the USA where he first studied at Gordon College and finally acquired a D.Miss. at Fuller Theological Seminary, Pasadena. He had a good contact with the Billy Graham Evangelical Association. Thanks to him, perhaps, the New India Bible College did not acquire any explicit Pentecostal character.[78] The succession in the leadership of the New India Evangelical Association went over to his son Mathew A. Philip.

Ponraj, S. (d. 1952)

S. Ponraj, a carpenter by profession, went to school for only two years. He was converted to the Pentecostal faith in Malaysia. When he returned to India, he worked as a married pastor of the Ceylon Pentecostal Mission in Trichy. He was

---

76. The names of the Australian missionaries are mentioned as Dart (or Todd) and Ebenezer (see The Pentecostal Mission n.d.: 12).

77. See also Saju 1994: 218, where 1930 is indicated as the date of birth of Abraham Philip. The year 1932 was given in the interview of the author with Thomas Philip.

78. See the creed printed in the prospect for the College (New India Bible College 1994: 9-19).

transferred from there in 1942 to Coimbatore, where he left the Ceylon Pentecostal Mission after a short while and became the cofounder of the Pentecostal Church of India. He also took part in the founding of the Apostolic Christian Assembly in Madras in 1948. Because he died unexpectedly at the early age of about fifty to fifty-five, just when a new church building was consecrated, there was no appointed successor to take over his ministry.

Poonen, Zac (b. 1939)

Zac Poonen grew up in Delhi. His parents were Thomas Christians but belonged to the Brethren. His father was a functionary of the central administration. Zac Poonen studied in Delhi and at nineteen became a marine officer. He was converted in 1959 and baptized in 1961. In 1964 he decided to give up his post in the marines. At this time, through his father, he was known to Bakht Singh and when on leave accompanied him on his preaching tours. In 1966 he was successfully demobilized. From then on he was a close associate of Bakht Singh, but because of differences with some fellow workers, he left him in 1969 and began a new work with the Union of Evangelical Students of India. In 1970 he joined the Bible Medical Missionary Fellowship. At this time he was active as an evangelist. As such he traveled much and spoke at numerous Keswick conventions at home and abroad until 1975, when he came over to Pentecostalism and founded the Christian Fellowship Centre.

Prabakaran, Justin (1951-1991)

Justin Prabakaran came from a Lutheran family. His father, John Sigamani (1912-1972), was a well-known pastor of the Arcot Lutheran Church.[79] Justin Prabakaran studied medicine and practiced in the neighborhood of Cuddalore. He then came in contact with the Pentecostal movement, and at the end of the 1970s, arranged big yearly retreats called Calvary Crusade on a large estate near Cuddalore. To these well-attended retreats he invited leading Pentecostal evangelists. At the beginning of the 1980s he himself experienced baptism by immersion, in the Assemblies of God. After the death of his first wife, he left his employment in 1983 and entered full-time ministry. He became a successful evangelist for the Assemblies of God. At this time he came into contact with the Faith Movement, which changed him. Before, he had worn saffron-colored clothes and a long beard, in the Sadhu style. Under the influence of the Faith Movement, he gave up this style of evangelism. At the same time, he came into conflict with his own church. When in 1987 he married his second wife,[80] she wore jewelry in the celebrations. This gave the Assemblies of God the occasion to cut him off. Prabakaran was believed to have said of a Tamil evangelist, after the evangelist had died of a

79. Wandall 1978: 185-86.
80. See Rajendran 1992: 22.

serious illness, that he was himself to blame because of his insufficiently strong faith. Prabakaran himself died of a brain tumor.

Rajamoni, P. S. (b. 1939)

P. S. Rajamoni comes from a village near Shenkottai, Tirunelveli District. His parents, originally Hindu, joined the Anglican Church. S. Adamdurai, his elder brother by ten years, converted to Pentecostal faith at the end of the 1950s, under the influence of the Edwards couple at Shenkottai, and belonged to the founding members of the congregation of the Assemblies of God in K. P. Valasai.[81] Later S. Adamdurai became pastor in Kovilpatti. Following his brother's example, P. S. Rajamoni was converted in 1957, received baptism in the Spirit the same day, and shortly afterwards was baptized by immersion. After high school he was in a technical trade school in Coimbatore (1958-1960). On completing these studies, he worked in public service for four years as a mechanic. In 1964 he gave this work up and studied for a year at the Tamil Bible Institute in Madurai and then changed to the Southern Asia Bible Institute, Bangalore. Finishing these studies, he was called as a teacher to the Tamil Bible Institute, Madurai. In 1976 to 1978 he studied at the Assemblies of God theological seminary in Springfield, Missouri, and finished with an M.A. Returning to India, he carried on with his teaching at the Tamil Bible Institute. In the 1970s P. S. Rajamoni collected considerable material on the history of the Assemblies of God in India.[82] Already during his teaching at the Tamil Bible Institute he was a speaker at evangelizations and was much sought after because of his elaborate biblical interpretations. In 1990 he left the Bible school and became the Indian leader of Decade of Harvest, a worldwide missionary campaign by the Assemblies of God.

Rajendran, M. (b. ca. 1942)

M. Rajendran comes from a village near Alangulam in Tirunelveli District. His parents were Hindus. At the age of seventeen he was admitted to the craft school of the Assemblies of God in K. P. Valasai. It is probably due to the influence of K. C. Andrews, who was the Indian pastor there at the time, that he was converted to Christianity at this American mission school. He was baptized and received the call to ministry. Immediately he went to study at the Tamil Bible Institute in Madurai, and on completion of his studies was made pastor in Idaiyankulam, Tirunelveli District. By mediation of Andrews his marriage was arranged, his wife being a relative of S. B. Daniel from Tiruvannamalai. M. Rajendran took up Daniel's offer to set up and direct an orphanage for the Indian Christian Assembly in Palayankottai. Rajendran is a well-known hymn writer and was increasingly active in evangelism in the mid-1970s. He has numerous overseas contacts. Partners

81. See Gabriel 1993: 86.
82. See Rajamoni n.d.

include Intermission, World Wide Sending from Holland, and Victor Mission (Ben Hanegraaff). His eldest son, R. Rajendran (b. 1968), received Spirit baptism at the age of nine. He completed high school (S.S.L.C.), received immersion baptism at the age of seventeen, and finally studied for four years at Southern Asia Bible College, Bangalore, graduating with a B.Th. He then went to Holland for ten months. He learned Dutch in order to be able to translate directly into Tamil for Dutch evangelists in India. He visits Europe nearly every year.

Rose, John (ca. 1904-1977)

John Rose came from a Christian family in Kanyakumari District. In 1926, he was converted to the Pentecostal faith.[83] He was a teacher in Malaysia but returned to India in 1933 as pastor of the Ceylon Pentecostal Mission and started a congregation in Kadamalaikuntu, Kanyakumari District. He later came in conflict with his church, since he refused to accept the obligation of celibacy for pastors. It seems that he was even called to the headquarters in Colombo and transferred as a punishment. As a result, he made himself independent along with the congregation he had founded in Kadamalaikuntu. When exactly this happened is difficult to establish. The church remained strongly bound to the teachings of the Ceylon Pentecostal Mission, but it was left open to work with other Pentecostal churches.

Sam Sunderam, M. K. (b. 1938)

M. K. Sam Sunderam's father, M. V. Kuttalam Pillai, was converted from Hinduism to Christianity in Coimbatore by S. Ponraj. Together with the eldest son, M. J. Rajamoni, they were foundation members of the Apostolic Christian Assembly. Sam Sunderam grew up in this atmosphere. He had his conversion experience in 1954 and in the same year received baptism by immersion and baptism in the Spirit. In 1959 he graduated with a B.Com. from Madras University. During his studies, he was already active in the congregation. Immediately after his studies he went into full-time ministry and was ordained as a pastor at New Year 1961. In the same year he was married, but his wife died childless. Then for almost thirty years he was active as assistant pastor under G. Sunderam, who systematically prepared him to be successor. His exceptional leadership qualities came into play when he assumed the leadership in 1989.

Samuel, Abraham (1930-1993)

Abraham Samuel was the son of P. M. Samuel. He studied in the USA between 1952 and 1956. First he attended the Elim Bible Institute, New York. Then he studied a year and a half at St. Louis College.[84] Returning in 1956 to India, he married a daughter of P. T. Chacko, and he returned to the USA with her, where she stud-

83. See Rose 1982: 2.
84. See Samuel 1980: 120.

ied at Indiana University and earned an M.A. They returned to India and Abraham Samuel began to assist his father. He had a special commitment to the church's social project. His wife became the head of the school. Long before the father's death, Abraham Samuel was systematically promoted by his father as successor, and he was chosen as State President of the Indian Pentecostal Church in Andhra Pradesh as well as Vice President of the General Council. After his father's death he was not chosen for his successor as General President, but in spite of that he was as influential as his father in Andhra Pradesh and Tamil Nadu. He died of a heart attack at Amsterdam's Schiphol Airport.

Samuel, A. C. (1900-1970)
A. C. Samuel belonged to the Thomas Christians and joined the Brethren, where he received immersion baptism when he was twenty-one years old. When he was twenty-five, he received the baptism of the Spirit and came to the Pentecostal movement. For some time he worked together with K. E. Abraham and studied at the Mt. Zion Bible School in Mulakuzha. In 1932, however, he went to Trivandrum and was working for the Assemblies of God with Martha Kucera. In 1935, he was ordained as a pastor of the Assemblies of God.[85]

Samuel, Noel (b. 1959)
Noel Samuel, son of Abraham Samuel, went to the USA in 1979, by the mediation of P. J. Titus, to study at Dallas Christian College. He returned to India in 1983. He married a U.S. citizen of Malayali origin and settled with her in the USA in 1985. There he studied at Regent University, Virginia Beach, and worked at Pat Robertson's nearby 700 Club. He completed his studies with an M.A. in 1990 and returned to India to help his father. In 1991 he succeeded him as Principal of the Bible school. On the death of his father, he was too young in the eyes of the well-established pastors of the Indian Pentecostal Church to succeed him as State President for Andhra Pradesh. He sought to take up his father's position in Tamil Nadu, but this failed because of the desire there for independence from Andhra Pradesh. However, he was State Secretary for Andhra Pradesh, remained principal of the Bible school, and worked on modernizing the administration of the church. In the 1990s, it was difficult to say whether he is likely in the future to have influence like that of his father.

Samuel, P. M. (1903-1981)
P. M. Samuel came from Keekozhoor in Kollam District. His parents belonged to the Mar Thoma Church. He was married at fifteen. In the Mar Thoma Church in 1920 he experienced his conversion and began theological studies in the seminary

85. See Sam 1983; Saju 1994: 68, 172.

of this church in Kottayam.[86] In the meantime he was in contact with the Brethren and was convinced of the need for baptism by immersion, which he received through Kunnapi Upadesi in 1926. At the invitation of a certain Rev. Kesari, he took part as guest preacher in evangelization campaigns in the churches of the London Missionary Society in 1927-1929.[87] Then for the first time during a visit to Madras, he came into close contact with the Pentecostal movement and experienced the power of the Holy Spirit during common prayer.[88] But, apparently under the influence of the Brethren, he refused at first to consider speaking in tongues as the initial evidence of baptism in the Spirit. In 1929 P. Paul invited him to Ceylon. There after some time he became convinced of Pentecostal teaching and finally received Spirit baptism with tongues. He returned to India and joined K. E. Abraham. From 1930 to 1932 he spent much time in Tamil Nadu, mostly in Nazareth, where he cooperated with the local congregation of the Ceylon Pentecostal Mission. He was also in close contact with Gopal Daniel in Madras. After living for a time in Kerala in 1932, he decided to go to Andhra Pradesh. In this province, which was unfamiliar to him, he first visited Lam Jeevaratnam in Gudivada. In 1932 he also took part in the rallies of M. Devadas in Rajahmundry, and from 1932 to 1936 he was guest preacher at evangelical rallies of the established churches. In 1936, when P. T. Chacko came to Eluru, they together founded the first congregation of the Indian Pentecostal Church in Andhra Pradesh. In 1940 P. M. Samuel settled in Vijayawada. During his frequent foreign trips, he went to Germany in 1957, where he made the acquaintance of Hermann Zaiss, so that the latter took part in a church rally in Eluru in 1958.[89] His foreign trips were not only to western countries, as in 1952 he visited Japan and the Philippines, and in 1959 Nigeria.[90]

Santhosam, B. A. James (b. 1948)

B. A. James Santhosam came from Melnedungal, a village near Pallipet, Chengalpattu District. His parents were Hindu. After failing the high school examination, he went to Madras and worked as a day laborer and then as a radio announcer. In 1971, on a trip as a salesman, he got to know Pastor Pammal James (of the Apostolic Church?), through whom he was converted to Christianity and received baptism by immersion. Thereupon he received the call to ministry. He went to

---

86. Saju 1994: 99.
87. Samuel 1980: 8. It is there reported that there was a great awakening in the London Missionary Society at the time.
88. Saju 1994: 101.
89. See Samuel 1989: 83-86, 134-35. Because Zaiss died in the same year, this contact didn't develop further. But apparently P. M. Samuel gained further financial aid through Ecclesia. On Zaiss, see Hutten 1989: 374-76.
90. See Samuel 1989: 122-26, 144-51.

the Tamil Bible Institute of the Assemblies of God in Madurai but soon had to leave since he did not pass the first intermediate test. He came back to his native village in 1972 and worked as pastor of the Apostolic Church under Benjamin Selvaratnam. In the course of time many of his family were converted to Christianity and he became a prominent evangelist in the region. In 1983 there was an opportunity for him to travel to Malaysia. There he had contacts with more Tamil partner churches, so that he saw the possibility in 1984 to leave the Apostolic Church and found his own Prince of Peace church. He seems to have had serious financial problems, but contact with Y. S. John Babu rescued him in 1987. In the early 1990s he was able to make various other contacts in the West. Partners for Prince of Peace came from various quarters: Peter Light, Cornerstone International Church, Southampton (probably through Y. S. John Babu); David Egli, Broken Arrow, USA (apparently close to Kenneth Hagin); David Fiksen, Praise Fellowship Church, Kasson, Minnesota.[91] But this appears not to have been a really stable partnership. At all events James Santhosam was in financial difficulties throughout the 1990s.

Shankar, Pappa (b. ca. 1930)
Pappa Shankar came from a Christian family in Tirunelveli. Her mother died when she was two and she was raised by her father. At thirteen she was married and compelled by her husband to return to Hinduism. She had to suffer all manner of chicanery, and in the 1950s she found help from a Baptist community and became a Christian again. A short time later she discovered the healing power of prayer. Many people began coming to see her and asked for her prayers. Impressed by her success in this, her husband also became a believer. At the beginning of the 1970s, she was undoubtedly among the best known of the healing evangelists in south India, but as a woman, life was especially hard for her. Soon she lost her preeminence, but continued her evangelistic work in smaller compass. Her husband had left her in the meantime, but her children continued to work with her. Since the 1980s, her work has mostly been in Andhra Pradesh.[92]

Singh, Pratap (b. 1943)
Pratap Singh comes from Aravankadu, Nilgiris District. His parents were Baptists who also attended worship in a Church of God congregation led by Pastor M. I. Thomas. He experienced conversion there in 1959, followed by Spirit baptism and call to ministry. He had just finished his high school (S.S.L.C.) and was invited by Dora Myers to the newly founded Bible school in Madurai. He studied here for two years and was then called to Mulakuzha as Office Secretary for Tamil Nadu. In the neighborhood of Mulakuzha he took over a small congregation. From 1967

91. See *Prince of Peace* Apr.-May, Oct.-Nov. 1993, April-June 1994.
92. See also Hoerschelmann 1977: 182-98.

to 1970 he studied at Lee College, Cleveland. In 1971 he declined the post of State Overseer of the Church of God for Tamil Nadu but helped Joseph Navamoni decisively in his legal action against P. Abraham. At the same time he was active as a pastor and helped the Bible school in Madras, which was destitute. When the school returned to Coimbatore in 1978, he took over the leadership until he left the Church of God in 1980. Pratap Singh was considered one of the best Tamil interpreters for western evangelists.

Solomon, John (b. 1952)

John Solomon comes from Madras and like his parents belongs to the Church of South India. He was converted at the end of 1970 by his brother William Devadoss, who was seven years older and already active as a Pentecostal pastor. A month later, in 1971, Solomon was baptized by immersion by G. Sunderam and half a year later received baptism in the Spirit. In the same year he secured his B.Com. and a position in a firm. A short time later he changed to Jesus Calls and as secretary coordinated the evangelistic activities of D. G. Dhinakaran from 1972 to 1978. He then became an independent evangelist and called his organization Miracle Ministry.

Stephen, S. S. S. (b. 1925)

S. S. S. Stephen came from Coimbatore. His family belonged to the Church of South India. From 1944 to 1950 he studied medicine at Stanley Medical College, Madras, and finished with a M.B.B.S. In Madras he was in close contact with Jehovah Shammah, and it was probably there that he received baptism by immersion. After his studies in 1951, he moved to Trichy, together with his wife who was also a doctor. His wife worked in the Church of South India Mission Hospital in Trichy, and he had a medical practice at nearby Lalgudi. In the beginning of the 1950s he experienced a conversion and became an active lay evangelist in the Church of South India. At the same time he joined a congregation that was close to Bakht Singh. He had his first contacts with the Pentecostal movement in the 1950s. At a rally of Paulaseer Lawrie at Trichy in 1961 he received baptism of the Spirit and then (another) immersion baptism in the name of Jesus. When he joined Paulaseer Lawrie, several members of the Bakht Singh congregation followed his example. After 1969 he severed ties with Paulaseer Lawrie and the congregation became independent. Later he moved his medical practice to Trichy, but till the 1990s he led his congregation, commonly called Dr. Stephen Assembly, on an honorary basis only.

Sunderam, G. (1909-1989)

G. Sunderam hailed from Palliyadi near Marthandam, Kanyakumari District. He was born as the fourth child out of eight children in a Christian family (London

Missionary Society). At the end of the 1920s he went to Malaysia, where one of his younger sisters lived with her husband. There he was employed as a teacher and came in contact with a Pentecostal congregation in which he was converted to the Pentecostal faith in 1929. He was employed as a teacher for three and a half years. After that he received the call to the ministry in 1932. First, he worked for a short period with a pastor, Titus by name, in Kuala Lumpur. Perhaps he experienced his conversion also in this congregation. Probably in 1932, he returned to India and became a pastor of the Ceylon Pentecostal Mission.[93] While he was leading a congregation in Royapuram, Madras, he came to know the woman who later became his wife, who was studying there at that time. As the love relationship between the two became known, the Ceylon Pentecostal Mission excommunicated him in 1942(?). He first went for a short period to Bangalore, where he seemed to have worked with Stephen Andrew, and where he was married by his long-time friend Pastor S. Ponraj from Coimbatore in 1945. The Ceylon Pentecostal Mission seemed to have exercised pressure on him, who had once been one of its popular pastors, so that Sunderam withdrew for some time to Ceylon, the home of his wife, in 1946(?).[94] From there, Ponraj brought him to Coimbatore in 1948. He took over his congregation, when Ponraj went to Madras. When Ponraj had to go back to Coimbatore, Sunderam relieved him in Madras. Sunderam seemed to have laid great value on the fact that his call to Madras must be attributed to a direct intervention of the Lord. This fact is reported in an oral tradition of the church in the following manner:

> One evening Ponraj left. He said, he will go to Coimbatore and send Sunderam to Madras to continue this work. He left this evening, we saw him off at the station. The next early morning, there was a knock. When we opened the man said: "I am Sunderam." We never knew Sunderam. So, he didn't go and send him. Sunderam came on his own. It was God's timing.[95]

By the 1950s, Sunderam had already become one of the most important Pentecostal leaders in Madras. The cooperation with his friend John Rose in the south of Tamil Nadu strengthened his position. Many pastors and evangelists in Tamil Nadu were influenced by him. Foreign contacts were also established, particularly with Pastor J. F. Rowlands from Bethesda Full Gospel Church in South Africa. In many aspects, Sunderam remained strongly influenced by the teachings of the Ceylon Pentecostal Mission, even though he held moderate views in many respects. Thus, for example, he baptized people wearing jewels.

93. See Hoerschelmann 1977: 165.
94. See George n.d.: 7.
95. Interview.

With one of the two founding families of the church (that is, the family of P. S. Chelladurai and of M. V. Kuttalam Pillai), he established family ties. Two sons of M. V. Kuttalam Pillai, M. K. Rajamoni and Sam Sunderam, were married to the younger sisters of the wife of Sunderam. Sunderam even chose Sam Sunderam to be his assistant and successor. M. K. Rajamoni, who worked as an engineer, also held an influential position in the congregation. It is remarkable that Sunderam did not attempt to make his own son his successor. When he died in 1989, his son Joshua Sunderam, who was about forty years old, was associate pastor of the main congregation.

Thamby, V. A. (b. 1941)

V. A. Thamby hailed from a Canaanite Syrian Orthodox family near Kuricha, Kerala. He did not finish high school and he did not acquire any other educational qualification. Shortly after his conversion to the Pentecostal faith, he received the baptism of immersion through P. C. George in 1962. Immediately after that, he went to Bethel Bible School in Punalur. Since his Syrian Orthodox relatives called on him there and protested loudly, a job for him in a rubber plantation was procured, but he remained there for only a short time. He started then to travel around as an Evangelist and among other things also with Operation Mobilisation and with P. C. George. In 1970, he married Mariamma Thamby, a Tamil woman from Nagercoil, who had studied for a B.Sc. degree. Since she had received a call to ministry, she wanted to marry a pastor. Many of her brothers and sisters went likewise into full-time ministry. One of her sisters married Ebenezer John, the son of M. O. John. Her brother Abraham took over the leadership of the New India Church of God in north India.

Thannickal, John (b. 1931)

The parents of John Thannickal belonged originally to the Mar Thoma Church and, through Sadhu Kochukunju, they came to the Indian Pentecostal Church. His father was pastor of a church in Othara, near Kumbanadu. In this Pentecostal home, John was converted at the age of ten. At thirteen he was baptized and committed himself to full-time ministry. He finished high school in 1953 and in the same year he went to the recently opened Southern Asia Bible Institute in Bangalore. Completing these studies in 1956, he was appointed to the library and teaching staff of the Bible school which also supported him to continue his studies at Union Biblical Seminary at Yeotmal in 1957-1958. Returning from there, he resumed his teaching and at the same time joined a further course at United Theological College, Bangalore, leading to a B.D. degree. Through John Wright, the young American missionary principal of the Southern Asia Bible Institute in 1960-1961, he gained a place at Wheaton College (Wheaton, Illinois) where he studied in 1965-1966 for an M.A. After this he returned to Southern Asia Bible Institute, and in 1968 he became the first indigenous District Superintendent of Central District, until T. C. George took over this post in 1973. In 1972-1974 Thannickal studied at Fuller Theological Seminary, Pasadena, and progressed to his D.Miss. At the 1976 Pentecostal World Conference in London he was elected to the advisory committee in his absence by the mediation of Y. Jeyaraj. This made him internationally known. In 1977 he gave up his teaching post at Southern Asia Bible College and undertook the foundation of an ashram project. This was interrupted when he was called to be leader at Bethel Bible School in Punalar to help it through a severe crisis. In connection with his membership of the advisory committee of the Pentecostal World Conference, he engaged in inter-church connections in the Indian Pentecostal movement. At the beginning of the 1980s he called together a Pentecostal pastors' fellowship in Bangalore and played a role in the founding of the Pentecostal Fellowship of India in 1991.

Thomas, N. (b. 1934)

N. Thomas by his own declaration was from a Hindu family, although his mother went to church (London Missionary Society). As he was attending high school in Marthandam, he took part in 1949 in a campaign by Bakht Singh in which he was converted. But this conversion remained, at first, without consequence. He was married in 1959, and after graduation was a teacher in the high school in Kattathurai. In 1962 he was seriously ill and was healed through the prayer of a pastor of the Full Gospel Pentecostal Church. At a convent of this church, where Henry Joseph was guest speaker, he was converted anew and became member of the church. In 1964 he fell ill again, and again was healed by prayer, whereupon he founded his own congregation in Kattathurai. But it was only a few years later, when he took early retirement and entered full-time ministry, that he was recognized as a pastor by the Full Gospel Pentecostal Church. John Rose built him up as his successor and in 1976 appointed him a deputy. Although some older pastors were against him because he had been too short a time in full-time ministry, a large majority of the church chose him as the new leader in 1978.

Thomas, P. J. (1915-1998)

P. J. Thomas, the younger son of P. V. John (Ayyapillai), was baptized in 1933 in the Assemblies of God and changed over to the Indian Pentecostal Church along with his father in 1938. By that time he seems to have been already working full time as pastor. For some time he was the head of the Free English School in Kumbanadu, which was run by the Indian Pentecostal Church from 1939 to 1945.[96] During 1941-1942, he studied Theology in Serampore College, West Bengal, and finished it with an L.Th. In 1946, on the recommendation of K. E. Abra-

---

96. See Mathew 1990: 72.

ham, he received an invitation from Charles Rolls to study in his Bible school at Sydney. Charles Rolls had stayed for many years in India as a missionary for the Brethren. After finishing the two-year studies, he went to the USA in 1948 and studied at Wheaton College in Illinois. In the same year, he accompanied K. E. Abraham in his preaching tour through the USA.[97] In 1952, he took a postgraduate degree, an M.A., and returned to India. After a short stay in Alwaye, he went to Tiruvalla, where he bought a piece of land and founded his Bible school, which was the beginning of Sharon Fellowship. P. J. Thomas was considered to be an important figure of integration in Kerala's Pentecostal movement.

Titus, P. J. (b. 1935)

P. J. Titus was born near Rani. His parents belonged to the Mar Thoma Church; he was converted in 1955 in a prayer group of this church. In the same year he finished high school. After a short time at the Ceylon Pentecostal Mission in Kerala he went to his uncle, P. M. Samuel, in Andhra Pradesh. From there he went to the Southern Asia Bible Institute, Bangalore, in 1956. He attended this school at the same time as Ernest Komanapalli. He then worked for five years as pastor of the Indian Pentecostal Church in Khammam District, Andhra Pradesh. In 1965 he obtained a place in a Bible school in the USA. Once in the USA, he pursued ten years of education in colleges and universities, finally finishing with a D.Min. from the Southern Methodist University, Dallas. Then he found employment in a Dallas firm and taught part time in the Evangelical Dallas Christian College. He retained the marks of his Indian culture. He was successful in leading a congregation of Indians coming from Kerala and provided an important reception point for Indian immigrants to the USA. At the beginning of the 1980s, he faced problems concerning his employment and entered a difficult phase in his life, with the result that he decided to return to India as a missionary to start the Church on the Rock Theological Seminary in Andhra Pradesh.

Ummaccen, Parattupara (d. 1957)

Parattupara Ummaccen hailed from Parattupara near Adur, Pathanamthitta District. He had founded the Brethren congregation in Thuvayur that got converted to the Pentecostal faith when he invited George E. Berg in 1911. Parattupara Ummaccen was pastor of the church in Thuvayur till 1931. Later he was also pastor in Punalur, where he died.[98]

Vasu, John (1909-1962)

John Vasu was born in a Hindu family. As the eldest son of the family, he was left in a Christian orphanage in Tiruvottiyur, Madras, which seemed to have been led

97. See Verghese 1974: 50.
98. See Saju 1994: 34-35, 40.

by a Norwegian woman missionary. There he was converted to Christianity and received the baptism of the Spirit in a tarrying meeting soon after. He received immersion baptism at the age of fifteen in 1924 and came into contact with Benjamin Jacob in 1926. He decided to go into full-time ministry and became a coworker in his congregation. In 1941 he married a high school teacher from a Lutheran family. They had a son, Prabhudoss Vasu. In 1949, John Vasu took part in the World Pentecostal Conference. After the death of Benjamin Jacob, he became the official leader of the Madras Pentecostal Assembly. Particularly because of his numerous foreign contacts, he was looked upon as one of the most influential Pentecostal leaders in Madras at the time.

Vasu, Prabhudoss (1942-1995)
Prabhudoss Vasu was the son of John Vasu. He graduated with a B.Sc. (mathematics) from Madras Christian College. At the time his father died, since he was too young for direct succession, he was appointed pastor in a branch congregation in Kelly's, Madras. He led the congregation together with his mother, who stood by him with her many years' experience. When his mother died in 1966, he went for a year to England to the International Bible Training Institute, Sussex. Henry Joseph had arranged this for him. On his return in 1967 he was pastor in Kelly's until the death of G. N. Chockalingam. When he took over the leadership of the Madras Pentecostal Assembly, he proved to be a committed pastor who was strongly in favor of cooperation between Pentecostal churches. Under him Madras Pentecostal Assembly was one of the first and most important partners of Intermission, which apparently had had contact since the mid-1960s. When Prabhudoss died after a repeated heart attack, his son Stanley Vasu (b. 1971) was studying in his last year for a master's in mathematics at Madras Christian College, so that he was considered by the elders of the congregation to be too young for immediate succession. However, despite this reservation and with no other viable option, Stanley Vasu succeeded his father immediately.

Yesudhason, Sadhu (b. ca. 1913)
Sadhu Yesudhason hailed from a Christian family (London Missionary Society) in Kadamalaikuntu, Kanyakumari District. After going to school for eight years, he became an agricultural laborer. In 1941, he experienced his conversion and came in close contact with Pentecostals.[99] First he went around as an evangelist in a sadhu dress and lived a celibate life. He then took over a congregation in Poovancode for some time. Not later than the end of the 1940s, he settled down in Kanjiracode and started Kirubasanam.

99. See Hoerschelmann 1977: 272, where it is mentioned that he was in contact with American missionaries in Madurai in the 1940s. Maybe this refers to the missionaries of the Assemblies of God in Madurai.

Yohannan, K. P. (b. 1950)

K. P. Yohannan hailed from Niranam, Kerala. His parents belonged to the Mar Thoma Church, but his mother had apparently close contact with the Indian Pentecostal Church. He experienced his conversion at the age of eight.[100] At the age of eighteen, he joined Operation Mobilisation and went to north India as an evangelist. During that time he strengthened his contact with the Pentecostal movement. In Chandigarh, he received the baptism of immersion through Pastor Samuel John of the Church of God, and he worked with Operation Mobilisation in north India until 1973. In 1971, he also studied for a month in Singapore in a Bible school founded by John Haggai. It is there where he met Bob Pierce, the founder of World Vision. In 1973, he came to know his later wife Gisela in a spring conference of Operation Mobilisation. He met her more often when he was sent to north India during the following summer. When Gisela went back to Germany, he gave up his work for the Operation Mobilisation and also went to Germany in December 1973 with the vague intention of studying in some Bible school. In Germany, where he got engaged to Gisela, he was given a chance to go to Criswell Bible Institute, Dallas. In 1974, he went to Dallas and married Gisela, who followed him to the USA. During his studies he had already taken charge of a congregation while his wife worked as a nurse. Perhaps in 1978, he left the congregation and concentrated on founding his own mission society, Gospel for Asia. In the winter of 1980/1981, he undertook a big preaching journey through the USA with a view to collecting some funds. A breakthrough occurred when he succeeded in getting access to American TV church. It all began when Lester Roloff supported him with his daily radio broadcasting, and a little later when televangelists Bob Walker (Christian Life Missions) and David Mains (Chapel of the Air) offered their support too.

---

100. See Yohannan 1994b: 23.

Missionaries and Leadership Positions

Indian Pentecostal Church

General Presidents

K. E. Abraham	?[1]-1974
P. M. Samuel	1974-1981
T. G. Oommen	1981-1985
P. L. Paramjothi	1985-1996
K. M. Joseph	1996-2000
T. S. Abraham	2000-

Assemblies of God

American Missionaries in Kerala[2]

Mary Chapman	1916-1927
John H. Burgess	1927-1950
Martha Kucera	1928-1963[3]

1. See Indian Pentecostal Church 1991.

2. The list is not complete. Only important missionaries are recorded. For a complete list see Assemblies of God, ca. 1995, where, however, the duration of stay in India is not mentioned, but only the time when the missionaries were in the service of the Assemblies of God. Moreover, one should notice that male western missionaries always came with their wives to India, but there were unmarried female missionaries.

3. The dates are taken from Assemblies of God ca. 1995. Perhaps Martha Kucera had already left India before 1963. However, she is still recorded in McLeish 1955: 181, for Trivandrum and in Warren 1959: 179, for Bangalore.

Mildred C. Ginn	1930-1972
Clarence T. Maloney	1937-1942
Lydia H. Graner	1937-1972
Robert Shaver	1950
Ernest A. Sorbo	1951-1982
Earl Stubbs	1975-(1979)

General Superintendents, South India Assemblies of God

Carl D. Holleman	1949-1954
A. C. Samuel	1954-1967[4]
C. Kunnjummen	1967-1979
Y. Jeyaraj	1979-1991
T. C. George	1991-

District Superintendents, Malayalam District

A. C. Samuel	1947-1967
C. Kunjummen	1967-1979
P. D. Johnson	1980-1990
T. J. Samuel	1991-

District Superintendents, Tamil District[5]

M. Benjamin	1948-1951
Robert W. Edwards	1952
S. V. Nallaiya	1953
Santhosam Philip	1954-1956
P. D. Manickam	1957
M. S. Joseph	1958
Y. Jeyaraj	1959-1961
S. Adamdurai	1962
Y. Jeyaraj	1963-

4. It seems that A. C. Samuel did not hold this office continuously but that there was one election period (about 1-2 years) when Victor Joseph (Tamil District) was General Superintendent (see Rajamoni n.d.: 74; Reginald 1995: 45).

5. See Rajamoni n.d.: 8,3; Benjamin 1981: 32.

Church of God

American Missionaries in India[6]

Robert F. Cook	1936-1950
George R. Cook	1936-1945
Hoyle Case	1938-1942
Edward Crick[7]	1943-1948
C. E. French	1947-1952
Paul Cook	1947-1948
Dora P. Myers	1950-1962
William Pospisil	1952-1972
Harold L. Turner	1957-1974
Robert J. Reesor	*1964-1969*
D. L. Lindsay	1967-1969

State Overseers, Kerala State[8]

U. Thomas	1965
P. C. Chacko	1966-1970
A. V. Abraham	1971-1978
M. V. Chacko	1978-1988
P. A. V. Sam	1988-2000
V. C. Itty	2000-2002
K. C. John	2002-

State Overseers, Kerala Division

K. J. Chacko	1972-1986
Y. Joseph	1986-1993
Sunny Varkey	1993-

6. See Conn 1959: 289; Varghese & George 1973: 56-66; Alexander 1980: 18; Myers n.d. The sources differ from one another regarding the dates. In uncertain cases years are given in italics.

7. Edward Crick had married a daughter of Robert F. Cook. He was stationed in India as an officer of the British Air Force (see Cook 1955: 237) and is therefore a special case.

8. See Verghese & George 1973: 50-52.

Ceylon Pentecostal Mission

Chief Pastors

P. Paul	1921-1945
Alwin R. de Alwis	1945-1962
Freddy Paul	1962-1973
A. C. Thomas	1973-1976
Jacob Ratnasingam	1976-1990
V. G. Samuel	1990-1991
Henry Ernest Paul	1991-1994
C. K. Lazarus	1994-1999
P. M. Thomas	1999-2007
T. U. Thomas	2001-2006
F. Wilson Joseph	2006-

Church Statistics

The real number of the followers of the south Indian Pentecostal movement can be ascertained only with difficulty. By counting the known churches, about 400,000 members were ascertained by the author for the year 1994. The details of this counting are presented in Tab. 1. All the churches with more than 1,000 members in a state are shown individually there. Smaller churches with fewer than 1,000 members are not mentioned by their names for the sake of clarity, but are summed up according to the region.[1] In the estimation, all the available resources were taken into consideration. For a realistic estimation of the membership figures, the knowledge that was gained from the interviews and personal observations was of special importance. Furthermore, it proved to be of great advantage that the author had worked together with the Church Growth Research Centre to undertake a census of all Christian churches of Madurai in 1994.[2] With the help of comprehensive lists of addresses of Pentecostal congregations, handed over to the author by individual Pentecostal leaders, he could undertake special statistical investigations into the smaller churches. Printed directories of churches with their addresses are also available in a few individual towns and regions of south India, which,

1. Because of this reason, two churches that are described in the main text of this present research will be missing in the list, because they had a membership below 1,000: The Christian Fellowship Centre had a main congregation in Bangalore with 200 members. In Kerala and Tamil Nadu, there were a few quite independent branch congregations with about 500 members altogether. Maranatha Visvasa Samajam, Vijayawada, had 300 in the main congregation; in the branch congregations, all of which are found in Andhra Pradesh, it had about 200 members.

2. See Vasantharaj Albert 1995.

however, are extremely incomplete with regard to statistical details and give only insufficient details about the Pentecostal churches.[3] The number of members of the individual churches given by the author is always a conservative assessment that gives the minimum size of a particular church. Thus, the figures given by some churches are often drastically reduced.[4] The real number of followers of the south Indian Pentecostal movement can be established as at least twice as high as the given minimal estimation in which, for example, non-baptized children are not taken into consideration. Only then a certain numerical comparison with the established churches in south India can be made.[5] In addition, it is also taken into consideration that in the estimation presented here, at the most, 80 percent of all the south Indian Pentecostal churches are covered. Thus, we arrive at a realistic and in no way too-highly-estimated number of about 1,000,000 followers for the south Indian Pentecostal movement.[6]

The attempt to determine in percentage the share of the Pentecostal movement in south Indian Christianity meets with great difficulties, since only insufficient statistical details are available even about the established churches. Therefore, the counting undertaken by the author is to be considered only as a rough approximation. According to this reckoning, about 6 percent of the Christians in south India are followers of the Pentecostal

---

3. A few statistical overviews about Christianity in India also contain references to the Pentecostal movement (see Philip 1934; McLeish & Watts 1951; McLeish 1955; Warren 1959; Barrett 1982: 377-79; Mar Aprem 1984: 126-31; Vasantharaj Albert 1989: 75-96). Regional church directories also contain references about Pentecostal congregations (see Forerunner Publishers 1988; Jacob 1993; Vasantharaj Albert 1995; Devaraj & Vasantharaj Albert 1995; Vasantharaj Albert & Rethinasamy 1997). However, only for Madras is there a directory with references about the number of followers, and here Pentecostal congregations are also covered (see Jaffarian 1981; Sunder Singh & Rajakumar 1989; Rajakumar 1994). Since 1993, a yearbook in the Malayalam language about the Pentecostal movement in Kerala references is published with numerous statistics, which however, are based on (as a rule much exaggerated) figures given by the churches and organizations themselves (see Sarosh T. Jacob 1993, 1994, 1995).

4. Thus, for example, the Indian Pentecostal Church in Kerala claims 250,000 followers, World Missionary Evangelism in Kerala 50,000, and the New India Bible Church 14,000 (see Sarosh T. Jacob 1995: 42). Only the Assemblies of God give quite reliable statistics on their membership (see, for example, George 1993).

5. See also Barrett 1982, which follows a similar procedure.

6. It is to be noted that in the case of the Pentecostal churches a roughly estimated 20 percent of the given followers keep an additional membership in an established church (see Bergunder 1999: appendix 2, table 8). This fact, however, is not statistically taken into consideration, since it is neither known to which established churches the people with double membership belong, nor is their exact percentage recorded.

Growth for selected churches of the South Indian Pentecostal Movement

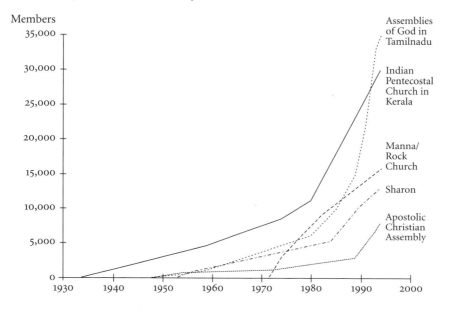

movement (see Tab. 2). The Pentecostals form, however, about 20 percent of the Protestant Christians of south India (see Tab. 3). The Pentecostals are strong particularly in Tamil Nadu. According to the information received there, about 9 percent of all Christians and about 26 percent of all Protestants are Pentecostals (see Tab. 4). Unfortunately, it is not possible with the help of the available data to get reliable details about the historical dimension of the growth of the south Indian Pentecostal movement. An overview about the growth of five Pentecostal churches with strong membership shows, however, that all these churches have seen a rapid increase only since the 1970s. According to the experiences of the author, this is a general trend. Everything supports the assumption that the sensational growth that led to the present numerical strength of the south Indian Pentecostal movement first began in the 1970s.

Tab. 1: South Indian Pentecostal Churches (1994)

Church	State[7]	Members
Assemblies of God, Andhra Pradesh	AP	3,500
Bible Mission	AP	10,000
Christ's Church	AP	1,000
Church of God of Prophecy	AP	6,000
Church of God, Andhra Pradesh	AP	4,000
Indian Pentecostal Church, Andhra Pradesh	AP	16,000
Jesus Christ Prayer & Evangelistic Ministries	AP	1,000
Smaller churches, Andhra Pradesh	AP	5,000
Smaller churches, Hyderabad	AP	4,000
Smaller churches, Vizag	AP	1,000
Manna/Rock Church	AP	16,000
New Testament Church	AP	1,000
Sion Fellowship	AP	5,500
World Missionary Evangelism, Andhra Pradesh	AP	11,000
Assemblies of God, Karnataka	KAK	8,000
Ceylon Pentecostal Mission, Karnataka	KAK	1,000
Gospel Prayer Hall	KAK	1,000
Smaller churches, Bangalore	KAK	3,000
Smaller churches, Karnataka	KAK	2,000
Philadelphia Church	KAK	1,000
Shekinah Gospel Prayer Fellowship	KAK	1,200
Apostolic Church of Pentecost	KER	1,200
Assemblies of God, Kerala	KER	16,000
Ceylon Pentecostal Mission, Kerala	KER	9,000
Church of God (M. E. Jacob)	KER	1,000
Church of God, Kerala Division	KER	7,000
Church of God, Kerala State	KER	13,000
Indian Pentecostal Assembly	KER	1,000
Indian Pentecostal Church, Kerala	KER	30,000
International Zion Assembly	KER	1,500
Smaller churches, Kerala	KER	12,000
New India Bible Church	KER	3,000
New India Church of God	KER	6,000
Sharon Fellowship	KER	13,000
United Pentecostal Church, Kerala	KER	2,000

7. AP = Andhra Pradesh; KAK = Karnataka; KER = Kerala; TN = Tamilnadu.

World Missionary Evangelism, Kerala	KER	7,000
Apostolic Christian Assembly	TN	8,000
Apostolic Fellowship Tabernacle	TN	2,000
Assemblies of God, Southern District	TN	5,000
Assemblies of God, Tamil Nadu	TN	35,000
Athumanesar	TN	1,000
Beginning Pentecostal Truth Church	TN	1,000
Body of Christ	TN	6,000
Ceylon Pentecostal Mission, Tamil Nadu	TN	15,000
Church of God, Tamil Nadu	TN	5,000
Full Gospel Pentecostal Church	TN	7,000
Good News Mission	TN	1,400
Good Samaritan Fellowship	TN	2,000
Good Shepherd Evangelical Church	TN	1,000
Indian Pentecostal Assemblies	TN	4,500
Indian Pentecostal Church, Tamil Nadu	TN	6,000
Jehovah Salvation Church	TN	2,000
Kirubasanam	TN	5,000
Smaller churches, Kanyakumari District	TN	8,000
Smaller churches, Coimbatore	TN	1,500
Smaller churches, Madras	TN	20,000
Smaller churches, Madurai	TN	5,000
Smaller churches, Tamil Nadu	TN	5,000
Smaller churches, Tirunelveli District	TN	3,000
Living Word Church	TN	2,000
Madras Pentecostal Assembly	TN	5,000
Maranatha	TN	3,500
Open Bible Church	TN	1,000
Prayer Garden Fellowship	TN	1,200
Prince of Peace	TN	2,000
Trinity Full Gospel Church	TN	1,500
United Pentecostal Church, Tamil Nadu	TN	1,500
World Missionary Evangelism, Tamil Nadu	TN	2,000
Zion Assemblies of God	TN	2,800

Members	396,800
Followers	ca. 800,000
Followers of churches not covered	ca. 200,000
Total number	ca. 1,000,000

Tab. 2: South Indian Christianity (1994)

Churches[8]	Followers	Percentage
Catholics	9,700,000	58.36%
Church of South India	2,070,000	12.45%
Syrian Orthodox Church	1,830,000	11.01%
Pentecostal churches	1,000,000	6.02%
Samavesam of Telugu Baptist Churches	660,000	3.97%
Lutherans	650,000	3.91%
Mar Thoma Church	460,000	2.77%
Others	250,000	1.50%
Total	16,620,000	100.00%

Tab. 3: Protestantism in South India (1994)

Churches	Followers	Percentage
Church of South India	2,070,000	40.67%
Pentecostal churches	1,000,000	19.65%
Samasevam of Telugu Baptist Churches	660,000	12.97%
Lutherans	650,000	12.77%
Mar Thoma Church	460,000	9.04%
Others	250,000	4.91%
Total	5,090,000	100.00%

Tab. 4: Protestantism in Tamil Nadu (1994)

Churches	Followers	Percentage
Church of South India	925,000	56.40%
Pentecostal churches	430,000	26.22%
Lutherans	210,000	12.80%
Others	75,000	04.57%
Total	1,640,000	100.00%

8. In order to arrive at comparative numbers of followers for the year 1994, different statements had to be reconciled with one another. Therefore, the statistics presented here are to be considered only as rough estimates. For more details see Bergunder 1999: 308-9.

List of Interviews

J. Balachandran cofounder of Good Samaritan Fellowship, founder and leader of Jesus Lives Ministry. Madurai, 29 March 1994.

Jesudason Jeyaraj professor of Old Testament in Tamil Nadu Theological College, brother-in-law of Joseph Balachandran. Madurai, 11 April 1994.

Dudley Thangaiah leader of New Life Assembly. Madurai, 13 April 1994.

D. Daniel professor of history at Kamaraj University, Madurai. Treasurer of Indian Pentecostal Church in Tamil Nadu. Madurai, 1 June 1994 and 5 October 1994.

G. Athisayam evangelist. Madurai, 1 June 1994.

Edwin Karunakaran leader of Rhema-Church. Madurai, 5 June 1994.

D. N. Rajan assistant pastor of Rhema-Church. Madurai, 6 June 1994.

S. S. Stephen retired pastor of Assemblies of God. Madurai, 8 June 1994.

M. O. John senior leader of the Pentecostal movement in Tamil Nadu. T. Kallupatti, 10 July 1994.

Ebenezer John leader of Elim Church of God. Thirumangalam, 10 June 1994.

M. Devaraj pastor of Church of God. Madurai, 12 June 1994.

J. Harris leader of Living Word. Madurai, 14 June 1994.

D. R. Jesudasan elder and cofounder of Assembly of Christ Jesus. Thanjavur, 16 June 1994.

V. Rowlands N. P. Kay representative of World Missionary Evangelism. Thanjavur, 17 June 1994.

Victor P. D. Kay   former representative of World Missionary Evangelism. Thanjavur, 17 June 1994.

Immanuel Francis   representative of World Missionary Evangelism. Thanjavur, 17 June 1994.

Robert John Milton   founder and leader of Emmanuel Prayer Fellowship. Thanjavur, 18 June 1994.

Sister Daisy   evangelist. Pattukottai, 18 June 1994.

Selvaraj   pastor of World Missionary Evangelism. Pattukottai, 18 June 1994.

C. M. Paul   evangelist. Pattukottai, 18 June 1994.

Asirvatham   founder and leader of Athumanesar. Thanjavur, 19 June 1994.

Y. Chellappa   senior leader of the Assemblies of God in Tamil Nadu. Madurai, 25 June 1994.

D. Robinson   pastor of Assemblies of God. Trichy, 5 July 1994.

Norman Basker   pastor of Assemblies of God. Trichy, 6 July 1994.

A. Jacob   Good Shepherd Ministries, former leader of Siloam. Trichy, 7 July 1994.

D. D. Vincent   leader of Peniel. Trichy, 7 July 1994.

George Victor   joint-secretary of Indian Pentecostal Church in Tamil Nadu. Trichy, 7 July 1994.

J. Jeyachandran   pastor of Assemblies of God. Thanjavur, 7 July 1994.

S. S. S. Stephen   founder and leader of Assembly of Christ Jesus. Trichy, 8 July 1994.

Paul Jesudoss   leader of Church of Jesus. Madurai, 9 July 1994.

Ranjit Singh   father of Mariamma Thamby. Nagercoil, 11 July 1994.

Sundara Dhas   retired pastor of Church of God. Nagercoil, 12 July 1994.

Gnanasigamony   independent pastor and senior leader of the Pentecostal movement in Kanyakumari District. Nagercoil, 12 July 1994.

S. Oliver   bookkeeper of Fellowship of Evangelical Friends. Nagercoil, 13 July 1994.

J. Jeyapaul   pastor of Church of God. Nagercoil. 13 July 1994.

J. D. Nirmala   leader of Apostolic Christian Perfecting Church. Nagercoil, 13 July 1994.

C. Simon   general treasurer of South India Assemblies of God. Attoor, 14 July 1994.

C. Selva Raj   leader of Beginning Pentecostal Truth Church. Malavilai, 14 July 1994.

Chellappan   pastor of Jehovah Pentecostal Church. Kalladimamoodu, 14 July 1994.

N. Thomas   leader of Full Gospel Pentecostal Church. Kattathurai, 15 July 1994.

Y. S. Devasundaram   leader of Jehovah Salvation Church. Nagercoil, 15 July 1994.

S. Jesudhasan   leader of India Philadelphia Church. Mekka Mandapam, 16 July 1994.

S. Samuel   founder and leader of Apostolic Pentecostal Mission. Palayankottai, 20 July 1994.

R. Rajendran   pastor and leader of a Bible school, son of M. Rajendran, Good News Mission. Palayankottai, 20 July 1994.

Ratna Paul   pastor of Assemblies of God. Palayankottai, 20 July 1994.

S. Chellappa   leader of Pentecostal Church of India. Palayankottai, 20 July 1994.

M. Sathya   retired independent pastor. Nazareth, 21 July 1994.

Edwin Prabahar   pastor of Assemblies of God. Nazareth, 21 July 1994.

Rethinam   pastor of Kirubasanam. Kanjiracode, 22 July 1994.

S. J. Dhas   leader of The Ceylon Pentecostal Mission. Nagercoil, 22 July 1994.

Deva Asir   leader of Manujothi Ashram, son of Paulaseer Lawrie. Odaimarichan, 23 July 1994.

V. J. Paulus   pastor of Assemblies of God. Palayankottai, 23 July 1994.

C. Zechariah   principal of Assemblies of God Tamil Nadu Bible College. Madurai, 25 August 1994.

Paul Thangiah   pastor of Assemblies of God. Bangalore, 31 August 1994.

P. P. Chinnadurai   founder and leader of Madurai Christian Centre, brother of P. S. Chelladurai Sr. Madurai, 2 September 1994

Rachel Daniel   sister of P. D. Johnson. Trivandrum, 6 September 1994.

Sam E. Edwin   principal of Zion Bible College, Zion Sangam. Vilangamuri, 6 September 1994.

A. Yovan   founder and leader of Sathya Daiva Sabha. Thozhukkal, 6 September 1994.

Edwin K. Raj   pastor of International Zion Assembly. Kovalam, 7 September 1994.

Titus Verghese   leader of Gospel Activity Centre. Trivandrum, 7 September 1994.

T. J. Rajan   secretary of Malayalam District Assemblies of God. Trivandrum, 7 September 1994.

G. Samuel   pastor of Indian Pentecostal Church. Trivandrum, 8 September 1994.

Habel G. Verghese   director of Asian Institute of Christian Education. Trivandrum, 8 September 1994.

T. J. Samuel   district superintendent of Malayalam District Assemblies of God. Punalur, 9 September 1994.

T. P. Verghese   teacher in Bethel Bible College of Assemblies of God. Punalur, 9 September 1994.

D. C. Samuel   founder and leader of India Pentecostal Assembly. Trivandrum, 10 September 1994.

Kunjunju Kutty   pastor of United Apostolic Church of God. Trivandrum, 10 September 1994.

C. A. Abraham   pastor of New Testament Church (Tiruvalla). Trivandrum, 10 September 1994.

K. C. Alexander   pastor of The Pentecostal Gospel Church. Trivandrum, 10 September 1994.

A. V. Verghese   pastor of Church of God Kerala State. Trivandrum, 11 September 1994.

Kalliyoor Kunjumon   leader and founder of Christian Acts Mission India. Trivandrum, 11 September 1994.

Y. Jeyaraj   senior leader of the Assemblies of God in India. Madurai, 14 September 1994.

Peter Prakasam   pastor of Indian Pentecostal Assemblies, son of Job Gnanaprakasam. Coimbatore, 16 September 1994.

D. A. Johnson   pastor of Trinity Prayer House, son of D. A. Sathiyanathan. Coimbatore, 16 September 1994.

Paul Ponraj   leader of Pentecostal Church of India. Coimbatore, 17 September 1994.

D. M. David Daniel   leader of Coimbatore Christian Centre. Coimbatore, 17 September 1994.

Arulanandam   founder and leader of Arulanandam Prayer House. Coimbatore, 18 September 1994.

Joel Anandaraj   founder and leader of The Apostolic Church. Coimbatore, 18 September 1994.

Peter Arumainayakam   leader of Zion Assemblies of God. Coimbatore, 19 September 1994.

Samuel Isaiah   elder of Livesey Memorial Church, Tatapad, son of J. C. Isaiah. Coimbatore, 19 September 1994.

S. Jeyasingh   founder and leader of Abundant Life Assembly. Coimbatore, 20 September 1994.

G. Gnanadhas   principal of Church of God Tamil Nadu Bible College. Coimbatore, 20 September 1994.

P. John   leader of Open Bible Church. Coimbatore, 21 September 1994.

Edwin Sunder Singh   pastor of United Pentecostal Church. Kodaikanal, 23 September 1994.

Sunny P. Samuel   pastor of Church of God Kerala State, personal Advisor of P. A. V. Sam. Mulakuzha, 26 September 1994.

P. J. Thomas   founder and leader of Sharon Fellowship. Tiruvalla, 27 September 1994.

Cherian Oommen   head of a department in Gospel For Asia. Tiruvalla, 27 September 1994.

V. A. Thampy   founder and leader of New India Church of God. Chingavanam, 27 September 1994.

Thomas Philip   founder and leader of New India Bible Church. Pallikachira Kavala, 27 September 1994.

T. S. Abraham   general secretary of Indian Pentecostal Church, son of K. E. Abraham. Kumbanadu, 28 September 1994.

O. M. Rajakutty   supervisor of World Missionary Evangelism. Kariamplavu, 28 September 1994.

Sunny Varkey   overseer of Church of God Kerala Division. Pakkil, 30 September 1994.

P. George   general superintendent, United Pentecostal Church in India. Adoor, 30 September 1994.

Samuel Mathew   teacher at Faith Theological Seminary. Manakala, 30 September 1994.

P. M. Philip   senior pastor of Indian Pentecostal Church. Vadavathoor, 1 October 1994.

K. M. Thomas   principal of the Bible Institute of the Apostolic Church of God. Manarcaud, 1 October 1994.

M. V. Chacko   former overseer of Church of God Kerala State. Eraviperoor, 1 October 1994.

Unni Jacob   wife of M. E. Jacob, the founder and leader of the independent Deva Saba. Mavelikara, 2 October 1994.

P. S. Rajamoni   leader of Decade of Harvest of Assemblies of God. Madurai, 3 October 1994.

P. S. Chelladurai Sr.   founder of Apostolic Fellowship Tabernacle. Madras, 14 October 1994.

Abraham Thomas   secretary of Tamil District Assemblies of God. Madras, 17 October 1994.

Henry D. Joseph   founder and leader of Maranatha. Madras, 18 October 1994.

Joseph Wilson   leader of Rainbow Ministry. Madras, 19 October 1994.

Wellesley Solomon   overseer of Church of God Tamil Nadu. Madras, 19 October 1994.

Sam Jebadurai   evangelist. Madras, 19 October 1994.

P. George   office secretary in Apostolic Christian Assembly. Madras, 20 October 1994.

Prabhudas Vasu   leader of Madras Pentecostal Assembly. Madras, 21 October 1994.

Sara Navroji   evangelist and leader of Zion Gospel Prayer Fellowship. Madras, 21 October 1994.

N. Jeevanandan   evangelist. Madras, 22 October 1994.

John Solomon   evangelist. Madras, 22 October 1994.

D. Mohan   pastor of Assemblies of God. Madras, 2 November 1994.

James Santhosam   founder and leader of Prince of Peace. Madras, 24 October 1994.

Chellam Asan   evangelist. Madras, 24 October 1994.

Sadhu Chellappa   evangelist. Madras, 25 October 1994.

Emmanuel Milton   founder and leader of Carmel Full Gospel Church. Madras, 25 October 1994.

Paul C. Martin   influential layman in The Pentecostal Mission, national director of Full Gospel Business Men's Fellowship. Madras, 26 October 1994.

Sam P. Chelladurai Jr.   leader of Apostolic Fellowship Tabernacle. Madras, 27 October 1994.

V. Ezekia Francis   evangelist, founder and leader of Berachah Prophetic Ministries. Madras, 27 October 1994.

Jochen Tewes   Indian representative of Intermission. Madras, 28 October 1994.

Manasse   pastor of the Pentecostal Mission. Madras, 28 October 1994.

M. Isaac   pastor of Apostolic Church. Madras, 28 October 1994.

Pappa Shankar   evangelist. Madras, 28 October 1994.

Dayanandan   cofounder and leader of Gospel Echoing Missionary Society. Madras, 29 October 1994.

Pratap Singh   founder and leader of Trinity Full Gospel Church. Madras, 1 November 1994.

Office-Manager (name unknown)   Siloam India. Madras, 1 November 1994.

Stephen Devakumar   founder and leader of Open Door Full Gospel Church. Madras, 3 November 1994.

Padma Mudaliar   evangelist. Madras, 3 November 1994.

Lamech Inbaraj   international coordinator of The Living Rock Ministries. Madras, 4 November 1994.

A. Christdoss   head of a department in Jesus Calls. Madras, 4 November 1994.

M. K. Sam Sunderam   leader of Apostolic Christian Assembly. Madras, 5 November 1994.

D. G. S. Dhinakaran   evangelist, founder and leader of Jesus Calls. Madras, 8 November 1994.

K. David Raju   leader of International Training Centre, brother of K. A. Paul. Vizag, 24 January 1995.

P. J. Titus   founder and leader of Church on the Rock Theological Seminary and New Testament Church. Vizag, 24 January 1995.

K. C. Mathews   founder and leader of New Life Compassion Pentecostal Church. Vizag, 25 January 1995.

A. G. Thankachan   founder and leader of College of Ministries. Vizag, 26 January 1995.

M. A. Paul   founder and leader of Christ's Church. Vizag, 26 January 1995.

Sukumar Patnaik   evangelist. Vizag, 27 January 1995.

K. R. Singh   leader of United Christian Interior Mission. Vizag, 28 January 1995.

N. Krupa Rao   founder and leader of Jesus Christ Prayer and Evangelistic Ministries. Vizag, 29 January 1995.

Godi Samuel   founder and leader of Good Shepherd Ministries, former chairman of World Missionary Evangelism. Srikakulam, 30 January 1995.

P. L. Paramjothi   senior leader of the Pentecostal movement in Andhra Pradesh, general president of Indian Pentecostal Church. Rajahmundry, 7 February 1995.

Isaac Komanapalli   chairman of World Missionary Evangelism. Narasapur, 8 February 1995.

D. Joseph   leader of Church of God of Prophecy. Rajahmundry, 9 February 1995.

Stephen David Kalyanapu   cofounder and leader of Shalom Pentecostal Ministries, son of K. R. David. Rajahmundry, 9 February 1995.

Reddi Stephen   overseer of Church of God in Andhra Pradesh. Kakinada, 10 February 1995.

P. John Lazarus   leader of Rock Ministries International. Rajahmundry, 11 February 1995.

A. S. W. Jaikumar   leader of Independent Full Gospel Church. Rajahmundry, 12 February 1995.

K. James   leader of Sharon Prayer House. Rajahmundry, 12 February 1995.

G. Rakshanandam   founder and leader of World Wide Faith Missions of India. Tadepalligudam, 13 February 1995.

John Selvaraj   leader of Bible Mission. Guntur, 21 February 1995.

G. Moses Choudary   founder and leader of Maranatha Visvasa Samajam. Vijayawada, 21 February 1995.

Noel Samuel   principal of Zion Bible College, secretary of Indian Pentecostal Church in Andhra Pradesh. son of Abraham Samuel. Vijayawada, 22 February 1995.

J. Yesanna   founder and leader of Hosanna Ministries. Guntur, 22 February 1995.

S. Ratna Raju   founder and leader of Bethesda Pentecostal Fellowship. Jaggaya Petah, 23 February 1995.

Gera Peter   District-Superintendent of Assemblies of God in Andhra Pradesh. Hyderabad, 1 March 1995.

P. P. Johnson regional overseer of New Testament Church. Hyderabad, 2 March 1995.

Mammen Mathews pastor of Indian Pentecostal Church. Secunderabad, 2 March 1995.

Y. S. John Babu founder and leader of Sion Fellowship. Hyderabad, 3 March 1995.

D. David Sudhakar founder and leader of Apostolic Fire Brand Assembly. Secunderabad, 4 March 1995.

P. Devaiah founder and leader of Bethany Full Gospel Church. Secunderabad, 4 March 1995.

A. N. Mathew pastor of Indian Pentecostal Church. Hyderabad, 5 March 1995.

Ernest Komanapalli founder of Rock Church Ministries. Hyderabad, 6 March 1995.

P. J. Honoch pastor of New Life Fellowship. Secunderabad, 6 March 1995.

R. A. Paul founder and leader of Full Gospel Mission. Hyderabad, 7 March 1995.

David Bollam founder and leader of Jesus Loves You Ministries. Hyderabad, 7 March 1995.

S. A. George leader of Full Gospel Church in India. Bangalore, 14 March 1995.

W. Ferdinand leader of Revival Centre Church. Bangalore, 14 March 1995.

Reuben M. Sahtiya Raj founder and leader of Agape Bible Fellowship. Bangalore, 15 March 1995.

T. C. George general superintendent of South India Assemblies of God. Bangalore, 15 March 1995.

Thomas Kutty leader of Church of the Foursquare Gospel in India. Bangalore, 16 March 1995.

Yeswanth Kumar pastor of Shekinah Gospel Prayer Fellowship. Bangalore, 16 March 1995.

F. Jackson founder and leader of Karnataka Maranatha Pentecostal Church. Bangalore, 16 March 1995.

G. Nickelson founder and leader of Philadelphia Church. Kolar Gold Fields, 17 March 1995.

Zac Poonen founder and leader of Christian Fellowship Centre. Bangalore, 18 March 1995.

Sister M. R. John leader of Bangalore Pentecostal Mission. Bangalore, 18 March 1995.

T. Daniel Paul leader of Grace Gospel Hall. Bangalore, 19 March 1995.

John Thannickal founder and leader of Nava Jeeva Ashram. Bangalore, 19 March 1995.

Johney Kutty Joshua founder and leader of Full Gospel Church of Karnataka. Bangalore, 20 March 1995.

K. V. Jeyavel founder and leader of Full Gospel Fellowship. Bangalore, 20 March 1995.

A. Stephen founder and leader of Cornerstone Ministries. Bangalore, 21 March 1995.

S. J. Berchmans evangelist, founder and leader of Prayer Garden Fellowship. Madras, 24 March 1995.

Sam Selvaraj founder and leader of Echo His Call Evangelistic Ministries. Madras, 25 March 1995.

M. S. Joseph pastor of Indian Pentecostal Church. Madras, 27 March 1995.

G. Rajakumar owner and editor of Thina Thutu. Madras, 28 March 1995.

A. J. Thamburaj, S.J. leader of the Catholic Charismatic movement. Madras, 28 March 1995.

Mrs. Manoharan daughter of Joel Joseph. Madras, 29 March 1995.

Charles Aaron pastor of Rose of Sharon Assembly of God. Madras, 30 March 1995.

S. Chandrasekaran founder and leader of Eleventh Hour Ministries. Madras, 31 March 1995.

John Joseph evangelist, founder and leader of Christ for Every Soul. Madras, 31 March 1995.

G. P. S. Robinson evangelist, founder and leader of Jesus Meets Ministries. Madras, 1 April 1995.

D. John Paul Anand founder and leader of Life Ministries Trust. Madras, 1 April 1995.

Bibliography

Abraham, K. E.:

1955. Prarambha Varshangal <malay.> (The Early Years of I.P.C.). Kumbanadu, Kerala: Abraham Foundation Printers.

1976. The Seven Paradises. Kumbanadu, Kerala: K. E. Abraham Foundation.

1983. Yesukristhuvinte Eliya Dassan <malay.> (Autobiography of Pastor K. E. Abraham). Kumbanadu, Kerala: K. E. Abraham Foundation.

Abraham, Aleyamma:

2004. Pentecostal Women in Kerala, their Contribution to the Mission of the Church. (Diss., Fuller Theological Seminary, School of Intercultural Studies). Pasadena, California.

Abraham, Sara:

1990. A Critical Evaluation of the Indian Pentecostal Church of God — Its Origin and Development in Kerala. (M.Th. Thesis, United Theological College). Bangalore.

Adhav, Shamsundar Manohar:

1979. Pandita Ramabai. Madras: Christian Literature Society.

Alexander, Estralda Y.:

1996. What Doth the Lord Require. Toward a Pentecostal Theology of Social Justice. Papers from the 25th Annual Meeting of the Society for Pentecostal Studies. Toronto.

Alexander, George P.:

1980. Development of the Church of God in India. (unpublished manuscript, Dixon Pentecostal Research Center, Lee College Library). Cleveland, Tennessee.

Alexander, Patrick H.:

1990. Art. Slain in the Spirit. In: Burgess, Stanley M.; McGee, Gary B.; Alexander, Patrick H. (eds.): Dictionary of Pentecostal and Charismatic Movements. Grand Rapids: Zondervan. 4th ed., pp. 789-91.

Anderson, Allan H.:

2000. Zion and Pentecost. The Spirituality and Experience of Pentecostal and Zionist/ Apostolic Churches in South Africa. (African Initiatives in Christian Mission; 6). Pretoria: University of South Africa Press.

2001. African Reformation. African Initiated Christianity in the 20th Century. Trenton: Africa World Press.

2007. Spreading the Flame. The Missionary Nature of Early Pentecostalism. London: SCM Press.

Anderson, Robert Mapes:

1979. Vision of the Disinherited. The Making of American Pentecostalism. New York; Oxford: Oxford University Press.

Andreasson, Barbro; Andreasson, Erik:

1989. Pingst i Indien. Dokumentation av Svensk Pingstmission i Indien. (Forsknings-rapporter i missionsvetenskap missionshistoria och missionsanthropologi; 6). Stockholm: MissionsInstitutet-PMU.

Andronov, M. S.:

1989. A Grammar of Modern and Classical Tamil. (1969). Madras: New Century Book House. 2nd ed.

Apostolic Christian Assembly:

n.d. Spiritual Questions. Madras: Divine Deliverance Publication.

1957. Memorandum of Association, Rules and Regulations. (mimeo). Madras.

1994. Annual Report 1993-1994. Madras.

Apostolic Church:

1976. Silver Jubilee 1951-1976, Souvenir. Madras.

Asirvatham, R. N.:

1994. paricutta vētākama ottavākkiya viḷakkavurai (paḻaiya tirupputal) (Concordance to the Tamil Bible [O.V.]). (1961). Madras: Evangelical Literature Service.

Assemblies of God:

1929. Constitution of the South India and Ceylon District Council of the General Council of the Assemblies of God. Minutes of the Conference Held at Yercaud, South India, April 16th 1929. Yercaud.

1962. Revised Constitution and By-Laws of the South Indian Assemblies of God, May 12, 1962. Trivandrum.

1977. Golden Jubilee. Assemblies of God, Bethel Bible College 1927-1977. Punalur, Kerala.

1984. vicuvāciyum, nērnilai aṟikkaiyum (Positive Confession). Madras.

1994. Constitution and By-Laws of the South India Assemblies of God (Revised and adopted on 23rd June 1994 in Madras). Bangalore.

ca. 1995. Liste der Missionare der Assemblies of God in Südindien. General Council of The Assemblies of God, Division of Foreign Mission. (unpublished manuscript from the Assemblies of God Archives). Springfield, Mo.

1995. Memorandum, Constitution and By-Laws of the General Council of the Assemblies of God. Entwurf.

Augustine, John S.:

1993. Dimensions of Fundamentalism. Sociological Soundings Emerging from an Empirical Probe into the Evangelical Upsurge in Madras. In: Augustine, John S. (ed.): Religious Fundamentalism. An Asian Perspective. Bangalore: South Asia Theological Research Institute, pp. 109-80.

Ayrookuzhiel, A. M. Abraham:

1983. The Sacred in Popular Hinduism. An Empirical Study in Chirakkal, North Malabar. Madras: Christian Literature Society.

Azariah, M.:

1983. Witnessing in India Today. Madras: United Evangelical Lutheran Churches.

1995. News from the Dioceses. Madras Diocese. Hyderabad: Church of South India, pp. 11-13.

Baago, Kaj:

1966. "Sheepstealing" in the 19th Century. In: Bulletin of the Church History Association of India. Serampore. November: 17-35.

Bain, Ian:

ca. 1938. Before Kings. Life Story of Lam Jeevaratnam. Reprinted from "The Pentecostal Testimony" of Toronto, Canada. London.

Bakht Singh:

n.d. How I got joy unspeakable and full of glory. Bombay: Gospel Literature Service.

1968. Skill of His Loving Hands. Bombay: Gospel Literature Service.

Balasundaram, Franklyn Jeyakumar:

1990. The Voice and the Voices or the History and the Development of the Charismatic Movement. A Theological Critique. In: Asia Journal of Theology. Singapore. 4: 225-52.

Barrett, David B.:

1982. World Christian Encyclopedia. A Comparative Study of Churches and Religions in the Modern World AD 1900-2000. Oxford: Oxford University Press.

1990. Art. Statistics, Global. In: Burgess, Stanley M.; McGee, Gary B.; Alexander, Patrick H. (eds.): Dictionary of Pentecostal and Charismatic Movements. Grand Rapids: Zondervan, 4th ed., pp. 810-30.

1995. Annual Statistical Table on Global Mission 1995. In: International Bulletin of Missionary Research. 30: 24-25.

Barrett, D., et al. (eds.):

2001. World Christian Encyclopedia. Oxford: Oxford University Press.

Barrett, Thomas Ball:

1927. When the Fire Fell and an Outline of My Life. Oslo.

Bartleman, Frank:
1980. Azusa Street. (1925). S. Plainfield, New Jersey: Bridge Publishing.

Bayly, Susan:
1994. Christianity and Competing Fundamentalisms in South Indian Society. In: Marty, Martin; Appleby, R. Scott (Hrsg.): Accounting for Fundamentalisms. The Dynamic Character of the Movement. (The Fundamentalism Project; 4). Chicago: Chicago University Press. S. 726-69.

Bays, Daniel:
1999. The Protestant Missionary Establishment and the Pentecostal Movement. In: Blumhofer, Edith L.; Spittler, Russell P.; Wacker, Grant (ed.): Pentecostal Currents in American Protestantism. Urbana: University of Illinois Press, pp. 50-67.

Benjamin, A.:
1981. Origin and Developments of Assemblies of God in Tamilnadu. (B.Th. Thesis, Southern Asia Bible College). Bangalore.

Bergunder, Michael:
1999. Die südindische Pfingstbewegung im 20. Jahrhundert. Eine historische und systematische Untersuchung. (Studien zur interkulturellen Geschichte des Christentums; 113). Frankfurt: Peter Lang.

2000a. Proselytismus in der Geschichte des indischen Christentums. Eine ökumenische Bestandsaufnahme. In: Heyden, Ulrich van der; Becker, Jürgen (eds.): Mission und Gewalt. Der Umgang christlicher Missionen mit Gewalt und die Ausbreitung des Christentums in Afrika und Asien in der Zeit von 1792 bis 1918/19. (Missionsgeschichtliches Archiv; 6). Stuttgart: Franz Steiner, pp. 371-84.

2000b. "Ministry of Compassion." D. G. S. Dhinakaran — Christian Healer-Prophet from Tamilnadu. In: Hedlund, Roger E. (ed.): Christianity Is Indian. The Emergence of an Indigenous Community. New Delhi: ISPCK, pp. 158-74.

2002a. The "Pure Tamil Movement" and Bible Translation. The Ecumenical Thiruviviliam of 1995. In: Brown, Judith M.; Frykenberg, Robert Eric (eds.): Christians, Cultural Interactions, and India's Religious Traditions. Grand Rapids: Eerdmans, pp. 212-31.

2002b. The Pentecostal Movement and Basic Ecclesial Communities in Latin America. Sociological Theories and Theological Debates. In: International Review of Mission. Geneva. 91: 163-86.

2003. From Pentecostal Healing Evangelist to Kalki Avatar. The Remarkable Life of Paulaseer Lawrie alias Shri Lahari Krishna (1921-1989). In: Robert E. Frykenberg (ed.): Christians and Missionaries in India. Cross-Cultural Communication since 1500. London: Curzon Press, pp. 357-75.

Bevans, S. B.:
1992. Models of Contextual Theology. Maryknoll, N.Y.: Orbis Books.

Biehl, Michael:
1990. Der Fall Sadhu Sundar Singh. Theologie zwischen den Kulturen. (Studien zur interkulturellen Geschichte des Christentums; 66). Frankfurt am Main: Peter Lang.

Bloch-Hoell, Nils:
1964. The Pentecostal Movement. Its Origin, Development, and Distinctive Character. Oslo: Universitetsforlaget.

Blumhofer, Edith L.:
2001. Consuming Fire. Pandita Ramabai and the Global Pentecostal Impulse. (unpublished manuscript).

Bosch, D. J.:
1991. Transforming Mission. Maryknoll, N.Y.: Orbis Books, pp. 420-57.

Brouwer, S., et al.:
1996. Exporting the American Gospel. London: Routledge.

Brown, L. W.:
1956. The Indian Christians of St. Thomas. An Account of the Ancient Syrian Church of Malabar. Cambridge: Cambridge University Press.

Bundy, David:
1992. Spiritual Advice to a Seeker. Letters to T. B. Barratt from Azusa Street, 1906. In: Pneuma. Gaithersburg, Maryland. 14: 159-70.

Burgess, John H.:
ca. 1934. Opportunities in South India and Ceylon. Springfield, Mo.: Foreign Missions Department, General Council of the Assemblies of God.

Burgess, Stanley M.:
2001. Pentecostalism in India. An Overview. In: Asian Journal of Pentecostal Studies. Baguio City. 4: 85-98.
2002. Art. India. II. Development and Growth of Pentecostalism in India (1910-1960). In: Burgess, Stanley M.; van der Maas, Eduard M. (eds.): The New International Dictionary of Pentecostal and Charismatic Movements. Grand Rapids: Zondervan, pp. 122-26.

Burgess, Stanley M.; van der Maas, Eduard M. (eds.):
2002. The New International Dictionary of Pentecostal and Charismatic Movements. Grand Rapids: Zondervan.

Bush, Timothy A. C.:
1992. The Development of the Perception of the Baptism in the Holy Spirit within the Pentecostal Movement in Great Britain. In: EPTA Bulletin. Frankfurt am Main. 11: 24-41.

C. O. T. R. Theological Seminary:
ca. 1984. Prospectus. Bheemunipatnam, Andhra Pradesh: Jyoti Press.

Caldwell, Robert:
1869. The Tinnevelly Shanars. (1849). Abridged Version in: Ziegenbalg, Bartholomaeus: Genealogy of the South-Indian Gods. A Manual of the Mythology and Religion of the People of Southern India, Including a description of Popular Hinduism. (Genealogie der Malabarischen Götter <engl.>). Madras, pp. 156-76.

Caplan, Lionel:
> 1987. Class and Culture in Urban India. Fundamentalism in a Christian Community. Oxford: Clarendon Press.
> 1989. Religion and Power. Essays on the Christian Community in Madras. Madras: Christian Literature Society.

Cerillo Jr., Augustus:
> 1997. Interpretative Approaches to the History of American Pentecostal Origins. In: Pneuma. Hagerstown, Md. 19: 29-52.

Cerillo Jr., Augustus; Wacker, Grant:
> 2002. Art. Bibliography and Historiography of Pentecostalism in the United States. In: Burgess, Stanley M.; van der Maas, Eduard M. (eds.): The New International Dictionary of Pentecostal and Charismatic Movements. Grand Rapids: Zondervan, pp. 382-405.

Ceuta, Ioan:
> 1994. The Pentecostal Apostolic Church of God in Romania 1944-1990. In: EPTA Bulletin. Nantwich, Cheshire. 13: 74-87.

Chacko, E. J.:
> 1986. Keralathile chila swathanthra sabhakal <malay.> (Some of the Free Churches in Kerala). Tiruvalla, Kerala: The Theological Literature Council.

Chan, Simon:
> 2000. Pentecostal Theology and the Christian Spiritual Tradition. (Journal of Pentecostal Theology Supplement Series; 21). Sheffield: Sheffield Academic Press.

Chandran, J. R.; Ficher, R.; Collison, J. G. F.; Peery, W. P.; Duraisingh, C. J.:
> 1985. The Concept of Baptism in the Judeo-Christian Tradition. In: Singh, Godwin R. (ed.): A Call to Discipleship. Baptism and Conversion. Delhi: ISPCK, pp. 16-63.

Chaturvedi, Vinayak (ed.):
> 2000. Mapping Subaltern Studies and the Postcolonial. London: Verso.

Chelladurai Sr., P. S.:
> 1995. The Father of Many Nations. The Life Story of P. Sam Chelladurai. An autobiography of P. Sam Chelladurai edited by Yolanda Beltran. First Draft. (unpublished manuscript). Madras.

Cherian, M. T.:
> 1995. Worship. In: Titus, P. J. (ed.): Christian Ministers' Manual. Bheemunipatnam, Andhra Pradesh: C.O.T.R. College of Ministries, pp. 9-12.

Chevreau, Guy:
> 1994. The Toronto Blessing. An Experience of Renewal and Revival. London: Marshall Pickering.

Chitty, Simon Casie:
> 1992. The Castes, Customs, Manners and Literature of the Tamils. (1934). Delhi: Asian Educational Service.

Bibliography

Choudary, G. Moses (Gullapalli Vinayak):

1980. Reaching and Discipling Caste Hindus in Andhra Pradesh, India. (A Class Term Paper, Church of God School of Theology). Cleveland, Tennessee.

Christopher Asir, A.:

1975. A Historical Survey of the Sectarian Church Groups in the C.S.I. Diocese of Tinneveli in the 20th Century. (B.D. Thesis, United Theological College). Bangalore.

Church Growth Research Centre:

1992. Data on People Groups, Castes, Tribes and Ethnolinguistic Groups of India. In: Sargunam, M. Ezra (ed.): Mission Mandate. A Compendium on the Perspective of Missions in India. Madras: Mission India 2000, pp. 585-725.

Church of God:

1976. General Assembly Minutes (Supplement) and Church of God (Full Gospel) in India Policy. Mulakuzha, Kerala.

1979. Church Teachings and Policies combined with Rules and Regulations. Reprinted and Published with the Approval of the Governing Body of the Society of the Church of God (Full Gospel) in India. Coimbatore.

1993. Convention Souvenir 1993. Suvisesha Nadam Voice Publishers. Jan.-Feb. 1993. Church of God (Full Gospel) in India, Kerala State. Mulakuzha, Kerala.

Church of God of Prophecy:

1995. Silver Jubilee Souvenir. The Church of God of Prophecy India 1970-1995. Rajahmundry.

Clarke, Sathianathan:

1998. Dalits and Christianity. Subaltern Religion and Liberation Theology in India. Delhi: Oxford University Press.

Collet, G. (ed.):

1990. Theologien der Dritten Welt. Immensee.

Conn, Charles W.:

1959. Where the Saints Have Trod. A History of Church of God Missions. Cleveland, Tennessee.

Cook, Robert F.:

1955. Half a Century of Divine Leading and 37 Years of Apostolic Achievements in South India. Cleveland, Tennessee: Church of God Foreign Missions Department.

Coulter, Dale M.:

2001. What Meaneth This? Pentecostals and Theological Inquiry. In: Journal of Pentecostal Theology. Sheffield. 10, 1: 38-64.

Cox, Harvey:

1996. Fire from Heaven. The Rise of Pentecostal Spirituality and the Reshaping of Religion in the Twenty-First Century. London: Cassell.

Creech, J.:
1996. "Visions of Glory," Church History 65.

Dale, L. D.:
1973. The Lightning from the East. Alcoa, Tennessee: Wings of Life.

Daniel, Johnson:
1981. The Origin and Development of Indian Pentecostal Church in Kerala. (B.Th. Thesis, Southern Asia Bible College). Bangalore.

Daniel, K. (ed.):
1993. Arise and Build, Hand Me Another Brick, Great Is God's Faithfulness. Souvenir C.O.T.R. & N.T.C. 1983-1993. Bheemunipatnam, Andhra Pradesh: Jyoti Press.

Daniel, K. V.:
1979. Brief History of Pentecostal Churches in Kerala with Special References to the Problems Facing Them Today. (B.D. Thesis, Union Biblical Seminary). Yavatmal, Maharashtra.

Daniels, David D.:
1999. "Everybody Bids You Welcome." A Multicultural Approach to North American Pentecostalism. In: Dempster, Murray W.; Klaus, Byron D.; Petersen, Douglas (eds.): The Globalization of Pentecostalism. A Religion Made to Travel. Oxford: Regnum Books International, pp. 222-52.

Dayton, Donald W.:
1987. Theological Roots of Pentecostalism. Grand Rapids: Francis Asbury Press.

Dempster, Murray W.:
1993. Christian Social Concern in Pentecostal Perspective. Reformulating Pentecostal Eschatology. In: Journal of Pentecostal Theology. Sheffield. 2: 51-64.

Devaraj, M.; Vasantharaj Albert, S. (eds.):
1995. Nilgiris Christian Directory. Madras: Church Growth Research Centre.

Devasahayam, K.:
1982. The Bible Mission. In: Religion and Society. Bangalore. 29: 55-101.

Devasundaram, Y. S.:
1981. What God Has Done. Nagercoil: Jehovah Salvation Church.

Dharmagnani, P. (ed.):
1990. In the Power of the Holy Spirit. Madras: Christian Literature Society.

Dhinakaran, D. G. S.:
1978. Love So Amazing. Madras: Christian Literature Society.
1979. Healing Stripes. Madras: Jesus Calls.
1987. I Am That I Am. Madras: Jesus Calls.
ca. 1995. Paricutta āviyin̠ varaṅkaḷ. Madurai: Word of Christ.

Dhinakaran, Stella:
n.d. The Rose Amidst Thorns. Madras: Jesus Calls.

Diehl, Carl Gustav:

1956. Instrument and Purpose. Studies on Rites and Rituals in South India. (Diss., Universität Lund). Lund: Gleerup.

1965. Church and Shrine. Intermingling Patterns of Culture in the Life of some Christian Groups in South India. Uppsala.

Dongre, Rajas Krishnarao; Patterson, Josephine F.:

1969. Pandita Ramabai. A Life of Faith and Prayer. Madras: Christian Literature Society. 2nd ed.

Downs, Frederick S.:

1992. North East India in the Nineteenth and Twentieth Centuries. (History of Christianity in India; V, 5). Bangalore: The Church History Association.

Dusing, Michael L.:

1995. The New Testament Church. In: Horton, Stanley M. (ed.): Systematic Theology. Revised Edition. Springfield, Mo.: Logion Press, pp. 525-66.

Easow, Thankachan P.:

1991. Glimpses of Christian Doctrines. A Brief Survey and Interpretation of Christian Doctrines, with Reference to Recent Developments in Indian Churches. Trivandrum: Christian Literature Service.

Eastern Full Gospel Mission:

1946. Memorandum, Rules and Regulations and the Statement of the Fundamental Truths. (Registered 6th April 1945). Gudivada.

Edwards, Doris M.:

n.d. The Good Fight: Robert Wade Edwards. Shencottah, Tamilnadu: A. G. Press.

Ellington, Scott A.:

1996. Pentecostalism and the Authority of Scripture. In: Journal of Pentecostal Theology. Sheffield. 9: 16-38.

Elmore, W. T.:

1984. Dravidian Gods in Modern Hinduism. (1913). New Delhi: Asian Educational Service.

Estborn, S.:

1958. Our Village Christians. A study of the life and faith of village Christians in Tamilnadu. Madras: Christian Literature Society.

Evangelisches Missionswerk in Deutschland (ed.):

1995. Gerechtigkeit für die Unberührbaren. Beiträge zur indischen Dalit-Theologie. (Weltmission heute Nr. 15). Hamburg.

Faupel, D. William:

1996. The Everlasting Gospel. The Significance of Eschatology in the Development of Pentecostal Thought. (Journal of Pentecostal Theology Supplement Series; 10). Sheffield: Sheffield Academic Press.

Fee, Gordon D.:

1985. Baptism in the Holy Spirit. The Issue of Separability and Subsequence. In: Pneuma. Pasadena, Calif. 7: 87-99.

Fiedler, Klaus:

1992. Ganz auf Vertrauen. Geschichte und Kirchenverständnis der Glaubensmissionen. Giessen; Basel: Brunnen.

Fleisch, D. Paul:

1983. Geschichte der Pfingstbewegung in Deutschland of 1900 bis 1950. (1957). Marburg an der Lahn: Francke-Buchhandlung.

Forerunner Publishers (ed.):

1988. Bangalore Christian Directory cum Sunday Diary — 1988. Incorporating the Names and Addresses of Churches and Christian Missions/Ministries in Bangalore. Bangalore.

Forrester, Duncan B.:

1980. Caste and Christianity. Attitudes and Policies on Caste of Anglo-Saxon Protestant Missionaries in India. (London Studies on South Asia; 1). London: Curzon.

Francis, V. Ezekia:

1990. Prayer — the Vital Breath of Life. Madras: Berachah Ministries.

Franz, Andreas:

1993. Mission ohne Grenzen. Hudson Taylor und die deutschsprachigen Glaubensmissionen. Giessen; Basel: Brunnen.

Freston, P.:

2001. Evangelicals and Politics in Asia, Africa and Latin America. Cambridge: Cambridge University Press.

Frodsham, Stanley Howard:

1946. With Signs Following. The Story of the Pentecostal Revival in the Twentieth Century. Springfield, Mo.: Gospel Publishing House.

Frölich, Richard:

1915. Tamulische Volksreligion. Ein Beitrag zu ihrer Darstellung und Kritik. Leipzig.

Frykenberg, Robert Eric:

1976. The Impact of Conversion and Social Reform upon Society in South India During the Late Company Period. In: Philips, C. H.; Wainwright, M. D. (eds.): Indian Society and the Beginnings of Modernization, c. 1830-1850. London: School of Oriental and African Studies, pp. 187-243.

Fuchs, Stephen:

1992. Godmen on the Warpath. A Study of Messianic Movements in India. New Delhi: Munshiram Manuharlal.

Gabriel, M.:

1993. The Assemblies of God Church in Tirunelveli 1940-1992. (M.Phil. Thesis, School of Historical Studies, Madurai Kamaraj University). Madurai.

Gee, Donald:

1967. Wind and Flame. Incorporating the former book "The Pentecostal Movement" with additional chapters bringing this work up-to-date. Croyden: Assemblies of God Publishing House.

Gee, Donald; Woodford, L. F. W.:

1948. We want to Understand. Joint Report of the Chairman and Secretary of the Overseas Mission Council of Assemblies of God in Great Britain & Ireland following their visit to China and India in the autumn of 1948. London: Assemblies of God Overseas Missions Council.

Geevargheese, K. Y.:

1987. The Future of the World (Biblical Eschatology). Jabalapur, Madhya Pradesh: Biblical Publications.

George, A. C.:

2001. Pentecostal Beginnings in Travancore, South India. In: Asian Journal of Pentecostal Studies. Baguio City. 4: 215-237.

George, Ebenezer Andrew:

1995. Evangelism and Church Planting Through Full Gospel Church in India. (M.Div. Thesis, Church of God School of Theology). Cleveland, Tennessee.

George, K. M.:

1991. Grace Through Gate of Cancer. Punnaveli, Kerala: Published by the author.

George, S. A.:

n.d. History of the 1st Pentecostal Church in Bangalore Now Known as Full Gospel Church in India. (unpublished manuscript). Bangalore.

George, Thackil Chacko:

1975. The Growth of the Pentecostal Churches in South India. (M.A. Thesis, Fuller Theological Seminary, School of World Mission). Pasadena, Calif.

1976. The Life and Growth of Churches in Bangalore. (D.Miss. Thesis, Fuller Theological Seminary, School of World Mission). Pasadena, Calif.

George, Thackil Chacko (ed.):

1993. Directory of Churches and Ministers. South India Assemblies of God (As of February 1993). Bangalore.

Gerloff, R. I.:

1992. A Plea for British Black Theologies. Frankfurt: Peter Lang.

Giese, Ernst:

1987. Und flicken die Netze. Dokumente zur Erweckungsgeschichte des 20. Jahrhunderts, herausgegeben of Prof. O. S. v. Bibra. (1976). Metzingen: Ernst Franz.

Gill, Kenneth D.:

1994. Toward a Contextualised Theology for the Third World. The Emergence and Development of Jesus' Name Pentecostalism in Mexico. (Studien zur interkulturellen Geschichte des Christentums; 90). Frankfurt am Main: Peter Lang.

Gitre, E. J.:

    2002. Art. Post, Ansel Howard. In: Burgess, Stanley M.; van der Maas, Eduard M. (eds.): The New International Dictionary of Pentecostal and Charismatic Movements. Grand Rapids: Zondervan, p. 994.

Gnanaprakasam, Job:

    1987/1993. iyēcu kiristuviṉ irantām varukai (The Second Coming of Jesus Christ). vol 2. Coimbatore: India Pentecostal Assemblies.

    1990. mūṉṟāvatu ulaka makā yuttam (Third World War). Coimbatore: India Pentecostal Assemblies. 3rd ed.

    1993. Jesus Is the Lord of A.D. 2000. In: Thannickal, John (ed.): Jesus Christ Is Lord. The Pentecostal Fellowship of India Conference, New Delhi, Nov. 3-7, 1993. Bangalore: Pentecostal Fellowship of India.

    1995. Aufzeichnungen zur Geschichte der Pfingstbewegung in Tamilnadu: (1) The Origin of the Pentecostal Truth Brought to Coimbatore. (2) History of the Ministry with the World Missionary Evangelism. (3) History of the Ministry of Rev. Job Gnanaprakasam. (4) History of the Pentecostal Ministries Fellowship of Coimbatore. (5) History of IPA/History of My Family. (unpublished manuscript). Coimbatore.

Gnanasekar, S.:

    1994. Christian Attitude Towards Cinema — A study based on the experience of Nagercoil Protestant Christians. (mimeo, Tamilnadu Theological College, PG Students Seminar). Madurai.

Gnaniah, Ebenezer:

    1994. Deliverance from Darkness to Light. Madras: Eleventh Hour Publications.

Goff Jr., James R.:

    1988. Fields White unto Harvest. Charles F. Parham and the Missionary Origins of Pentecostalism. Fayetteville: University of Arkansas Press.

Gokak, Vinayak Krishna:

    1989. Bhagavan Sri Sathya Sai Baba. The Man and the Avatar. An Interpretation. New Delhi: Abhinav Publications. 3rd ed.

Grafe, Hugald:

    1990. The History of Christianity in Tamilnadu from 1800 to 1975. (Erlanger Monographien aus Mission und Ökumene; 9). Erlangen: Verlag der Ev.-Luth. Mission.

Grafe, Hugald (ed.):

    1981. Evangelische Kirche in Indien. Auskunft und Einblicke. (Erlanger Taschenbücher; 51). Erlangen: Verlag der Ev.-Luth. Mission.

Griffith, R. Marie; Roebuck, David G.:

    2002. Art. Women, Role of. In: Burgess, Stanley M.; van der Maas, Eduard M. (eds.): The New International Dictionary of Pentecostal and Charismatic Movements. Grand Rapids: Zondervan, pp. 1203-9.

Grossmann, Siegfried:

1990. Der Geist ist Leben. Wuppertal und Kassel: Oncken.

Gründer, H.:

1992. Welteroberung und Christentum. Gütersloh: Gütersloher Verl.-Haus Mohn.

Grundmann, Christoffer H.:

1997. Leibhaftigkeit des Heils. Ein missionstheologischer Diskurs über das Heilen in den zionistischen Kirchen im südlichen Afrika. (Hamburger Theologische Studien; 11). Hamburg: Lit Verlag.

Hardgrave, Jr., Robert L.:

1969. The Nadars of Tamilnadu. The Political Culture of a Community in Change. Berkeley: University of California Press.

Harrell, Jr., David Edwin:

1975. All Things Are Possible. The Healing and Charismatic Revivals in Modern America. Bloomington, Indiana: Indiana University Press.

1985. Oral Roberts. An American Life. Bloomington: Indiana University Press.

Hedlund, R. E.:

1999. Indian Instituted Churches. In: Mission Studies 16.1: 26-42.

2000a. Quest for Identity. Delhi: ISPCK.

2001. Previews of Christian Indigeneity in India. In: Journal of Asian Mission. Quezon City. 3, 2: 213-30.

2002a. Art. Apostolic Christian Assembly (India). In: Burgess, Stanley M.; van der Maas, Eduard M. (eds.): The New International Dictionary of Pentecostal and Charismatic Movements. Grand Rapids: Zondervan, p. 322.

2002b. Art. Indian Pentecostal Church of God. In: Burgess, Stanley M.; van der Maas, Eduard M. (eds.): The New International Dictionary of Pentecostal and Charismatic Movements. Grand Rapids: Zondervan, pp. 778-79.

2002c. Art. Indigenous Churches. In: Burgess, Stanley M.; van der Maas, Eduard M. (eds.): The New International Dictionary of Pentecostal and Charismatic Movements. Grand Rapids: Zondervan, pp. 779-84.

Hedlund, R. E. (ed.):

2000b. Christianity Is Indian. New Delhi: ISPCK.

Hellmann-Rajanayagam, Dagmar:

1984. Tamil. Sprache als politisches Symbol. (Beiträge zur Südasienforschung; 74). Wiesbaden: Franz Steiner.

Henke, Frederick G.:

1909. The Gift of Tongues and Related Phenomena at the Present Day. In: American Journal of Theology. Chicago. 13: 193-206.

Hewett, James Allen:

1990a. Art. Daoud, Mounir Aziz. In: Burgess, Stanley M.; McGee, Gary B.; Alexander, Patrick H. (eds.): Dictionary of Pentecostal and Charismatic Movements. Grand Rapids: Zondervan. 4th ed., p. 237.

1990b. Art. Wyatt, Thomas. In: Burgess, Stanley M.; McGee, Gary B.; Alexander, Patrick H. (eds.): Dictionary of Pentecostal and Charismatic Movements. Grand Rapids: Zondervan. 4th ed., p. 906.

1990c. Art. Douglas, John Elwood. In: Burgess, Stanley M.; McGee, Gary B.; Alexander, Patrick H. (eds.): Dictionary of Pentecostal and Charismatic Movements. Grand Rapids: Zondervan. 4th ed., p. 248.

Hminga, Chhangte Lal:

1987. The Life and Witness of the Churches in Mizoram. (1976). Serkawn, Mizoram: Literature Committee, Baptist Church of Mizoram.

Hocken, Peter D.:

2002a. Art. Church, Theology of the. In: Burgess, Stanley M.; van der Maas, Eduard M. (eds.): The New International Dictionary of Pentecostal and Charismatic Movements. Grand Rapids: Zondervan, pp. 544-51.

2002b. Art. Harper, Michael Claude. In: Burgess, Stanley M.; van der Maas, Eduard M. (eds.): The New International Dictionary of Pentecostal and Charismatic Movements. Grand Rapids: Zondervan, pp. 689-90.

2002c. Art. Charismatic Movement. In: Burgess, Stanley M.; van der Maas, Eduard M. (eds.): The New International Dictionary of Pentecostal and Charismatic Movements. Grand Rapids: Zondervan, pp. 477-519.

1996. Theological Reflections on the "Toronto Blessing." Papers from the 25th Annual Meeting of the Society for Pentecostal Studies. Toronto.

Hodges, Melvin L.:

1999. The Indigenous Church. (1959). Springfield, Mo.: Gospel Publishing House. 11th ed.

Hoefer, Herbert E.:

1991. Churchless Christianity. A Report of Research Among Non-baptised Believers in Christ in Rural and Urban Tamilnadu, India, with Practical and Theological Reflections. Madras: Gurukul Publications.

Hoerschelmann, Werner:

1972. English Transcript of an Interview with Henry D. Joseph, Madras. 21/05/1972. (unpublished manuscript).

1973. English Transcript of an Interview with Sadhu Yesudhason, Kanjiracode. 11/02/1973. (unpublished manuscript).

1977. Christliche Gurus. Darstellung von Selbstverständnis und Funktion indigenen Christseins durch unabhängige, charismatisch geführte Gruppen in Südindien. (Studien zur Interkulturellen Geschichte des Christentums; 12). Frankfurt am Main: Peter Lang.

1998. Christian Gurus. A study on the life and work of Christian Charismatic Leaders in South India. Chennai: Gurukul Lutheran Theological College and Research Institute.

Hollenweger, Walter J.:

1965/1967. Handbuch der Pfingstbewegung. 10 Bde. Genf.

1988. The Pentecostals. (Enthusiastisches Christentum <engl.>). (1972). Peabody, Mass.: Hendrickson Publishers. 3rd ed.

1993. Verheißung und Verhängnis der Pfingstbewegung. In: Evangelische Theologie. Gütersloh. 53: 265-88.

1996. Von der Azusa-Street zum Toronto-Phänomen. Geschichtliche Wurzeln der Pfingstbewegung. In: Concilium. Mainz. 32: 209-16.

1997. Charismatisch-pfingstliches Christentum. Herkunft, Situation, Ökumenische Chancen. Göttingen: Vandenhoeck & Ruprecht. [Engl. as Pentecostalism, 1998]

Horn, J. Nico:

1989. From Rags to Riches. An analysis of the Faith movement and its relation to the classical Pentecostal movement. Pretoria: University of South Africa.

Horton, Harold:

1976. The Gifts of the Spirit. (1934). Nottingham: Assemblies of God Gospel Publishing House. 10th ed.

Horton, Stanley M.:

1995. The Last Things. In: Horton, Stanley M. (ed.): Systematic Theology. Revised Edition. Springfield, Mo.: Logion Press, pp. 597-638.

Houtart, François:

1974. Religion and Ideology in Sri Lanka. Bangalore: TPI.

Hunt, W. S.:

1920/1933. The Anglican Church in Travancore and Cochin 1816-1916. 2 vols. Kottayam.

Hunter, Harold D.:

1996. "Wir sind die Kirche." Neuer Kongregationalismus aus der Sicht der Pfingstbewegung. In: Concilium. Mainz. 32: 217-20.

1997. Beniah at the Apostolic Crossroads. Little Noticed Crosscurrents of B. H. Irwin, Charles Fox Parham, Frank Sandford, A. J. Tomlinson. In: Cyberjournal for Pentecostal-Charismatic Research. www.pctii/cyberj/hunter.html (01/03/2001). No. 1.

2002 International Pentecostal Holiness Church. In: www.pctii.org/arc/iphc.html (13/03/2002)

Hutchison, W. R.:

1987. Errand to the world. Chicago: University of Chicago Press.

Hutten, Kurt:

1989. Seher, Grübler, Enthusiasten. Das Buch der traditionellen Sekten und religiösen Sonderbewegungen. Stuttgart: Quell Verlag. 14th ed.

idea e. V. — Evangelische Nachrichtenagentur (ed.):

1995. Gottes Geist oder Gotteslästerung? Die Diskussion um den Toronto-Segen verschärft sich. Eine zweite Dokumentation mit Kommentaren, Analysen und Berichten zu einem umstrittenen charismatischen Phänomen. (idea Dokumentation 10/95). Wetzlar: idea.

India Full Gospel Bible College:

n.d. Prospectus. Andersonpet, Karnataka.

India Missions Association:

1994. Orissa State. Unreached Areas. Pincodewise Status Report as on May 1994. Madras.

Indian Pentecostal Assemblies:

1991. Bethel Faith Sparkling Bible College. Commemoration of 10th year, March 1991. Souvenir. Coimbatore.

Indian Pentecostal Church:

1974. Jubilee Souvenir 1924-1974. <eng./malay.>. Kumbanadu, Kerala.

1982. Golden Jubilee Souvenir, 1932-1982. Indian Pentecostal Church of God, Andhra Pradesh. Vijayawada.

1991. Memorandum of Association and Constitution of the Indian Pentecostal Church of God. Kumbanadu, Kerala.

1992. Golden Jubilee Souvenir, 1942-1992. Zion Bible College, Gunadala. Vijayawada.

Ingram, J. H.:

1936. Final report on my trip to India. In: The Church of God Evangel. Cleveland, Tennessee. 8. August, pp. 10-12, 15.

Jacob, Chinnappa (ed.):

1993. Twin Cities Christian Directory. Hyderabad-Secunderabad. Secunderabad: GIFTS of A.P.

Jacob, Mathew:

1995. "Evangelism Is My Life." Interview with Rev. Fr. Rufus Pereira, Editor of Charisindia and Director of the First Catholic-Charismatic Bible College in India. In: Faith Today. New Delhi. November, pp. 43-44.

Jaffarian, Michael E. (ed.):

1981. The Madras Christian Directory. Madras: Church Growth Research Centre.

Jain, Madhu:

1996. Marriage. A Search for Intimacy. In: India Today. New Delhi. Nr. 24, 31. December, pp. 78-85.

Jeevanandam, N.:

ca. 1993. Autobiographische Aufzeichnungen in englischer Sprache. (unpublished manuscript). Madras.

Jeevaratnam, Lam:

1948. Concerning Demons. Questions and Answers. (1936). Gudivada, Andhra Pradesh. 4th ed.

Jesus Calls:

ca. 1992. Campaign Preparation Manual (For the use of the campaign organizers only). Madras.

Jeyachandran, P.:

1991. A Critical Analysis of the Ideology and Practice of Communications in Bro. Dhinakaran's (Jesus Calls) Ministry. (M.Th. Thesis, Tamilnadu Theological College). Madurai.

Jeyanesan, P.:

1990. kōlār taṅka vayal pakutiyiluḷla pentēkōstē iyakkam parriya camūkaviyal, uḷaviyal marrum iraiyiyal cārnta oru matippīṭu. (B.D. Thesis, Tamilnadu Theological College). Madurai.

Jeyaraj, Robert (ed.):

1995. The General Council of the Assemblies of God of India, February 20-22, 1995, New Delhi. New Delhi.

Job, E. J. Chandran:

1989. Guide to Divine Healing. Bombay: Published by the author.

John, George; Palavesamuthu, Daniel (eds.):

ca. 1990. anāti kirubai. (teyvīka viṭutalai veḷiyīṭu; 1). cennai: appōstala kiristava cabai.

John, M. O.:

n.d. My Witness unto Christ. (Edited by M. J. Xavier). T. Kalupatti.

Johns, Cheryl Bridges:

1995. The Adolescence of Pentecostalism. In Search of a Legitimate Sectarian Identity. In: Pneuma. Gaithersburg, Md. 17: 3-17.

Johnson, I. C.:

1971. A Study of the Theories and Practices of the Pentecostal Movement in India in the Light of the Lutheran Understanding of the Christian Faith. (B.D. Thesis, Gurukul College). Madras.

Johnson, P. D.:

1976. vākkurutiyin niraivērram (Promise Fulfilled). Trivandrum: Assemblies of God.

Jongeneel, Jan A. B. (ed.):

1992. Pentecost, Mission and Ecumenism. Essays on Intercultural Theology. Festschrift of Professor Walter J. Hollenweger. (Studien zur interkulturellen Geschichte des Christentums; 75). Frankfurt am Main: Peter Lang.

Judah, J. Stillson:

1967. The History and Philosophy of the Metaphysical Movements in America. Philadelphia: Westminster.

Kärkkäinen, Veli-Matti:

2002. Toward a Pneumatological Theology of Religions. A Pentecostal-Charismatic Inquiry. In: International Review of Mission. Geneva. 91: 187-98.

Kariyil, Antony:

1995. Church and Society in Kerala. A Sociological Study. New Delhi: Intercultural Publications.

Ketcham, Maynard L.:
1973. History of Pentecost. (unpublished manuscript).

Kim, Dongsoo:
1999. The Healing of Han in Korean Pentecostalism. In: Journal of Pentecostal Theology. Sheffield. 15: 123-39.

Komanapalli, Ernest P.:
ca. 1991. Burning Heart. A Life Sketch of Pastor P. L. Paramjothi. Antarvedipalem, Andhra Pradesh: I.P.C. Ministries. 2nd ed.

Kosambi M. (ed.):
2000. Pandita Ramabai Through Her Own Words. Delhi: Oxford University Press.

Koshy, George:
1989. Mystery of Apostasy. The Church Through the Centuries. Bombay: Published by the author.

Künzlen, Gottfried:
1994. Der Neue Mensch. Eine Untersuchung zur säkularen Religionsgeschichte der Moderne. München: Wilhelm Fink.

Kutty, T. S. Samuel:
2000. The Place and Contribution of Dalits in Select Pentecostal Churches in Central Kerala from 1922-1972. New Delhi: ISPCK.

Land, Steven J.:
1993. Pentecostal Spirituality. A Passion for the Kingdom. (Journal of Pentecostal Theology Supplement Series; 1). Sheffield: Sheffield Academic Press.

Lange, Dieter:
1981. Eine Gemeinschaft bricht sich Bahn. Die deutsche Gemeinschaftsbewegung im ausgehenden 19. und beginnenden 20. Jahrhundert und ihre Stellung zu Kirche, Theologie und Pfingstbewegung. Berlin: Evangelische Verlagsanstalt. 2nd ed.

Lazarus, Sam (ed.):
1992. Proclaiming Christ. A Handbook of Indigenous Missions in India. Madras: Church Growth Association of India.

Lederle, Henry I.:
1988. Treasures Old and New. Interpretations of "Spirit-Baptism" in the Charismatic Renewal Movement. Peabody, Mass.: Hendrickson.

Leggett, Dennis:
1989. The Assemblies of God Statement on Sanctification (A Brief Review by Calvin and Wesley). In: Pneuma. Gaithersburg, Md. 11: 113-22.

Leembruggen-Kallberg, Elisabeth:
2002. Art. Sri Lanka. In: Burgess, Stanley M.; van der Maas, Eduard M. (eds.): The New International Dictionary of Pentecostal and Charismatic Movements. Grand Rapids: Zondervan, pp. 248-53.

Lim, David:

1995. Spiritual Gifts. In: Horton, Stanley M. (ed.): Systematic Theology. Revised Edition. Springfield, Mo.: Logion Press, pp. 457-88.

Livesey, Margaret:

n.d. Together with God. o. O.: Hulme and Whitehead.

Luke, P. Y.; Carman, John B.:

1968. Village Christians and Hindu Culture. Study of a Rural Church in Andhra Pradesh, South India. London: Lutterworth.

Lutgendorf, Philip:

1994. The Life of a Text. Performing the Râmcaritmânas of Tulsidas. Delhi: Oxford University Press.

MacNicol, Nicol:

1926. Pandita Ramabai. Calcutta: Association Press.

1930. Pandita Ramabai. Die Mutter der Ausgestoßenen. Stuttgart; Basel: Evang. Missionsverlag.

MacRobert, Iain:

1988. The Black Roots and White Racism of Early Pentecostalism in the USA. Basingstoke: Macmillan.

1992. The Black Roots of Pentecostalism. In: Jongeneel, Jan A. B. (ed.): Pentecost, Mission and Ecumenism. Essays on Intercultural Theology. Festschrift of Professor Walter J. Hollenweger. (Studien zur interkulturellen Geschichte des Christentums; 75). Frankfurt am Main: Peter Lang, pp. 73-84.

Madras Pentecostal Assembly:

1934. Memorandum of Association of the Madras Pentecostal Assembly (Tamil), 17.08.1934. (unpublished manuscript). Madras.

Mahoney, Ralph (ed.):

1993. The Shepherd's Staff. India Edition. Madras: India Bible Literature.

Maier, Gerhard:

1995. Gemeindeaufbau und Gemeindewachstum. Zur Geschichte, Theologie und Praxis der "church growth"–Bewegung. (Erlanger Monographien aus Mission und Ökumene; 22). Erlangen: Verlag der Ev.-Luth. Mission.

Maloney, Doris:

n.d. Clarence T. Maloney. Ready to Go. N.p.: By the author.

Mar Aprem:

1984. Indian Christian Directory. Bangalore: Bangalore Parish, Church of the East.

Maranatha:

1988. Silver Jubilee Souvenir, 1963-1988. Madras.

Mark, Ivar R.:

1973. The Origin and Development of the Charismatic Movement in India. (M.Th. Thesis, Howard University).

Martin, Chandran Paul (ed.):

1992. UELCI Directory 1992. Madras: United Evangelical Lutheran Churches in India.

Martin, David:

1990. Tongues of Fire. The Explosion of Protestantism in Latin America. Oxford: Basil Blackwell.

2002. Pentecostalism. The World Their Parish. Oxford: Blackwell.

Martin, Francis:

1990. Art. Knowledge, Word of. In: Burgess, Stanley M.; McGee, Gary B.; Alexander, Patrick H. (ed.): Dictionary of Pentecostal and Charismatic Movements. Grand Rapids: Zondervan. 4th ed., pp. 527-29.

Mascarenhas, Fio:

1977. Historical Note on the Charismatic Renewal in India. In: Word and Worship. Bangalore. 10, 1: 78-80.

Masilamani-Meyer, Eveline:

2004. Guardians of Tamilnadu. Folk Deities, Folk Religion, Hindu Themes. (Neue Hallesche Berichte; 5). Halle: Verlag der Franckeschen Stiftungen.

Mathew, A. C.:

1992. Christian Baptism. Madras: Christian Literature Society.

Mathew, Samuel:

1990. The Pentecostal Churches in Kerala and Its Witness in the Socio-Political Life. (M.Th. Thesis, Serampore University). Kottayam.

Matthew, Thomson K.:

2002. Art. Abraham, K. E. In: Burgess, Stanley M.; van der Maas, Eduard M. (eds.): The New International Dictionary of Pentecostal and Charismatic Movements. Grand Rapids: Zondervan, p. 305.

Mauss, Marcel:

1990. Die Gabe. Form und Funktion des Austauschs in archaischen Gesellschaften (Essai sur le don <German translation>). (1950). Frankfurt am Main: Suhrkamp.

Maxwell, David:

1995. Witches, Prophets and Avenging Spirits. The Second Christian Movement in North East Zimbabwe. In: Journal of Religion in Africa. Leiden. 25: 309-39.

1999. Historicizing Christian Independency. The Southern African Pentecostal Movement c. 1908-60. In: Journal of African History. Cambridge. 40: 243-64.

McClung, Grant:

1985. From Bridges (McGavran 1955) to Waves (Wagner 1983). Pentecostals and the Church Growth Movement. In: Pneuma. Pasadena, Calif. 7: 5-18.

1990. Art. Evangelists. In: Burgess, Stanley M.; McGee, Gary B.; Alexander, Patrick H. (eds.): Dictionary of Pentecostal and Charismatic Movements. Grand Rapids: Zondervan. 4th ed., pp. 288-89.

McConnell, D. R.:

1990. Ein anderes Evangelium? Eine historische und biblische Analyse der modernen Glaubensbewegung. (A Different Gospel <German translation>). (1988). Hamburg: Verlag C. M. Fliß.

McCracken, Horace:

1943. History of Church of God Missions. Cleveland: Church of God World Missions Board.

McGavran, Donald:

1979. Understanding the Church in India (Ethnic Realities and the Church). Bombay: Gospel Literature Service.

McGee, Gary B.:

1986. "This Gospel . . . Shall Be Preached." A History and Theology of Assemblies of God Foreign Missions to 1959. Springfield, Mo.: Gospel Publishing House.

1990a. Art. Garr, Alfred Goodrich Sr. In: Burgess, Stanley M.; McGee, Gary B.; Alexander, Patrick H. (eds.): Dictionary of Pentecostal and Charismatic Movements. Grand Rapids: Zondervan. 4th ed., pp. 328-29.

1990b. Art. Burgess, John Harry. In: Burgess, Stanley M.; McGee, Gary B.; Alexander, Patrick H. (eds.): Dictionary of Pentecostal and Charismatic Movements. Grand Rapids: Zondervan. 4th ed., pp. 102-3.

1996a. From East to West. The Early Pentecostal Movement in India and Its Influence in the West. Papers from the 25th Annual Meeting of the Society for Pentecostal Studies. Toronto.

1996b. Pentecostal Phenomena and Revivals in India. Implications for Indigenous Church Leadership. In: International Bulletin of Missionary Research. New Haven. 20: 112-17.

1999. "Latter Rain" Falling in the East. Early Twentieth-Century Pentecostalism in India and the Debate over Speaking in Tongues. In: Church History. Red Bank, New Jersey. 68: 648-65.

2001. Shortcut to Language Preparations? Radical Evangelicals, Missions, and the Gift of Tongues. In: International Bulletin of Missionary Research. New Haven. 25: 118-23.

2002. Art. India. I. Pentecostal and Pentecostal-like Movements (1860-1910). In: Burgess, Stanley M.; van der Maas, Eduard M. (eds.): The New International Dictionary of Pentecostal and Charismatic Movements. Grand Rapids: Zondervan, pp. 118-22.

McGee, Gary B. (ed.):

1991. Initial Evidence. Historical and Biblical Perspectives on the Pentecostal Doctrine of Spirit Baptism. Peabody, Mass.: Hendrickson Publishers.

McGee, Gary B.; Rodgers, Darrin J.:

2002. Art. Abrams, Minnie F. In: Burgess, Stanley M.; van der Maas, Eduard M. (eds.): The New International Dictionary of Pentecostal and Charismatic Movements. Grand Rapids: Zondervan, pp. 305-6.

McLeish, Alexander:
1955. The Christian Handbook of India 1954-55. (Published for the National Christian Council of India). Mhow, Madhya Pradesh: World Dominion Press.

McLeish, Alexander; Watts, Lincoln:
1951. Directory of Churches and Missions in India and Pakistan 1951. (Published for the Christian Council). Ootacamund, Tamilnadu: World Dominion Press.

Melzer, Friso:
1976. Christliche Ashrams in Südindien. Begegnungen mit Bruderschaften. (Erlanger Taschenbücher; 37). Erlangen: Verlag der Ev.-Luth. Mission.

Meyer, Eveline:
1986. Ankalaparamecuvari. A Goddess of Tamilnadu, Her Myths and Cult. (Beiträge zur Südasienforschung; 107). Stuttgart: Steiner.

Mlecko, Joel D.:
1982. The Guru in Hindu Tradition. In: Numen. Leiden. 29: 33-61.

Moffatt, Michael:
1979. An Untouchable Community in South India. Structure and Consensus. Princeton: Princeton University Press.

Mohan, D.:
1989. New Life Assembly of God Church Built through Faith. Madras: New Life Assembly of God Church.

Moltmann, Jürgen; Kuschel, Karl-Josef (eds.):
1996. Die Pfingstbewegung als ökumenische Herausforderung. In: Concilium. Mainz. 32: 207-96.

Monai, C. P.:
1994. New India Daiva Sabha Charithram <malay.> (History of New India Church of God). Chingavanam: New India Church of God.

Moore-Gilbert B. J.:
1997. Postcolonial Theory. London: Verso.

Moorhead, Max Wood:
1920. The Latter Rain in Calcutta, India. In: The Pentecostal Evangel. Springfield, Mo. 17. April.

Morgan, Louis:
2002. Art. Cook, Robert F. In: Burgess, Stanley M.; van der Maas, Eduard M. (eds.): The New International Dictionary of Pentecostal and Charismatic Movements. Grand Rapids: Zondervan, pp. 560-61.

Mundadan, A. Mathias:
1984. History of Christianity in India from the Beginning up till the Middle of the Sixteenth Century (up to 1542). (CHAI History of Christianity in India, Volume 1). Bangalore: Church History Association of India.

342

Myers, Dora P.:

n.d. My Life's Story. (unpublished manuscript, Dixon Pentecostal Research Centre, Lee College Library). Cleveland, Tennessee.

1960. Daiva Sabha Charithram <malay.> (Church of God History). Mulakuzha, Kerala: Church of God in India.

Nava Jeevan Public School:

1994. Decennary Celebrations 1984 to 1994, Souvenir. Bheemunipatnam, Andhra Pradesh.

Neill, Stephen:

1964. A History of Christian Missions. Harmondsworth: Penguin.

n.d. Out of Bondage. Christ and the Indian Villager. London: Cargate Press.

Nelson, Amirtharaj:

1975. A New Day in Madras. A Study of Protestant Churches in Madras. (Zugleich: D.Miss. Thesis, Fuller Theological Seminary, School of World Mission, 1974). Pasadena, Calif.: William Carey Library.

Neuman, H. Terris:

1990. Cultic Origins of Word-Faith Theology within the Charismatic Movement. In: Pneuma. Gaithersburg, Md. 12: 32-55.

New India Bible College:

1994. Catalogue 1994-1995. Changanacherry, Kerala.

New Life Assembly of God Church:

1994. 20th Anniversary Souvenir. 7th March 1994. Madras.

Nichol, John Thomas:

1966. Pentecostalism. New York: Harper and Row.

Nickelson, G.:

1993. A Man Who Trusts God. (Autobiographische Aufzeichnungen). (unpublished manuscript). Kolar Gold Fields.

Oommen, T. G.:

1979. I.P.C.yum Anpathu Varshathe Sevana Charithravum <malay.> (I.P.C. and History of Fifty Years Ministry). Mallapally, Kerala: Mallapally Printers.

1984. Atmakatha <malay.> (Life History). Jeleeb Al Shyoukh, Kuwait: Kuwait I.P.C.

Oosthuizen, Gerhardus C.:

1975. Pentecostal Penetration into the Indian Community in Metropolitan Durban, South Africa. Durban: Human Sciences Research Council Pretoria, South Africa.

Orr, J. Edwin:

1973. The Flaming Tongue. Chicago: Moody Press.

1976. Evangelical Awakenings in Southern Asia. Minneapolis, Minnesota: Bethany Fellowship. 2nd ed.

Parathazham, Paul:
1996. Neo-Pentecostalism in India. Preliminary Report of a National Survey. In: Word and Worship. Bangalore. 29: 81-101.

Parker, Christián:
1996. Popular Religion and Modernization in Latin America. A Different Logic (Otra lógica en América Latina <engl.>). (1993). Maryknoll, N.Y.: Orbis.

Parker, Stephen E.:
1996. Led by the Spirit. Toward a Practical Theology of Pentecostal Discernment and Decision Making. (Journal of Pentecostal Theology Supplement Series; 7). Sheffield: Sheffield Academic Press.

Pastor Chacko's family members (eds.):
1980. Pastor P. T. Chacko. A Man of God. Kumbanadu, Kerala: Hebron Printing House.

Paul, K. R.; Paul, Lydia:
1977. eṅkaḷ cāṭciyum cabaiyiṉ ūḷiyamum. Bangalore: Gospel Prayer Hall.

Paul, M. Victor:
1990. Parish Renewal. In: Andhra Christian Theological College (ed.): Reflections on Theology Today. Papers Presented by the ACTC-Faculty During the Academic Year 1988-89 on Theology and the Mission and Ministry of the Church. Hyderabad, pp. 104-7.

Pentecostal Fellowship of India:
1991. Inaugural Convention Madras 1991. Souvenir. Madras.

Petersen, Douglas:
1996. Not by Might nor by Power. A Pentecostal Theology of Social Concern in Latin America. Oxford: Regnum Books International.

Pfister, Raymond:
1995. Soixante ans de Pentecôtisme en Alsace. (Studien zur interkulturellen Geschichte des Christentums; 93). Strasburg: Peter Lang.

Philip, P. O.:
1934. Directory of Christian Missions in India, Burma and Ceylon, Incorporating a Decennial Survey. 1934-1935. Nagpur, Maharashtra: The National Christian Council.

Plakkottam, Joseph L.:
1995. The Role of the Catholic Charismatic Renewal in "Evangelization 2000" in India. (unpublished manuscript). Hyderabad.

Poloma, Margaret M.:
1995. Charisma, Institutionalization and Social Change. In: Pneuma. Gaithersburg, Md. 17: 245-52.
1996. By Their Fruits . . . : A Sociological and Theological Assessment of the "Toronto Blessing." Papers from the 25th Annual Meeting of the Society for Pentecostal Studies. Toronto.

Poonen, Zac:

n.d. The Truth That We Believe. Bangalore: Christian Fellowship Centre.
1982. Secrets of Victory. Bangalore: Hidden Treasures.
1990. A Good Foundation. Katunayake, Sri Lanka: New Life Literature.
1994. Know Your Enemy. A guide for young people to overcome Satan. Katunayake, Sri Lanka: New Life Literature.

Pothen, Abraham T.:

1988. The India Pentecostal Church of God and Its Contribution to Church Growth. (M.A. Thesis, Fuller Theological Seminary, School of World Mission). Pasadena, Calif.
1990. Indigenous Cross-Cultural Missions in India, and Their Contribution to Church Growth. With Special Emphasis on Pentecostal-Charismatic Missions. (Ph.D. Thesis, Fuller Theological Seminary, School of World Mission). Pasadena, Calif.

Powers, Janet Evert:

2000. Missionary Tongues? In: Journal of Pentecostal Theology. Sheffield. 17: 39-55.

Prabakaran, Justin:

1989. vētam ariya vētam. Madras: Rainbow Church.
1990. kēḷuṅkaḷ koṭukkappaṭum. Madras: Rainbow Church.

Prabhakaran, M. E.:

1990. Andhra Christians — Some Demographic and Ecclesial Issues. In: Religion and Society. Bangalore. 37: 4-28.

Prasad, Ram D.:

1990. Kalki Maha Avatar. Odaimarichan, Tamilnadu: Shri Lahari Krishna Publications.

Pulikottil, Paulson:

2001. As East and West Met in God's Own Country. Encounter of Western Pentecostalism with Native Pentecostalism in Kerala. In: Cyberjournal for Pentecostal-Charismatic Research. www.pctii/cyberj (2/9/2001) No. 10.

Purdy, Vernon L.:

1995. Divine Healing. In: Horton, Stanley M. (ed.): Systematic Theology. Revised Edition. Springfield, Mo.: Logion Press, pp. 489-525.

Rajakumar, A. (ed.):

1994. Madras Christian Directory. Madras: Church Growth Research Centre.

Rajamani, C.:

1981. The Cult of Muthukutty Swami. (M.Th. Thesis, United Theological College). Bangalore.

Rajamoni, P. S.:

n.d. Private notes on the history of the Assemblies of God in Tamilnadu: (1) Interview with Y. Jeyaraj, August 1976. (2) Interview with David Stewart, 15.10.1976. (3) Interview with Kenneth Weigel, summer 1976. (4) Interview with Ernest Sorbo, summer 1976. (5) E. Sorbo: Eurasia Group Report during the School of Missions, June 1976.

(6) Fragments from an interview with Doris Edwards. (7) Letter of Carl Holleman to P. S. Rajamoni, 26/11/1973. (8) Nine lecture preparations in Tamil on the history of the Assemblies of God in India. (unpublished manuscript). Madurai.
1989. iṉṉum oru vāḻkkai iruntāl. K. P. Valasai, Tamilnadu: Paripoorna Jeevan Press.

Rajendran, S. T. (ed.):
1992. tēcattiṉ tīrkkatarici. niṉaivu malar. Madras: Rainbow Church.

Rajakutty, O. M.:
1994. World Missionary Evangelism of India (With special reference to the ministry of Kerala State). (unpublished manuscript). Kariamplave, Kerala.

Rao, Kande Prasad:
1991. The Law Relating to Marriages of Christians in India. Hyderabad: Asia Law House.

Ratnasingam, Jacob (ed.):
1985. An Exposition of the Book of Revelation. (1975). (Publication No. 1). Madras: The Pentecostal Mission. 2nd ed.

Reed, David Arthur:
1978. Origins and Development of the Theology of Oneness Pentecostalism in the United States. (Ph.D. diss., Boston University). Boston.

Reginald, N.:
1995. A Study of the Growth of the Churches in the Southern District of the Assemblies of God, from 1981-1994. (M.Th. Thesis, South Asia Institute of Advanced Christian Studies). Bangalore.

Reimer, Ingrid:
1991. Evangelistisch-missionarische Werke und Einrichtungen im deutschsprachigen Raum. Einzeldarstellungen — Übersichten — Adressen. Stuttgart: Christliches Verlagshaus.

Riss, Richard Michael:
1987. Latter Rain. The Latter Rain Movement of 1948 and the Mid-Twentieth-Century Evangelical Awakening. Mississauga, Ont.: Honeycomb Visual Productions.
1990. Art. Women, Role of. In: Burgess, Stanley M.; McGee, Gary B.; Alexander, Patrick H. (eds.): Dictionary of Pentecostal and Charismatic Movements. Grand Rapids: Zondervan. 4th ed., pp. 893-99.

Robeck, Jr., Cecil M.:
1990a. Art. National Association of Evangelicals. In: Burgess, Stanley M.; McGee, Gary B.; Alexander, Patrick H. (eds.): Dictionary of Pentecostal and Charismatic Movements. Grand Rapids: Zondervan. 4th ed., pp. 634-36.
1992. The Social Concern of Early American Pentecostalism. In: Jongeneel, Jan A. B. (ed.): Pentecost, Mission and Ecumenism. Essays on Intercultural Theology. Festschrift of Professor Walter J. Hollenweger. (Studien zur interkulturellen Geschichte des Christentums; 75). Frankfurt am Main: Peter Lang, pp. 97-106.
1993. Pentecostal Origins from a Global Perspective. In: Hunter, Harold D.; Hocken, Pe-

ter D. (eds.): All Together in One Place. Theological Papers from the Brighton Conference on World Evangelization. (Journal of Pentecostal Theology Supplement Series; 4). Sheffield: Sheffield Academic Press, pp. 166-80.

1999. Making Sense of Pentecostalism in a Global Context. Papers from the 28th Annual Meeting of the Society for Pentecostal Studies. Springfield, Mo.

2002. Art. Azusa Street Revival. In: Burgess, Stanley M.; van der Maas, Eduard M. (eds.): The New International Dictionary of Pentecostal and Charismatic Movements. Grand Rapids: Zondervan, pp. 344-49.

Robinson, Elizabeth B.:

1990a. Art. Schoonmaker, Christian H. In: Burgess, Stanley M.; McGee, Gary B.; Alexander, Patrick H. (eds.): Dictionary of Pentecostal and Charismatic Movements. Grand Rapids: Zondervan. 4th ed., pp. 770-71.

1990b. Art. Cummings, Robert Wallace. In: Burgess, Stanley M.; McGee, Gary B.; Alexander, Patrick H. (eds.): Dictionary of Pentecostal and Charismatic Movements. Grand Rapids: Zondervan. 4th ed., p. 232.

Rose, J. John:

1982. oruvicai oppukkoṭukkappaṭṭa vicuvācam. Kadamalaikuntu, Tamilnadu: Full Gospel Pentecostal Church.

Rosenkranz, G.:

1977. Die christliche Mission. München: Chr. Kaiser, pp. 218-19.

Rothermund, Dieter (ed.):

1995. Indien. Kultur, Geschichte, Politik, Wirtschaft, Umwelt. Ein Handbuch. München: C. H. Beck.

Rouse, R., Neill, S.:

1994. A History of the Ecumenical Movement, 1517-1968. Geneva: World Council of Churches.

Rzepkowski, Horst:

1991. Art. Indien. In: Bäumer, Remigius; Scheffczyk, Leo (eds.): Marienlexikon. St. Ottilien: EOS Verlag, pp. 296-300.

Saju:

1994. Kerala Pentekosthu Charithram <malay.> (Kerala Pentecostal History). Kottayam, Kerala: Good News Publication.

Sam, L.:

1983. Pastor A. C. Samuel. A Short Biography <malay.>. Trivandrum, Kerala: Pastor T. J. Rajan.

Sam Mathews, K.:

1990. An Assessment of the Dawn and Growth of the Indigenous Pentecostal Movement in the State of Andhra Pradesh. (M.Th. Thesis, South Asia Institute of Advanced Christian Studies). Bangalore.

Samuel, P. Frederick S.:

1988. Urban Evangelism Model — III. Pastor Sam Chelladurai's Apostolic Fellowship Tabernacle. Church Growth Research Centre. (unpublished manuscript). Madras.

Samuel, P. M.:

1980. Autobiography. Vijayawada, Andhra Pradesh: The Zion Printing House.

1989. eṉṉai pelappaṭuttiṉavarālē (autobiography <tam.>). (cīyōṉ pūrikaiyiṉ ciṟappu veliyīṭu; 1). tiruppaccūr, ceṅkai māvaṭṭam: intiya pentekostē tēvacapai, tamiḻnāṭu.

Samuel, Reddimalla:

1971. A Study of the Bakht Singh Movement, Its Origin and Growth Especially in Andhra Pradesh. (B.D. Thesis, United Theological College). Bangalore.

Santhosam, B. A. James:

1990. Jesus Met Me. Madras: Prince of Peace Ministries.

Sargunam, M. Ezra:

1974. Multiplying Churches in Modern India. An Experiment in Madras. Madras: Federation of Evangelical Churches in India.

ca. 1994. Church Planting among the Responsive People Groups of India. (unpublished manuscript). Madras.

1994. Religious Toleration and Social Harmony. Madras: Dayan Publishers.

Sargunam, M. Ezra (ed.):

1992. Mission Mandate. A Compendium on the Perspective of Missions in India. Madras: Mission India 2000.

Sarosh T. Jacob:

1993. Pentecostal Yearbook — 1993 <malay.>. Pathanapuram, Kerala: Yearbook Committee.

1994. Pentecostal Yearbook — 1994 <malay.>. Pathanapuram, Kerala: Yearbook Committee.

1995. Pentecostal Yearbook — 1995 <malay.>. Pathanapuram, Kerala: Yearbook Committee.

Satyavrata, Ivan Moses:

ca. 1994. Foundations for Christian Maturity. Bangalore: Full Gospel Assembly of God.

Schäfer, Klaus:

1993. "Demonstration of the Spirit and of Power." A Necessary Critical Note on the Recent Mass "Healing Festival" in Hyderabad. In: Bangalore Theological Forum. Bangalore. 25, 2 & 3: 37-48.

Schmidgall, Paul

1997. 90 Jahre deutsche Pfingstbewegung. Erzhausen: Leuchter-Verlag.

Schmieder, Lucida:

1982. Geisttaufe. Ein Beitrag zur neueren Glaubensgeschichte. (Paderborner Theologische Studien; 13). Paderborn: Schöningh.

Schoonmaker, Christian H.:

1908. My Baptism in the Holy Spirit. In: Cloud of Witnesses to Pentecost in India. Pamphlet Number Six. Bombay. November.

Selva Raj, C.:

ca. 1986. The Rising Up of the Righteous Man from India and the Great Wonders to Happen Through Him in the World. Malavilai, Tamilnadu: Beginning Pentecostal Truth Church.

Sepúlveda, Juan:

1999. Indigenous Pentecostalism and the Chilean Experience. In: Anderson, Allan H.; Hollenweger, Walter J. (eds.): Pentecostals after a Century. Global Perspectives on a Movement in Transition. (Journal of Pentecostal Theology Supplement Series; 15). Sheffield: Sheffield Academic Press, pp. 111-34.

Sesselmann, Matthias:

1988. Die Geschichte des Jesus Treff. Rinteln: Werner Hoppe.

Shalm, George:

1954. Tamil Nad Toiler. Tamil Nad Pentecostal Church, Associated with the Apostolic Church of Pentecost of Canada. Kodaikanal, Tamilnadu.

Shankar, Pappa:

1990/1991. Seven Letters to Rajiv Gandhi (Dates: 20/07/90; 20/11/90; 15/04/91; 10/05/91; 17/05/91). Two Formal Letters of Acknowledgement After Reception of the Letters by Rajiv Gandhi (Dates: 26/07/90; 30/11/90). (unpublished manuscript). Madras.

Shemeth, Scott:

1990. Art. Ketcham, Maynard L. In: Burgess, Stanley M.; McGee, Gary B.; Alexander, Patrick H. (eds.): Dictionary of Pentecostal and Charismatic Movements. Grand Rapids: Zondervan. 4th ed., p. 519.

Sheppard, Gerald T.:

1984. Pentecostals and the Hermeneutics of Dispensationalism. The Anatomy of an Uneasy Relationship. In: Pneuma. Pasadena, Calif. 6, 2: 5-33.

Shinde, Benjamin Prasad:

1974. The Contribution of the Assemblies of God to Church Growth in India. (M.A. Thesis, Fuller Theological Seminary, School of World Mission). Pasadena, Calif.

1975. Animism in Popular Hinduism. Survey of the literature and a viewpoint. (D.Miss., Fuller Theological Seminary, School of World Mission). Pasadena, Calif.

Sich, D.; Diesfeld, H. J.; Deigner, A.; Habermann, M. (eds.):

1993. Medizin und Kultur. Eine Propädeutik für Studierende der Medizin und der Ethnologie mit vier Seminaren in Kulturvergleichender Medizinischer Anthropologie. Frankfurt am Main.

Sion Fellowship:

ca. 1990. Newsletter. Hyderabad.

Smail, Thomas; Walker, Andrew; Wright, Nigel:

1994. "Revelation Knowledge" and Knowledge of Revelation. The Faith Movement and the Question of Heresy. In: Journal of Pentecostal Theology. Sheffield. 5: 57-77.

Smith, James K. A.:

1997. The Closing of the Book. Pentecostals, Evangelicals, and Sacred Writings. In: Journal of Pentecostal Theology. Sheffield. 11: 49-71.

Snell, Jeffrey T.:

1992. Beyond the Individual and into the World. A Call to Participation in the Larger Purposes of the Spirit on the Basis of Pentecostal Theology. In: Pneuma. Gaithersburg, Md. 14: 43-57.

Solivan, Samuel:

1998. The Spirit, Pathos and Liberation. Toward a Hispanic Pentecostal Theology. (Journal of Pentecostal Theology Supplement Series; 14). Sheffield: Sheffield Academic Press.

Solomon Raj, P.:

1986a. The Influence of Pentecostal Teaching on Some Folk Christian Religions in India. In: International Review of Mission. Geneva. 75: 39-46.

1986b. A Christian Folk Religion in India. A Study of the Small Church Movement in Andhra Pradesh, with a Special Reference to the Bible Mission of Devadas. (Studien zur Interkulturellen Geschichte des Christentums; 40). Frankfurt am Main: Peter Lang.

1995. Father Devadas and the Story of a Folk Church in India. In: Dharma Deepika. Madras. 1: 61-68.

Southern Asia Bible College:

1991. Chronicle. Forty years of ministerial training 1951-1991. Bangalore.

Spittler, Russell P.:

1994. Are Pentecostals and Charismatics Fundamentalists? A Review of American Uses of Theses Categories. In: Poewe, Karla (ed.): Charismatic Christianity as a Global Culture. Columbia, S.C.: University of South Carolina Press, pp. 103-16.

Srinivasan, Ranganayaki:

1991. Bhagwan Sri Yogi Ramsuratkumar. His Divine Life and Message. Nagercoil, Tamilnadu: Yogi Ramsuratkumar Manthralayam Trust.

Stanley, J. Simon:

1988. God's Next Move. Madras: Yesudasan Publications.

Stephen, M.:

1995. The Challenge of the Pentecostal Churches Today. An Insider's View. In: Jeevadhara. Kottayam, Kerala. 25: 274-81.

1999. Towards a Pentecostal Theology and Ethics. Kottayam: Chraisthava Bodhi Publications.

Stepper, Frank:

1995. Die Geschichte der charismatischen Bewegung. Ihre Entwicklung in lutherischen Kirchen, baptistischen, methodistischen, pfingstkirchlichen und freien Gemeinden sowie der katholischen Kirche. (idea Dokumentation 16/95). Wetzlar: idea.

Stout, Glen:

1994. Be Fruitful and Multiply. Visakhapatnam: Alpha Book Centre.

Stotts, George R.:

1981. Le Pentecôtisme au pays de Voltaire. Craponne: Viens et Vois.

Sullivan, Francis A.

2002. Art. Jeyaraj, Yesudian. In: Burgess, Stanley M.; van der Maas, Eduard M. (eds.): The New International Dictionary of Pentecostal and Charismatic Movements. Grand Rapids: Zondervan, pp. 809-10.

Sundara Rao, R. R.:

1990. Speaking in Tongues. A Socio-Cultural Investigation of Religious Experience. In: Gurukul Journal of Theological Studies. Madras. 1, 2: 41-52.

Sunder Raj, Ebe; Moses, Dhanapal; Samuel, Lynda (eds.):

1992. Management of Indian Missions. Madras: India Missions Association.

Sunder Singh, P. S.; Rajakumar, A. (eds.):

1989. Madras Christian Directory. Madras: Church Growth Research Centre.

Sundkler, Bengt Gustaf Malcolm:

1954. Church of South India. The Movement Towards Union 1900-1947. London: Lutterworth Press.

Surya Prakash, P.:

1993. Implications of Revival Preachings in India. In: The South Indian Churchman. Hyderabad. June-July: 3-6.

Synan, Vinson:

1971. The Holiness-Pentecostal Movement in the United States. Grand Rapids: Eerdmans.

Tamilnadu Theological College (ed.):

1989. Educated by the People of God. 20th Annual Report 1988-89. For the Governing Council April 11, 1989. Madurai.

Tan, D.:

2002. Art. Malaysia. In: Burgess, Stanley M.; van der Maas, Eduard M. (eds.): The New International Dictionary of Pentecostal and Charismatic Movements. Grand Rapids: Zondervan. S. 170-73.

Taves, Ann:

1999. Fits, Trances, and Visions. Experiencing Religion and Explaining Experience from Wesley to James. Princeton: Princeton University Press.

Thamby, V. A.:

1993. Our Own Personal and Family Profile. (unpublished manuscript). Chingavanam, Kerala.

Thannickal, John:

1975. Ashram. A Communicating Community. (D.Miss. Thesis, School of World Mission, Fuller Theological Seminary). Pasadena, Calif.

Thannickal, John (ed.):

1993. Jesus Christ Is Lord. The Pentecostal Fellowship of India Conference, New Delhi, Nov. 3-7, 1993. Bangalore: Pentecostal Fellowship of India.

The Pentecostal Mission:

n.d. The Biography of Pastor Paul. Madras.

1984. Doctrine, Rules and Regulation, 13/01/1984. (unpublished manuscript). Madras.

ca. 1985. Deeper Truths (Which Are Indispensable to Be Ready for His Coming). Madras: Pentecost Press Trust.

1986. Divine Healing Messages. (Publication No. 3). Madras: Pentecost Press Trust.

1987a. Baptism of the Holy Spirit. (Publication No. 11). Madras: Pentecost Press Trust.

1987b. Water Baptism. (Publication No. 8). Madras: Pentecost Press Trust.

1989. The Doctrine Concerning Worldliness. Madras: Pentecost Press Trust.

1993. New Testament Ministry (Part-I). A Study of the New Testament Ministry Compared with the Old Testament Levitical Priesthood. (Publication No. 11). Madras: Pentecost Press Trust.

1994. Divine Healing. (1980). (Publication No. 1). Madras: Pentecost Press Trust.

Thekkedath, Joseph:

1982. History of Christianity in India from the Middle of the Sixteenth to the End of the Seventeenth Century (1542-1700). (CHAI History of Christianity in India, Volume 2). Bangalore: Church History Association of India.

Titus, P. J.:

1992. The New Vision of Glory for World Missions. Dallas: Christ for India, Inc. Ministries.

Titus, P. J. (ed.):

n.d. Guidelines for the National Association for Theological Accreditation (NATA). NATA is the Accrediting Body of NAPTI. Bheemunipatnam, Andhra Pradesh: Jyoti Press.

1994. Manual of the National Association of Pentecostal Theological Institutions (NAPTI). Bheemunipatnam, Andhra Pradesh: Jyoti Press.

1995. Christian Ministers' Manual. Bheemunipatnam, Andhra Pradesh: C.O.T.R. College of Ministries.

University of Madras (ed.):

1982. Tamil Lexicon. (1924-1939). 7 vols. Madras: Macmillan India Press.

Varghese, Jose:

1980. The Origin and Development of Assemblies of God in Kerala. (B.Th. Thesis, Southern Asia Bible College). Bangalore.

Varghese, Kunjappan:

1999. Reformation Brings Revival. A Historical Survey of K. E. Abraham and his contributions in the founding of the Indian Pentecostal Church. Deerfield, Ill.: Ph.D. thesis, Trinity Evangelical Divinity School.

Varghese, T. M.; George, E. V.:

1973. Fifty Years. Short Story of the Church of God in India <malay.>. Mulakuzha: C.G.I. Press.

Varghese, T. P.:

1982. A Historical Analysis of the Growth and Development of the Pentecostal Churches in Kerala with Special Reference to the Church of God (Full Gospel) in India. (B.D. Thesis, United Theological College). Bangalore.

Vasantharaj Albert, S. (ed.):

1989. A Portrait of India. Madras: Church Growth Research Centre.
1995. Madurai Christian Directory. Madras: Church Growth Research Centre.

Vasantharaj Albert, S.; Rethinasamy, E. Johnson (eds.):

1997. Thanjavur Christian Directory. Madras: Church Growth Research Centre.

Vasu, N. G. John:

ca. 1950. My Mites to My Master. Madras: Madras Pentecostal Assembly.

Vasu, Stanley:

1995. Balm of Gilead. A special edition in memory of Pastor Prabhudoss Vasu. Madras: Madras Pentecostal Assembly.

Vaughan, John N.:

1984. The World's Twenty Largest Churches. Grand Rapids: Baker.

Verghese, Habel G.:

1974. K. E. Abraham. An Apostle from Modern India. (A Brief Life Story of Rev. Dr. K. E. Abraham). Kadambanad, Kerala: The Christian Literature Service of India.

Verghese, Paul (ed.):

1974. Die syrischen Kirchen in Indien. (Die Kirchen der Welt, Band XIII). Stuttgart: Evangelisches Verlagswerk.

Vimala Grace Darly, P.:

1989. The Indian Pentecostal Church in Kerala 1924-1954. (M.Phil. Thesis, School of Historical Studies, Madurai Kamaraj University). Madurai.

Visvanathan, Susan:

1993. The Christians of Kerala. History, Belief and Ritual among the Yakoba. Madras: Oxford University Press.

Wacker, Grant:

1990. Art. Bibliography and Historiography of Pentecostalism (U.S.). In: Burgess, Stanley M.; McGee, Gary B.; Alexander, Patrick H. (eds.): Dictionary of Pentecostal and Charismatic Movements. Grand Rapids: Zondervan. 4th ed., pp. 65-76.

1993. The Travail of a Broken Family. Radical Evangelical Responses to Early Pentecostalism. (Conference Papers, 23rd Annual Meeting of the Society for Pentecostal Studies, November 11-13). Guadalajara, Mexico.

2001. Heaven Below. Early Pentecostals and American Culture. Cambridge, Mass.: Harvard University Press.

Wandall, Povl:

1978. The Origin and Growth of the Arcot Lutheran Church. Madras: Christian Literature Society.

Warren, Hugh:

1959. The Christian Handbook of India 1959. Nagpur, Maharashtra: The National Christian Council of India.

Weaver, C. Douglas:

1987. The Healer-Prophet, William Marrion Branham. A Study of the Prophetic in American Pentecostalism. Macon, Georgia: Mercer University Press.

Webster, John C. B.:

1992. The Dalit Christians. A History. Delhi: I.S.P.C.K.

Whitehead, Henry:

1988. The Village Gods of South India. (1921). New Delhi: Asian Educational Service.

Wilfred, Felix:

1992. Zeitgenössische Strömungen in einigen Hauptbereichen der Theologie in Indien. In: Wilfred, Felix; Thomas, M. M. (ed.): Theologiegeschichte der Dritten Welt, Indien. (Kaiser-Taschenbücher; 108). München: Kaiser, pp. 269-333.

1996. Art. Indien, IV Gegenwart, 2. Katholische Kirche. In: Lexikon für Theologie und Kirche. 3rd ed. Freiburg im Breisgau. 5: 455-65.

Williams, Frank:

1962. When the Stars Fall. Nugegoda.

Wilson, D.:

1994. A Comparative Study of the Liturgical Worship of Church of South India and the Worship of Sectarian Groups. (P.G. Diploma Thesis, Tamilnadu Theological College). Madurai.

Wilson, Everett A.:

1990. Art. Norton, Albert. In: Burgess, Stanley M.; McGee, Gary B.; Alexander, Patrick H. (ed.): Dictionary of Pentecostal and Charismatic Movements. Grand Rapids: Zondervan. 4th ed., p. 641.

1999. They Crossed the Red Sea, Didn't They? Critical History and Pentecostal Beginnings. In: Dempster, Murray W.; Klaus, Byron D.; Petersen, Douglas (eds.): The

Globalization of Pentecostalism. A Religion Made to Travel. Oxford: Regnum Books International, pp. 85-115.

Wingate, Andrew:

1986. The Secret Christians of Sivakasi, Tamilnadu. One Pattern of Conversion in a South Indian Town. In: Religion and Society. Bangalore. 33: 73-87.

1997. The Church and Conversion. A Study of Recent Conversions to and from Christianity in the Tamil Area of South India. Delhi: ISPCK.

World Missionary Evangelism:

n.d. New Amended Memorandum of Association. (Registered No. 182/1969). (mimeo). Hyderabad.

1989. Silver Jubilee Souvenir. World Missionary Evangelism. Silver Jubilee Convention-Srikakulam (India). Srikakulam, Andhra Pradesh.

Worsfeld, James E.:

1991. The Origins of the Apostolic Church in Great Britain, with a Breviate of its Early Missionary Endeavours. Thorndon, Wellington: Julian Literature Trust.

Wyckoff, John W.:

1995. The Baptism in the Holy Spirit. In: Horton, Stanley M. (ed.): Systematic Theology. Revised Edition. Springfield, Mo.: Logion Press, pp. 423-55.

Yadav, Yogendra:

1996. The Maturing of a Democracy. In: India Today. New Delhi. Nr. 16, 31. August, pp. 28-43.

Yohannan, K. P.:

1994a. Living in the Light of Eternity. Tiruvalla, Kerala: Gospel for Asia Publications.

1994b. Weltmission auf neuen Wegen. (Revolution in World Missions <German translation>). (1986). Kreuzlingen: Dynamis Verlag.

Yong, Amos:

2000. Discerning the Spirit(s). A Pentecostal-Charismatic Contribution to Christian Theology of Religions. (Journal of Pentecostal Theology Supplement Series; 20). Sheffield: Sheffield Academic Press.

Young, R. J. C.:

2001. Postcolonialism. London: Blackwell.

Younger, Paul:

1989. Hindu-Christian Worship Settings in South India. In: Coward, Harold (ed.): Hindu-Christian Dialogue. Perspectives and Encounters. Maryknoll, N.Y.: Orbis Books.

Zechariah, Chelliah:

1981. Missiological Strategy for the Assemblies of God in Tamilnadu. (D.Miss. Thesis, Fuller Theological Seminary, School of World Mission). Pasadena, Calif.

Ziegenbalg, Bartholomaeus:

1867. Genealogie der Malabarischen Götter. Madras: Christian Knowledge Society's Press.

Maps

NORTH INDIA

SOUTH
INDIA

ANDHRA PRADESH

KARNATAKA

KERALA

TAMIL NADU

KARNATAKA

⊙ Kasargod

⊙ Kannur

WYNAD

⊙ Kalpetta

⊙ Kozhikode

• 10

⊙ Malappuram

TAMIL NADU

⊙ Palakkad

⊙ Thrissur

• 11

IDUKKI

⊙ Ernakulam

⊙ Pienave

Kottayam
⊙
• 9
• 8 • 7
• 1 • 2 • 3
Alappuzha ⊙ • 6 • 5 • 4
• 12
• 13
Pathanamthitta
• 14
• 15 • 16
⊙ Kollam

Trivandrum
⊙
• 17 • 18

Kerala

Adur 14
Alwaye 11
Changanacherry 7
Chengannur 6
Chingavanam 8
Kariamplave 4
Kayankulam 13
Kottarakara 15
Kovalam 17
Kumbanadu 2
Mavelikara 12
Mulakuzha 5
Neyyatinkara 18
Nilambur 10
Pakkil 9
Punalur 16
Rani 3
Tiruvalla 1

Tamilnadu

Alangulam	7
Aravankadu	27
Coonoor	28
Idaiyankulam	5
Kalaiyarkoil	14
Kanjiracode	2
Kattathurai	3
Kodai Road	19
Kodaikanal	20
Kotagiri	29
Kovilpatti	11
Lalgudi	21
Malavilai	4
Manarkudi	23
Marthandam	1
Nazareth	10
Palayankottai	6
Pallipet	31
Paramakuddi	13
Pollachi	22
Rajapalaiyam	12
Sankarankovil	9
Shengottai	8
T. Kalupatti	16
Tiruchengodu	26
Tirumangalam	17
Tirupattur	30
Tiruvannamalai	24
Usilampatti	18
Uttamapalayam	15
Villupuram	251

Karnataka
    Dodballapur   2
    Kolar Gold Fields   1

Andhra Pradesh

Amalapuram	9
Antarvedipalem	8
Armoor	2
Bheemunipatnam	11
Gudivada	4
Narasapur	6
Rajahmundry	10
Secunderabad	1
Tadepalligudam	7
Vijayawada	3
Vuyyuru	5

Index

Aaron, Charles, 70, 320
Abraham, A. V., 303
Abraham, K. C., 75
Abraham, K. E., 28-29, 32-33, 37-40, 55, 93, 183, 191n.1, 195-96, 200, 255-56, 258-59, 262-64, 283, 291-92, 298, 301, 315
Abraham, P., 20, 72
Abraham, Philip, 97n.19
Abraham, Sadhu, 74-75
Abraham, T. S., 38-40, 75, 93, 256, 315
Abraham, Valson, 40, 256
Abrams, Minnie F., 23, 26
ACM Theological Seminary (Philippinen), 257
Adamdurai, S., 69, 70, 289, 302
Administration, 38-39, 45-51, 54, 56, 73, 78, 80, 95, 98, 100, 211, 219, 237, 280, 288, 291
Adur, 26, 51, 111-12, 298
Africa, 1, 4, 6, 7, 9, 13, 127, 247, 248n.2, 249-51, 259, 271, 283, 284n.71, 295
African Instituted Churches (AIC), 13
Alangulam, 289
alcohol, 139-40, 182-83, 189
Aldwinckle, 25, 259, 283
Allen, A. A., 50, 51n.38
Allenkottai, 265
All-India Pentecostal Fellowship, 109, 110n.9

Aluva. *See* Alwaye
Alwaye Settlement School, 259
Alwaye, 256, 258, 298
Alwin, 29, 32, 41-43, 64, 72, 256, 260, 285, 304
Amalapuram, 280
America, 37, 43, 69-72, 98-99, 101, 107, 127-28, 144, 160, 248
Ammapatti, 275
Amsterdam, 97, 291
Ancient Pattern Pentecostal Church, 101
Anderson Church of God, 238, 276
Anderson, Rufus, 250
Andhra Christian Theological College, 242
Andhra Evangelical Lutheran Church, 17, 103n.26, 113, 242
Andhra Pradesh, 16-18, 32n.45, 35-39, 46-48, 55, 63, 74-75, 86-87, 89n.14, 92-105, 109, 113-14, 131, 141, 180, 185, 221, 237, 238, 259, 263, 265-66, 274, 276, 278, 280, 286, 291-93, 298, 305, 308
Andrew, Stephen, 35, 295
Andrews, K. C., 289
Anglican, 7n.26, 15, 269, 281, 289
Antarvedipalem, 36, 94, 214, 265, 285
Apostolic Christian Assembly, 66-67, 76n.50, 77-80, 144n.22, 149n.12, 158,

159n.40, 185, 210, 220, 223, 260-61, 273, 277, 284, 288, 290
Apostolic Church of Pentecost, 111-12
Apostolic Church, 41n.14, 251, 292-93
Apostolic Faith Mission, 264
Apostolic Fellowship Tabernacle, 66, 80, 122n.7
Aramada, 279
Aravankadu, 293
Armoor, 104, 274
Arumainayakam, C. P. D., 273
Arumainayakam, Lawrence, 257
Arumainayakam, Peter, 62, 82-83, 256
ashram project, 88, 297
ashram, 88, 108, 111, 116-19, 252n.20, 272, 278, 282
Asia, 1, 4, 7n.26
Asian Theological Association, 110n.12
Asirvatham, D., 112
Assemblies of God Bible College (Mattersey), 257, 271
Assemblies of God Theological Seminary (Springfield), 289
Assemblies of God, 19n.75, 25, 27-31, 32nn.41,42, 34-36, 44-47, 58-62, 68-71, 77, 81-83, 86-88, 99-100, 110, 114n.24, 121, 122n.6, 129, 138n.2, 140n.12, 144, 168, 185, 188, 201-2, 204, 207, 209, 211-13, 218, 226, 229n.48, 231n.1, 232n.6, 233, 250-51, 255-56, 258-60, 262, 264, 270-71, 273-76, 280-81, 286, 288-89, 291, 293, 297, 299n.99
Assembly of Christ Jesus, 112
Athumanesar, 112
Augustine, John S., 233
Australia, 23, 50, 52, 101, 103, 160, 287
Austria, 117
Avatar, 118n.48
Awrey, Daniel, 9
Azariah, M., 232, 242
Azusa Street, 3, 5, 6-11, 24, 27, 264

Babu, Y. S. John, 104-5, 274, 293
Bai Aiman, Mary, 25
Bakht Singh, 238, 277, 284, 288, 294, 297
Balachandran, Joseph, 90, 257-58
Bangalore, 19n.76, 24-27, 35, 46, 71, 86-90,

100n.22, 109n.7, 110, 121n.3, 135n.13, 144, 152, 157, 160, 163, 186, 188, 201, 221, 241, 243, 261-62, 264, 266, 271, 279-80, 281n.63, 286, 289-90, 295-98, 301n.3, 305n.1
baptism, 56, 59, 65, 68, 72n.43, 113n.19, 114, 140-41, 185-87, 195, 203, 205, 223-24, 226, 236, 239-40, 241n.38, 241n.40, 255, 257-62, 266, 270, 272, 274-77, 278, 282-85, 288, 290-92, 294, 296, 299-300
Baptists, 17, 102, 261, 263, 293
Barrett, David B., 1, 23
Barrington College, 279
Bartleman, Frank, 9
Basker, Dawson, 261
Basker, Norman, 70
beard, 288
Becker, Karl, 76
Beginning Pentecostal Truth Church, 111, 115-16
Believer's Church, 54
Bellary, 87, 100n.22
Benjamin, M., 35, 59-61, 71-72, 275, 302
Berchmans, S. J., 108, 221, 240, 257
Berg, George E., 9, 24-27, 35, 255, 264, 283, 298
Berlin, 135
Bethel Bible School (College), 31, 44, 46, 110, 201, 253, 275-76, 281, 296-97
Bethel Bible Training School (Newark), 258
Bethel Church, 95, 278
Bethesda Praying Centre, 268
Bezwada. See Vijayawada
Bharoshagar Mission College, 276
Bheemunipatnam, 101, 215
Bhimili. See Bheemunipatnam
Bible Medical Missionary Fellowship, 288
Bible Mission, 113-15
Bible reading, 108, 140, 272
Bible school, 28, 31, 33, 39, 40, 44-46, 48, 50-53, 56, 59-62, 67, 69, 71-72, 78-80, 82-84, 86-88, 89n.14, 91, 93, 100, 102n.23, 104-5, 111-12, 114, 132, 196, 200-202, 207, 210, 235, 259, 263, 265, 270-73, 275-78, 281, 283-84, 289, 291, 293-94, 296-98, 300

Bihar, 118
Billy Graham Evangelical Association, 287
black magic, 124-25, 147-48, 149, 151, 156-58, 162
Blessing Youth Mission, 102, 227n.41
blessing, 122-24, 130, 133-35, 137, 143, 163, 216-17, 220, 223, 227, 268
Blumhofer, Edith L., 24
Bombay University, 287
Bombay, 25, 48, 104, 142, 240n.35, 281
Bouncil, 25
branch churches, 44, 79-80, 83-84, 89, 104, 113, 210, 261, 271. *See also* branch congregations
branch congregations, 67, 77-78, 82-83, 96, 103, 105, 261, 305n.1. *See also* branch churches
Branham, W. M., 108, 117-18, 281-82
Brethren (Open Plymouth), 4, 15, 26, 28, 30, 33, 55, 185, 238, 239n.32, 255, 262, 275, 279, 283, 288, 291-92, 298
Brethren Mission, 24, 238n.32
British Assemblies of God, 32n.41, 34-36, 58, 61-62, 82, 93, 114, 256, 260, 270, 273
Buchanan, C. T., 259, 261
Burgess, John H., 31, 44-45, 258, 270, 275, 301
Burgess, Stanley M., 251
burial, 224-25
Burma, 276

Calicut. *See* Kozhikode
call to ministry, 130, 172n.74, 178, 192-93, 195, 204, 226, 263, 265, 270, 273, 276, 279, 284-85, 289, 292-93, 295-96
Caplan, Lionel, 147, 151
carols. *See* hymns
Case, Hoyle, 34, 303
caste, 16-18, 29-30, 45, 49, 54, 105-6, 232, 234, 252, 263
catholics, 214, 231, 234, 310
celibacy, 64, 65n.23, 74, 116, 159, 255, 264, 278-79, 290, 299
Central Bible Institute (College), 258, 270
Ceylon Pentecostal Mission, 29-32, 35, 41, 43-44, 63-67, 72-74, 114n.28, 116n.36,

140, 151, 154, 159, 166-68, 170, 182, 185, 189, 202-3, 209, 211, 224, 236, 255-56, 260, 264, 265, 272, 274, 277-78, 284-85, 287-88, 290, 292, 295, 298
Ceylon, 9, 24n.10, 28-29, 32, 41-43, 256, 272, 274, 279, 281-82, 285-87, 292
Chacko, K. J., 56, 303
Chacko, M. V., 49-50, 303
Chacko, P. T., 36, 92-94, 97, 256, 258-59, 285, 290, 292, 303
Chandigarh, 300
Chandrapillai, Philip, 44
Chandy, A., 44
Changanacherry, 52, 287
chants. *See* hymns
Chapel of the Air, 300
Chapman, Mary, 28, 31, 206, 255, 259, 275, 283, 301
charismatic churches, 121, 237, 247
charismatic movement, 1, 89, 121-22, 151, 231-32, 240-42, 257
Chelladurai Jr., Sam P., 80-81, 259-60
Chelladurai Sr., P. S., 66, 80, 109, 259, 260, 267, 271, 296
Chellappa, S., 262, 264
Chellappa, Sadhu, 108, 252, 261-62
Chellappa, Y., 312
Chengalpattu District, 292
Chengannur, 28-30, 52, 255, 275
Chennai. *See* Madras
Cherian Jacob, Thangamma, 66
Cherian, C. T., 259
Cherian, K. C., 33, 37-38, 256, 262-63
Cherian, Oommen, 315
Chicago Evangelization Society, 5
Chidambaranar District, 27, 69
child blessing, 223
Chingavanam, 52
Cho, Paul Yonggi, 122, 227
Choti, 30
Choudary, G. Moses (Gullapalli Vinayak), 105-6, 263, 318, 252n.20
Christ for Every Soul, 278
Christ for India, 101
Christensen, Jean, 84, 266
Christian and Missionary Alliance, 5, 10, 25

Christian Fellowship Centre, 19n.76, 89, 90, 121n.3, 288, 305n.1
Christian Life Missions, 300
Christian Medical College (Ludhiana), 57n.52
Christian Medical College (Vellore), 281
Christian Mission Service, 97, 264, 275
Christliche Initiative für Indien, 77
Christmas, 225-26, 267n.34
Christ's Church, 121n.3
church building, 28, 34, 60-61, 83, 87, 89, 94, 103, 219, 265, 275, 288
church discipline, 240
church foundation, 54, 117
church growth movement, 70, 105-6, 229, 252n.20
church membership, 28, 78, 232, 239-40, 267-68, 281, 307
Church Missionary Society, 30, 271-72, 286
Church of God of Prophecy, 99, 115, 191n.1
Church of God School of Theology, 105, 263
Church of God, 30, 33-35, 48-50, 55-56, 58-61, 71, 72n.43, 76, 82, 99, 138, 144, 185, 187, 209, 211, 231, 251-52, 263-64, 271, 275, 284n.71, 293-94, 300
Church of South India, 17-18, 68, 89n.14, 102, 116n.38, 171n.71, 204, 212, 223, 228n.43, 232n.6, 241n.37, 243, 251, 257, 265, 267-69, 277-78, 281-82, 284, 294
Church on the Rock Theological Seminary, 101, 215, 298
church songs, 221
Churches of Christ, 238
cinema, 81, 138, 183, 188-89
Clement de Alwis, 256
Cleveland, 99, 251, 263-64, 294
clothes, 182-84, 288
Cochin, 224
Coimbatore, 35, 61-63, 65-66, 72, 76-77, 82-83, 109n.7, 176, 218, 220, 256, 260-61, 266-67, 269-70, 288-90, 294-95
Colombo, 31, 32n.41, 42, 281, 287, 290
Cometh, Karin, 94
Communists, 61

Compassion International, 97
Conney, Arthur, 35n.63
contextual, 88, 106, 123, 125, 128, 220, 248-49, 252, 262
contextuality. See contextual
Continental Bible College, 80
convention, 23, 26, 30, 33, 40, 59, 82, 95, 109, 226, 260, 270, 285, 287
conversion, 16, 30, 36, 52, 105, 113n.19, 126, 130, 138-39, 140, 144, 170, 172, 176, 178, 181, 203, 223, 226, 228n.43, 231n.1, 233-34, 240, 255, 261, 263, 273-74, 275, 277, 281, 282n.67, 283-84, 285, 287, 290-91, 293-97, 299-300
Cook, G. A., 10n.45
Cook, George R., 303
Cook, Paul, 303, 48
Cook, Robert F., 25, 27-35, 48, 60, 144, 255, 258, 263-64, 275, 283, 303
Coonoor, 24-25, 46, 271
Cornerstone International Church, 293
court cases, 39-40, 57, 72, 75, 275
Courts, R., 98
Coxe, Herbert, 25
Crick, Edward, 303
Criswell Bible Institute (Dallas), 300
critique within Pentecostalism, 158-59, 168, 219
Cuddalore, 266, 288
Cummings, 258

Dalits, 16, 18, 29-30, 45, 53-57, 106, 112, 123n.1, 232n.6, 234, 242, 253n.21
Dallas Christian College, 291, 298
Dallas, 251n.17, 298, 300
Daniel Paul, T., 89, 286, 261
Daniel, S. P., 266
Daniel, Gopal, 35n.58, 60n.8, 292
Daniel, Joe, 239n.32, 261
Daniel, N., 239n.32
Daniel, S. B., 65, 67, 84, 262, 264, 289
Daniel, T., 261
Daniels, D. M. David, 314
Danish missionary, 31
Daoud, M. A., 50
Dart, 287n.76
daughter, 7, 23, 80, 90, 93, 98, 148, 164,

169, 171, 173, 198, 256, 259, 261-62, 265, 271, 276, 280, 282-83, 286, 290, 303n.7. *See also* woman
David, C. T., 58
David, K. R., 94, 265, 276
Dayton, Donald W., 3, 5n.18
Decade of Harvest, 289
Dehradun, 286
Delhi, 120, 283, 288
demonology, 125, 147, 149
demons, 54, 150, 243
Devadas, M., 113-15, 292
Devadoss, William, 294
Devanesan, Sadhu, 115-17
Devasahayam, K. P., 102n.23
Devasundaram, Y. S., 68, 84, 109, 265-66
devil, 134, 148-49, 159
Dhass, S. J., 73
Dhinakaran, D. G. S., 108, 132, 134, 154, 160-61, 174, 203, 226, 240, 241n.41, 262, 266-68, 273, 294, 317
Dhinakaran, Paul, 134-35, 155, 176, 269
Dhinakaran, Stella, 269n.41
Dickens, E. M., 34n.57
discerning the spirits, 151
Disciples of Christ, 238n.32
dispensationalist teaching, 136
Dr. Stephen Assembly. *See* Assembly of Christ Jesus
Dodballapur, 25, 264
Doon Bible College, 286
double membership, 224
Douglas, John E., 51, 55, 75, 95-96, 98, 197, 214
Dowdy, Naomi, 70, 207
dream, 37, 131
D'Souza, James, 240n.35

Eady, C. S., 87, 286
Easter, 225-26
Eastern Full Gospel Mission, 36, 273
East Godavari District, 280
Ebenezer, 283, 287n.76
ecumenism, 4, 115, 231-43, 249, 252
edifying literature, 18, 108, 222, 272
education, 40, 44, 56, 74, 101, 125-26, 134,

157, 182-83, 192, 199, 200-202, 234-35, 263, 271, 198. *See also* training
Edwards, Doris, 58-59, 69, 270, 274-75, 289
Edwards, Richard, 59
Edwards, Robert W., 58-59, 69, 270, 274-75, 281n.63, 302
Egli, David, 293
Elim Bible College, 80
Elim Bible Institute, 38, 256, 259, 276, 290
Elim Church of God, 276
Eluru, 32n.45, 36, 102n.23, 114, 259, 263, 285, 292
England, 9, 36, 67, 79-80, 89-90, 101, 239n.32, 271, 273, 277, 279, 282, 299
eschatology, 136n.15-16
ethics, 181, 183, 185, 187, 189
Ethiopia, 287
Eucharist, 257
Europe, 7, 9, 17, 42, 62, 67, 93, 127, 144, 242-43, 247-48, 274, 290
European Pentecostal Theological Association, 248
Evangelical Church of India, 239
Evangelical Fellowship of Vishakapatnam, 109n.7
evangelicalism, 1-3, 240, 249
evangelist, 7, 9, 18, 26-27, 32, 60n.8, 68, 75-76, 78-79, 84, 95-96, 102, 107-9, 113, 117, 124, 131-32, 134-35, 141, 143, 150-52, 154-59, 161, 163, 167, 169, 172-75, 178-80, 191, 193, 196, 200, 203-4, 206-7, 216-19, 224, 226, 235-36, 238, 240, 255, 258, 260, 262, 265-66, 268-70, 272-74, 276-77, 279, 281-84, 285n.74, 288, 290, 293-96, 299-300
evangelization, 5, 51, 58, 88, 90, 103, 257-58, 273, 283, 293
evil spirits, 123-26, 147-48, 150-51, 155-56, 158
exorcism, 124-26, 133, 143, 146-47, 155-58, 161, 165, 166, 232-33
Ezhavas, 17n.66

Faith Home, 42-43, 64, 74, 116n.36, 260, 272, 285
faith mission, 5, 9-10, 26, 96, 195, 218

Faith Movement, 79-81, 83, 122, 204, 260, 298
Faith Theological Seminary, 51, 110n.12
family, 62, 90, 93n.6, 94n.8, 95, 99, 100n.22, 115n.33, 123, 128, 148-49, 153, 155, 164, 168, 171, 174, 178, 180, 184, 197, 204-5, 217, 219, 224, 226-28, 256-66, 269n.41, 270-78, 280-82, 284, 286, 288, 290, 293-94, 296-99. *See also* sons
fast, 131-32, 155, 163, 180, 205, 225, 272
Faupel, D. William, 6, 11
feet washing, 223
fellowships, 107, 109, 121-22, 237-38, 260
Fiksen, David, 293
finances, 27-29, 33, 38-39, 45, 50-51, 53-55, 57, 59, 69-70, 74-77, 80, 83, 85, 90, 92, 95-96, 98-99, 101-5, 153, 189, 196, 201, 210-11, 216-19, 238, 255, 264-65, 272, 282, 292n.89, 293
Fisher, Elmer Kirk, 263
fortune-telling, 173
Foth, Oliver, 59-60
Fourth Man Gospel Team, 277
France, 41n.14, 42
Francis, Immanuel, 212
Freda, 256
French, C. E., 48, 303
Frodsham, Stanley H., 3
Full Gospel Assembly, 221
Full Gospel Church in India, 35n.63
Full Gospel Churches Association (Trichy), 109n.7
Full Gospel Leaders Fellowship of Andhra Pradesh, 109n.7, 280
Fuller Theological Seminary, 256, 280, 287, 297
full-time evangelist, 51
full-time ministry, 49, 66, 74, 89, 112, 151-54, 191, 194-95, 200, 203, 215-19, 233-34, 243, 260-61, 264, 267, 271, 273, 275, 279, 281, 283, 285-86, 288, 290, 296-97, 299
full-time pastor, 103, 195
full-time service, 74
full-time to work, 80, 103
fundamentalism, 3, 8, 128, 238
funeral, 224-25. *See also* burial

Garr, A. G., 9, 24
Gee, Donald, 3, 67, 110, 270
George, A. C., 86n.1, 87
George, P. C., 296
George, P., 315-16
George Raju, E. M., 109n.7
George, S. A., 35n.63
George, T. C., 86n.1, 201, 297, 302
Germany, 8, 76-77, 117-18, 264n.23, 271, 292, 300
gifts of the Spirit, 8, 114, 133, 146-80, 267
Gimenez, John, 286
Ginn, Mildred C., 302
Glassey, Jennie, 6
Gnanakan, Ken, 110
Gnanaprakasam, Job, 62-63, 66, 75-76, 83, 109n.7, 136, 261, 270-71
Godavari Delta Mission, 278
Good News Mission, 84, 309
Good Samaritan Fellowship, 257, 309
Good Shepherd Evangelical Church, 77n.52, 309
Gordan, A. J., 5
Gospel Echoing Missionary Society, 227n.41
Gospel for Asia, 53-54, 57, 300
Gospel Prayer Hall, 35n.63, 88-89, 266, 286, 308
Gospel to the Unreached Millions, 101
Graham, Billy, 287
Graner, Lydia H., 302
growth, 1, 16n.64, 18, 37-39, 41, 43, 45-50, 52-53, 55-57, 63, 67, 69-70, 72-74, 77-78, 81-83, 87, 89, 99, 105-6, 108, 163, 186, 204-5, 210-11, 219, 224, 228-30, 239, 240n.35, 251, 252n.20, 305, 307
Gudivada, 35n.57, 97, 273, 292
Guinn, Colleen, 71
Guinness, Fanny and Grattan, 5
Gulf countries, 38
Guntur, 100n.22, 273, 276
Guru, 160-61, 200-201
Gurukul, 241n.39
Guru-Shishya System, 61, 74, 78, 200, 202

Haggai, John, 300
Hagin, Kenneth, 122, 293

Hamburg, 77n.52

Hanegraaf, Ben, 84, 290

Harper, Michael, 89

Harris, J., 83, 210, 260, 271, 311

healing evangelist, 107, 117, 150, 154, 156, 158, 161, 167, 169, 178, 281, 293

healing, 8, 11, 69, 81, 108, 112, 115, 125-26, 129, 143, 146-47, 150, 152, 154-55, 158-72, 174, 178, 203, 205, 222-23, 229, 232-33, 240n.35, 243, 257, 266, 268, 269n.40, 270-72, 274, 276, 281, 285-86, 293

Hebron Bible School (College), 33, 39-40, 89n.14, 200, 259

Hedlund, Roger, 251

Henke, Frederick, 7

Hinduism, 16n.65, 19, 56, 84, 106n.35, 123-25, 148-49, 151, 155-56, 158, 161, 178, 224, 233-34, 260, 262, 276, 290, 293

Hinn, Benny, 122n.4

Hobday, Victor, 112n.17

Hoefer, Herbert E., 233

Hoerschelmann, Werner, 116n.36, 233

holiness, 3, 5, 42n.17, 65, 71, 85, 90, 121, 129, 136, 144, 145, 181, 183-85, 187-90, 199, 202, 212, 226, 239

Holland, 290

Holleman, Carl, 46, 302

Hollenweger, Walter J., 248

Holy Spirit, 3n.11, 5-6, 132-33, 139, 141-42, 144-45, 152, 154, 164, 173, 177, 186, 195, 266, 269n.44, 292

Houghton, Graham, 239, 278

Hyderabad, 92, 94, 97, 100, 104-5, 109n.7, 174, 176-77, 221, 228, 242, 278, 280. *See also* Secunderabad

hymns, 108, 220-21, 257-58, 285

Idaiyankulam, 289

ill. *See* illness

illness, 123, 124n.6, 126, 147, 149, 151-53, 167, 170-71, 194, 229, 281, 289

images, 268

immersion baptism, 65, 72, 113, 140, 186, 223-24, 239-41, 255, 257-62, 265-66, 270-71, 275, 277-78, 281-85, 288-92, 294, 296, 299-300. *See also* baptism

Independent Church of God in India, 55

Independent Full Gospel Church, 113, 276

India Bible College, 40, 53, 287

India Bible Institute, 283

India Gospel Outreach, 256

Indian Pentecostal Assemblies, 76n.50, 82-83, 271, 276

Indian Pentecostal Church, 29-30, 32-33, 36-40, 50-51, 55, 63-64, 74-75, 92-97, 99, 101-2, 104, 142, 144n.22, 145, 182-83, 185, 202, 209, 211-12, 219-20, 224, 231, 236-37, 251-52, 255-56, 259, 263-65, 274-76, 278-79, 285, 291-92, 296-98, 300-301, 306

Indore, 112n.17

infant baptism, 56, 114, 140, 223, 240-41, 282

Ingram, J. H., 33

initial evidence, 2, 5, 24, 114, 121, 142, 238, 292

Intermission, 78-79, 84, 90, 109, 271, 277, 290, 299

International Bible Training Institute, 277, 299

International Full Gospel Church, 276

International Gospel Centre, 97

International Levites Camp, 84

International Ministerial Association (St. Louis), 276

International Zion Assembly, 57

Isaac, Solomon, 112n.17

Isaiah, J. C., 62-63, 261

Jacob, A., 76-77, 197

Jacob, Benjamin, 25, 34, 259, 283, 287, 299

Jacob, Gideon, 67n.29, 77n.52

Jacob, P. I., 287

Jacob, Thangamma Cherian, 66

Jaffna, 41, 273

Jaikumar, A. S. W., 113, 276

James, Pammal, 292

Japan, 8-10, 292

Jebadurai, Sam, 108, 203, 272

Jeevanandam, N., 76, 108, 142, 225, 257, 259, 273

Jeevaratnam, Lam, 35, 114n.24, 273-74, 292

Jerusalem, 64, 115n.33, 116, 118, 279

Jesudian, D. R., 112

Jesus Calls, 132, 134-35, 148, 155, 160n.43, 162, 174, 267-69, 294
Jesus Christ Prayer and Evangelistic Ministries, 121n.3
Jesus Lives Evangelistic Ministries, 257
Jesus only churches, 111
jewelry. *See* ornaments
Jeyaraj, Y., 32n.42, 46n.25, 59, 69, 274, 297, 302
Jeyavel, K. V., 109n.7
Job, E. J. Chandran, 168, 170
John, A. J., 31, 275
John Babu, Y. S., 104-5, 274, 293
John, Ebenezer, 276, 296, 311
John, K. C., 303
John, M. O., 58, 63, 74, 97, 275, 296, 311
John, P. V., 31, 276, 297
John, Samuel, 300
Johns, Cheryl Bridges, 128
Johnson, D. A., 314
Johnson, P. D., 45-46, 302
Jonah, A. N., 113, 276, 282
Joseph, Alex, 80
Joseph, Charles Finney, 80, 109, 286
Joseph, D., 99
Joseph, F. Wilson, 304
Joseph, Henry, 66-67, 79-80, 81, 83, 109n.7, 110, 272, 277, 297, 299
Joseph, Joel, 280
Joseph, John, 108, 204, 240, 269, 277-78
Joseph, K. M., 301
Joseph, K. S., 36, 95, 278-79
Joseph, M., 112n.17
Joseph, M. S., 75, 302
Joseph, Victor, 302n.4
Joseph, Y., 303

K. E. Abraham Foundation, 39-40
Kadamalaikuntu, 290, 299
Kakinada, 99, 102n.24, 263, 285
Kalupatti, T., 275
Kammas, 17n.66
Kanjiracode, 299
Kannada, 18n.74, 86, 185n.11
Kanyakumari District, 16, 44-47, 63, 68, 72n.43, 84-85, 109n.7, 116, 118n.48, 265-66, 279, 290, 294, 299

Karamala, 283
Kariamplave, 283
Karnataka, 35, 39, 46, 86-89, 91, 100, 185, 263
Karunya Institute of Technology, 267-69
Kattathurai, 85, 297
Kay, Stephen, 279
Kay, V. Rowlands N. P., 279
Kay, Victor P. D., 63, 275, 278-79
Kayankulam, 276
Keekozhoor, 291
Kerala Pentecostal Fellowship Convention, 109n.7, 287
Kerala, 14-15, 17, 24-27, 29-34, 36-41, 43-57, 61, 63, 66, 72-75, 86, 89, 92-93, 96-97, 99-101, 109-12, 144-45, 157, 171, 184-85, 206, 212, 223, 231-32, 238, 240, 252-53, 256, 259-60, 270, 275, 277, 279, 283, 286-87, 292, 296, 298, 300-301, 303, 305n.1, 306n.3
Keswick conventions, 7, 23, 288
Keswick, 7
Ketcham, Maynard L., 110
Khammam District, 298
Khan, John A. D., 238n.32, 276
Kirubasanam, 68, 115, 265, 299
Klinge, Erwin, 264n.23
Kochi. *See* Cochin
Kochukunju, Sadhu, 63, 68, 262, 265, 277, 279, 296
Kodaikanal, 75, 111
Kodai Road, 61
Kolar Gold Fields, 26, 35, 86, 90, 286
Kollam, 26, 31, 291
Komanapalli, Benjamin, 278
Komanapalli, Carl, 278, 286
Komanapalli, Ernest, 86, 100-101, 109-10, 278-80, 286, 298
Komanapalli, Isaac, 98, 185n.12, 265, 278
Komanapalli, Sudarshan J., 280
Korean, 7, 11, 88
Koshy, T. G., 51
Kotagiri, 88, 271
Kottarakara, 26-27, 44, 264, 275
Kottayam District, 52
Kottayam, 56, 111, 218, 283, 287, 292
Kovalam, 56-57

Kovilpatti, 27, 69-70, 289
Kozhikode, 262
Krishna District, 265, 273, 285
Kristukula Ashram, 272
Krupa Rao, N., 102-3
Kuala Lumpur, 295
Kucera, Martha, 31, 291, 301
Kumar, Ramsurat, 160-61
Kumar, Yeswanth, 89, 280
Kumbanadu, 29-30, 32-33, 38-40, 89, 255-56, 258, 263, 296-97
Kunjummen, C., 44-46, 280, 302
Kunnam, 283
Kuricha, 296
Kuschel, Karl-Josef, 248n.6
Kuttalam Pillai, M. V., 290, 296

Laharinagar, 282
Lalgudi, 294
Lamech, M. V., 87
Last Supper, 135, 223, 279
Latin America, 1, 7, 127, 247, 248n.2, 249-51
Latter Rain, 3n.11, 6, 37
Lawrie Ministries, 282
Lawrie, Deva Eevu, 282
Lawrie, Devadayavu, 282
Lawrie, Devaseer, 113, 119, 282
Lawrie, Paulaseer, 107-8, 111-13, 117-18, 161, 273, 276-78, 281-82, 294
lay(people), 18, 70, 72, 84, 130-31, 170, 172, 241, 272, 277
laying on of hands, 141, 145, 151-52, 155-56, 164
Laymen's Evangelical Fellowship, 238
Lazarus, C. K., 73, 304
Lazarus, John, 286
Lazarus, Mohan C., 272n.48
Lee College, 263, 294
Liberation theology, 125, 242, 253n.21
Light, Peter, 293
Lindsay, D. L., 303
Livesey, Lawrence, 35n.57, 35n.60, 61-63, 82, 256, 270-71
Livesey, Margaret, 35n.57, 61n.13, 62-63, 82, 256, 270-71
Living Word Church, 83, 122n.7, 210

London Missionary Society, 56, 265, 279, 297, 299
Lord's Supper, 135, 223, 279
Lörrach near Basel, 262
Los Angeles, 6, 7, 9, 263-64
Lowry, H. W., 60
Luce, Alice E., 26
Ludowici, 263
Lutherans, Lutheran family, 15, 214, 257, 273-74, 288, 299

Macden, Freddy, 261
Madigas, 17
Madras Christian College, 116n.38, 281-82, 299
Madras Pentecostal Assembly, 25, 34-35, 67, 81-82, 159, 299
Madras Pentecostal Fellowship, 109n.7
Madras University, 290
Madras, 25, 33-35, 41n.14, 42, 57, 61, 66-67, 70, 72-73, 76-83, 87, 105n.31, 108-10, 112, 122, 132, 141, 148, 152, 164-65, 174-75, 177, 185, 187, 207, 210, 214, 216, 218, 220, 223, 225, 227-29, 232-34, 238n.32, 241n.39, 243, 257, 258n.9, 259-62, 266-68, 272-73, 277-78, 280, 283-88, 292, 294-95, 298-99, 306n.3
Madurai District, 257, 262
Madurai, 35, 59-61, 69-71, 77, 83, 122n.7, 153, 210, 241, 257, 260-61, 271-72, 275-76, 279, 289, 293, 299n.99, 305
Maharashtra, 23, 46, 157, 179
Mains, David, 300
Malankara Full Gospel Church, 29
Malankara Pentecostal Church, 28-29
Malappuram District, 275
Malas, 17
Malavilai, 116
Malayalam, 18n.74, 44-45, 46n.24, 47-48, 54, 270, 281, 287, 302, 306n.3
Malayalis, 43, 72
Malaysia, 67, 278, 287, 290, 293, 295
Maloney, Clarence Jr., 270
Maloney, Clarence T., 270, 302
Mammen, Umman, 26-27
Manasse, C., 255, 259, 282
Manavalapuram, 265

Mangalore, 33, 262, 266

Manickam, P. D., 302

Manna, 100-101, 278, 280, 286, 317

Manoraj, David, 262

Manoramabai, 32

Manujothi Ashram, 108, 111, 117-19, 278, 282

Maranatha Bible Training Institute, 79

Maranatha Faith Ministries, 263

Maranatha Visvasa Samajam, 19n.76, 105, 305n.1

Maranatha, 67, 76n.50, 79, 80, 83, 257, 272, 277, 309

marriage license, 65, 224

marriage, 4, 41, 65, 67, 77n.52, 80, 90, 93, 97, 113, 131, 160, 173, 178, 183, 188, 204-5, 224-25, 236, 255-56, 258-59, 261-66, 268n.6, 269-71, 275-77, 279-84, 286-93, 295-97, 299-300, 303n.7

Marshall, Tom, 243

Marthandam, 294, 297

Mar Thoma Church, 15, 17, 30, 241n.40, 258-59, 262, 276-77, 283, 287, 291, 296, 298, 300

Martin, David, 127

Martin, P. C., 72

Mascarenhas, Fio, 240n.35

Mathew, A. C., 241

Mathew, C. S., 51n.40, 54-55, 283

Mathew, I. C., 99n.20

Mattai, Pandalam, 25-27, 283

Mattersey, 257, 271

Mauss, Marcel, 217n.17

Mavelikara, 31, 259, 275, 280

May, Spencer E., 61

McGavran, Donald, 105, 152n.20

McGee, Gary B., 10n.44, 24

Mead, Samuel J., 9

medicine, 125, 146, 152, 157, 161, 166, 168-70, 282, 288, 294

Megnanapuram, 271

Melnedungal, 292

Meluveli, 262-63

Methodists, 17

Ministry to the Interior, 278

ministry, 64, 191-208. *See also* full-time ministry

Miracle Ministry, 294

miracle worker, 161. *See also* wonder worker

miracle, 129, 146, 153, 155, 161-66, 172, 269n.40, 294

Miriam Children's Homes, 101

missionary, missionaries, 5-7, 9-10, 15, 23-25, 27-28, 31-36, 43, 41n.14, 44-49, 56, 59-62, 69-71, 79, 84, 86-88, 90, 92, 94-95, 97, 110-13, 114n, 125-26, 144, 200-201, 206-7, 213-14, 238n.31, 250-51, 258n.9, 259-60, 264, 270-71, 273, 277-78, 280, 286-87, 298-99

modernity, 128-29, 189

Moffatt, Michael, 123n.1, 125n.10

Mohan, D., 70, 207, 229, 273

Moltmann, Jürgen, 248n.6

Moody Bible Institute. See Chicago Evangelization Society

Moody, Dwight L., 5

Moorhead, Max Wood, 24n.12

Morar, James, 276

Moses, Paul, 81

Mott, John R., 5

Mt. Zion Bible School, 291

Mudaliar, Nataraja, 76, 283

Mudaliar, Padma, 108, 206, 284

Mukti Mission, 7, 23-25

Mulakuzha, 28, 61, 255, 264, 291, 293

Mumbai. *See* Bombay

Murthy, A. K., 286

Murugesan, M., 35, 260, 285

Muskegon, 258

Muthuramalingam District, 257-58

Muttu, R., 75

Myers, Dora P., 48, 61, 206, 293, 303

Nadars, 16, 54, 57, 118n.48, 232, 234

Nagercoil, 72n.43, 73-74, 84, 118n.48, 282, 284, 296

Nagpur, 276

Nallaiya, S. V., 302

Narasapur, 36, 95, 278

National Association of Pentecostal Theological Institutions, 110

Nava Jeeva Ashram, 88

Navroji, Sarah, 72n.43, 108, 221, 284

Nazareth, 35, 271, 274, 281-82, 292
Netherland. *See* Holland
New India Bible Church, 52-53, 287,
306n.4, 308
New India Bible College, 53, 287
New India Church of God, 52, 296, 308
New India Evangelistic Association, 53
New Life Assemblies, 71
New Testament Church, 101, 308
Neyyatinkara, 56
Nickelson, G., 90, 198
Nigeria, 287, 292
Nilambur, 275
Nilgiris District, 33, 89, 264, 293
Nizamabad, 274
North America. *See* America
North Arcot District, 102, 272
Northeast India, 14, 23, 112n.16
North India, 14, 25, 32n.41, 36, 52, 54, 98,
110, 112, 227n.41, 251, 277-78, 296, 300
Norton, Albert, 25

offerings, 78
oil, 126, 155, 160
Oommen, George, 86n.1
Oommen, T. G., 301
Ooty, 33, 264
Open Bible Church, 309
Open Bible Standard Church, 278n.58
Operation Mobilisation, 296, 300
Order of St. Luke, 282
ordination, 56, 67, 199, 202, 204, 206-8,
235
Ordo Salutis, 138, 144-45, 181
Oriental Missionary Society, 239n.33, 278
ornaments, 60, 62, 71, 181, 183-88, 223, 277,
288
Orr, Edwin, 7, 24
Osteen, John, 261
Othara, 296

Packiam, Soorna, 68, 84, 265
Padiri, Umman, 27n.21
Pakkil, 56
Palayankottai, 35, 65-67, 70, 83-84, 266,
271-72, 281, 289
Pallipet, 292

Palliyadi, 294
Paramjothi, P. L., 94-97, 100, 265, 280,
286, 301
Paraniam, 282
Parattupara, 298
Parham, Charles, 5, 6, 9n.35, 11
parousia, 11
Pasadena, 256, 280, 287, 297
Pastors' Conference (Trivandrum), 109
Pastors' Fellowship (Bangalore) = Pente-
costal Pastors' Fellowship
Pathanamthitta District, 51, 111, 262, 298
Paul, Daniel, 89-90
Paul, Ebenezer, 272n.48
Paul, Ernest, 304
Paul, Freddy, 42-43, 304
Paul, K. A., 101-2
Paul, K. R., 87-90, 160, 266, 269, 286
Paul, M. A., 103
Paul, M. Victor, 242
Paul, P., 29, 31-33, 41-43, 167, 279, 286-87,
292, 304
Paul, Ratna, 70
Pentecostal Assemblies of the World, 111
Pentecostal Church of India, 63, 65-66,
75, 262, 266, 271, 288
Pentecostal Fellowship Madras, 109n.7
Pentecostal Fellowship of India, 110, 280,
297
Pentecostal Fellowship of Kanyakumari
District, 109n.7
Pentecostal Fellowship of Tirunelveli Dis-
trict, 109n.7
Pentecostal Mission. *See* Ceylon Pente-
costal Mission
Pentecostal Pastors' Fellowship
(Bangalore), 109n.7, 297
Pentecostal Pastors' Fellowship
(Coimbatore), 109n.7
Pentecostal Pastors' Fellowship of Greater
Hyderabad, 109n.7
Pentecostal World Conference, 2, 110, 279
Pentecostal Young People's Association,
256
Pereira, Rufus, 240
Perinbam, Paul, 74
persecution, 101, 165, 198

Peter, Gera, 87, 90, 100
Pethrus, Lewi, 33, 37
Philadelphia Church, 35n.63, 90, 308
Philip, Abraham, 53, 287n.77
Philip, Mathew A., 287
Philip, P., 74
Philip, P. S., 110n.13
Philip, Santhosam, 274, 302
Philip, Thomas, 52-53, 287
Philippinen, 257, 292
Pierson, Arthur Tappan, 5
politics, 136, 190
Pollachi, 35, 61n.13, 270
Ponnammal, Sannyasini, 260
Ponraj, Paul, 66
Ponraj, S., 65-67, 260, 287, 290, 295
Poona, 231n.2, 253n.21
Poonen, Zac, 89-90, 135, 167, 181, 215-17, 284, 288
Poornachandra Rao, G. D., 102
Poovancode, 299
Pospisil, William, 48-49, 56, 303
possession, 124, 148, 151, 160, 222
Power Encounter, 88
Prabakaran, Justin, 31, 179, 204, 229, 288-89
Praise Fellowship Church, 293
Prakasam, David, 83, 110, 271
Prayer Garden Fellowship, 258, 309
prayer oil, 126, 155, 160
prayer, 23, 26, 35, 51-52, 56, 59, 62, 68, 70, 73, 88-89, 102-3, 112-15, 117n.44, 121n.3, 126, 129-31, 133-37, 141-43, 148, 155, 160, 162-64, 173, 176, 178-80, 183, 192, 194, 196, 205-6, 210, 217, 220, 222, 225-29, 233, 237, 240-41, 243, 255, 258, 260, 263, 265-68, 272, 279-80, 283, 285-86, 302-3, 307-8
premillennialism, 4-6, 136
Prince of Peace, 104-5, 293, 309
property, 28, 38, 39, 43, 55, 59, 74, 79, 87, 93-94, 101, 104, 116, 265, 272, 282
prophecy, 4, 8, 130-31, 141, 146, 153, 172-80, 194
proselytism, 17, 235, 239
prosperity gospel, 81, 122, 189
Pulikottil, Paulson, 251-52

Punalur, 27n.21, 44, 201, 253n.21, 275, 281, 296, 298
Pune. See Poona
Puttenkavu, 255, 275

Quilon. See Kollam

radio, 267-68, 285, 292, 300
Rainbow Church, 81, 122n.7
Raj, C. Selva, 116
Raj, Edwin K., 57
Rajamoni, M. J., 290
Rajamoni, M. K., 296
Rajamoni, P. S., 289
Rajapalaiyam, 256
Rajaratnam, P., 36, 94, 179-80, 279
Rajendran, M., 83-84, 289
Rajendran, R., 84, 290
Raju, E. M. George, 109n.7
Raju, Spurgeon, 286
Rakshanandam, G., 286
Ramabai, Pandita, 23-24
Ramanathapuram District, 257
Rangoon, 36, 179-80, 276
Rani, 283, 298
Ranipettai, 261
Rao, G. D. Poorna-Chandra, 102
Rao, N. Krupa, 102-4
rapture, 114, 118, 136
Ratnasingam, Jacob, 304
Reddis, 17n.66
Regent University, 291
registration, 28, 32, 34, 39-40, 46, 48, 50-52, 56-57, 65, 69, 72-73, 83, 93, 96, 98, 100-101, 103, 109, 134, 219, 224, 259, 264, 275
resurrection, 4, 114, 116, 207-8
revelation, 118, 151, 175
revival, 3, 5-11, 23-24, 107, 135, 205, 225, 241, 257, 263, 268
Richter, Emil, 264n.23
Roberts, Clarence W., 60, 71
Roberts, Oral, 74
Roberts, Owen, 257
Robinson, J., 34
Rochester Bible Training School, 258
Rock Church (Virginia Beach), 280, 286

Rock Church, 100-101, 307-8
Rock Ministries International, 286
Rolls, Charles, 298
Roloff, Lester, 300
Rose, John, 62, 65, 67, 84, 290, 295, 297
Rowlands, J. F., 283, 284n.71, 295
Ryan, M. L., 10

Sadhu, 63, 288, 299
Sai Baba, 160-61
St. Louis College, 290
St. Louis, 276
St. Xavier's College, 281
Saju, 30
Salayam Palayam, 273
Salem District, 34n.57, 261
Salvation Army, 281, 281n.63
Sam, P. A. V., 49-50
Samuel, Abraham, 74-75, 93, 97-98, 290-91
Samuel, A. C., 31, 44-45, 283, 291, 302
Samuel, Godi, 98
Samuel, M. S., 259
Samuel, Noel, 75, 97, 110n.13, 291
Samuel, P. M., 32, 36-37, 39, 39n.9, 63, 74-75, 92-97, 113-14, 179, 191n.1, 192, 259, 265, 275-76, 278-79, 285, 290-92, 298, 301
Samuel, T. J., 46, 302
Samuel, V. G., 304
sanctification, 138, 144-45, 181
Sandford, Frank, 6
Sandy, Robert, 89, 280
Sankarankovil, 261
Santhosam, James, 104-5, 292-93
Santhosam, Philip, 274, 302
Sargunam, M. Ezra, 293n.33
Schambach, W., 50
Schley, Richard, 79n.55
Schneider, Achim, 79
Schoonmaker, Christian H., 25
Scism, Ellis L., 111-12
Scism, Harry, 112
Second Coming of Christ, 6, 64, 136
secularization, 127-28
Secunderabad, 93-94, 256, 259. *See also* Hyderabad

Selva Raj, C., 116
Selvaratnam, Benjamin, 41, 293
Serampore College, 259, 297
Serampore University, 110n.12
700 Club, 291
sexual, 42, 183, 189, 235
Shalm, George, 111-12
Shankar, Pappa, 108, 180, 293
Shankar, S., 272n.48
Sharon Bible School, 50
Sharon Fellowship, 51, 298, 308
Shaver, Robert, 302
Shekinah Church, 81
Shekinah Gospel Prayer Fellowship, 89, 280, 308
sickness. *See* illness
Sigamani, John, 288
Siloam, 76-77, 197
Silvanus, 67
Simon, K. V., 255
Simpson, A. B., 5
Simson, Wolfgang, 262
sin, 138-39, 144-45, 147, 149-50, 154-55, 166, 181-82, 189
sin, 138-39, 144-45, 147, 149-50, 154-55, 166, 181-82, 189
Singapore, 70, 110, 207, 300
Singh, Bakht, 238, 277, 284, 288, 294, 297
Singh, Pratap, 71, 82, 293-94
Singh, Sunder, 139n.3
Singhalese (language), 41-42
Singhalese, 31, 42, 256, 272
Sion Fellowship, 104, 274, 308
Sivaganga, 257
slain in the Spirit, 122
smoke, 138, 183, 189
social activities. *See* social works
social engagement. *See* social works
social work, 78, 101, 212-15
social works, 53, 77-78, 101, 189, 212-15
Society for the Propagation of the Gospel, 266, 274, 278, 281
Solomon, John, 204, 240, 269, 294
Solomon, Wellesley, 72
sons, 40, 80, 119, 148, 192, 256, 265, 278, 286, 296
Sorbo, Ernest A., 44-45, 47, 302

sorcery, 148-49, 156-59

South Africa, 7n.26, 9, 271, 283, 295

South Arcot District, 273

South Asia Institute of Advanced Christian Studies, 239, 243

Southern Asia Bible Institute (College), 86-88, 279, 289, 296, 298

Southern Methodist University (Dallas), 298

South Madras Pastors' Fellowship, 109n.7

Spiers, Donald M., 74

Spirit baptism, 2, 5, 102, 114, 130, 133, 140-43, 152, 173, 195, 225-26, 238, 257, 261, 265-66, 269, 276, 278, 284, 290, 292-93

Spittler, Russell P., 128

split, 1, 12, 38, 64, 70, 87, 96, 103, 197, 263

Springfield, 258, 270-71, 289

Srikakulam, 102n.23

Sri Lanka, 43n.18, 71, 73, 267n.34, 272

Stanley Medical College, 294

Stephen, K. N., 56-57

Stephen, Reddi, 99, 105

Stephen, S. S. S., 112, 113n.19, 271, 294

Stephen, T., 56-57

Stewart, David, 69-70

Stubbs, Earl, 45-47, 100, 302

Subramaniam, S., 285

succession, 60, 71, 73, 76, 78, 80, 89, 97-99, 210-11, 276, 287, 299

suicide, 139, 175

Sundar Singh, Sadhu, 139

Sunday school, 170, 225

Sunderam, G., 66-67, 77-80, 185-87, 210, 260, 267-77, 279, 284, 294-95

Sunderam, Joshua, 296

Sunderam, Sam, 66-67, 78, 277, 290, 296

Surya Prakash, P., 241n.40

Sussex, 277, 299

Swahn, Carl, 33, 35, 262

Sweden, 25, 33, 37, 93, 271

Switzerland, 117, 264n.23, 279

Sydney, 171n.71, 298

Syrian Orthodox Church, 15, 17, 251n.17, 255, 262

Tadepalligudam, 278, 286

Tamil Bible Institute (College), 70-71, 271, 286, 289, 293

Tamil Evangelical Lutheran Church, 17, 261, 284

Tamil Nadu, 14, 16, 17n.66, 34-35, 39, 41, 43, 46n.24, 47-48, 58-61, 63, 65, 68-77, 79, 82-83, 86, 96-98, 108, 109n.7, 111-13, 118n.48, 122n.6, 123, 144, 160, 180, 184-85, 188, 192-93, 199, 206, 222-23, 233, 237n.30, 238, 239n.33, 240n.35, 241nn.39,41, 258-59, 270, 274, 276, 279, 282, 284, 291-95, 305n.1, 307

Tamil, 18n.74, 26, 42, 44-47, 61, 63, 69, 73-74, 75n.48, 87, 89-90, 104, 108, 122n.6, 123n.1, 124, 136n.18, 148, 152, 157, 160, 170, 209, 212, 220, 222, 229n.48, 251n.17, 258, 261, 267, 270, 272, 280, 283, 285, 290, 293-94, 296, 302n.4

Tamilnadu Theological College, 241nn.39,41

Tamils, 25, 27, 41-44, 63, 65, 72, 74-75, 87, 107, 109, 123, 131-32, 134, 136, 151-52, 154, 156-57, 159, 163, 167, 174, 177-79, 186, 192-93, 199, 204, 212-14, 216, 218, 222, 235-36, 258, 273, 278

Tanjore. See Thanjavur

Tarrying Meeting, 141, 225, 259, 287, 299

Taylor, Hudson, 5

Taylor, William, 9

television, 183, 189, 267-68, 300

Telugu Baptist Church, 15

Telugu, 18n.74, 36, 87, 94-97, 99, 100-101, 267n.34

Terrell, David, 229n.48

testimony, 142, 148, 155, 162, 176-77

Tewes, Jochen, 79n.55, 90, 109n.7

Thamburaj, A. J., 240n.35

Thamby, Mariamma, 52

Thamby, V. A., 51-52, 296

Thangaiah, A. R., 71

Thanjavur, 17n.66, 25, 63, 111-13, 188, 275, 277-79

Thannickal, John, 46, 86n.1, 88, 110, 239, 252n.20, 280, 296-97

Thesaiyan, 265-66

Thomas Christians, 15-17, 29-30, 34n.51,

37, 43, 45-46, 49-57, 111, 231n.1, 252, 275, 280, 288, 291

Thomas, A. C., 42-43, 304

Thomas, M. I., 293

Thomas, M. M., 275

Thomas, N., 85, 297

Thomas, P. C., 259

Thomas, P. J., 50-51, 109n.7, 276, 297-98

Thomas, T. K., 97n.19, 285

Thomas, U., 303

Thomas, V. T., 259

Thrichur. *See* Thrissur District

Thrissur District, 240n.35

Thuvayur, 26-27, 298

Timothy, Lois, 56n.51

Tiruchchirappalli. *See* Trichy

Tirumangalam, 276

Tirunelveli District, 47n.26, 61, 109n.7, 257, 261, 266, 272, 289

Tirunelveli, 112, 118, 260, 282, 293

Tirupattur, 272

Tiruvalla, 30, 50, 51n.41, 54, 258, 298

Tiruvanathapuram. *See* Trivandrum

Tiruvannamalai, 84, 289

Titus, G. V., 276

Titus, P. J., 86m1, 101, 110, 215, 225, 291, 295, 298

tongues-speaking, 2, 5-11, 24, 114, 121, 125, 127, 130, 132, 141-43, 146, 220, 238n.32, 241n.40, 249, 292

Topeka, 3

Toronto blessing, 122

training, 44, 70-71, 78-79, 82, 86-88, 200-203, 207, 212, 225, 239, 257, 261, 263, 270-71, 273, 284. *See also* education

Travancore, 47n.26, 224n.34

Trichy, 70, 76, 77n.52, 109n.7, 112, 113n.19, 257, 260, 266, 278, 287, 294

Trinity Christian Centre (Singapore), 70, 207

Trinity Full Gospel Church, 82

Trivandrum District, 56, 279, 282-83

Trivandrum, 27, 31, 109n.7, 259, 291, 301n.3

Turner, Harold, 99, 263, 303

Tuticorin, 35

Tutyko, Tom, 266

Udagamandalam. *See* Ooty

Ummaccen, Paruttupara, 26, 27

Umman Padiri, 27n.21

Union Biblical Seminary, 296

Union Christian College, 258

Union of Evangelical Students, 288

United Pentecostal Church, 111-12

United Theological College, 234n.39-40, 296

Upper Room Mission (Los Angeles), 263

Upper Room, 103

USA 9, 27, 31, 33, 44, 47, 50-54, 60, 69, 80, 86-87, 89, 93, 95, 97-98, 100-105, 113, 114n.22, 117-18, 122n.6, 138, 183, 201, 217, 237-38, 258-59, 263, 265, 268n.40, 270-71, 274, 278-82, 286-87, 290-91, 293, 298, 300. *See also* America

Usilampatti, 17n.66, 257

Valasai, K. P., 58-60, 69, 213, 270, 274-75, 289

Varkey, Sunny, 303

Vasu, John, 34, 67-68, 81, 110, 298-99

Vasu, Prabhudoss, 81-82, 110, 299

Vasu, Stanley, 82, 299

Vellalas, 17n.66

Vellore, 102, 178, 261, 266, 281

Venn, Henry, 250

Verghese, P. E., 99

Verghese, T. M., 34, 48-49

Vickramasingapuram, 61

Victor Mission, 290

Vijayawada, 19n.76, 92-93, 97-98, 102, 105, 263, 285, 292, 305n.1

Villupuram, 273

Vincent, Alan, 104, 274

Virginia Beach, 280, 286, 291

Vishakapatnam. *See* Vizag

vision, 114, 130-31, 139, 193, 194-95, 205, 209-10, 286

Vizag, 101-3, 109n.7, 121n.3

Vuyyuru, 285

Walker, Bob, 300

Warangal District, 265

Warangal, 97n.19, 265, 285

way of the Cross, 268

Wesley College, 281
Wesley, John, 181
Wesleyan, 3
West Godavari Dt., 36, 274
West Herts Community Church, 104
Wheaton College, 296, 298
wife, 6, 25, 34, 44, 52, 66-67, 69, 76, 88,
    100, 115, 131, 153, 156, 159, 164, 168, 171,
    173, 184, 196, 204, 227-28, 255, 258-59,
    264, 269, 277, 279, 286, 288, 289, 290-91,
    294-96, 300
Williams, Paul, 71
Wilson, Everett, 11
Wilson, Joseph, 316
Wingate, Andrew, 228n.43
Wings of Healing, 285
witchcraft, 148-49, 157-59
woman, 6, 10, 34, 41, 52, 66, 68-69, 71, 74,
    102, 108, 111, 114-16, 159-60, 171, 172-73,
    184, 191, 204, 206-8, 221-22, 225, 227,
    239, 241-42, 260, 277, 281-82, 284-85,
    293, 295-96, 299. See also wife
wonder worker, 160, 217. See also miracle
    worker
World Missionary Conference at Edin-
    burgh, 4
World Missionary Evangelism, 51, 55, 75-
    78, 83, 85, 92, 95-99, 102n.23, 209, 211,
214, 237, 251n.17, 252, 265, 271, 278-79,
    283-84, 306n.4
World Pentecostal Conference, 76, 299
World Vision, 79, 300
World Wide Faith Missions of India, 286
World Wide Mission, 97
World Wide Sending, 290
Wright, John, 296
Wyatt, Thomas, 95, 214, 285

Yeotmal, 296
Yesudhason, Sadhu, 68, 115n.33, 299
Yesunamam. See Jesus only churches
Yesunesan, 265-66
Yohannan, K. P., 53-54, 300
Yohannan, Pokayil, 30
Young Partner's Plan, 133-35, 268
Younger, Paul, 220
Youth for Christ, 257

Zaiss, Hermann, 292
Zechariah, Chelliah, 71, 232n.6
Ziegenbalg, Bartholomaeus, 149
Zion Assemblies of God, 82-83, 218
Zion Bible Institute (Rhode Island), 271
Zion Gospel Prayer Fellowship, 206
Zion Sangham, 56-57